Henry Bullinger

Shepherd of the Churches

Henry Bullinger
(1504-1575)

Shepherd of the Churches

George M. Ella

Go *publications*

Go Publications
The Cairn, Hill Top, Eggleston, Co. Durham, DL12 0AU, ENGLAND

First Published 2007

British Library Cataloguing in Publication Data available

ISBN 978 095486243 5

For information on other Go Publications titles and New Focus magazine:

www.go-publications.co.uk

www.go-newfocus.co.uk

Printed and bound in Great Britain by Lightning Source UK Ltd

Dedication

This book is dedicated to the Protestant Reformation Society which seeks bravely to maintain the revival doctrines of the Reformation at a time when deadening secularism and pseudo-religion are striving to quench the Spirit in modern evangelism and pastoral work.

Contents

Illustrations

Page

Foreword One

George Ella has taken the unusual step of asking two of his friends to write a foreword to this book. His reason is that the reception of Henry Bullinger over the centuries on the Continent has been different to that of the English-speaking world. In Germany, for example, any discussion of Bullinger will be linked with a study of Martin Bucer, Bullinger's fellow Reformer in the German-speaking, non-Lutheran, states.

Bucer and Bullinger are still known and respected in continental Europe and their works are experiencing something of a revival. Yet both men have lost their position as major Reformers in the English-speaking world where they are eclipsed by Martin Luther and John Calvin. Dr. Ella has therefore invited Prof. Thomas Shirrmacher, a notable German Reformed scholar, and myself to view Bullinger from these two aspects. Prof. Shirrmacher's foreword deals with the book in relation to the Continental situation and his own work at the Martin Bucer Seminary where he trains Reformed ministers, whereas I view the book from the point of view of an English-speaking reader and pastor.

This biography of Henry Bullinger is the first full-length study of his life and works ever to appear in the English language. Today he is almost unknown amongst English-speaking Christians, yet he was the best known theologian in Britain during the entire Reformation period. Bullinger of Zürich, and the equally forgotten Martin Bucer of Strasbourg, reintroduced the doctrines of grace to the churches long before Calvin. In fact, former scholars called Bucer and Bullinger either 'The Fathers of the Reformed Churches' or even 'The Fathers of Calvinism'. Bucer began his reforms at the same time as Luther but he soon overtook him in reforming fervour.

After Bullinger's conversion and an initial two years' period of intense reading leading up to 1522, he then out-classed and out-stripped both Luther and Bucer by producing some eighty-six works on the doctrines of grace during the following six years. At the same time, young Bullinger produced numerous commentaries, started on a long period of educational reforms and undertook an enormous international correspondence with the world's leading theologians and statesmen. Bullinger was the first to practise a Reformed Lord's Supper pre-dating even Zwingli by a few years and his writings on the Covenant of Grace, which became the backbone of Reformed theology, were produced between 1525 and 1534, a number of years before other Reformers took up the theme to any extent.

Not only is Bullinger a forgotten Reformer, the German-Swiss Reformation which he pioneered, as opposed to the later Franco-Genevan Reformation which allied tentatively with the Swiss some twenty years after, can also truly be called the forgotten Reformation. Nowadays, few are aware that the Swiss-German Protestants produced the first complete Bible in High German, translated from the original languages by a team of godly linguistic experts several years before Luther published his 'Luther Bible'. Perhaps the Luther Bible has established itself more in international notice because unlike Bullinger and his team, Luther placed his own name on the title page. The Swiss called their translation simply 'The Bible', which God had given to mankind. It was Bullinger's doctrine of the Word of God which thrilled the English Reformers and encouraged them to 'go and do likewise' in producing several standard works on this theme. So, too, it was the doctrines of the Swiss Reformation which became the basic reading of trainee ministers of the gospel in England and their doctrines were those exported to the New World during the times of Reformer King Edward VI and good Queen Bess.

Bullinger's Decades, now once again available, became the systematic theology of English theological students before any of Calvin's works of a comparable size were written or reached England. Bullinger's Reformed works went into hundreds of editions as the Reformation spread. When Geneva did get around to publishing Calvin's works, the Council ruled that this should only take place if Bullinger's latest works were also printed to balance them off. When Calvin died, the Council told Beza, to put Bullinger at the top of his list of predecessors worth following.

Another of the Swiss Reformation's achievements under Bullinger was the reformation of schools and universities. This involved the production of suitable text books, the setting up of institutes to study the Semitic and Classical languages, and the establishment of colleges for missionary training. These colleges also housed academic departments for the study of botany, zoology and the natural sciences. Switzerland served as Protestant pioneers in these academic fields and induced many other countries to follow their lead. In the field of humanitarian and social help, Bullinger set up parish offices to help the poor and find employment for those out of work which led to the canton of Zürich becoming free of poverty. Bullinger was also instrumental, here following Zwingli's lead, in stopping the recruiting of mercenaries from the Protestant cantons of Switzerland by the French.

Much of George Ella's book is taken up with outlining the national and international impact Bullinger had on his contemporary world. In doing so, he has had to combat many myths and faulty interpretations of history which have developed in post-Reformation times. Perhaps the most surprising fact Dr Ella brings to light is the unfounded distinction between Zürich and Geneva during the period from the fifteen-twenties to the fifteen-seventies. Modern 'Calvinists' tend to view Geneva as 'the City on a Hill', where peace, prosperity and spiritual growth reigned in government, Church and people, making the city a veritable Heaven on earth. Many Reformed writers even portray Calvin as having everything firmly in hand and acting as the main instrument for good in the city over several decades. Ella shows that this is quite wrong as contemporary records depict Geneva as a city in turmoil, where the church was beset with poverty and both political and ecclesiological revolutions were common.

The author depicts Calvin as having a tough time because of his attitude to the Councils, his fellow clergy, church members, the Swiss states, alleged heresies and a number of Reformed doctrines. Indeed, Geneva banned Calvin from the city from 1538 to 1541 and at regular intervals he was threatened with expulsion and witnessed protests against him in the streets. This antagonism continued until just a few years before Calvin's death in 1564. Ella claims furthermore that Calvin's Francophile politics were harmful to the gospel and his constant wish to 'go it alone' proved more negative than positive. Indeed, on Ella's evidence, Calvin can be blamed for much of the fierce turmoil Geneva experienced in the sixteenth century. In contrast, Dr. Ella depicts Zürich as truly representing Bullinger's 'City on a Hill' where unity was nurtured between Church, government and people. He also presents Calvin as Bullinger's oft-times rebellious protégé, who, nevertheless, always looked to Bullinger to help him out of troubles often of his own making such as his ill-thought-out transactions with the Lutherans, the Emperor and French Roman Catholics and his blunders in dealing with Bolsec, Castellio and Servetus.

This book is, however, no mere 'history'. Dr. Ella believes that the Reformed churches of today have isolated themselves historically and doctrinally from the teaching of the Reformation and this need to be corrected. He sees Bullinger as the Reformer best suited to exercise such corrections because of the highly pastoral way he dealt with error. The author is critical of some modern pseudo-Christian activities, practised under the name of 'Reformed'. For example, he believes that the old view of the Word of God as infallible and inerrant has been weakened by Reformed men opening the doors to the rationalistic speculations of pseudo 'Higher Critical scholars'. He also believes the doctrine of justification, taught by the Scriptures and passed on by Luther, Bucer and Bullinger, has been exchanged for Melanchthon's more speculative and legal ideas and predestination and election are now taught as if they were the earned products of belief, not the instrument and origin of it. In short, the author believes the modern Reformed movement has radically changed the doctrines which were once delivered to the saints in the Scriptures and revived in the Reformation.

George Ella reintroduces us to Bullinger, believing that if the churches today study what really brought the Reformation to life through his ministry, this might move them to pray, once again, that grace and gospel might triumph over law and legal bondage as it did in his day. The author's wish is that the churches might once again see Christ in all His glories as the hope of the world rather than base their 'faith' on a trust in historical myths and dead-letter doctrines learnt by rote and not experienced in the heart. My friend and brother, George Ella, thus presents the life of Bullinger as an antidote to today's miseries in the churches. Bullinger's doctrines were not legal but full of the grace which Christ still offers to His people. Thus, by returning to the ways of our fathers in the faith which they obtained by grace only, we might once again learn to serve Christ as our true Saviour and no longer pay lip service to the traditions of men.

Peter L. Meney

Foreword Two

This book is a masterpiece of research and does not just follow trodden paths, but is willing to take a new look at the whole picture even though this might shake loved and much defended traditions and 'myths'. It is written in Bullinger-style, as it has to criticise a lot of other researchers and theologians, but does not do so in an aggressive or proud spirit, but with a pastoral and humble goal to unite us all in the one faith given to us once for all in the revelation of Jesus Christ and Holy Scripture.

Dr Ella calls Bullinger 'the forgotten Reformer' and says this is true in a similar sense only of Martin Bucer (1491-1551). As our theological seminary with campuses in all German speaking countries calls itself 'Martin Bucer Seminary', and as we have done a lot of research on our patron, I have much experience with pastors and theologians asking me, who Bucer was, a man who was at least as famous as Martin Luther in his day.[1] I also have much experience with 'Calvinists' (to whom I belong myself) asking me, what confession we have, not knowing that Calvin owed most of his 'Calvinism' to his elder friend Bucer and to Bullinger. So let me take the freedom to compare Bullinger's and Bucer's fate among church historians a little.

Bonn is the former residence of the Archbishop of Cologne. His huge castle nowadays is used by one of the major universities of Germany. The Bonn office of Martin Bucer Seminary near the Cathedral where Bucer preached is located in the inner city of Bonn, actually door to door to the Jesuit college, where not only Beethoven studied, but which was also the organising office of the Counter-Reformation, which destroyed much of the work of Bucer and others. Martin Bucer, reformed Reformer of Strasbourg, lived, preached and wrote in Bonn for one year to prepare the reformation of the state of Cologne on behalf of the Archbishop until the Archbishop was dismissed. Later his proposed church order and liturgy for Cologne was used by Archbishop Cranmer in the Reformation of England – together with the influence of Bullinger's writings – a major reason why Britain became Reformed and not Lutheran in theology. At the end of his life Bucer fled to England, taught at Cambridge, helped Cranmer to revise the Book of

[1] See Thomas Schirrmacher. "Einheit durch Hören auf die Schrift und aufeinander: Martin Bucers theologisches und praktisches Programm ...". S. 9-74 in: Thomas Schirrmacher (ed.). Anwalt der Liebe - Martin Bucer als Theologe und Seelsorger. Jahrbuch des Martin Bucer Seminars 1 (2001). VKW: Bonn, 2001 and other essays in this volume.

Common Prayer and wrote his major treatise 'De regno Christi' (1550), an ethics demanding the Church to transform every part of society under Christ's rule.

Most people, even most historians, still see Bucer and Bullinger as second generation reformers. It is true in the sense that both had read writings by Luther prior to their 'conversions', and both gave Luther credit all their lives to being the beginner, even after Luther started to blame both as heretics and inspired by the devil. But reading Luther prior to their 'conversion' took place in 1518 which does not make them 'second generation reformers'. Otherwise Philip Melanchton would have to be a second generation reformer, especially as in the beginning he just copied Luther's teaching, while Bucer and Bullinger prove in their first writings 1518-1519 that they followed Luther in general, but departed from him at certain points, which later became to be known as 'Reformed'. But compared to other Reformers, especially those in Switzerland – including the later famous Zwingli and Calvin – they were not only first generation reformers, but even years ahead in their earliest statement of typical protestant positions, 6 years earlier than Zwingli and 18 years earlier than Calvin.

Bucer became first a follower of Erasmus of Rotterdam and then, after moving to Heidelberg, one of the earliest followers of Luther through Luther's disputation in 1518, when Luther himself still had a lot of questions. In 1519 he had his first public disputation as a reformer. And already by 1520 he had written a book explaining justification and departing from Luther in the question of good works after regeneration – the beginning of his Reformed theology. The Holy Spirit, says Bucer, fulfils the third use of the law within Christians. Bucer was released from his order in 1521 and in 1522 was one of the first of the Reformers to marry. Excommunicated in 1523 he fled to Strasbourg to become the leader of the Reformation there for two decades.

Dr Ella proves in detail: When Zwingli for the first denied the worship of idols in the church in June 1524, and denied the teaching of transubstantiation as well as ending the Catholic mass in Zürich at Easter 1525, both Bullinger and Bucer had already started the reformation in their cities and by 1525 were already well-known authors of bestselling theological books.

Around 1525 there where three theologians who were the most respected leaders of the Reformation in Europe: Luther, Bucer and Bullinger. Bucer and Bullinger during their lifetimes were more widely known in all of Europe than either Luther or Calvin. Their books were published and translated, they were asked for counsel by other Reformers, kings and rulers, manuscripts were put before them to obtain their judgment. Bullinger wrote with his "119 works and 12,000 letters" (Dr Ella) more books, tracts and letters than both

Luther's and Calvin's together. Bucer, who surely was not such an eloquent writer as Bullinger, nevertheless wrote thick books on Romans, on exegesis, dogma, ethics[2] and counselling, becoming the model for Calvin, who studied in Bucer's huge library in Strasbourg and followed Bucer in many of his writings by form and content. Often what is called 'Calvinism' in reality stems from Bullinger or from Bucer. All editions of Calvin's 'Institutes', especially the first 1536 edition and the 1550 edition, show heavy influence by Bucer and Bullinger, so that it is an irony, that church historians nowadays present Bullinger as a preserver of Calvin's thought. Bullinger and Bucer were the first to write on predestination, on the third use of the law or the new 'Reformed' type of church leadership by a combination of lay and theologically trained elders – nowadays the local church structure of virtually every denomination. John Calvin sat at Bucer's feet for three years during his exile from Geneva, as evidenced notably in his theological views of the Church, the Eucharist and the ecumenical idea to bring the different wings of reformation together. Bucer was a profuse biblical commentator and his verse by verse exegesis was the beginning of modern exegesis, becoming a source for Calvin's lectures and commentaries on the whole Bible (with the exception of Revelation – which was only commented on by Bullinger).

Without Bullinger and Bucer, Calvin's history in Geneva and probably in Switzerland would have come to an end when he was expelled from Geneva. Both arranged a new task in Bucer's Strasbourg and it is said, that it is there where Calvin became a 'Calvinist'. Both negotiated Calvin's way back to Geneva. Without them, particularly Bullinger, Calvin never would have returned to Geneva.

Bucer and Bullinger are the only reformers of the 16th century who had a great impact on all three branches of the Protestant Church; Lutheran, Reformed and Anglican, and in the three major language blocs, the German, the French and the English speaking world.

It was Luther, Bucer and Bullinger who started a new era of theological education long before the Geneva Academy; Luther together with Melanchthon by taking over the existing theological faculties in Saxony, Bucer and Bullinger by starting very early famous schools in Strasbourg and Zürich. These attracted students from all over Europe, who later became reformers in their home countries. Victor Shepherd wrote of Bullinger: "Apart from him the theological 'shape' of late sixteenth and early seventeenth century England is unimaginable. Without him the first waves of English Puritans wouldn't have thrived."[3]

---

[2] See my review See my review "Martin Bucer und das Recht" (Rezension). Zeitschrift für Kirchengeschichte 115 (2004) 3: 416-419.

[3] http://www.victorshepherd.on.ca/other%20writings/heinrich_bullinger.htm.

Taking this into account, one is astonished, that Shepherd – like many others – nevertheless starts his essay with a centuries old, but typical myth: "Unlike the first generation of Reformation 'pioneers' (e.g., Martin Luther, born 1483 and Ulrich Zwingli, 1484) Bullinger was a consolidator. While adding his own perspective to Protestant theology it was his genius to be less an innovator than someone who could gather up and 'package' the gospel riches that hungry people craved in Switzerland and elsewhere."[4] A statement like this does not become truer by one author copying it from the other. The very dates of their earliest publications speak against it.

Heinrich (engl. Henry) Bullinger published the first ever treatise devoted to explaining the covenant in 1534, that is two years before Calvin developed covenant theology in later editions of his Institutes. Bullinger's 'A Brief Exposition of the One and Eternal Testament or Covenant of God' (1534) was the first book devoted to the subject of the covenant in 1500 years of the Christian church and a milestone in the history of dogma similar to Anselm of Canterbury's 'Cur deus homo'. Because of its influence on the subsequent development of the doctrine of the covenant, Charles S. McCoy and J. Wayne Baker like Dr Ella rightly call it the fountainhead of covenant theology.[5] Perhaps this is something Christians on the European continent are coming to see more clearly.[6]

There is another advantage of Bucer and Bullinger over the other major reformers. I would have preferred rather to have worked and lived with Bullinger and Bucer, than with Calvin or Luther. I fear, Luther and Calvin would have easily either called me a heretic or fought me because of some personal misunderstanding! Not so Bucer and Bullinger! They both were very gentle and had a pastoral and friendly spirit even in necessary struggles. Bucer and Bullinger were the two reformers who constantly tried to reconcile the different fringes of the Reformation. They were always in the middle, whenever there was a chance to get Lutherans and Reformed together in discussion with the Anabaptists, to negotiate with Roman Catholic opponents, or to find peaceful ways within the Reformed camp. They longed for spiritual peace as much as they longed for doctrinal purity. Where other Reformers have a long record of fighting fellow-Reformers or departing from fellowship with them, Bucer and Bullinger have long records of bringing people together to find a common biblical base, where division seemed

---

[4] http://www.victorshepherd.on.ca/other%20writings/heinrich_bullinger.htm.

[5] Charles S. McCoy, and J. Wayne Baker. Fountainhead of Federalism: Heinrich Bullinger and the Covenant Tradition. Westminster/John Knox Press: Louisville (KY), 1991. S. 11; cf. J. Wayne Baker. Heinrich Bullinger on the Covenant: The Other Reformed Tradition. Athens (OH): Ohio University Press, 1980.

[6] Eg Martin Hohl. Heinrich Bullinger und seine Bundestheologie. RVB: Hamburg, 2001.

otherwise to be inevitable. Thus it is not by chance, that Bullinger's and Bucer's view and practice of church discipline is so much warmer and liveable than that of Luther, Zwingli or Calvin. It is also not by chance, that Bullinger and Bucer wrote more on counselling than all the other reformers and wrote more on family and marriage, as both obtained strength from their wives and left us unsurpassed praises of their beloved spouses who lived and worked with them.

Nobody at the time of the Reformation devoted so much attention to studying the problems caused by the conflicting views arising during the Reformation as these two did[7] and their solutions to these problems have survived the years. Bucer was identified so closely with a spirit of understanding that Bullinger called people who strove for unity amongst the brethren 'buceristic'.[8]

Bucer is best known as a Christian diplomat trying to achieve the unity of the Protestants or even all Christians. He played a major role in virtually every meeting of Lutherans with Reformed, initiating the discussion of Luther and Zwingli in Marburg (1529). In the late 1530s and early 1540s he was the leading Protestant negotiator for agreement with the Roman Catholic Church in Germany, especially in the conferences of Leipzig (1539), Hagenau and Worms (1540), and Regensburg (1541). No Reformer was more on the road to organise the Reformation at other places and wrote more books and pamphlets for other Reformers. And even if Bullinger thought that Bucer could be going too far in bringing people together, he nevertheless backed every theological dispute Bucer organised for the unity of the church.

No reformers had more connections with the Reformations in all the European countries and with all branches of Christianity than Bucer and Bullinger. Bucer and Bullinger had the whole Christian world, yes, even the whole world, in view and were never satisfied to have problems solved for themselves if others still needed help.

There is also a big difference here between Bullinger and Bucer. Bullinger hardly travelled and never left Switzerland. Through an astonishing correspondence, Bullinger exerted influence on theologians everywhere. He corresponded with Swiss, German, and English theologians, he wrote to kings, princes, and queens. Bucer was a great letter writer too, but was constantly on the road in all of Europe, reforming, negotiating, connecting and discussing. He helped with the reformation on the spot in Strasbourg,

---

[7] Vgl. Gottfried Bender. Die Irenik Martin Bucers in ihren Anfängen. Studia Irenica 5. Gerstenberg: Hildesheim, 1975. S. 149-153.

[8] Bullinger to Blaurer on 10.10.1544, quoted from Willem van't Spijker. "Martin Bucer, Pietist unter den Reformatoren?". S. 88-101 in: Jan van den Berg, Jan P. van Dooren (Hg.). Pietismus und Reveil. Kerkhistorische Bijdragen 7. E. J. Brill: Leiden, 1978. S. 101.

France, Southern Germany, Hessia, Cologne and England, always living there for at least some months. Both achieved the same end and no other Reformer, not even Luther and Melanchthon, had such a wide circle of friends, partners and students. They were Europeans in the best sense and when they died, the English mourned their passing as a calamity as if they had been British Reformers.

Bullinger was also a master systematic theologian, even though many historians only see him as a pastor, organisor and multiplicator. The '*Decades*', Bullinger's main theological work, is a collection of 50 Latin teaching-sermons (five books of ten sermons each, hence the title '*Decades*'), which grew out of Bullinger's work as a teacher. They deal with all the important 'loci' of the evangelical faith and demonstrate Bullinger's personal imprint on the Reformation. The *Decades* are comparable to Calvin's *Institutes* in length, scope and influence.

Eduard Böhl (1836-1903), longtime professor of Systematic Theology in Vienna, was the last Bible believing 'Calvinist' on a chair at a State University in German-speaking Europe.[9] Deeply rooted in Luther's and Calvin's thoughts and writings, he nevertheless thought Bullinger's writing to be the best way to revive Reformed thinking in Europe's churches. Böhl's Systematic Theology, which we re-edited and still use at our seminary as a Reformed text book, [10] is very much built on Bullinger's thoughts. This is the reason why we can use this text book also for non-Reformed students, because it starts out with what is common to all Christians and discusses the differences in a pastoral way. Böhl gave his first lecture on 11 April, 1864 in Vienna on the Second Helvetic Confession.[11] He sees Bullinger as the man who unified the different branches of the Reformed camp and reformation in general in an exegetical and pastoral way. He advises Reformed churches all over Europe to follow Bullinger in the way he presents the Reformed message and not to use an aggressive approach, which starts out with complicated teachings, which are under debate even among Reformed theologians. His motto following Bullinger is 'Christianus mihi nomen – Reformatus cognomen!'.[12] To that end he published a critical edition of 'The

---

[9] See my biography of Böhl "'Festwerden im Glauben an Christum': Leben und Werk Eduard Böhls". S. 137-163 in: Im geistlichen Kampf um die Wahrheit. Festschrift zum 25jährigen Bestehen der STH Immanuel-Verlag: Riehen (CH), 1995 (Fundamentum 3/1995). "'Festwerden im Glauben an Christum': Leben und Werk Eduards Böhls". S. 11-38 bzw. 13-45 in: Eduard Böhl. Dogmatik. Hänssler Theologie. Hänssler: Neuhausen, 19951; RVB: Hamburg, 20042.

[10] Eduard Böhl. Dogmatik. Hänssler Theologie. Hänssler: Neuhausen, 19951; RVB: Hamburg, 20042.

[11] Eduard Böhl. Die Zweite Helvetische Confession: Eine Antrittsrede. Wilhelm Braumüller: Wien, 1864.

[12] Ibid.: Preface "Christian is my name, Reformed is my second name".

Second Helvetic Confession' for its 300 year jubilee.[13] He persuaded synods all over Europe, especially in Austria and Hungary, to accept the Second Helvetic Confession as their confessional standard.

The Swiss Reformation, outside Geneva, produced two remarkable and beautiful confessions: The First and the Second Helvetic Confessions. The First Helvetic Confession was co-authored by Bullinger. The famous Second Helvetic Confession was written as Bullinger's personal statement of faith. Friedrich III, Elector of the Palatine (1559-1576) was so impressed, that he used Bullinger's confession as justification for his change from the Lutheran to the Reformed faith in 1566. He also used it widely for uniting Reformed churches, following the Swiss example, and finally used its structure as initiator and possible co-author of the famous Heidelberg Catechism.

When we at the Martin Bucer Seminary edited the German version of the three Chicago Declarations, especially the Chicago Declaration on Biblical Inerrancy, to distance ourselves from a liberal theology using higher criticism of the Bible, we – perhaps different to the American editors – as Europeans wanted to prove that these hermeneutical views are not new and not just the result of debates in the USA in the 20th century. We considered many texts, but it became obvious that we must include Bullinger's articles on the Bible from the beginning of his Second Helvetic Confession.[14] Long before the Westminster Confession started out with a similar clear cut statement on the Bible, Bullinger had laid out a doctrine of Scripture which not only became standard in the Reformed world, but is nowadays common to all Bible believing Christians. As Dr Ella shows in detail, no other Reformer thought and wrote more on the doctrine of Scripture than Bullinger, especially in books published in 1538 and 1572 as well as in a book written in the 1520s and rediscovered in 1991. All other Reformers built on 'sola scriptura', but only a few gave the doctrine detailed discussion. I personally think that Bullinger's writings alone can still be used today despite being separated from us by almost half a millennium. It is more or less Bullinger's view of Scripture which nowadays binds together all branches of Christianity who believe in the infallibility of Scripture![15]

Most Reformed churches on the European continent are liberal anyway and not so much concerned about the roots of Reformed dogmatics. Even though these churches are very rich compared to churches in other countries and their theological faculties are financed by the State, they have done little

---

[13] Eduard Böhl. Confessio Helvetica Posterior olim ab Henrico Bullingero ... ad fidem editionis principis ... G. Braumüller: Wien, 1866. S. 1-95 (Text mit textkritischen Anmerkungen).
[14] Cf. William Traub. "Die Lehre von der Schrift in den reformierten Bekenntnisschriften". Bibel und Gemeinde 97 (1997) 2: 98-116.
[15] See ibid.

to research the publications of many of the Reformers, or even to edit historical-critical editions and workable translations. Two thirds of the writings of Martin Bucer still have not been republished since the 19th century and most of his letters and many major works by him are still totally unpublished and rarely accessible.[16] Heinrich Bullinger's works, at present, are being published in a critical edition for the first time, even though quite slowly. The vast majority of the non-German writings of these two reformers have never been translated into German and only a few titles are in print.

The latest German edition as well as a computer version of the Latin version of Bullinger's 'Summa' is thus not published by the Swiss Reformed churches or one of the big liberal publishers, but by a local Evangelical church.[17]

Thomas Schirrmacher

---

[16] See my review of a new edition of his writings for the (failed) reformation of Cologne/Bonn: "Martin Bucer Schriften zur Kölner Reformation" (Rezension). Zeitschrift für Kirchengeschichte 116 (2005) 1: 120-122.

[17] Heinrich Bullinger. Christliches Glaubensleben: Summa christenlicher Religion 1556. Limache Verlag: o. O. (Basle), 1995.

Henry Bullinger (1504–1575)

Introduction

Henry Bullinger's Unique Position in Church History

The Reformation's neglected heroes

It has long been my conviction that not half of the story of the Reformation has been told. Happily, great men and women of God who were true pioneers and upholders of reform are now being rediscovered causing a radical alteration in our knowledge and even convictions concerning how the true faith was revived after centuries of papal superstition. Since the nineteen fifties, however, the attention of the Reformed Churches has centred on the so-called Puritan Age, often called The Second Reformation, which emphasises the testimony of men and women of God who graced this earth in the seventeenth century. Since the 19th century the comparatively little research that has been done on the earlier Reformers has almost exclusively concentrated on the pioneering influence of Luther and the consolidating influence of Calvin. Luther, however, sadly set himself against much of the work of more consistent Reformers, viewing Zwingli and Bullinger as 'Anabaptists'. Calvin, who came closer to Luther at times than his Swiss-German contemporaries thought-wise, was a second-generation Reformer who built on the work of a number of spiritual giants. These are now forgotten and overshadowed by Calvin's subsequent fame which has become out of proportion as a consequence of neglect regarding Calvin's great mentors. The result is that the majority of the great pioneer Reformers on the European Continent such as Martin Bucer (1491-1551), Wolfgang Capito (c.1478-1541), Valerand Poullain (1515-1557), Berchtold Haller (1492-1536), Oswald Myconius (1488-1552), Conrad Pellican (1478-1556), Oecolampadius (1482-1531), Peter Viret (1511-1571), William Farel (1489-1565), Peter Martyr Vermigli (1500-1562),[1] Jerome Zanchi (1516-1590) and Henry Bullinger (1504-1575) are as little known today as are the English pioneers Robert Greathead (c.1168), Thomas Bradwardine (c.1290-1349), John Wycliffe (c.1329-1384), John Colet (c.1466-1519), William Tyndale (c.1494-1536), Miles Coverdale (1488-1569), Thomas Lever (1521-1577), John Jewel (1522-1571) and Edmund Grindal (c.1519-1583). Indeed, many of these Reformers, both Englishmen and Continentals, had an international reputation and influence which was far wider than that of the later Puritans. The immediate freshness, and spontaneity of these early contenders for hitherto lost truths provides us with a glorious witness second to none. Knowledge of their experimental heart-religion at the dawn of the Reformation when the churches again discovered their first-love to Christ is essential to our own present-day Christian well-being. In seeing how God has worked in the past, we learn to trust Him all the more in the future. Sadly, such little interest is shown concerning the faith of our fathers today that the bulk of our Reformed churches, if asked to name Reformed names which have been God's agents in transforming the churches, would remember John Calvin (1509-1564), Charles Haddon Spurgeon (1834-1892), Dr Martyn Lloyd-Jones (1899-1981) and perhaps George Whitefield (1714-1770) and Benjamin Breckinridge Warfield (1851-1921). They would thus be almost ignorant of the great men and women who carved out the Reformed path with a spiritual stubbornness which has been abandoned because of our modern views of live-and-let-live and lack of interest in vital, Christian religion.

---

[1] Usually the surname is dropped.

Switzerland at the dawn of the Reformation

The earlier history of the Reformation in Switzerland, especially in the German-speaking areas, tends to be a neglected topic for study in the English-speaking world. The German Reformers Luther and Melanchthon are familiar names to most and Frenchman John Calvin, so indelibly associated with Geneva, is no stranger. But Bullinger, Zwingli, Haller, Oecolampadius, Myconius, Farel, Viret, Vadian, Pellican, Bibliander, Simler, Gualter and a host of other fine Swiss Reformers are sadly not even known by name by those who live beyond the European Continent and even appear lost to most Continental Christians. This, in spite of the fact that their contemporaries called them the Fathers of the Reformed Churches. This is a most deplorable state as in Reformation times, the new awakening drew the churches of the nations far closer together than they are now and just as the English Reformers were well-known to the Continentals, so the names of the above-mentioned pioneers were household words in Great Britain and many of their works avidly read. Furthermore, the Reformation in Switzerland came early and spread rapidly. The independent German-Swiss were rarely under the yoke of great dukes as in Germany or under the threat of a foreign take-over as in Geneva. Often entire communities could vote freely to become Protestant or remain papist with no pressure placed on them by popes, prelates or princes. Indeed, Switzerland[2] began to be won for the Reformation in the early 1520s, starting in the Zürich area under the teaching of Zwingli and Bullinger, followed by Bern, Basle and Schaffhausen who were mostly evangelised from Zürich. It was initially a German-speaking urban movement, only slowly moving into the French, Romansh and Italian speaking territories which it never fully gained.

The population of Switzerland was small in the 16th century, starting at around 800,000 inhabitants and rising up to a million by 1600. There were no great cities of note. Basle had approximately 9,500 inhabitants, followed in size by Zürich with 8,000 inhabitants. However, there were around 60,000 inhabitants in the surrounding *Landshaft* governed by

[2] Geneva was not yet Reformed and not yet part of Switzerland.

Zürich, approximating to the present-day canton of Zürich. Bern and Sankt Gallen had each around 5,000 inhabitants and Lucerne (Luzern) was a little smaller. Politically speaking, Switzerland as it is governed today did not exist. A number of city cantons and provinces had founded different kinds of confederacies which never fully united the entire country and often included states which are now part of other nations. Nor had the Swiss states or cantons a common language. Upper German dialects, various Swiss-German dialects, French, Italian and Rhaeto-Romanic made communications between the common people of the cantons most difficult – as it still does. Zwingli and Bullinger strove to use an over-regional form of German years before Luther but the disadvantages of this strategy were almost as great as the advantages before the Swiss became used to the new system.

All the leaders both in church and state used Latin as a *lingua franca*, but turned to various German dialects more and more as the sixteenth century progressed. A letter dated 11 December, 1531 from Berchtold Haller to Bullinger, for instance, illustrates this trend as Haller starts off in Swiss-German but the bulk of the letter is such a mixture of German and Latin that the two languages appear to be used as one.[3] To make matters more complicated, the main linguistic divisions often gave rise to political and religious barriers. Many of the major towns often found themselves forming political unions against Zürich such as the 1524 union of Lucerne, Uri, Schwyz, Unterwalden and Zug, known thereafter as the *Fünf Orte* who protested against the larger city's political and ecclesiastical policies and preferred an alliance with Roman Catholic Austria Anterior to one with their Protestant neighbours. Similar opposition was shown French-speaking Geneva both from the Savoy and the German cantons who each wished to 'liberate' her in their own opposite ways. Likewise, too, each group of confederates whether Roman Catholic or Protestant wished to emphasise that they were forming their alliance to preserve the Christian religion. Thus during 1527-1529 Zürich, Constance, Bern, Basle, Schaffhausen, Biel and Mülhausen united under

[3] *Heinrich Bullinger Werke, Briefe der Jahre 1524-1531*, pp. 234-237.

the name of *Christliches Burgrecht*[4] whereas the Roman Catholic *Fünf Orte*, Solothurn, Freiburg and Austria Anterior called themselves the *Christliche Vereinigung.*[5] Often, the Reformation in one city took a different course than that in another. As cantons became Reformed, this political confusion became worse as the Protestant districts swore to keep the confederacies under the patronage of God whereas the Fünf Orte, took an oath in the name of God and the saints. The trouble in Locarno, referred to when we come to discuss Bullinger's international reputation, started because the confederacy who ruled the city-state were divided over religious and language issues. At times, when Bern, Basle and Geneva quarrelled, these Reformed cantons refused to allow their citizens full inter-church fellowship.

Other cantons, whether papist or Reformed, often fell out with Zürich over the question of selling mercenary soldiers to the French. This was stopped by Zwingli and Bullinger in Zürich, though other areas such as near-by Zug still gained a good deal of their income via exporting soldiers. It was a horrific experience for Bullinger to hear that the popish kings of France were using Swiss mercenaries to slaughter the French Protestants and one of the many reasons why Bullinger, unlike Calvin, would not hear of a political allegiance with France. The political and religious state of the Swiss cities and rural areas became more complicated and less independent when various Swiss territories entered into confederacies with bordering German and French areas. Thus the largest confederacy of thirteen cantons including Appenzell, Basle, Bern, Freiburg, Schaffhausen, Schwyz, Solothurn, Lucerne, Unterwalden, Glarus, Uri, Zürich and Zug called the *Gemeine Herrschaften* (Common Dominions) often functioned as a Swiss-only confederacy but it was at times extended to include other territories (*Zugewandte Orte*) which included besides Swiss Sankt Gallen and Neuchâtel, parts of Alsace and the Black Forest. Geneva, roughly the size of Basle, became an associated member of this widened confederacy much later on in the century because of Bern's opposition and the Genevan desire to ally with France

[4] Christian Civil Rights.
[5] Christian Union.

rather than Protestant Switzerland. Geneva, with the entire Pays de Vaud (Waadtland), was under the rule of the Savoy until 1536. In that year, Bern opposed the Roman Catholic Emperor Charles V by ridding the city of Savoyard troops. From then on, Bern, who took a strong anti-Calvin line for most of this period, influenced the politics and religion of Geneva strongly and remained in control of the city until 1564, the year of Calvin's death, when Bern entered into permanent peace treaties with the Savoy and paved the way for Geneva's Swiss membership. It was not until 1584 that Geneva was able to gain membership of the *Eidgenossenschaft*[6] with leading cantons such as Zürich. Most certainly one of the major reasons why Geneva did not enter the Swiss fold earlier was the major quarrels Calvin had with cantons such as Bern and Basle. However, even Geneva's entrance into the Swiss Eidgenossenschaft was at risk after Calvin's death when the city became bankrupt in 1583 and the Duke of Savoy, urged on by the pope, attempted to retake both the city and her surrounding domains. Geneva begged England for help and Queen Elizabeth wrote to the Confederacy and the main Swiss-German Protestant cities of Zürich, Bern, Basle and Schaffhausen, urging them to hurry to the support of Geneva, otherwise she would be lost to the Reformation. Meanwhile, Archbishop Whitgift and other Church and state dignitaries collected money to help the poor city-state.[7] Help, too, came in from other Protestant Swiss and German cities.

One of the last to join the *Gemeine Herrschaften* was Basle, though the city was one of the first to be won over for the Reformation through Oecolampadius and Myconius, formerly of Zürich. To complicate matters from the 1520s onwards mutual defence treaties were drawn up by various Swiss cities and neighbouring cities in Upper Germany. These non-Swiss associates, such as Constance and Strasburg joined with the Swiss Protestants which escalated Roman Catholic fears, especially in the central Swiss Roman Catholic cantons who founded a Roman Catholic League at Waldshut in 1529. This polarisation soon led to the Kappel

---

[6] Confederacy of Swiss states under one oath.

[7] See Queen Elizabeth's letters to the Swiss authorities in Zürich Letters, Second Series, pp. 315-319.

wars. The close association of the Swiss Protestants with Strasburg helps to explain Martin Bucer's enormous influence in forming Swiss Reformed theology.

Ulrich Zwingli and the Swiss Reformation

The fact that Ulrich (Huldrych) Zwingli (1484-1531) took over as Superintendent of the Great Minster in Zürich in December 1518 has caused many to claim that Zwingli was the first to start the Swiss Reformation. However, it was not until June 1524 that Zwingli seriously challenged the use of images in worship and it was first in 1525 that Zwingli rejected the doctrine of transubstantiation. This stand was more because of the humanistic teaching of Erasmus and his disagreements with the Lutherans than any deep theological reason. Indeed, Erasmus himself spotted this connection between himself and Zwingli. The Zürich Reformer wrote to Vadian on May 28, 1525, sending him a copy of his newly published *Taufbüchlein*,[8] and told him:

"When Erasmus of Rotterdam received my *Commentary*,[9] he exclaimed, as a friend of his reports 'My good Zwingli, what do you write that I have not first written?' I tell you this that you may see how far self esteem can carry us. Would that Erasmus had treated my arguments with his pen! The world would then have been persuaded, so that I should not labour under such a burden of enmity. I always preferred to stay in the background, but the Lord did not wish it; and his will be done. Would that the name of Erasmus had been attached to my book!" [10]

During Easter of 1525, Zwingli abolished the mass and had the images removed from his church, an act which has moved many a church historian to claim that this was a 'first' in Switzerland. However, only a few miles away, in the small town of Kappel am Albis, later to become

[8] Booklet on Baptism.
[9] *Commentary on True and False Religion*, published March, 1525.
[10] Taken from 69D Zwingli to Vadian, *The Sources of Swiss Anabaptism: The Grebel Letters and Related Documents*, p. 376.

famous for the wars and treaties between the papist and Reformed powers, eighteen-year-old Henry Bullinger had been preaching down popery in the abbey school since January, 1523 and had taken a firm stand against transubstantiation, fully supported by the Abbot. This work was not confined to the abbey school over which teenager Bullinger was placed but he also taught the full Reformed faith in the lectures he was commissioned to give to the monks. Thus though Zürich and Kappel both abolished the popish mass in 1525, it was Bullinger's Kappel who first came under a thorough-going Reformed teaching. Indeed, both Leo Jud (1482-1542) and Bullinger were openly preaching and writing against the use of images in churches as early, or, as in Jud's case,[11] earlier, than Zwingli. Bullinger was training ministers to go out and preach the Reformed faith several years before Zwingli followed his example. We must also acknowledge the fact that at this time, young, brilliant Bullinger had no official office in the church and Zwingli was a man of great ecclesiastical and political power. By the grace of God, the spiritual giant Zwingli, with one brief exception mentioned below, never regarded the youngster Bullinger as his rival and gradually came not only to love him but to admire and follow him. It appears that modern scholarship is, on the whole, not abreast of this fact and the most modern learned volumes coming from renowned Swiss and American publishing houses still refer to Bullinger as if his fame was merely in carrying on Zwinglian traditions. The fact that Bullinger was thoroughly Reformed in faith and teaching before ever he met Zwingli is seemingly lost to those who merely refer to Bullinger as 'Zwingli's successor'.

The rediscovery of Henry Bullinger

Perhaps no Reformer has been neglected in modern times so much as Swiss-born Heinrich Bullinger,[12] whose birth 500 years ago is being

[11] A sermon of Jud's from 1 September 1523 is extant entitled *wie man uss der gottlichen gschrift bewären möcht und recht wäre, dass man die götzen uss den kilchen tuon sölle.* After this sermon, images were thrown out of several churches until Jud and Zwingli actually put a stop to it.

[12] Called Henry Bullinger in English works.

celebrated this year.[13] Indeed, Bullinger is invariably called 'the forgotten Reformer', though this could equally be said of Bullinger's contemporary Martin Bucer[14] who also played a formative role in the Reformation. This neglect regarding Bullinger's and Bucer's fame is particularly frustrating because if we erase such key figures from church history, we can never rightly understand such contemporary Swiss and Genevan Reformers as Zwingli and Calvin, either. Nor can we judge accurately the development of the Reformation in Britain, Germany, Eastern Europe, Italy and France. In particular, Calvin is still a popular subject for Reformed biographers and systematic theologians but as such works invariably lack the briefest discussion concerning Calvin's enormous dependence on Bullinger, Bucer and other first generation Reformers, their value is greatly reduced. So, too, such appraisals of Calvin's teaching tend to give Calvin an importance as a pioneer Reformer which would be most difficult to defend historically. Until very recently, Bullinger hardly ever appeared as a figure of note in any of our modern church history or theological books. Indeed, the situation concerning Bullinger and Calvin is very similar to what has been happening in our understanding of Whitefield and Wesley. In my youth, I was brought up to look on Wesley as the pioneer of the Great Awakening of the Eighteenth Century. He was the one to collect all the 'firsts'. He was the first to take the gospel to the streets, first to try and awaken the Church of England and first to revive North America etc.. Then, in the late 1950's, George Whitefield was re-discovered and suddenly Wesley's fame grew less as it became known that much that had been attributed to John Wesley had been, in God's Providence, really the work of Whitefield. It is this author's contention that Calvin, with all his obvious abilities as a Reformer, has been placed on a pedestal which rightly belongs to Bullinger who eclipsed his French friend in almost all areas. Indeed, had it not been for Bullinger's strong leadership over Calvin and the enormous influence Bullinger exerted on

[13] 2004, the year this book was written.
[14] For recent brief introductions to Bucer's life and works see Philip H. Eveson's two essays entitled *Martin Bucer (1491-1551)* in Issues 457-458 of the Banner of Truth Magazine and my essay *Martin Bucer: Moderator of the Reformation* in New Focus, Vol. 6, No. 04.

his doctrines and the fatherly and brotherly way Bullinger supported Calvin in all his battles, Calvin would never have remained in Geneva from 1541-1564 and never have been half the Reformer he was. Bullinger's advantage over Calvin was that Zürich at that time, as Bullinger repeatedly testifies, was a City on a Hill in the spiritual sense that Church and state lived in almost constant, peaceful harmony. On the other hand, the scene at Geneva was one of turbulence and strife both within the Church and within the State and also in their constant conflicts with each other. We never hear of Bullinger denouncing his fellow ministers, citizens and Council in the denigrating way Calvin did the ministers, Church, citizenship and Council of Geneva up to the last few years of his life. It must also be said with equal truthfulness that the peace of Zürich was largely Bullinger's making and the problems which arose in Geneva, which Bullinger was invariably looked upon to solve, were often because of Calvin's lack of diplomacy and lack of control over his temper, tongue and pen. Ernst Stähelin, a great admirer of Calvin, nevertheless sees Calvin's temper as one of his more negative characteristics which caused many to distrust him. In his biography of Calvin, he excuses his subject by saying:

"Whoever has read his letters knows only too well how his irritable, choleric temperament, especially when spontaneously vented against his intimate friends, led to his putting on paper remarks which were not meant to be taken as severely as they sounded. In any case, it is safer, when faced with (Calvin's) contradictory testimonies to accept only those which were written later in times of tranquillity and clear-headedness rather than his outbreaks of wrath when under pressure."[15]

Fritz Büsser, who has written widely on Calvin and Bullinger for half a century writes of Calvin's 'exaggerations and thoughtlessness'[16]. Modern lovers of Calvin often excuse him by saying that in those days hard, biting language was not against the decorum of the times. If this

[15] *John Calvin: Leben und ausgewählten Schriften,* Band 1, p. 441.
[16] *Calvin's Urteil über sich selbst,* p. 17.

were true, then one must ask why Calvin's most intimate friends such as Bullinger and Haller were always urging him to tame his language.

Gottfried W. Locher in his excellent, detailed study of Bullinger's and Calvin's contributions to the Reformation, sees the difference between Bullinger and Calvin in the two men's personal experience and aims reflected in their different attitudes to the cities they served. Bullinger wrote primarily for the pastoral edification of the Zürich Church under his care in which he was very much at home physically and spiritually because the gospel fell on fertile soil there. Calvin's position was much different. He was a refugee who never felt at home in the Old Geneva of the pre-fifties and his main theological aim was to aid and build up the persecuted Church in France, a country in which the gospel had been forbidden. Locher can thus say concerning Calvin, "The city-state Geneva was for him a base; his battle-front was in France."[17] Until very recently, however, such a diagnosis of the relationship between Bullinger and Calvin and Zürich and Geneva would have been judged to be lacking totally in objectivity. The following brief survey of works on the Swiss and Continental Reformation will suffice to illustrate this fact.

Bullinger ignored

In 1904 Professor Heinrich Boehmer of Leipzig published his *Luther im Lichte der neueren Forschung*. The work quickly ran into five editions and was translated into several languages, including English. A re-written and enlarged edition was published in 1930 under the title *Luther & the Reformation in the Light of Modern Research*. In this work, purporting to be an extensive and detailed study of Luther in particular and the Reformation in general, Ignatius of Loyola is mentioned on fifteen pages, Calvin on fourteen, Zwingli on nine, but Bullinger's part in the many debates and controversies with Luther is completely ignored and his name not so much as mentioned in the entire book. Between 1890 and 1911, B. J. Kidd compiled his 742 paged work for the Oxford Clarendon Press entitled *Documents Illustrative of the Continental Reformation*. When

[17] *Bullinger und Calvin – Probleme des Vergleichs Ihrer Theologie*, Gesammelte Aufsätze zum 4000. Todestag, p. 4 and footnote 15.

dealing with the Genevan Reformation, Kidd produces documents up to the year 1564, the year of Calvin's death. When listing documents to do with the Zürich Reformation, Kidd produces nothing after 1531, the year of Zwingli's death but the start of the Reformed Church under Bullinger. The true 'father' of the Swiss Reformation is not even mentioned once in the lengthy index. His name, however, is mentioned in a brief 'aside' when dealing with Calvin's most erratic doctrine of the Lord's Supper under the title 'Calvinism in Europe', stating that Bullinger "opened the way for the reception of the Genevan doctrine of the sacraments in German Switzerland" in 1549.[18] As Bullinger had been writing since the early 1520s on the subject and had not altered his position one bit and as Calvin first adopted this position in 1549, only to drop it later, this statement can only be classified as erroneous and misleading.

August Lang in his 1913 work on the Swiss Reformation entitled *Zwingli and Calvin* which he dedicated to the Theological Faculty of Geneva University, again leaves Bullinger almost entirely out of the Reformation picture. The man who took the Reformation far beyond Zwingli and succeeded in shaping it and consolidating it to a far greater extent than Calvin receives a very brief mention as if he had merely played a small caretaker role between the reigns of two giants. In 1952, V. H. H. Green brought out his *Renaissance and Reformation: A Survey of European History between 1450 and 1660.* This work was quickly reprinted nine times in the fifties and sixties and became a 'standard' for many readers and scholars. Yet in Chapter X on the Swiss Reformers, Green devotes the first section to Zwingli, the second to Calvin and Section 3 to the influence of Calvinism. Nothing is said concerning Bullinger's work. The Zürich Reformer is mentioned once in the body copy and once in a footnote but both references are historically incorrect. On page 164 Green writes "The English Reformers, for instance, were much affected by their correspondence with his (Zwingli's) son-in-law and successor, Heinrich Bullinger." Bullinger was, indeed, Zwingli's successor at Zürich but he had maintained a successful ministry for eight

[18] Op. cit., p. 318.

years in Kappel and Bremgarten before that. He was not, however, Zwingli's son-in-law. Green is confusing Heinrich Bullinger with his son of that name by Anna Adlischwyler. This Heinrich Bullinger was born three years after Zwingli died and married Anna Gualter who was the daughter of Rudolf Gualter (1519-1586), *Bullinger's successor* and Regula Zwingli, daughter of Ulrich Zwingli.[19] Henry Bullinger Junior was thus son-in-law to Rudolf Gualter and Gualter was son-in-law to Ulrich Zwingli. Regula died on November 14, 1565[20] and, some time afterwards, Gualter married Anna Blaurer, the niece of the Constance Reformer Ambrose Blaurer (1492-1564), also called Blaarer and Blarer.

In his second reference to Bullinger in a footnote on page 166, the author claims that Zürich accepted 'Calvin's sacramental system' in the *Consensus Tigurinus*. This oft-repeated statement does not fit the facts. The agreement was initiated by Zürich in the early forties as soon as Bullinger's diplomacy had helped greatly in reinstating exiled Calvin back in Geneva. Thereafter, Bullinger stressed in his letters, especially to Vadian that he thought Calvin's views were not so wide from his own and with him union was far more probable than with Luther. The *Consensus* bore Zürich's name and reflected Bullinger's doctrines which had remained unchanged since the early twenties as he stated in a letter to Leonhard Sörin of Moravia in September 1545. Furthermore, Bullinger published his *Von den Sakramenten* (On the Sacraments) in 1545[21] which in no way differs in doctrine from the 1549 *Consensus* with Calvin. Sörin had complained about Calvin's views not being fully Reformed according to his taste and Bullinger gave him the diplomatic answer, "If he teaches as you say, do not follow him but the truth!".[22]

---

[19] The misunderstanding that Bullinger was Zwingli's son in law is also asserted in Lindsay's *History of the Reformation*, written in 1907. Lindsay gives as his source Müller, Die Bekentnisschriften der reformierten Kirchen, p. 159.

[20] Blanke and Leuschauer give 1565 as the date of Regula's death on p. 156 of their *Henry Bullinger* but 1569 on p. 291. The earlier date is to be accepted as Regula died of the same plague that killed Anna Bullinger and other members of the family in 1564-65.

[21] The Lutherans begged Bullinger to delay publication of this work so as not to weaken their position before the Emperor in the Smalcaldian War. Pestalozzi says that Bullinger first sent Calvin a copy in 1547, p. 376.

[22] Pestalozzi, p. 375.

Calvin was compelled to drop a number of his more Lutheran tenets for reasons given in the detailed analysis of the events leading to the *Consensus Tigurinus* given later in this work. Besides, Farel also took part in the *Consensus* and it was at his initiative that Calvin travelled to Zürich to consult with Bullinger in the first place. Though Calvin occasionally threatened, especially at the time of the predestination controversy, to pull out of the *Consensus*, he never did for diplomatic reasons but continued to write and teach contrary to it. Thus the *Consensus* united Zürich and Geneva politically more than it did in doctrine. Concerning the latter, Bruce Gordon, echoing Amy Nelson Burnett, is certainly correct in saying that the *Consensus* " by no means knitted together their views on the Lord's Supper. There was also the fundamental difference of mentality: the Swiss Republican and the Frenchman who believed in an essentially aristocratic structure of the church did not share a common view of the world."[23]

G. W. Bromiley did a little to rectify the neglect of Bullinger in his anthology entitled *Zwingli and Bullinger* in Volume XXIV in the series The Library of Christian Classics published in 1954. However, he deals with five separate works of Zwingli on 230 pages but he allows only 42 pages for one work of Bullinger's, though Bullinger was arguably the more prolific writer and carried the Reformation much further than Zwingli. When, however, Owen Chadwick came to review the work in *The Journal of Theological Studies* in the same year, he spent all his comments on Zwingli and mentions Bullinger merely by saying that Gualter, Zwingli's translator into Latin, was closer to Bullinger than he was to Zwingli. Bromiley's comments on Bullinger and his sermon reproduced in the book are not mentioned at all in the review.

One of Britain's leading writers on the Reformation was A. G. Dickens. I had occasion to criticise Dickens' most unsatisfactory account of the English exiles at Frankfurt during the Marian persecutions in an appendix to my book *The Troublemakers at Frankfurt*. His handling of Bullinger, too, cannot escape criticism. In his book *Martin Luther and the*

[23] Architect of Reformation, p. 25.

Reformation in the 1970 edition, Dickens mentions the fact that Bullinger 'wrote the most famous of the attacks upon Anabaptists', not realising that it was what Dickens called 'the poor, heroic Anabaptists' who attacked the Bremgarten and Zürich churches first and that Bullinger's 'attack' was thus a defence against faulty criticism. He also refers to Bullinger's agreement with Calvin on the Lord's Supper in 1549 and mentions briefly in a comparison with Tyndale, Bucer and Oecolampadius, Bullinger's pioneer work on the covenant.[24] This exhausts all Dickens has to say about this major Reformer. Yet when Dickens comes repeatedly to discuss the Reformation in Switzerland, he mentions Zwingli but sees the Frenchman Calvin as the formative spirit behind the Reformed churches and their distinctive characteristics which separated them from Lutheranism.[25] Never a word is said about Bullinger's major Reforming initiative of the Swiss-German cantons, confederacies and *Eidgenossenschaften*.

In a more recent work published by the Cambridge University Press in 1994 entitled *The Reformation in National Context*, Kaspar von Greyerz, who appears to be a Swiss citizen, traces the Zwinglian Reformation in Zürich up to Zwingli's death in 1531 and then takes a great leap through time and geography and continues with Calvin at Geneva, not so much as even mentioning Bullinger's name. Needless to say, Calvin was only twenty-two when Zwingli died and still a papist whereas the active life of Bullinger after his conversion and as a Reformer ran exactly parallel to Zwingli's but then continued for another forty years far beyond Zwingli's and Calvin's deaths. This utter neglect of Bullinger at home and abroad is as serious as if the English were to omit Cromwell from the history of the Great Rebellion or John Wycliffe from the history of England's rejection of the papacy. Besides, such neglect draws with it a further neglect of Bullinger's enormous influence not only throughout Switzerland, including Geneva, but in such countries as Hungary, Poland, Romania, Holland, France, Italy and England. Bullinger was one of the most central figures, if not *the* central figure, in the international outreach of the

[24] See pages 101, 123 and 130.
[25] See especially p. 93 and entries on Switzerland.

Reformation. This has led Fritz Büsser, the greatest Bullinger and Calvin scholar alive today, when considering the international impact of Bullinger's theology, to argue, "In spite of the usual and still current practice of calling Reformed Christians 'Calvinists', especially in Eastern Europe, it was not the Genevans but Bullinger and the Zürich ministers, notably by means of the Second Helvetic Confession, who gave the Reformed churches and their theology their special characteristics."[26] Thus, if the life, work and witness of Bullinger is banned from our history and theology books, no true understanding of the Reformation is possible.

A further example of Swiss neglect of their major Reformer has been demonstrated regularly in the *Theologishe Zeitschrift* published by the Theological Faculty of Basle University. In Peter Bühler's article *Der Abendmahlsstreit der Reformatoren und seine aktuellen Implikationen* of 1979 on the 1528 Bern disputation, we read of the influence of Luther, Zwingli, Calvin and Oecolampadius concerning the Lord's Supper but nothing about the direct and strong influence of Bullinger on the 1528 Disputation through his numerous pioneer works on the Lord's Supper prior to that date. So, too, Franz-Josef Sladeczek in his 1988 study of the Bernese *Bildersturm* (storming the images) of 1528, also refers to Zwingli's influence, fully ignoring the early work of Bullinger on the subject. Indeed, it was Oecolampadius of Basle who encouraged Bullinger to publish his works of 1524-27 against popish practices at least a year before the Disputation. Furthermore, Bullinger, though only twenty-four years of age at the time, took an active part in all the proceedings. Yet the nearest Sladeczek comes to mentioning Bullinger is when he reproduces a picture from Bullinger's *History of the Reformation* depicting the *Bildersturm*. Indeed, much of what we know about the *Bildersturm* and the 1528 Disputation in general, comes from Bullinger's pen. Given such almost total silence regarding Bullinger's vast importance to the history of the Reformation, it came as no surprise for this author to read on the morning of his writing this account that the nearby Landeskirche (state-church) of Lippe was celebrating the 400th

[26] Büllinger biography, Vol. 2, p. 300.

anniversary of their acceptance of the 'Reformed Confession' and the 'Reformed Lord's Supper'. This confession and order for celebrating the Lord's Supper, the news agency (epd) reported, were products of "the doctrines of the Swiss Reformation of Calvin and Zwingli". The confession named arose as a direct appeal to Bullinger from the German states and the form of Lord's Supper used was worked out through Bullinger's almost ten-year endeavour to win Calvin over to the Reformed view of the ordinance. Furthermore, Zwingli's confessional works and views on the Lord's Supper were not prominent in the German Reformed churches of 1605, the year Lippe became Reformed. The main Reformer in this process, Bullinger, is thus totally forgotten in the Lippe Church of 2005, which is celebrating its acceptance of the Reformation four hundred years ago.[27]

In the few decades immediately preceding 2004, the five-hundredth anniversary of Bullinger's birth, some effort was made in modern scholarship to evaluate the global influence of Bullinger but this was still not carried out by in-depth studies and still left Bullinger in the shade of those whom he illuminated. Bob Scrivner in his *Comparative Overview* when drawing conclusions from his collection of essays in *The Reformation in National Context* places Bullinger in his 'famous five' group of Reformers, saying:

"Luther, Zwingli and Calvin contributed the major Reformation doctrines: Melanchthon gains his place because of his important modifications to Luther's theology, producing internal disputes which were to weaken Lutheranism more than any of the efforts of Luther's Catholic opponents: Bullinger joins the list because of his pivotal role in disseminating Helvetic doctrine throughout Europe in ways that made him as influential as Calvin in the shaping of the Reformed tradition."[28]

This is a good start to a new appreciation of Bullinger, or rather the beginning of a re-discovery of historical and theological facts, but it still

---

[27] *400 Jahre Reformation in Lippe*, WAZ, 28 May, 2005, p. WKU1_X.
[28] Op. cit., p. 217.

fails to see how much the doctrines of the other four of the 'famous five' were influenced and even moulded by Bullinger and how Bullinger's greatest influence on the Reformation was during his own lifetime and for the following century whereas Calvin's influence was mostly post-mortem and for reasons given below which were neither strictly doctrinal nor Reformed.

Recognition of Bullinger is now growing

A still more encouraging note was sounded by J. Wayne Baker in his *Heinrich Bullinger and the Covenant: The Other Reformed Tradition*, published in 1980. Baker states in his Prologue:

"It was Bullinger who preserved the Swiss Reformation after the death of Zwingli, and it was he who assured the essential theological unity of Reformed Protestantism with the First and Second Helvetic Confessions. During his forty-five-year tenure as leader of the Zürich church his importance in Reformed circles was unsurpassed, except perhaps by Calvin. Bullinger's influence was partly due to the many evangelical exiles, especially those from England and Italy, who went to Zürich. Mostly, however, this influence resulted from his voluminous writings and correspondence. He published a total of 119 works, not including titles that appeared posthumously or in later translations and editions. His extant correspondence numbers more than twelve thousand pieces, letters to and from nearly every prominent ecclesiastical and political leader of his day. His works have been traced to almost every part of Europe, including Poland, Hungary, Romania, Italy, and Spain, and his books crossed the seas with the Dutch and English colonists.

Bullinger's importance in the historical development of the Reformed tradition is thus indisputable. But the precise nature of his influence is largely yet to be determined. He is still among the least known of the leading sixteenth-century Reformers, especially amongst English readers. Not only does Bullinger lack a biography in English, but general histories of the Reformation contain very little about him. Invariably he is presented simply as Zwingli's successor and alter ego. This paucity of knowledge about Bullinger and his thought has made Bullinger the phantom figure of the Reformation."[29]

Baker, in spite of great leaps in Bullinger research accomplished since 1980, is still correct in affirming that if Bullinger is known at all nowadays, it is invariably as a younger assistant of Zwingli's who always remained in his shadow. Yet Bullinger was once rightly called 'the common shepherd of all Christian churches' and had an international reputation which far surpassed that of Luther, Zwingli and Calvin. Indeed, few people today appear to know that Bullinger produced far more Christian writings of equal, and often superior, character than these three Reformers together. Nevertheless, by the 19th century, his star had sadly waned. In 1828, in commemoration of the Bernese Reformation, Johannes Friedrich Franz was commissioned to write a Denkschrift (memorial report) which he entitled *Remarkable features in the life of the Zürich Superintendent Henry Bullinger as also his travel instructions to his eldest son Heinrich, student at Strasburg and Wittenburg.*[30] The address was dedicated to the student population of Bern and Franz confessed that though most of our Reformation heroes have been remembered through biographies and their services were continually being praised by posterity, worthy Bullinger's life has been totally neglected. As a result Professor Felix Nüscheler, who had just completed a biography of Zwingli, started to write a life of Bullinger but found the Zürich Reformer's theology too 'Reformed' for his liking and broke off the enterprise.

Little was done for another thirty years until in 1858 Carl Pestalozzi surprised the Reformed world by producing a major biography on

---

[29] Prologue, pp. xi-xii. Current catalogues of Bullinger's published works include almost 800 works and editions. Baker estimated that some 300 works of Bullinger's were still unpublished but since 1980 a number of these have been published by the Theologisher Verlag Zürich (TVZ) and various works have been made available from private organisations over the internet.

[30] *Merkwürdige Züge aus dem Leben des Züricherischen Antistes Heinrich Bullinger, nebst dessen Reiseinstruktion und Briefen an seinen ältesten Sohn Heinrich, auf den Lehranstalten zu Strassburg und Wittenberg. Der studierenden Jugund auf das dritte Reformations-Jubiläum der Stadt und Republik Bern 1828 gewidmet.* Von Joh. Friedr. Franz, evangel. Pfarrer zu Mogelsberg, Kantons St. Gallen, Bern, bei F. F. Burgdorfer, 1828.

Bullinger, *Heinrich Bullinger: Leben und ausgewählte Schriften* in his mammoth series on the fathers and founders of the Reformed Church,[31] making rightful claims for Bullinger which the uninitiated thought most pretentious. Many a follower of Calvin was most surprised to discover that such a proficient scholar as Pestalozzi looked on Bullinger as the Reformer's 16th century contemporaries had viewed him, that is, as the Founding Father of the Reformed Church. Again, there was a long period of biographical inactivity until Fritz Blanke published a work on the younger Bullinger in 1942.[32] In 1990, Immanuel Leuschner added a much longer section to the volume describing Bullinger's ministry in Zürich. This joint work was then named, following Pestalozzi's interpretation, *Heinrich Bullinger: Vater der Reformierten Kirche*.[33] Though this joint work lacks a comprehensive coverage of Bullinger's doctrines, it indicates clearly that Bullinger's light has been hid under a bushel for far too long and that there are many Bullinger tracks which still need to be followed closely.

Fritz Büsser, well-known amongst students of Bullinger for very many years (b. 1923), has done us all a great service in publishing his two-volumed *Heinrich Bullinger: Leben, Werk und Wirkung*.[34] The first volume appeared in 2004 but the second volume, awaited eagerly by lovers of true Reformation theology, was delayed until November, 2005. It was worth withholding the publication of my own work so that I might check what the greatest living expert on Bullinger has to say. Büsser's major contribution has gone a long way to remove Bullinger's light from under its bushel and has followed many hitherto forgotten tracks in rediscovering his subject. Nor does Büsser neglect to deal with Bullinger's doctrines. Büsser's aim, as he states himself in his

[31] *Leben und ausgewählte Schriften der Väter und Begründer der reformierte Kirche. Teil V. Heinrich Bullinger.*

[32] *Der Junge Bullinger*, Zwingli Verlag.

[33] Father of the Reformed Church. See Blanke's and Leuschner's *Heinrich Bullinger: Vater der Reformierte Kirche*; and Blanke's editorial work in *Exegetische Schriften aus den Jahren 1525-1526*; *Briefe der Jahre 1524-1531*; *Briefe des Jahres 1532*; *Briefe des Jahres 1533* and *Beschreibendes Verzeichnis der Literatur über Heinrich Bullinger*, all available at the Theologischer Verlag Zürich.

[34] Henry Bullinger: Life, Work and Influence.

Introductions, is to rehabilitate Bullinger so that the present generation will view him as did his own, that is "as father and mother not only of the Zürich Church but also of her sisters in France and Germany."[35] The sheer scope and depth of this new study of the Swiss Reformation in the German language leaves the work without competition in any other tongue, nor does it appear that there are scholars in other countries who are able to produce a similar work. Büsser has done better than any other scholar up to date in setting Bullinger in first a pan-Swiss and then an international setting. In doing so, he shows he has done deep research into the Swiss Reformation as a whole, uncovering facts concerning central and important figures such as Berchtold and Johannes Haller, leaders of the Bernese Reformation, whose witness cannot be ignored by anyone wishing to understand how the Swiss Reformation, under God, came to be. The volumes covering some 700 pages, however, may be daunting for English-speaking readers as, though written in High German, they contain very many Swiss-German quotes and demand of the reader a previous background knowledge of the Swiss political and religious ins and outs of the sixteenth century. The work goes into enormous detail in explaining the Zürich situation which is most necessary for understanding Bullinger but the mass of information, if translated into English, would perhaps be too specialized for the average English-speaking Christian who is more interested in gaining an overview of the Swiss Reformation rather than intricate and detailed knowledge of local Zürich affairs. My main disappointment regarding the first volume was the lack of an index but happily, the second volume includes a fairly comprehensive index of names and places recorded in both volumes. Historians, pastors, theological students and lovers of Church History in general will not be pleased at the lack of a subject index. Of a more popular kind, Patrik Müller has authored a sixty-four paged, heavily illustrated work in German on Bullinger as a reformer, church politician and historian. On the doctrinal side, Cornelis P. Venema has produced a fine study of Bullinger's doctrine of predestination[36] in the English language.

---

[35] Op. cit., Vol. 2, p. IX. Büsser is quoting F. Hotman, a contemporary of Bullinger's.
[36] Published 2002.

Modern reappraisals of Bullinger have their weaknesses

Until very recently few modern scholars shared Baker's 1980 insight into Bullinger's importance. The current five hundredth anniversary of Bullinger's birth (2004) has produced many excellent lengthy studies by a number of Swiss and North American authors and a number of first-class English newspaper articles and lectures have provided new insights into Bullinger's teaching and awakened new interest in the Reformation period. The internet, too, has featured a bevy of articles on Bullinger and conferences over Bullinger themes have been held world-wide. Amongst works in German, Peter Opitz has provided us with a highly academic study of 485 pages on Bullinger's popular theological work the *Decades*, sadly without an index which reduces its utility considerably. However, to tackle Opitz' major contribution to Bullinger studies, one needs to be moderately fluent in several German dialects, including the very different Swiss-German language and have a good basic command of the Latin language in order to follow the arguments. I found myself reading Opitz with four dictionaries on my writing-desk.

Emidio Campi has produced a collection of lectures in German given by various Continental scholars, which happily includes an index of persons and places besides Scripture references prepared by Doris Klee. Bruce Gordon and Emidio Campi have also gathered together a collection of essays, this time written or translated into English, illustrating Bullinger as the 'Architect of Reformation'. These essay collections open up many new venues in Bullinger studies but are to be enjoyed with caution. Many of these new fields have not been adequately researched, yet conclusions have been drawn which are often speculative and could lead further research on wild goose chases. Most of these modern authors fail to emphasise that Bullinger was the pastor of the common man as they are obviously and legitimately not writing for such readers themselves but for scholars and students.

Another weakness of this new academic approach to Bullinger is that such writers tend to tackle Bullinger's doctrines in the opposite manner to the way Bullinger himself taught them. The Zürich Reformer emphasised the comprehensiveness and unity of the gospel, but each facet of Bullinger's gospel of unity is analysed in such a way that Bullinger's major message is lost. We are given jig-saw pieces with no indication that they might make a complete picture. Indeed, we are told that these isolated studies prove that a complete picture does not exist. So, for instance, by defining Bullinger's doctrine of the covenant most narrowly, Edward Dowey in his essay *Heinrich Bullinger as Theologian: Thematic, Comprehensive, and Schematic* can claim that his Second Helvetic Confession has nothing of Bullinger's covenant teaching in it. He then asks why, if covenant teaching were so important for Bullinger, he left it out of so many of his works? Other scholars with their more comprehensive view of Bullinger's covenant teaching, see it everywhere in the Reformer's writings.

Such isolated part-studies and the development of academic theories are obviously more of interest to the specialist scholar than the general believer who wishes to benefit from Bullinger's highly pastoral ministry. Yet Bullinger's reforms are so often particularised and emphasised as if he were a go-it-alone individual who set up an alternative Reformation rather than kept to *the* Reformation. Indeed, though Bullinger's importance as a Reformation figure is far more emphasised in these modern works than has been the case for many decades, the question raised is not so much whether Bullinger was indeed the Father and Shepherd of the Reformed Churches as his contemporaries held but whether he was or not the mere founder of an alternative religious tradition which died with his death. Thus, since J. Wayne Baker came up with his 1980 subtitle *The Other Reformed Tradition* to his work on Bullinger's doctrine of the covenant, this theme has dominated much of subsequent scholarship to the exclusion of the great influence Bullinger had on the entire international field of the sixteenth century Reformation. So, too, the false idea has developed that the Lutheran-Calvinistic Reformation represented one Reformed line but the Bullinger Reformation was a mere side channel or off-shoot.

This writer's conclusion is that though Bullinger's one-time greatness is now increasingly recognised, it is rather the greatness of a by-gone historical figure which is portrayed who was eclipsed by contemporary and subsequent Reformed orthodoxy. This writer's understanding of the evidence both new and old is that Bullinger not only spoke to a far-gone age as a major Reformer and a sign-post and path-finder pointing out the way further, true Reform must take, he was, and still is the best guide along that route. In his *Second Helvetic Confession* his *Decades*, his catechetical, doctrinal, exegetical and historical works and in his vast correspondence, he still states clearer than any other Continental Reformer what true Reformation entails.

Correcting negative trends

Indeed, apart from producing the first comprehensive biography of Bullinger in English, this book has been written to correct several negative trends in modern Bullinger studies. The prevailing modern view that Bullinger went his own way in comparison to the run-of-the-mill Reformers needs to be scrutinised carefully. The idea that Bullinger isolated himself from the main 'Calvinistic' stream of Reformers will be shown to be indefensible. The idea that Calvin and his theology ought to be used as a term of reference as to what 'Reformed' means and Bullinger is to be judged according to how he squares up alongside Calvin will be shown to be nothing but reversing Bullinger's and Calvin's roles in the historical development of the Reformation. Thus the teaching that Bullinger is a mere 'Reformer in the Wings'[37] is also rejected. My aim in this work is to demonstrate clearly that rather than go it alone along a side-track of Reformed thought, Bullinger marched ahead on the true path of Reformed orthodoxy, leading his contemporaries along the way. Like a sure Swiss mountain guide who takes those in his care safely over dangerous terrain, Bullinger led Reformed scholars, pastors, politicians and the so-called common man from the perilous path of Rome safely along Reformed paths. Rather than serving as an under-guide to Calvin, Bullinger was famed throughout Europe as a Reformer long before Calvin himself became Reformed, and long after he died. Indeed, I wish

[37] See Venema's *Heinrich Bullinger and the Doctrine of Predestination: Author of 'the Other Reformed Tradition'?*.

to show that Calvin would hardly have survived in the pages of history as the great Reformer he undoubtedly was without the leading influence, care and endless patience of Bullinger. Rather than see Calvin as the mentor and initiator of the Reformed Churches as has become the fashion in recent years, this honour should be given to his tutor and friend Henry Bullinger. Indeed, Biblical, Pauline theology which was at the heart of the Reformed movement is to be found in its evangelistic, pastoral and exegetic purity far more in Bullinger's teaching than in that of Calvin who left much untidiness of thought in his doctrines of the Scripture, the Church, the Trinity, Christology, the covenant of grace, justification, the order of salvation, the Lord's Supper and especially predestination. Indeed, though Calvin was strongly institutionally-minded in his ecclesiology, he could never decide to which branch of the institutionalised Reformed churches he belonged. Lutheranism for him was too 'German', the Swiss Church was too democratic and people-orientated and the French church built on French social structures which he would have liked to have led, if not founded, could not be realised because France was almost entirely in the hands of dictator kings and papists. All this leads this author to conclude that Bullinger must be seen as the Reformation's central pivotal figure and Calvin should be compared with him to see if Genevan doctrines ever reached the Zürich standard. Furthermore, the anti-trinitarian teaching which wrecked the churches of Poland and the Baltic States, the two opposites of Hyper-Calvinism and so-called Moderate Calvinism, Pelagianism and New Divinity teaching, all arose in Geneva during the time of Calvin, Beza and the Turretins whereas Zürich stood constant in the faith. So too, the period covered in Geneva from Calvin to Alphons Turretin was one of intense political, religious and economic turmoil, whereas Zürich enjoyed a long period of peace and prosperity. Where this was broken, it was not because of political unrest but the outcome of plagues and natural catastrophes. Trying to solve the major problem why Calvin's name has survived in theological discussion whereas Bullinger's has faded from history so long, Gottfried W. Locher suggests the reason is to be found in the pastoral, practical nature of Bullinger's message which has gained less notice in a theological world of theoretical doctrinal discussions. In other words, practical soul-care has been cultured theologically far less than head-care or what Locher calls the more 'theoretical-timeless system' (theoretisch-zeitloseren System) of the modern understanding of Calvinism.[38]

Any biography of Bullinger must include John Calvin

Any biography of Bullinger therefore must be a biography of Calvin, too; at least for the years 1536-1564 which cover Calvin's life from his first becoming assistant theological lecturer to Farel and finally a successful Reformer in the much-changed Geneva of the early 1560s which had suddenly found a brief period of peace. In parallel with new discoveries made concerning the historian and theologian Bullinger and the position of Zürich in the development of the Reformation, there has also been a reassessment of the life and work of John Calvin. As Richard C. Gamble says in his essay on current trends in Calvin Research, "Calvin research continues to explode".[39] Indeed, works such as Alexandre Ganoczy's *The Young Calvin*,[40] and Wilhelm H. Neuser's *Calvinus Sacrae Scripturae Professor*[41] have quite altered the traditional approach to the Genevan Reformer and debunked a number of myths surrounding his name. Past scholars have tended to concentrate their studies on Calvinism as a theological system rather than Calvin as a historical figure and often the Calvin of history has been given second rank behind Calvin the theologian, leaving a great breach between the two. Indeed, Calvin's history as Beza's and Colladon's biographies illustrate, has mostly been written backwards as those who knew him in the later years of his life, back-projected the mature Calvin onto the younger, immature Reformer. This tendency to view Calvin as always being the same man, with the same influence, from his youth to the end of his life has also been projected onto Calvin's turbulent sojourn in Geneva and even onto his

[38] *Bullinger und Calvin*, p. 1.
[39] *Calvinus Sacrae Scripturae Professor*, p. 108.
[40] First published in French in 1966 and in English in 1987.
[41] Published in 1994 with essays by 18 scholars who reassessed various branches of Calvin scholarship.

theology. Calvin is said to have ruled over a Geneva which was heaven on earth and stood, like the Church within its boundaries, always solidly behind him. That Calvin had a long struggle with both the Genevan Church and the Genevan council, besides with his own temper and often varying theological position, from 1536 to the late fifties has been quite left out of studies by most evangelical, Reformed scholars. These have been more interested in presenting what has come to be called 'Calvinism pure'[42] as a finished and fixed system rather than the Calvinism which grew out of a definite historical, ecclesiastical, social and political background. Furthermore, this 'Calvinism' which has been accepted as the sole work of Calvin for so long is now discovered to have been fostered by a number of Reformers amongst whom Calvin's position as the alleged greatest must be seriously challenged. Amongst these mentors of Calvin who have been more or less ignored in Calvin studies until recently are the well-known and much researched figures of Luther, Melanchthon and Zwingli but also, and more especially, the lesser known but most certainly not less important figures of Bucer and Bullinger, two Reformers who certainly held to a Calvinism before Calvin. Bullinger was to exert so much influence on Calvin that one can truly speak of Bullinger not only as Calvin's mentor but of Calvin as Bullinger's protégé.

The alleged different theologies of Bullinger and Calvin

In this book, too, I would like to contest the idea that Bullinger and Calvin represented radically different theologies although their emphasis and approach often took individual paths. Though undoubtedly Bullinger's emphasis was more on the practical and pastoral side, as Gottfried W. Locher points out,[43] this does not mean that Bullinger was lacking in clear doctrinal and theological acumen. The facts are that Bullinger called Calvin his best friend and neither Calvin nor Bullinger ever thought that their theologies were basically different. The untidiness

---

[42] See W.G.T Shedd's helpful book *Calvinism: Pure & Mixed. A Defence of the Westminster Standards.*
[43] *Bullinger und Calvin*, p. 1.

in Calvin's theology and thinking mentioned above certainly ought to warn scholars against concluding that Calvin's theological teaching took either a more comprehensive or more markedly Reformed line than Bullinger's. Indeed, though he was confident that his teaching reflected Bullingerite orthodoxy, his ever changing views of the Lord's Supper and predestination did tend to strain this basic agreement but never amounted to what one could call 'a different theology' as Calvin was always sure to change back when tackled by Bullinger. When Jerome Bolsec (d. 1585) claimed that he followed Bullinger rather than Calvin, as if the two differed on essentials, the Genevan Reformer promptly called him a liar and worse as he was certain that he was one with Bullinger on doctrine, especially election and predestination, the doctrines Bolsec allegedly challenged. Calvin's differences in formulating his theology of individual doctrines, in comparison with Bullinger's more integrated over-view was merely because he could not mould them into the one overall conception of the work of God in Christ for His Church which was so intrinsically Bullinger's special gift. There was an internal tension amongst most of Calvin's doctrines which made it difficult for him to fit them together. Calvin's didactic theories based on his humanist background and personal preference led him to think in compartments and he thus became the systematic champion of catalogued doctrine. This is Calvin's special genius but it does not, of necessity, lead to the idea that he was the greatest Reformer because of this gift. Bullinger's greater talent, I believe, lay in his ability to see the wholeness and unity of the Biblical gospel and put it over pastorally to his people without complicating it with analytical fervour. He always had the whole counsel of God in his theological sights. This does not mean that Bullinger was unable to think systematically but the parts of his thinking were always subordinate to the whole. This enabled him to be more systematic than Calvin at times as in his doctrines of the covenant, predestination and the sacraments. This was certainly because, once Bullinger had found their position in his total theological overview, he could return to the individual doctrines and view them better from all sides. In all this, his main purpose was to put the message over to the ordinary believer, rather than the student or theologian. Thus when scholars such as Schulthess-Rechberg say that Calvin was the better teacher but Bullinger the better pastor, they are not saying that Calvin was the better or greater Reformer, or that they provided alternative Reformations, but that Bullinger was able to apply what Reformed men call the 'whole counsel of God' better to the needy sinner. This explains the enormous success of Bullinger's own, private statement of faith which became the widest accepted creed of all the Reformed churches under the title *The Second Helvetic Confession.*

The dangers of over-systematising doctrine

Whenever Calvin isolated the doctrines of the Bible in order to analyse and systematise them, he left them with rough edges which made it difficult for him to fit them together again in a comprehensive over-view. This is nowhere clearer than in Calvin's teaching on predestination in his *Institutes*, Book III, Chap. XXIII:7 where Calvin apparently teaches that God's so-called double-predestination is irrespective of man's fallen nature and that God acts arbitrarily in election. Another example is Calvin's pamphlet war with Pighius in which Calvin argues for predestination without embedding his arguments in his overall teaching of the covenant and the work of Christ. A dozen quotes from other works of Calvin might contradict this but the shock many a reader has on reading such extreme apologetic works might cause them to reject Calvin's teaching en bloc, as did a number of ministers and refugees in Geneva to their peril. Because of his basic view of God as all-sovereign, seen irrespective of the distinctive Persons and offices within the Trinity, Calvin tended to look on election and predestination as an immediate act of God. Such thinking leads to the complicated and highly theoretical Lapsarian controversy concerning whether the elect were predestinated to salvation and/or the reprobate to damnation before (Supralapsarian) or after (Infralapsarian) the fall. Such a discussion for Bullinger was too speculative, unedifying, highly theoretical and most un-pastoral and practical. Most important, the Scriptures never dealt with sin and the fall in this context. Sinners are not elected causatively because of their own deeds or non-deeds but by grace. Thus sinners are elected *infra-Christum.*

It is neither unfallen man nor sinful man who is dealt with directly by God in election and predestined salvation. Within the economy of the Godhead, the Father deals directly with the Son on behalf of those who are in Christ. Predestination occurs thus through and in Christ. To discuss predestination outside of Christ's salvation is to speak of philosophical abstractions and theories. Elect sinners are predestinated in Christ, there is no predestination for those outside of Christ but the damnation they enter into by their own sin.

So, too, in his *Institutes*, Calvin differs from Bullinger in placing regeneration chronologically before justification,[44] and interprets being justified by faith as a justification which ensues because of faith previously held. This is difficult to harmonise with Calvin's doctrine of predestination and many present day 'Calvinists' would find this view difficult to harmonise with Scripture. Calvin views regeneration as bringing the life of believers into concord and harmony with the righteousness of God.[45] He then sees justification as the confirmation of this righteous faith given to the elect.[46] Calvin's order is therefore, regeneration, faith, repentance, justification. Calvin apparently adopted this view to ensure that justification was seen as coming via faith, but it jeopardises the Biblical – and traditional 'Calvinistic' – doctrine that God justifies the sinner whilst he is at enmity with God (Romans 4:5; 5:9-10). In this teaching, Calvin is nearer his own enemy, Osiander, than his friends Martin Bucer and Henry Bullinger. Indeed, Calvin's teaching on justification is spoilt by his formulating the doctrine amidst hefty polemics against Osiander where objective balance was called for in defining so essential a doctrine. Again, Calvin corrects this elsewhere but Bullinger rarely, if ever, shows such inconsistencies in his work. The worst one can say about Bullinger on doctrine is that he often does not say enough, but at least, he never says too much.

---

[44] *Institutes*, Vol. 1, Book III, Chapter III, p. 508 ff.. See especially Vol. 2, Book III, Chapter XI, p. 37.
[45] Vol. 2, Book III, Chapter VI, 1, p. 2.
[46] Vol. 2, Book III, Chapter XI, p. 36.

First encounters with Bullinger

I was first introduced to Bullinger by reading through the Parker Society's four volume collection of our Reformers' correspondence some ten years ago and became fascinated with the way the English Reformers, from the Archbishop to the lowest clergy and from Kings and Queens down to common servants addressed Bullinger as if they were in awe of him. At first, I could hardly understand the reverence they paid him and the deep trust they had in him and why, to use an apt phrase of Bruce Gordon's regarding Bullinger, he was 'one of the most widely consulted figures of the age.'[47] Then I purchased an incomplete second-hand collection of Bullinger's *Decades* in Scotland which whetted my appetite for more, especially on reading Bullinger's fine work on the covenant of grace, justification and predestination. Then I found two much-used volumes of Bullinger's further writings in a Swedish Church in Minnesota and bought a third through an English used-books dealer. I then began to read Bullinger intensively, adding volumes month by month which I purchased from Switzerland and Holland. The fact that Bullinger's works are available in so many different countries attest to their former great international impact. Soon, I discovered the secret of why those English Reformers looked to Bullinger as their main mentor and friend and now realize with them what an enormous asset Bullinger was and still is to the Church of the Lord Jesus Christ and how there has hardly been a man like him since apostolic days.

Sadly, Bullinger's primary works are still unknown to the bulk of today's English-speaking Christian readers though many of his earlier works have been republished in Swiss-German and Latin and more are being printed yearly. In his works it is most interesting to note that Bullinger, who rarely wrote of himself, has done much to foster the reputation of Luther, Zwingli and Calvin, especially through his diaries and histories of the Reformation. Bullinger is, indeed, one of our best sources for knowledge of their lives. Our biographical knowledge, for instance, of Zwingli is chiefly through Bullinger's writings on him and

[47] Architect of Reformation, p. 17.

his diligence in printing Zwingli's works. Indeed, as Bullinger was in close contact with most of the great ecclesiastical and political men of the Reformation and corresponded daily with his fellow Reformers, he presents us with a day to day overview of God's work on the Continent and in England which is provided by no other writer. Thus Rainer Henrich writes of Bullinger's *International News Network.*[48] However, humble as he was, Bullinger pointed his readers to others rather than himself, playing down his own role in his writings. Thus, though the *Consensus Tigurinus* was chiefly the product of Bullinger's research into the Lord's Supper from the early fifteen-twenties on, he put Calvin's name to it and merged his own name into the general epithet 'the ministers of Zürich'. It would be thus folly to neglect what Bullinger has to say concerning his fellow Reformers, but it would be a greater folly to believe that Bullinger played no major and transformative part in these events and thus neglect his own enormous contribution to the founding and establishing of the Reformed faith.

Comparing Bullinger with his contemporary Reformers

Great as Luther's, Zwingli's and Calvin's works are, a careful student will note that Bullinger is in no way inferior to them and often proves the sounder, more pastoral and most balanced teacher. Luther's attitude to his 'rival' Reformers, especially of the Swiss Schools, was often deplorable if not downright shocking. The fierce Wittenberg pastor had often an aggressive, intolerant faith which, as in his teaching on the Lord's Supper, displays much of Rome and even superstition. Much of Luther is lost to the modern scholar because he is invariably viewed through the eyes of Philip Melanchthon (1497-1560) who radically misinterpreted Luther on justification and predestination and turned a movement of the Spirit into a well-organised church institution which helped divide Lutheranism into the extremes of the Philippites on the one side and the Gnesio-Lutherans on the other. Also the over-influential Hamburg pastor Joachim Westphal (1511-1574) almost destroyed the original Lutheran

[48] See 'Bullinger's Correspondence: An International News Network' in *Architect of Reformation* (eds. Gordon and Campi).

piety with his inquisitorial temper and theological narrow-mindedness. On the other hand, Calvin's works, good as they are, nevertheless, prove at times to be too highly defensive and even complaining and argumentative to be clear in their theological significance. They also frequently leave the pastoral for the philosophical, polemic and legal. So, too, Calvin lacked Bullinger's consistency. Thus it is possible for Louis Berkhof in his *Systematic Theology* to place Calvin in the Supralapsarian camp which, today, is tantamount to calling him a Hyper-Calvinist, whereas present-day writers such as Dr Alan Clifford claim that Calvin was a thorough-going Amyraldian. This, for some modern Reformed Christians, is tantamount to calling Calvin an Arminian. Indeed, R.T. Kendall shocked the Reformed world in 1979 by presenting Calvin as a conditional Universalist. None of the findings of these scholars are thoroughly inaccurate, they have merely analysed one part of Calvin's teaching without realising that Calvin speaks elsewhere in another voice, according to the situation and period of development he is in and the controversies he was involved in at the time of writing. It is interesting to note that Dr Alan Clifford defends Moïse Amyraut against criticism by saying that such criticism does not apply to the 'mature' Amyraut. However, Clifford uses what many scholars would think was the 'immature' Calvin to 'prove' that doctrines he believes Amyraut had from Calvin were 'mature'.[49]

Bullinger in his pastoral letters to Calvin and in his defence of his Sublapsarian view of sin and salvation given to Bartholomew Traheron (who understood Calvin solely in a Hyper-Calvinist sense), pointed out the inconsistency within Calvin's thinking and that his special interpretation of a reprobation irrespective of the fall and the responsibility of the sinner was a new teaching neither found in Scripture nor in the early church. So too, the theological and pastoral quality of Calvin's earlier works is greatly inferior to his later writings. Thus, where Luther is Biblical and authoritative on justification and exegetically weak on the Lord's Supper, Calvin's teaching on justification is not fitted

[49] See Clifford's *Amyraut Affirmed*, Charenton Reformed Publishing, 2004 and my review article of that name in New Focus, Issue , 2005.

Biblically into the pan-Scriptural doctrine of salvation. His most detailed account of justification in his *Institutes* is too coloured by his personal animosities against Osiander and stands in sharp contrast to his more calm expositions in his commentaries. Calvin's teaching on the Lord's Supper is also rarely consistent and constant and he invariably opens up more problems with his revisions which are then left unsolved. Calvin's tendency to fall out with his most intimate co-workers earned him many enemies who might otherwise have remained his friends. In contrast, Bullinger always remains clearly Bullinger and all testify to the fact that at seventy, he was still the same Bullinger that he was at twenty and held to the same beliefs. There is also a didactic, objective clarity in his works and tidiness in his thinking which amazes those who turn to him with an open mind.

Bullinger the mediator

Bullinger was thus as well-balanced in his character as in his writings and so he was able to compose, clear precise theological statements without getting emotional and upset and without giving the impression that he had an axe to grind. Because of such outstanding characteristics, he was far more able than both Luther and Calvin to referee in theological debates and maintain good contact with both sides, without compromising his own views or falling out with anybody. This is shown by Bullinger's sound testimony in his disputations with the Catabaptists; his work in bringing Lutherans and Reformed together concerning the Lord's Supper; his ability to present Zwingli in a better light to the Senate and foreign critics; his Herculean efforts at bringing peace to the German and French-speaking Swiss churches, his successful efforts in December 1533 to arbitrate between Leo Jud and the Senate[50] and win him from his Schwenckfeld and war-mongering ways, his mediation in the Genevan-Poland-Lithuanian Antitrinitarian controversy and his mediation between the Precisians and Anglicans in England on the vestment issue. Thus, where Luther and Calvin made enemies, Bullinger lived at peace with all

[50] The result, for Jud, was that he withdrew from politics and church affairs and concentrated on his lecturing and translating what came to be called the Zürich Bible.

men of Reformed persuasion, though Luther and Calvin's more extreme followers occasionally called him names. The records show, however, that such insults were often followed by apologies in an effort to keep Bullinger as a valued correspondent and friend. This love of peace and harmony often caused Bullinger disappointments which, however, rarely burdened him. For instance, when the Zürich Senate refused to allow him to publish his commentary on Revelation, he merely dropped the matter and worked on other, more acceptable, projects, knowing that the right time for his commentary would come. This mediating work of Bullinger's is acknowledged by Koenigsberger and Mosse in their *Europe in the Sixteenth Century* where they write after describing the death of Zwingli:

"Defeat did not end the Reformation in Zürich or its influence. Heinrich Bullinger, Zwingli's successor, was a man no less remarkable than the reformer himself, though his talents took a different direction. Bullinger had the makings of a mediator, and he was consulted in all the great quarrels among the different branches of the Reformation. When English Protestants fled during the reign of Queen Mary they made use of his services, not only as a host but also as a mediator in their own quarrels. During the reign of Elizabeth he was consulted by both the Puritans and the queen, though he finally sided with the English government in the controversy over the use of the vestment or cope during religious service. His reputation was pre-eminent, though Calvin's was to eclipse it. Bullinger himself brought the Zürich Reformation into close contact with that of Geneva, preparing the way for the common front of the two Reformations with the acceptance by both of the Consensus Tigurinus (1549). All Zwinglian churches in Switzerland joined this agreement in points of theology."[51]

Koenigsberger and Mosse seem to be more impressed by Bullinger as a mediator than a theologian and their view of the vestment controversy in England and the signing of the *Consensus Tigurinus* is not quite

---

[51] Op. cit. p. 139.

accurate. Bullinger, unlike Zwingli[52] and Calvin, wore no vestments himself but was able to unite the archbishops, bishops and the vast majority of the English Puritan ministers in taking a moderate line concerning ecclesiastical robes. Even quite radical Puritans such as Hooper, Foxe, Sampson and Humphrey followed Bullinger's advice as did more conservative Puritans such as Grindal and Jewel. Concerning the *Consensus Tigurinus*, this brought Genevan theology into line with Bullinger's as the name suggests. It is quite wrong to call the various Swiss churches which signed the consensus 'Zwinglian' as their theologies by 1549 had matured greatly since the 1520s. Indeed, Zwingli's view of the Lord's Supper, which we know of mainly via Bullinger, was certainly far more comprehensive than the simple 'remembrance celebration' which goes nowadays under the heading 'Zwinglian'. It was the *First Helvetic Confession* in which Calvin played no part, the *Consensus Tigurinus* which was mainly formulated in Bullinger's terms and the *Second Helvetic Confession* penned by Bullinger alone that united the Swiss churches. Even when Calvin's final version of his *Institutes* came out in 1559, the Genevan Council insisted that it should only be printed in conjunction with Bullinger's *Decades* and Beza's *Confession of the Christian Faith*,[53] thus ensuring a sound, pan-Reformation teaching on the whole counsel of God.

Mediating on behalf of Farel

A typical example of Bullinger's masterly method of bringing peace to angry contestants was the way in which he assisted William Farel at Neuchâtel (Neuenburg). After his exile from Geneva with Calvin in 1538, Farel started a work at Neuchâtel but soon brought down the wrath of the Council on his head for criticising their lack of Christian testimony from the pulpit. Things came to a head in the summer of 1541. A leading citizen, a lady of very ill repute, who was mixed up in a notorious divorce suit, refused to be counselled by Farel who appealed to the Council for

[52] Zwingli used the old gala dress of the Upper Class citizens which had become obsolete but which he retained as a pulpit garment.
[53] *Confessio christianae fidei.*

support but the councilmen ignored him. Farel then condemned the wayward life of the lady from the pulpit and also complained that the Council were doing nothing about the lax morals displayed by prominent citizens. Calvin was on his way to Geneva from Strasburg at the time but called on Farel to give him support. Soon there was a good deal of unrest in the city. The Bernese, who still held the reins at Neuchâtel, resented ministers telling councilmen what to do. One leading Councilman, Schultheiß von Wattenwyl, told the ministers that preachers were like servants and could be dismissed whenever the Council so wished and without giving notice. Farel replied that he was not a servant of the Council but had been employed by the Church and would be dismissed by the Church and as the Church wanted and needed him in the present conflict, he intended to stay.

In the same year the Council of Neuchâtel, fully backed by Protestant Bern, voted to defrock the preacher. Farel and his fellow Neuchâtel ministers, Myconius in Basle and Ambrose Blaurer in Constance all turned to Bullinger, asking him to mediate. Bullinger wrote a lengthy treatise to the secular Council both defending Farel and explaining to the politicians that they had no spiritual jurisdiction over the pulpit. He also wrote to Farel, telling him that his calling as Superintendent of the Neuchâtel Church was to keep to the Word of God in all matters and where rebuke is needed from the pulpit, it must come. Part of preaching the forgiveness of sin is that sin must be called *sin* instead of being circumscribed in flowery language. Abandoning his flock was no answer to pressure from Bern. Bullinger also addressed the junior clergy, advising them to support their Superintendent and not to allow divisions to occur in their ranks. Bullinger advised the clergy to call a general synod of ministers, councilmen and pious citizens and draw up a general statement as to what the duty of a godly minister was according to 1 Timothy 5:17. Bullinger then wrote to the Council, explaining how necessary a free church was for the health of the community and for the discipline of the church. However, the appointment of ministers is not the responsibility of the Council but the Church. Naturally, the Council can object to the nominee, but the congregation must be allowed to examine all nominees and appoint their choice by general vote. Lastly, Bullinger turned to the congregation and told them what a godly gift they had in their pastors. He told the congregation that if Farel had been a pastor as some of them wished who gave them nothing but fair words but no firm leadership, they would be most unhappy and feel neglected in the end. He said of Farel, "He is just like a father, burning for love to his children, upright in all his deeds, he cannot flatter."[54] Besides Bullinger, the letter was signed by Leo Jud, Kasper Megander (1495-1545), Erasmus Fabritius, Conrad Pellican, Theodor Bibliander (1504-1564), and all the other Zürich ministers.

The Council melted at once and Bullinger received a reply from Neuchâtel saying, "We have never received a letter which we have listened to and accepted with so much joy. Nor one which has served so much to illuminate our hearts, comfort and strengthen us. This we can declare before God."[55] They told Bullinger, "We all have felt the wonderful power of God in your letter. You have touched on all the points where Satan can break into the flock of Christ and have totally disarmed the enemy."[56] Then Bullinger was told by the Bern government that they were prepared to put up with Farel as long as he did not step beyond his calling. Providence came to Farel's rescue. The plague struck Neuchâtel but Farel stuck to his post, and thus won the hearts of citizens and government. After January 1542, nobody challenged Farel again.

Mediating on behalf of Jud and the Zürich poor

A similar situation occurred in 1532 when Leo Jud scolded the Zürich Senate for being too weak in their dealings with the papist cantons. The Senate threatened Jud with dismissal and complained that it was the Zürich church that had caused all the trouble in the first place. Bullinger was able to show the Senate that they had published a mandate admitting sole responsibility for the war. He pointed out to Jud that the preachers had all promised not to dabble in the political affairs of the city which

---

[54] Pestalozzi, pp. 248-250.
[55] Ibid, p. 250.
[56] *Heinrich Bullinger der Nachfolger Zwinglis*, p. 57.

went beyond their Christian duties. Bullinger then obtained from the Senate the right of the preachers to admonish those clearly guilty of un-Christian behaviour and they even promised Bullinger that if he thought a Senator was acting unworthy of his position, Bullinger could stand before the Senate and argue his case. Peace was thus restored in a way that left the church with a greater freedom. Thus, Bullinger's appearance before the Council came to be a fairly regular event, if not a fixed feature of Bullinger's public work as a mediator between citizens and the Council. As usual, he kept an exact record of these appearances which he named *Fürträge*[57] and preserved a record of what he said. These *Fürträge* were usually on behalf of the city's poor people so that they need not go begging from door to door but received financial help, food, clothing and employment. Bullinger also used the opportunity to plead for better medicinal services in the city and the setting up of hospitals. Like William Cowper and John Newton who were given money to help the poor by wealthy friends, Bullinger believed in helping the 'deserving poor' but refused to help those who squandered their own and public funds or lived grossly immoral lives. Those deserving poor who had fallen into poverty through no fault of their own, were given a special metal badge so that when they visited the soup kitchens of the city, they could be recognised. In this work, Bullinger's own experience as a beggar student helped him considerably and also his conviction that when those who had, helped those who had not, the community would mutually profit by this charity and be moulded into one. Bullinger also used his *Fürträg*e to encourage the building of new roads and workhouses for convicted criminals so that they learnt to help themselves and society legally. He even used the opportunity to help develop the textile trade in the city.

Mediating on behalf of Calvin

It appears to be a forgotten fact amongst modern students of the Reformation that Calvin's reconciliation with Geneva after his exile from the city in 1538-41, was, to a very large extent, due to Bullinger's

[57] As opposed to *Vorträge*. The meaning is to appeal on behalf of someone else as in *Fürbitte*.

mediating work between Bern, Strasburg and Geneva. This was initially at Calvin's request, though soon afterwards, Calvin gave up the idea of returning to his former post. Bullinger's blunt frankness in prompting a very unwilling Calvin to return to Geneva was very similar to Farel's efforts to induce his unwilling friend to settle down in the city-state in the first place. However, Bullinger had to persuade not only Calvin to leave Strasburg, but also a very unwilling Strasburg to give him up and a very unwilling Bern to tolerate Calvin at Geneva again. So too, from 1542 to 1557, Bullinger saved Calvin from being re-exiled from Geneva or leaving of his own accord a number of times. All these tasks Bullinger mastered as only he could. Kolfhaus is thus quite correct in affirming that when Calvin returned to Geneva, Calvin, "would never have survived the heavy theological and ecclesiastical battles but for the energetic help Bullinger and his followers gave him."[58]

Calvin has won great acclamation for his method of dealing with Caroli, Servetus, Castellio and Bolsec in his controversies with them concerning the Trinity and predestination but we seldom hear that Calvin had turned to Bullinger for a solution in each case and it was largely through Bullinger's initiative and intervention that peace was restored at Geneva after each incident. Bullinger was also called on by Geneva's Council to advise them on their internal problems at times when they were not on good-speaking terms with Calvin. Bullinger avoided Calvin's clumsy, head-on confrontations and decided the matter solely on the grounds of Scripture and diplomacy rather than extreme views and personal temper. At times, Calvin was angry with Bullinger for often using milder methods than his, as in the case of Bolsec, but he always accepted Bullinger's terms in the end and was pleased with Bullinger's results. When Calvin complained that all were against him, Bullinger invariably replied with words such as in a letter to his friend dated 3 March, 1555, "Let us, dear Calvin, honoured brother, rather bear with patience whatever the Lord has laid on our shoulders. Such are the times and such are the dispositions of unthankful people from whom we can

[58] *Der Verkehr Calvins mit Bullinger*, p. 42.

expect nothing else ... I urge you honoured Sir and dear brother to bear these attacks calmly. You know how our Redeemer was treated by His people and that the Apostle had to complain more over the infidelity of false brethren than over open, unjust enemies."[59] Bullinger's constant assistance, advice and, indeed, leadership in solving the problems of Geneva led the city to take a great interest in Bullinger's works and saw to it that the Genevan printers kept the public up to date by printing them. Though many contested Bullinger at times, they rarely succeeded in becoming his enemies and often, as in the above mentioned cases of dispute, both sides turned to Bullinger for his final word. Bullinger's patience with Zwingli's development in his teaching on the Lord's Supper and Calvin's ever changing views on the ordinance and predestination was due to his respect for both friends and love of unity over essentials and tolerance over minor points.

The length of Bullinger's activity compared with Calvin's

It must also be remembered that Bullinger was converted to the Reformed faith a dozen years before Calvin and he had received a reputation as a Reformed teacher and writer over a decade before Calvin took up his pen to defend the Reformed faith. According to his own list in his diary, between 1520[60] and 1528, Bullinger had written some seventy works in Latin and German and by 1531 many more had been added including a large number of commentaries,[61] histories and apologetic works, especially against the Catabaptists. However, scholars such as Staedke have shown that Bullinger had penned numerous works before 1528 which he had not added to his list, probably thinking they were too unimportant to mention. Hans Georg Zimmermann looked into the matter and found 86 works from Bullinger's pen before 1528.[62] So, too, it must be borne in mind that in the middle twenties, even leading Reformers and theological writers sent their works to Bullinger for approval or wrote, as

---

[59] Bolsec-Akten von 1551 und 4 Privatbriefe an Calvin von 1552-1555 in Peter Walser's *Die Prädestination bei Heinrigh Bullinger*, pp. 179-180.
[60] Bullinger authored five Latin works whilst still at Cologne.
[61] The commentaries were mostly written during Bullinger's two years at Bremgarten.
[62] *Heinrich Bullinger*, pp. 50-51.

did Leo Jud in the early summer of 1526, asking him to look over his work on Erasmus' and Luther's teaching on the Eucharist and add further material to the book.[63] Bullinger was now an internationally recognised authority on the Reformation, whereas Calvin's interests were still centred in furthering the philosophy of Seneca and reading humanistic works. Furthermore, a study of Bullinger's earlier works show that by 1531, he had consolidated and formulated the theological position on which he was to build all his life and which was of great influence on Calvin. Fritz Büsser therefore writes, "Amongst the Reformers, there is no single instance of any one who authored so many and such versatile writings before his twenty-fifth birthday as the Kappel schoolmaster."[64] Through his *Ratio Studiorum*, young Bullinger had also become well-known as an educator of note. Zürich pastor Schulthess-Rechberg says of these early writings:

"All these works display the quality of Bullinger's writing, he masters his subject with a care that covers everything and leaves no room for questions or possible contrary arguments. He develops his thoughts with surety, transparency, clarity of expression, seriousness, dignity and warmth. The reader finds that he is holding the hand of a trustworthy, sincere and benevolent guide."[65]

Bullinger always viewed Calvin's works with respect and felt a great kinship in the faith with him. However, he found too much of the philosopher and lawyer in Calvin and not enough of the pastor, counsellor and lover of souls. He felt that Calvin's way of subordinating the covenant and the gospel to the doctrine of predestination[66] isolated it from its meaningful context which led to misinterpretations of the providential

---

[63] *Heinrich Bullinger Werke, Briefe der Jahre 1524-1531*, pp. 117-118.
[64] Ibid, p. 50.
[65] Ibid, p. 7.
[66] I am aware of the modern theory, propagated by moderate Calvinists of such as the Banner of Truth Trust in England and the Founders Journal in the U.S.A., that Calvin did not subordinate his gospel under his doctrine of predestination, but this is obviously because these new interpreters of Calvin wish to keep the name of 'Calvinist' yet understand predestination at best in Bullingerian terms and at worst in Arminian dogmatism.

love and care of God for His world and the work of Christ. Above all, Bullinger found he had to be very patient with Calvin's temper and usually found himself telling his friend to calm down.

Comparing the earliest biographies of Bullinger and Calvin

The fact that Bullinger was firmly established as a major Reformer long before his death yet Calvin's importance had yet to be spelt out is made clear by their earliest biographers. Josias Simler (1530-1576) wrote on Bullinger in 1575, immediately after his death and a biography of Calvin was produced in 1564-1565 shortly after Calvin died. It was published as *Vie de Calvin* in a preface to the second edition of Calvin's *Commentary on Joshua* and attributed to Beza. Peter Wilcox in his *Lectures of John Calvin and the Nature of his Audience* states, "The work is attributed there to Bèza; but in fact was written by Nicolas Colladon."[67] Fritz Büsser, however, believes that Colladon wrote a separate work but kept to the apologetic style of Beza, defending Calvin from charges of heresy.[68] Simler's biography is factual, historical, chronological and deals with Bullinger's great international influence amongst his contemporaries whereas Beza's (or Colladon's) work is almost purely apologetic. He is so busy proving that Calvin was not a heretic but an orthodox saint that actual details of Calvin's work as scholar, pastor and teacher are rarely given. The saint is portrayed as a giant-killer in his battles against 'filthy and stinking monsters' and 'apostates' of 'cursed memory' such as Caroli, Bolsec, Servetus, and the Anti-Trinitarians. Indeed, the author paints several men pitch black who were accepted by a large section of the Reformed churches of the day and would be quite comparable today with Bible believing Methodists and the so-called Moderate Calvinists. However, victory over Calvin's enemies was not gained without very strong leadership and support from the Swiss-Germans. The battlefield was mapped out to a great extent by Bullinger and in these campaigns

[67] Archiv für Reformationsgeschichte, Jahrgang 87, pp.136-137. Colladon (Collander) assisted Beza in the Genevan school and became its Rector. In 1566, he was appointed Professor of Divinity.

[68] *Die Prophezei*, pp. 205-206. See Büsser's comparison of Beza's apologetic work and Simler's more biographical presentation.

Bullinger was certainly a very active general, whatever part Calvin might have played at his side. Simler had no difficulty in filling his work on Bullinger with biographical details rather than dealing apologetically with controversies. Bullinger was never challenged as Calvin was and had hardly ever given cause for criticism in the way Calvin had. The *Vie de Calvin* sought to establish Calvin's integrity after his death in the face of acute criticism whereas Simler wrote the obituary of one who was well established as a pillar of the Reformed faith before he left his teens. We find thus that Simler gives us far more insight into the life of the Zürich Church than does the *Vie de Calvin* concerning Calvin's Church at Geneva. Indeed, Simler deals with Bullinger's continued influence in Genevan ecclesiastical and political affairs, showing what a major role he played in the Genevan Reformation. Büsser shows how subsequent biographers of Calvin have striven to describe their hero in the same matter of fact, sober terms Simler has portrayed Bullinger but the *Vie de Calvin*'s basic apologetic emphasis still remains. Here, too, Büsser drives home the point made here albeit with his tongue in his cheek, pointing out that Simler added 25 epitaphs, including one of Beza's, to Bullinger's biography, whereas Beza (or Colladon) could only find 14 for his work on Calvin.

The history of 'Calvinism' in the English-speaking world reassessed

The new interest in Bullinger in Great Britain and the United States is increasingly taking note of the fact that the development of 'Calvinism' in the New World, resulted from the work of Bullinger, Bucer and Martyr. Also that the foundation for world-wide Calvinism was laid during the time of Henry VIII and Edward VI, with Bullinger being the 'most prominent' Reformer. At this early stage, Bucer's, Martyr's and Bullinger's influence on the English Church was enormous but Calvin had still not gained much of a reputation in other countries and, in the case of the Elizabethan Settlement, Calvin's name was not highly respected in England. There was a small group of Precisians and Ultra-Puritans who claimed their allegiance to Calvin at this time but Calvin argued that they had misunderstood him. Thus, though John Knox and

Christopher Goodman claimed Calvin as their supporter and mentor in their revolutionary works, Calvin himself washed his hands of any such support. Goodman himself lived to condemn along with Alexander Nowell the separatist revolutionaries who claimed wrongly that Calvin was their ideological father. This problem will be addressed in more detail later in this work. All in all, however, in spite of the rebuffs Calvin obtained from Elizabeth and Sir William Cecil, Calvin respected the Church of England highly and, in private letters, confessed that he was not able to go as far as the Anglicans in his Geneva Reformation because of lack of support in his church.[69] Bullinger had no such problems in his. Also with regards to Bullinger's influence in England, his analysis – and defence – of Elizabeth and the Reformed Church of England is vastly superior to Knox's fanatical and most undiplomatic *Blast of a Trumpet*. It was also typical of the British more-Calvinistic-than-Calvin party in England that they resorted to Parliament for their reforms and not Convocation and did not rule out armed rebellion. Indeed, after condemning Elizabeth for her peaceful reforming principles, Knox begged her to send him troops so that he could enforce his reformation in Scotland. In this, too, Knox did not heed his alleged Genevan master.

Geneva was never a fit pattern of a Christian state.

Finally, modern Calvinists, in the tradition of the early American Calvinists who allegedly sought to found a church state on the pattern of Geneva, greatly err in their conceptions of that city. One has only to read the minutes of the council, consistory and Calvin and Beza's own writings to see that church and state in Geneva often clashed violently with each other and equally often Christian morals and ethics did not appear to make much headway amongst presumed 'Reformed' citizens. Calvin's own denunciations of the citizens and church of Geneva and especially his fellow-ministers prior to the time when the French refugees more or less took over the city, makes for alarming reading. Here again,

---

[69] See also Horton Davies on *The Worship of the English Puritans* for further sources on this subject as also the Parker Society's volumes of Whitgift's works, Lindberg's *The European Reformations*, and my own *The Troublemakers at Frankfurt*.

the Puritan picture of the state under godly control is not that of Calvin and his Geneva but is rather that of Bullinger and his Zürich. There a much greater harmony existed between preachers, pastors, university, council and people. Contrary to this objective view, John Knox is often quoted totally out of context for his praise of Geneva as ‘evidence’ that a Heaven on earth existed there during the 25 years of Calvin’s sojourn. Apart from the obvious fact that Calvin’s opinion of Knox was nowhere near as high as Knox’s opinion of Calvin, we must contextualize Knox’s praise of Geneva. In volume 5 of Laing’s edition of his works in his essay *On Predestination*, he *excuses* rather than *defends* the city in the face of accusations of political and doctrinal chaos. Indeed, in his defence of Geneva on pages 211-216, Knox paints a far more chaotic picture of the city than most of Geneva’s critics past and present, showing that it was Calvin’s severe discipline which caused much of the chaos, which Knox, nevertheless, justifies. It was this severe Church discipline, not shared by the bulk of the Swiss Reformers, which moved Knox to think that Geneva was the ‘City on a Hill’ in which true Christian discipline lay. Clearly Knox believed that the death, destruction and political revolt which he so dramatically describes were the natural consequences of the revolt against his ideal church discipline which ‘proved’ for him that the Genevan church was doing its Christian duty in provoking such opposition. His ‘church’ was thus a church without salt and leaven which had forgotten that it was there to win the city-state rather than to ruin it. Beza admitted this in a letter to Knox,[70] preserved in Laing’s report of the reception of Bullinger’s Confession in Scotland in the above volume, saying that the growth of the Genevan church was through ‘the ruins of others’, i.e. due to the persecutions in France and the steady influx of French refugees but not through the evangelism of the city. Actually, and happily, neither Calvin nor Beza shared Knox’s extreme revolutionary view of Geneva and both Church and state banned his highly controversial political and revolutionary books. The chaos in Geneva which Knox depicts, according to the Swiss records of the day, however, indicates that all was not well

[70] Laing, Vol. 6, p. 563.

with the church by any estimation. Referring to the time when Knox saw the Genevan Church as Heaven working against the world, Johannes Haller who led the Bernese oversight of the Genevan Church, complains that ministers in Calvin's Geneva look deeper into their drinking cups than the Scriptures and are thoroughly split amongst themselves in matters of doctrine and politics. He adds that the situation is worsening.[71] Thus, when quoting Bullinger on the ideal state, Fritz Büsser, referring to Alain Dufour's *Le Mythe de Genéve*, points out that we must distinguish between myth and historical reality. The reality is that Zürich, was for a lengthier period and with greater objective justification internationally recognized as the centre and fountain of the Reformed Church, contrary to what the now tottering 'Calvin Legend' would have us believe.[72] Bullinger believed that the mark of a healthy church was that it permeated and transformed all social and political orders and worked as a fruitful leaven in the state. His description of the 'City on a Hill' in *Decades* II was, however, not merely the Reformer's own personal testimony to his beloved Zürich but that of numerous English refugees who found asylum there. This is why Peter Martyr turned down two invitations to join Calvin at Geneva because he had felt himself called to the spiritual capital of Zürich soon after his conversion and once there, he never wanted to depart this side of Heaven. Of the nigh ideal city in which he dwelt, Bullinger says:

"What is, I pray you, more to be delighted in, than the good platform of a well ordered city, wherein there is (as one did say)[73] the church well grounded; wherein God is rightly worshipped; and wherein the word of God in faith and charity is duly obeyed, so far forth as it pleaseth God to

---

[71]See Büsser's chapter (Vol. 2) entitled *Bullinger und Bern*, especially pages 88-90, for excerpts on this topic from the 600 letters of Haller that have been preserved.

[72] See Section Zürich – Eine Stadt auf dem Berg, in *Heinrich Bullinger: Leben, Werk und Wirkung*, Band 1, p. 115. Büsser also takes up this theme in his Die Prophesei, 'Die Wirkung der Apokalypse-Auslegung Bullingers and passim in his comparison of Bullinger and Calvin, pp. 200-219. Referring to B. Hall's *The Calvin Legend*, Alister E. McGrath in his *Johann Calvin*, p. 370 complains that scholarship has a long way to go before 'fairy tales' concerning Calvin are eliminated from popular views of Calvin.

[73] Most likely Jerome as Bullinger was talking about his views in the context.

give the gift of grace; wherein also the magistrate doth defend good discipline and upright laws; wherein the citizens are obedient and at unity among themselves, having their assemblies for true religion and matters of justice; wherein they use to have honest meetings in the church, in the court, and places of common exercise; wherein they apply themselves to virtue and the study of learning, seeking an honest living by such sciences as man's life hath need of, by tillage, by merchandise, and other handy occupations; wherein children are honestly trained up, parents recompensed for their pains, the poor maintained of alms, and strangers harboured in their distress? There are therefore in this commonweal virgins, married women, children, old men, matrons, widows, and fatherless children. If any (by the naughty disposition of nature) transgress the laws, they are worthily punished; the guiltless are defended; peace, justice, and civility doth flourish, and is upheld."[74]

Bullinger was able to work well with the eight Lord Mayors who succeeded one another during his pastorate in Zürich and they nearly all, as Bullinger testifies, performed great services for the gospel and the city. Though Bullinger insisted that he had no political ambitions, nevertheless, and perhaps because of this stand, the Lord Mayors and Council often turned to Bullinger for advice. Such an acceptance amongst the political leaders was denied Calvin until the last few years of his life.

---

[74] *Decades*, Vol. I, Second Decade, Sermon V, p. 276.

Chapter 1

The Reformer in the Making

Son of a Roman Catholic Parish Priest

Johann Heinrich Bullinger[1] started his earthly pilgrimage in the tiny Swiss town of Bremgarten, fifteen kilometres west of Zürich where the Reuss River takes a sharp bend and flows through the Aargau. It was three o'clock in the morning on 18 July, 1504. Bremgarten had then a population of 800 and belonged to a confederacy of free communities (die freien Ämtern) founded in 1415 and formerly governed from Constance but at the time of Bullinger's birth from Baden. The citizens of these districts possessed a large number of rights which were not enjoyed by bordering Swiss and Upper German states. Politically, all the Swiss-German cantons belonged to the German Empire, but Maximillian I who died in 1519 and his successor Charles V who died in 1558 did not interfere much in Swiss affairs. Charles' brother Ferdinand, who took over the imperial crown, was forced to carry on this policy because of his controversies with Pope Paul IV. The Bullinger family had resided in Bremgarten for well over two hundred years and were of affluent means and possessed a large area of land which, apart from their large orchard and vineyard, they used mainly for hunting, fishing and recreation. Apparently, the family did not need to trade or farm for a living as they

[1] Bullinger the elder named all his sons 'Johann' (Hans).

had a number of revenues from land and property. The house in which young Bullinger was born was, for some now unknown reason, called "The Wild Man"[2] and such a figure decorated the Bullinger coat of arms. In later years, Bullinger's English friends were to tease him by pretending that he lived at a public house. Though built in the Middle Ages, the house is still standing in Market Street,[3] but the impressive sign of the Wild Man has gone and has been substituted by a less eye-catching emblem with the street number 66 painted on it.

Bullinger was the youngest of seven children, five boys and two girls, born to Heinrich Bullinger (1469-1533) and Anna Wiederkehr in their common law marriage.[4] Anna, described quaintly by Carl Pestalozzi as "pretty, homely and strong",[5] was the daughter of a wealthy miller and Councillor. This alliance is worthy of particular note as Heinrich Sen., educated in Swabia and Saxony, was a former organist and deacon at the Bremgarten Parish Church but was now in charge of the parish as *Leutpriester*[6] with twelve assistant-priests under him. Church historians have suggested that Heinrich Senior must have regularly bribed the church authorities to allow him to live in a common-law marriage as a priest but this is mere speculation. Switzerland was ruled democratically in a way otherwise unknown in Europe. It was thus not the church authorities who appointed Bullinger Sen., but the local parishioners who chose him because of his obvious abilities. Our subject's famous contemporaries Leo Jud and Felix Manz were also sons of parish priests. Pestalozzi comments that in those days, godly ministers had common-law wives whereas the immoral clergy refused to be bound to their various lady-friends.[7] Heinrich's alliance with Anna, however, did not receive the blessing of Anna's father and brothers who continually threatened to murder him. The couple were obliged to flee Bremgarten on several

---

[2] Zum Wildenmann.
[3] Marktgasse 66. The Bullinger family was later called Bucher.
[4] Schulthess-Rechberg in his *Heinrich Bullinger der Nachfolger Zwinglis*, p. 2, claims that Henry was the third son. As two older brothers died in childhood, the reference is to the Bullingers' third surviving son.
[5] *Heinrich Bullinger: Leben und ausgewählte Schriften*, p. 5.
[6] Secular or lay priest, i.e. he was not a member of a monk's order.
[7] Ibid, p. 5.

occasions and Heinrich worked as a chaplain in Arbon, Schwyz, Wädenschyl and Constance moving on with Anna every time their pursuers caught up with them. The Wiederkehr family appealed to the Bishop of Constance against Heinrich who passed the matter on to the Archbishop of Mainz. A trial was arranged at Mainz and Heinrich took Anna with him and pleaded on the grounds of mutual love and local laws to keep her. Heinrich won the case but the Wiederkehrs remained hostile. Soon afterwards, however, both Anna's mercenary brothers died in battle and Anna's father left Bremgarten for his place of birth in Dietikon, where he soon died. Heinrich and Anna then returned to Bremgarten and in 1506, in spite of having a wife and children, Heinrich was appointed parish priest by the popular vote both of the congregation and the town council.

Heinrich's and Anna's method of naming their five sons[8] reflects an ancient practice of giving the same saint's name to each child. This is still a tradition today in some German-speaking areas where boys are even given female saint names. So, too, it is an old Germanic custom to name a son after a dead brother.[9] This author has several male friends and acquaintances who bear the name of a deceased uncle or brother or the middle name 'Maria" (Mary). Keeping to these two traditions, Heinrich and Anna named all their boys 'Johann' (Hans) and when Johann Heinrich died as an infant, his younger brother, our subject, was given his name.

Heinrich the elder was never a slave of the papal system and exercised a measure of independence in his church. In 1519 the notorious Franciscan Bernard Samson, the Swiss equivalent of Luther's thorn in the flesh Tetzel, visited Bremgarten. Pope Leo X had granted Cardinal Christopher Forlivio, General of the Discalced (barefoot) Friars, the right to sell indulgences and Forlivio sent Samson to the Swiss churches to carry out his nefarious work. If anything, Samson was worse than Johann Tetzel because he sold indulgences not only for sins already committed

---

[8] Johann Heinrich, Johann Erhart, Johann Reinhart, Hans Bernhard and Johann Heinrich.

[9] I found this custom, too, amongst 18th century Europeans in North America whilst doing research for my book *Isaac McCoy: Apostle of the Western Trail.*

but for sins yet to come. He is said to have extorted 800,000 gold crowns from the Swiss. Heinrich refused to allow the man to enter his church and sell his bogus certificates of indulgence from the pulpit. This caused no end of trouble with the secular and church authorities but when anyone queried his action, Bullinger merely told them that Samson had no legal powers in his parish and he was solely responsible for how his pulpit should be used. Henry Bullinger Jun. wrote extensively on the debate between Samson and his father in his *Chronicle*. The indulgence-monger called Heinrich Sen. a 'cheeky beast' and 'a devil', put a ban on him and told him that he would raise the entire confederacy against him at Zürich. Heinrich replied that would not help him a bit because he would get there before Samson and inform the statesmen and clergy of his side of the story. Heinrich duly appeared before the Zürich Assembly where Zwingli, who had been ordained priest at the Great Minster two months before, also sat. It turned out that Samson had not carried out the necessary formalities before visiting the churches which entailed asking the Bishop of Constance for permission and paying the necessary fees. Thus the assembly made Samson take back the ban he had placed on Heinrich and leave the Swiss cantons at once. However, Samson was permitted to take his heavy-laden wagon full of extorted gold across the Alps to Rome. This was Zwingli's first encounter with the Bullingers and he learnt early in his Zürich ministry what stuff they were made of. Years later, Henry Bullinger, our subject, wrote a detailed account of his parents' ministry in the town. He tells how the Wild Man was a house with open doors where the rich and the poor could find comfort and strength. His father's wealth was used to look after the poor and under-fed in the town and many a mouth and purse was filled in his house. Anna, not content with feeding the needy at her home, went from house to house with her husband, he seeing to their spiritual needs and she catering for the sick with medicine and food. Heinrich kept up his hunt and had a large pack of dogs and Bremgarten's inhabitants and visitors to the town all profited from Heinrich's game. Above all, Henry told his children, his father was a good preacher and pastor and his flock loved him.[10] Of Heinrich and Anna's five sons, two died in childhood, their eldest son Johannes put the life of a mercenary and papist behind him to become a Reformed minister, hampered somewhat by war wounds which refused to heal. Hans Bernard, the second son, was a mercenary wastrel and brought great sorrow to his parents. Henry, the youngest son, became the pride of his parents' hearts.

On 12 May, 1509 young Henry was enrolled as a pupil at the town's Latin school. He was still not five years of age and the specified entrance age was seven. The rules for entrance stipulated fluency in speaking Swiss-German but the two teachers at the school, Johann and Abraham Schatt, considered that Henry was well able to hold his own in speech and general knowledge with children over two years his senior. Henry's entire education up to his twelfth year was limited to reading and writing Latin compositions and liturgical singing. The children were not allowed to communicate in any language other than Latin during school hours. The only religious education Henry received was through the singing lessons. Three terrible experiences each brought the threat of death to young Henry whilst a child. He was kidnapped by a thug and held at ransom but was happily rescued. Then he received a deep wound in his neck and was thought to be bleeding to death. Though he could neither eat nor drink for five whole days, he recovered. To cap all, Henry was smitten by the plague and this time actually given up for dead and his funeral arranged. As the burial procession was assembling, he recovered and in time was able to complete his elementary schooling none the worse for all his troubles. Above all, Bullinger learnt to pray and recite the Lord's Prayer and Christian Creeds off by heart before he was three years of age. As an infant, he used to climb up into his father's pulpit and recite, "I believe in God the Father Almighty, maker of heaven and earth" as if he were already preaching to the hundreds who two decades later flocked to hear his sermons.

---

[10] Pestalozzi reproduces this work in his biography and collection of writings, p. 5 ff..

Singing for his supper

On 11 June, 1516 Henry was sent to far away Emmerich, a town built on the right-hand shore of the river Rhine on the North-Western German border to the Netherlands.[11] There, in November of that year, he was to further his education at St Martin's School which traced its origins back to the missionary work of Northumbria's Willibrord (658-739).[12] Bullinger left home so early so as to make the long journey, mostly on foot. At the same age, his father had wandered on foot from Switzerland to Saxony, Thuringia, Franconia and Swabia in search of a higher education so Henrich did not expect less from his own son. Henry reached Emmerich on 4 July after a whole series of adventures. Emmerich was in the county of Cleves, known to the English through Henry VIII's brief marriage to Anne of Cleves. The most likely reasons for his parents' decision to send Henry to Emmerich is that his eight-year older brother, Johannes Reinhart, was already a pupil there and also assisted in the teaching. Johannes was of particular help to Henry in the latter's Latin studies. Johannes, however, was a restless youth who had already left schools in Rotweil, Bern and Heidelberg. A second reason was that Henry's cousin, Michael Wüst had been enrolled at St Martin's and the two boys are thought to have made the journey together. A further and major reason was that the Emmerich school was in the hands of German and Dutch teachers, both priests and secular scholars who were dedicated Christians of a more evangelical and humanistic nature and the school had a reputation of being 'reformed', though not in the full sense of the Protestant Reformation. According to Pestalozzi, the school was run by the Brethren of the Common Life (Brüder des gemeinsamen Lebens) with whom Thomas à Kempis, from nearby Kempen, was associated. This theory is, however, contested by Fritz Blanke in his *Heinrich Bullinger: Vater der Reformierten Kirche*, who emphasises the

---

[11] Pestalozzi presumes from this fact that the Bremgarten school was a mere elementary school but Blanke and Büsser show that between 1462 and 1526 at least 50 scholars matriculated from the school to the various German-speaking universities.

[12] See Hans Georg vom Berg's article 'Die "Brueder vom Gemeinsamen Leben" und die Stiftsschule von St Martin zu Emmerich. Zur Frage des Einflusses der Devotio Moderna auf den Jungen Bullinger' in *Gesammelte Aufsätze zum 400. Todestag*, Erste Band.

humanistic teaching in the school.[13] As both the Brethren of the Common Life and Humanists were active in Emmerich at this time, both influences on the school are probable. The school had a very good reputation in the early sixteenth century and usually catered for some 800 pupils. Nevertheless, Emmerich was to be no bed of roses for Henry whose affluent father could have provided his son with a luxurious life as a student. Heinrich Bullinger told his twelve-year old son that his accommodation in a private home[14] and clothing would be provided by his parents but for food and other necessities of life he would have to go begging from door to door. This had also been Henry's father's lot as a child. He explained to his son that this was so he might learn to understand the position of those who live perpetually in poverty. As Henry had a good voice, like Tommy Tucker in the nursery rhyme, he literally 'sang for his supper' for the next three years.

At Emmerich, the papal religion was seen as the major educational impulse and soon Henry decided that he would become a Carthusian monk.[15] Humanism had made some inroads in the school but, at the time, this did not seem to have influenced Henry, though learning Greek helped his future calling as a preacher. Teaching in the school was entirely in Latin which was also the compulsory language for all the students' written work. Most of the courses offered were classical and Bullinger tells us in his *Diary* that they dealt with the works of Cicero, Pliny the Younger, Jerome, Virgil, Horace and Battista von Mantua, the latter being a priest who sought reform towards the end of the 15th century and the beginning of the 16th century. The names of Bullinger's teachers have been preserved. These were Kaspar von Glogau, Petrus Homphäus, Matthias Bredenbach, Peter von Cochem and Johan Aelius from Münster.[16] Two of Bullinger's closest friends at Emmerich were local

---

[13] See pp. 23-33.

[14] Bullinger lodged at the home of Cornelius Holländer, a citizen of Emmerich.

[15] So Schulthess-Rechberg but Blanke in his biography claims that Bullinger's school was a free humanistic school independent of the monks. See *Heinrich Bullinger: Vater der reformierten Kirche*, p. 30.

[16] There is some doubt as to who headed the school at this time. See Hans Georg vom Berg's above mentioned work, p. 5.

boys Eberhard von Jülich and Hermann von Meurs but Michael Wüst, his cousin and fellow-pupil, became his friend for life.

The students were required to deliver a speech in Latin each week on the particular subject they were studying at the time. Discipline at the school was very strict but Bullinger actually professed to enjoy it and in later years expressed his thankfulness for it. The students were supervised by trained staff during all their studies and were expected to be occupied with useful work at all times. This life free of idleness became a pattern of Bullinger's life so that he was always up at three or four in the morning and active until nine or ten in the evening. At Emmerich, the students were taught systems of researching, filing, cataloguing and preserving knowledge but also how best to organise their own lives to make them generally useful to mankind. It is no wonder that the order to which the school was said to be attached was commonly called 'the Bee Hive'.

When only fifteen, Bullinger matriculated at Cologne University, and followed his brother who had left Emmerich for Cologne a year or so earlier.[17] Henry made the journey with his cousin Michael who remained his companion in studies. Cologne at that time was the centre of opposition against the New Learning but it was at Cologne that Bullinger was faced more and more with the teaching of Erasmus and those who placed the Scriptures over Aristotelian logic and ethics. Cologne was the largest and most wealthy city in Germany, the centre of Rome's power and the metropolitan seat of the large and lucrative bishoprics of Liege, Utrecht, Münster and Osnabrück. Even more prestige was given the city through its being the seat of the Roman Catholic Archbishop. Cologne's crowning claim to glory, however, was that it preserved the supposed bones of the Three Wise Men in a large golden, bejewelled casket behind the Cathedral High Altar. Here, too, in a special room, piled up from the floor to the ceiling could be found the bones of 11,000 virgins who were alleged martyred for their faithfulness to Saint Ursula. These features alone made the citizens of Cologne feel that their city was the most

[17] Büsser and a few other scholars assume that Henry made a swift visit to Bremgarten before matriculating but no evidence is given.

heavenly on earth.[18] One could not move more than a few yards in Cologne without viewing a church, chapel or monastery and without seeing priests go hurrying by in their full regalia. The German mystics under the leadership of Master Eckart and Johannes Tauler had also settled in large numbers in Cologne and also Albert the Great and Thomas Aquinas. Here, too, Scotsman John Duns Scotus had breathed his last and was buried. Thus there were mystical features in Cologne's religion and a permanent strife went on between the Dominican Aquinians who claimed that religion was a matter of logic and Franciscan Scotians who made religion a product of the will. The only other German city to pride themselves on being more true to Rome than Cologne was Aix la Chapelle (Aachen), who boasted parts of the skull of Charles the Great himself who is still celebrated as a saint in that part of Germany.[19]

Finding the truth as it is in Jesus

On Henry's arrival at Cologne in the late summer of 1519, he registered at the Bursa Montis,[20] the equivalent of a modern college, as a poor scholar. This meant that he did not have to pay student fees and could take the examinations for half of the usual price. He soon discovered that an increasing number in the city were teaching that religion is neither a matter of man's logic nor man's will but of God's will revealed in Scripture. Two of the Arts Professors, Johann Matthäus Phrissemius and Arnold von Wesel were Humanists. Nevertheless, Cologne became the first and only German university to publicly damn Luther's writings. Erasmus of Rotterdam, now at Cologne, used his

[18] The supposed bones, now a pile of dust, have been stolen several times by rival Roman Catholic factions for various purposes and the shrine plundered of its jewels by thieves. The present shrine is a re-make of what the original shrine was supposed to have looked like. Taking the dubious story of how the bones came to Cologne and how they 'disappeared' so often, one must be a very devoted 'believer' indeed to stand in the queues waiting to pray before the shrine at the High Altar as I witnessed people doing recently.

[19] In the year of writing, the skull bones have been reset in a bust of solid gold and set up in the Aix Cathedral for devotees to honour. On a recent historical tour of the churches around Aachen, I asked our priest-guide what factors determined the importance and seniority of the churches. "The number of relics", he answered.

[20] Named after Gerhard and Lambertus ter Stege van's Heerenberg (de Mont). The Bursa was the oldest in the university and thus carried the name *Bursa antiquissima*.

influence to curb the university's anti-Reformed reaction and gained a wide following. This became clear to the Roman Catholic authorities when Hieronymus Alexander, the pope's inquisitor, was sent to Germany in October 1520 with his bag of bulls. His first stop was at Cologne, otherwise called 'Germany's Rome'. He had expected to be received there as a conquering hero but to his amazement, few took notice of him. Instead, he saw anti-papal posters hung all over the city. The university, city authorities and the clergy had stopped persecuting the Lutherans. Erasmus, however, soon gave in to Rome's pressure and Cologne once again followed him blindly. Luther's works were again burned on 15th November, the very day on which 16 year-old Bullinger received his Bachelor of Arts degree. It had taken Henry only a year to master a three-years' course. So brilliant was his memory that he was said to have learnt the 9,900 lines of Virgil's *Aeneid* off by-heart in next to no time. A number of teen-age writings, including his essay *Flee from Lusts* have been preserved and show that even before he professed faith in Christ, Bullinger must have led a nigh immaculate life. Our subject had been, however, very wise in his choice of college and tutors. Matthius Frischheim,[21] Johann Sobius, Arnold von Wesel[22] and Johann Cäsarius were certainly staunch forerunners of the Reformation in their teaching and kept up correspondence with their protégé in the years to come. Now Bullinger studied Quintilian, Cicero, Virgil, Gellius, Macrobius, Pliny, Solinus, Mela, Justin, Homer and Erasmus and worked hard at rhetoric, logic, essay writing and the Greek language.

During this time, Bullinger learnt a real lesson in personal thrift. Heinrich Bullinger had sent his son 118 Guilders to finance his studies at Cologne and had bought him a complete change of clothing to last him until he took his Master's degree. Finding himself with cash in hand for the first time in his life, Bullinger joined several other students, who had also received money from their fathers, in visiting a sweet shop. The selfless proprietor soon realised that the young men were recklessly spending their parents' hard-earned money and refused to serve the

[21] Also called Johann Matthias Frissemius.
[22] Also called Arnoldus von Halderen.

youths, telling them in stern language to be gone or he would thrash the living daylights out of them for squandering good money. Bullinger kept this retailer in memory all his life as one who put the welfare of his customers above his commercial interests.

Bullinger now decided to study both the papists' and Luther's positions carefully. The Leipzig Disputation of 1519 had opened the ears of many Christians seeking Reform. By the time of the now-famous Reichstag at Worms in 1521, many in Germany felt that Rome's tyranny was fading. Bullinger avidly read Luther's *Babylonian Captivity* and *The Freedom of a Christian* published in 1520 and also Melanchthon's *Loci Communes*, a compendium of theology based on Paul's Epistle to the Romans, published the year after. Bullinger gained access to the local Dominican library which had a good store of works on the Fathers and consulted Peter Lombard and Gratian on them. Studying literally day and night, although it was not in his MA curriculum, Bullinger read as much as he could find on theology. He discovered that the Roman Catholic writers claimed their authority came from the Church Fathers and so he made a careful study of the sermons and expository works of the earliest Christian saints, especially John Chrysostom on Matthew's gospel, Origen, Ambrose and Augustine. He found that they appealed to Scripture, so Bullinger bought his first New Testament and he tells us in his diary account of his conversion that he read it day and night throughout 1521-1522 parallel with Jerome's commentaries. He discovered that not only did the Church Fathers teach in full opposition to Rome's 16th century novelties but that the Scriptures presented the faith and fellowship of Christians in a radically more spiritual and far less legal and 'churchy' manner than Rome. He also discovered that Luther, who was now under the pope's bull *Exsurge domine*, stood much closer to the Church Fathers than the 12th and 13th century papist scholars he had been studying and who professed to interpret the Church Fathers correctly.

Soon, Bullinger was reading that justification is by God-given faith alone and that salvation is by God's good grace and not man's dubious 'good works'. He stopped attending the mass and all ideas of becoming a monk vanished. Then Bullinger experienced faith in the Lord Jesus Christ and in His works alone. A year later, on 30 November 1523, he wrote to Rudolf Asper telling him how he had come to see how the canons and decretals of the Roman Catholic Church stood in stark contrast to the Word of God, but now he had found the true source of precious, heavenly food. "I did not confer with flesh and blood but I asked God to give me His Spirit and with renewed disposition consulted my Bible. This I now read continually and earnestly," he tells Asper, stressing that they should now allow the Scriptures to be their sole guide (Richtschnur) in matters of faith and Christian practice. Bullinger also tells Asper of his initial doubts that everything that was necessary for a lively faith could be contained in the Scriptures and not the Church but he explained that when he came to read Paul's letter to the Romans, all his doubts fled. There he found all that was necessary for salvation, the law, the gospel, teaching on sin, punishment, grace and forgiveness, faith, righteousness, Christ, God, good works, love, hope, sorrow, saints and sinners, strength and weakness and how to behave before friends and enemies. He explained that the early Christians were content to live according to the Word and rejected every dogma or deed which contradicted them.[23] In all these early letters, speaking of his love for the Word, Bullinger emphasised that the main message of Scripture is Matthew 17:5 "This is my beloved Son, in whom I am well pleased; hear ye him." So too, in a letter to Bartholomäus Stocker and Leo Jud dated 17 April, 1525 urging them to leave Scholasticism and view the Reformed Lord's Supper as that of the Scriptures and the early church, Bullinger says how in 1521 he went through a time of spiritual struggle and doubt until he found such peace with God that the most severe storms could not loosen his anchor.[24] Thus the greatest Reformed preacher and theologian of the sixteenth century found Christ in a city given over to the rule of Rome.

Though it is true that Bullinger was not led to Christ by any of the budding Reformers of the time and he found saving truth in the Scriptures, his conversion and trust in Reformed principles was not

[23] The letter is given in Pestalozzi, p. 28-30.

[24] See *Heinrich Bullinger Werke, Briefe der Jahre 1524-1531* for Bullinger's earliest letters expressing his faith and strong intention to reform the Swiss Church.

without human aid. This aid, however, came in the form of ancient books rather than contemporary pulpits. He learnt to distinguish between the heresies of Rome and the truth of Scripture through works such as Tertullian's *Against Heresies* and his various anti-Gnostic writings. It was Lactantius who showed Bullinger the folly of worshipping idols and images and Cyprian warned him from believing the traditions of men rather than the truths of the gospel. Through him, Bullinger also learnt the true, Biblical doctrine of the Lord's Supper. Augustine was a major influence on Bullinger, teaching him the doctrine of the covenant which became central to both his teaching and that of the entire Reformation. So, too, from Augustine, Bullinger learnt the doctrines of grace. However, Bullinger never quoted the Church Fathers as if he were quoting divine oracles. After repeating what they had said, he would add, "those were the words of humans, now let us listen to the Word of God." This Word, he always emphasised, is older and greater than the Church.[25]

Commenting on the speed and intensity of Bullinger's conversion at the time, Fritz Büsser points out that Bullinger, who never studied theology and therefore became a student of a particular school, had a unique conversion in comparison to the other great Continental Reformers. He explains how Luther came to faith through anxiety concerning his own soul's security, Zwingli because of his anxiety for the future of the Swiss Confederacies, Calvin through Humanism after a lengthy time of wavering but Bullinger was immediately gripped by the Scriptures, or rather by God through His Word and was led to spend the rest of his life in the service of expounding its treasures.[26]

Bullinger, now 17 years of age, gained his MA and returned home to Bremgarten in April, 1522 after an absence of almost six years. Bullinger tells us that he was as foolish as the rest in his love of university degrees but once he put the university behind him, he never used his academic titles, dropping them in his contempt of all that had to do with popish pomp and false honour. Though he was given the highest church titles possible in Zürich such as 'Antistes', he always signed himself either

[25] See Schulthess-Rechberg, pp. 26-27.
[26] Büsser, Vol. I, p. 26.

'Pfarrer', 'Diener des Wortes' or 'Diener der Kirche zu Zürich'.[27] Perhaps this is why, when young Bullinger founded the training colleges at Kappel and Zürich, although they quickly gained university status, no titles were given. Thus we rarely find contemporary records calling the Zürich academy a university but the most common names for the institution were simply *Prophezei*, *scola*, *Pfarrerschule* (ministers' school), *Collegium* or *Carolinum*. The latter name was because of an old statue of Charles the Great on the college premises. Nowadays, it is customary to refer to Bullinger's institute of learning as the *Scola Tigurina*. The upper classes of the Latin School were often called the *Grossmünster School*, *Obere Schule* or *Schola superior* and the lower classes held in the Fraumünster were called the *Schola inferior* or *Abbatissana*.[28] Bullinger wrote a history of his schools in his *History of the Reformation* (Reformationsgeschichte) but a number of known Bullinger schools are not mentioned in this work.

All doors in Bremgarten found open

How would his father, a Roman priest, take the news of his conversion? How would the church authorities in his canton accept him as the teacher he now wished to be? Bullinger realised that as a witness for Christ, he could not hide his faith. He resolved to tell one and all of his new life in Christ. Bullinger was warmly received by his family without a word of reproach. He immediately received a call to take over an abbey school in the Black Forest. On visiting the place, he found the monks idle, worldly and leading immoral lives, so he returned home at once. His father then allowed Bullinger to continue his studies of the church fathers, chiefly Tertullian, Athanasius and Cyprian for some eight months whilst looking for a post. These home-studies expanded to include works of the early church historian and apologist Lactantius, those of Luther and other early Reformers, besides general church history and Reformed doctrine. During these months of learning, Bullinger

[27] Pastor, Servant of the Word, Servant of the Church at Zürich.

[28] See also Kurt Rüetschi's 'Bullinger als Schulchronist', *Gesammelte Aufsätze zum 400. Todestag*, Erster Band.

realised the evils of the papist love of tradition, and declared, "Habit without truth is an ancient error. One must not make habit the rule of practice but truth must prevail!"[29]

Then the Cistercian abbot, Wolfgang Joner,[30] invited Bullinger to take over the abbey school at Kappel am Albis, a three hours' walk away.[31] Bullinger, now eighteen-years of age, visited Joner, gave him his testimony and told him that he could not possibly take the monk's oath, put on a monk's clothing or attend mass and he must be free to maintain his own testimony of faith and wanted nothing to do with a life of idleness. The abbot, was obviously pleased to find such an honest, sincere young man, accepted all his conditions and made him superintendent of the abbey school on the spot! When the monks were at mass, Bullinger was allowed to retire on his own for a time of prayer and worship.

The teenage Headmaster started on his new calling in the ancient abbey[32] on 17 January, 1523. Bullinger immediately drew up a new curriculum and the tiny school grew and flourished. For the next six years, the young Reformer, after teaching the children, daily expounded through 21 of the 27 New Testament books at the monastery but also gave lectures on Erasmus, Augustine, Jerome, Chrysostom and Melanchthon's *Loci Communes*. He found that the monks could hardly understand a word of Latin and thus preached regularly in Swiss-German. He also, with Joner's permission, invited the secular workers, servants and the entire town population to hear his teaching. Soon on lecture days a procession of hearers visited Kappel from nearby Zug to sit under Bullinger's ministry which caused the papist clergy at Zug to plot against him.

Bullinger always confessed that his Kappel years were the happiest time of his life. Soon, the eighteen-year-old became well-known in the canton as a leading Reformer. As Christoffel points out, 17 January, 1523 marks the beginning of the Reformation in Switzerland because Zwingli

[29] Pestalozzi, p. 19.
[30] Abbot since 1519. The abbey had been increasingly viewing the Reformation positively for several years.
[31] Bremgarten was also a three-hours' walk from Zürich.
[32] Founded 1185.

had not yet made an open confession of separation from Rome and not broken with Rome's traditions. He believed strongly at this time that if he faithfully preached the word, Reforms would naturally follow but they must not be pushed.[33] Twelve days after Bullinger began his teaching ministry in Kappel, Zwingli addressed the first Zürich *Religionsgespräch* (Disputation) with his 67 reforming theses[34] which he published soon after but this was an internal act within the papal set-up and was not seen then as a major break with Rome. Bullinger was present at the disputation and when he read Zwingli's published explanations a few months later, he wrote in his diary that he was very much drawn to the older man because he had been a fiery contender himself for the same reforms for the past four years. Bullinger was all for an open condemnation of Rome's novelties but as students of Bullinger's moved out into the surrounding cantons with their new learning and faith, they met up with great hardships. At Zug especially, Bullinger's followers were persecuted as heretics and the city even threatened to storm the Kappel abbey and leave it in ashes. Once Bullinger and a number of students were surrounded by a group of Zug's thugs, twenty-strong, who knew Bullinger and were out to harass him. However, when the thugs approached Bullinger, they apparently did not recognise him and left him and his party in peace. Bullinger wrote, "God shut their eyes so that they did not recognise us, although they knew us well enough."[35] Bullinger's precarious situation is made clear in a letter he sent to a friend who had studied with him at Cologne. Bullinger writes:

"I am very happy here. I live in a rich abbey, surrounded by flowery fields and woods out of which the birds sing sweetly and have every opportunity to lecture on theological and linguistic subjects … Yet I hang fully on Christ's cross and dare not step a straw's breadth beyond Zürich's borders if I do not wish to risk my life by sword or fire. But this is all to my taste, to be cast off by men for the sake of the sweet name of

---

[33] *Heinrich Bullinger und Seine Gattin*, pp. 13-14.
[34] Commonly called the *Schlussreden* (Conclusion).
[35] Pestalozzi, p. 24.

Christ (1 Corinthians 4:13) as I have long deserved far more terrible things because of my sins. Pray to God for me, that He would strengthen in me and all believers what He in grace has begun and that we in death might rejoice with the holy Ignatius: We are ready for the wild animals: for fire, for the sword; for the cross that we might only see Jesus, our Lord and Redeemer."[36]

The reformation in Kappel and Bremgarten

Changes made at Kappel were enormous and swift. By 1524 the images had been removed from the abbey church. The mass was abolished in 1525 and by March 1526 the entire order of monks was meeting at the Lord's Table in the Reformed manner. On the day of the first Reformed communion meal, all the monks, including the abbot, discarded their robes and renounced their monkish oaths. Instead of the usual mechanical liturgies, they gathered around the Scriptures for practical Bible study. Though some monks left to become Christian craftsmen and farmers,[37] many stayed on to be further educated by Bullinger and eventually became Reformed preachers in the Swiss cantons. Several works of Bullinger are extant from this very early period, including a thesis on the reliability of the Scriptures as the Word of God written at the request of Wolfgang Joner for critics in general who had questioned Bullinger's and Joner's Reformed stand and in particular for Rudolf Asper who had been closely attached to Joner but now led the criticism.[38] It is significant to note that the learned and more experienced Joner asked Bullinger to take on this task, though the main criticism was levelled at himself by his former friends. However, in this letter, we gain deep insight as to the conversion process of Bullinger as he came to see that salvation was by allegiance to God's written and Living Word. In the thesis, Bullinger shows that we cannot rely on church traditions and the Fathers for our understanding of Scripture as these are often

[36] Quoted in Pestalozzi, pp. 24-25.
[37] The abbey had long been a training school for farmers and viniculturists.
[38] *De scripturae negotio*, found in Gäbler's and Herkenrath's Gesammelte Aufsätze zum 400 Todestag, 1975, Band I, pp. 29-48 and *Heinrich Bullinger Werke*, Dritte Abteilung, Band 2, pp. 19-31, with copious notes.

contradictory. The Scriptures as the breath of the Spirit are their own interpreter and lead to a knowledge of Christ. Thus the true theologian or pastor uses the Scripture as his infallible standard and not tradition or the Scholastics. Bullinger also emphasises the unity of Scripture and the continued line of revelation in both Testaments. When the Scriptures speak, Christ speaks. Though Bullinger was still in his teens, in this study of the Word of God he is one of the very first, if not the first, to emphasise the rediscovery of *sola scriptura* as revealed by the whole canon. Luther, Zwingli and Calvin all tended to speak of the Word of God in Scripture rather than Scripture being the Word of God, all three Reformers finding some part of the canon which did not meet their criteria. So, too, the other Reformers emphasised that a Word of God for one person was not a Word of God for the next. This dualistic view of the Scriptures could only lead to strife as to which part of Scripture was the Word of God and for whom. We have this ancient source of sect-building in the modern Barthian and Pentecostalist view of the Scriptures which maintains that what is plain text to some are Spirit-filled words to others. Such 'I-am-holier-than-thou' enthusiasts fostered numerous split-offs from the Reformed Swiss churches during the 16th century. Bullinger maintained that the spiritual unity of the entire Scriptures and its full use in matters of faith and practice as applying to all men everywhere as a pointer to Christ and His salvation was the sole and absolute criterion for the true Church. Here Bullinger was pointing the way which was to make him a true pioneer of Reformed, Biblical theology and far superior in his exegesis than most other Reformers. He refused to view Christian doctrines in isolation from one another. He would not separate law from gospel as if there were no law in gospel and no gospel in the law. Similarly, he refused to separate justification from sanctification, as justification meant the gift of a lively, working faith, which contemporaries such as Melanchthon were now claiming were two separate stages in the believer's life. So, too, we find no distinction in Bullinger's theology between the freedom from guilt or fault and the freedom from punishment which goes with justification. When Christ rids His people of the one, he rids them of the other.[39] This doctrine, held by such great English Reformers and Puritans as Tobias Crisp, has been declared by many a modern Reformed party to be Antinomian. Such critics promote the idea that justification secures pardon from punishment but pardon from guilt comes via sincere obedience and post-justification sanctification and holiness. Bullinger rejected such an interpretation of God's grace and man's responsibility. Interesting enough, such modern Anti-Antinomians always air such criticism in the name of Calvin but the Frenchman was not one whit behind his friend and mentor as his defence of the believer's freedom from guilt and punishment through Christ's work alone is clearly stated in *Institutes* III. 4.29.

This lively working faith for Bullinger is only possible once the sinner has been taken into Christ's loving care and can say, "Christ lives within me" (Galatians 2:20 ff). In much modern Reformed thought, this merging of justification with sanctification is frowned on as being the old teaching of Rome. However, Bullinger was not talking of the Roman doctrine of infused righteousness but of imputed righteousness with the corollary of a life in Christ. A life in which a union of persons, however difficult to imagine or describe, is obviously according to Scripture a Christian state as Galatians 2:20 ff points out. This indwelling of Christ in the believer is a theme which goes through the whole of the New Testament as in Colossians 1:27-29, "Christ in you, the hope of glory: Whom we preach, warning every man, and teaching every man in all wisdom; that we may present every man perfect in Christ Jesus: Whereunto I also labour, striving according to his working, which worketh in me mightily." Is this not the same truth as in another of Bullinger's favourite verses, "Wherefore, my beloved, as ye have always obeyed, not as in my presence only, but now much more in my absence, work out your own salvation with fear and trembling. For it is God which worketh in you both to will and do of his good pleasure," (Philippians 2:12-13)?

---

[39] *Decades* I, p. 108.

Bullinger gave such examples to show that true theology was not separating parts from the whole and claimed that this was an exercise for Scholastics, philosophers and heretics. So, too, Bullinger did not separate providence from predestination and election, nor did he separate election from the preaching and reception of the gospel and the New Birth. Neither did he separate God's actions in time in which He sees the beginning from the end, from God's actions in eternity. In the same way, Bullinger did not separate covenant baptism from its pan-Biblical context in both the Old and New Testaments. One of Bullinger's earliest contributions to the Reformed faith in which he preceded Zwingli by at least two years, was his insistence on the unity of the Old and New Testaments which proved a basis for his covenant teaching of one covenant of grace between both Testaments. Indeed, he saw both law and gospel as being anchored in the five books of Moses with the prophets showing how their true fulfilment would occur and the New Testament showing how that fulfilment was established. Thus the Old Testament is God's promises and the New Testament is God's fulfilments. Bullinger felt that once one began to separate the attributes of salvation, the historical and prophetical teaching of the Scripture, the work of Christ and the teaching of the ordinances from each other, one lost the good news of salvation and left people merely picking at what suited them as if the gospel were divided. Thus he stressed that there was one Word of God, truly in harmony with itself with Christ as its centre who filled it out totally with His glorious Work radiated throughout both Testaments.

Even in these very early years, we find Bullinger exercising an enormous influence on the clergy of the surrounding cantons. Already in 1523, he had sought to win the Canton Zug priests, in particular Rudolf Weingartner, formerly of Zürich, Werner Steiner and Bartholomäus Stocker for the Reformed gospel. Foremost in Bullinger's teaching at this time was the Reformed view of the Lord's Supper over and against the idolatrous mass of the papists. Between 1523 and 1527, he wrote no less than eleven theses on the subject before other major Reformers on the Continent had begun to make this a key issue. Indeed, for at least two years, he must have been the only Swiss Reformer to have openly held to the Reformed position. Luther was totally opposed to the Reformed position on the Lord's Supper, Bucer was too cautious to come out with any really significant statement and Zwingli's policy of wanting to move Reforms only when he could carry all the Swiss with him and his dislike of working out formulas which did not grow directly out of his preaching, made him slow to take up his pen on the subject. Still, today, it is very difficult to work out exactly what Zwingli believed regarding the ordinance.[40]

The middle 1520s was a convenient time for the Reformation in Zug as Chief Magistrate Leonard Steiner, Werner Steiner's uncle, had decided not to take action against Protestant influence in the canton. However, the papist clergy allied with the Fünf Orte in the Beckenrieder Union of 8 April, 1524 and clamoured for the Senate to declare Bullinger's preaching illegal in the canton. Bullinger's life was threatened and he replied by sending manuscript after manuscript to the canton outlining the Reformed gospel. One of these works sent to Werner Steiner entitled *De cruce et patientia*, has survived in part but the entire essay *De sacrifitio missae*[41] sent at the request of Rudolf Weingartner on 16 November, 1524 to Jakob Frey in Wohlen, Canton Aargau has been preserved in several copies. This document was probably the first amongst the Swiss cantons to openly challenge the papist doctrine of transubstantiation and gained a hefty reaction from the papists. *De sacrifitio missae* was quickly followed by works sent to Zug in both Swiss-German and Latin such as *Von dem namen Christi Jesus, unsers seligmachers* (1524), *Wider das Gotzenbrot* (1525) and *De institutione eucharistiae* (1525). In these works, Bullinger bravely railed at the papist for making a Christ out of bread and turning the communion wine into 'a commercial business'. A work named *Zwei Gespräche über das Abendmahl* sent to a V. Brandenburg of Zug during Bullinger's Kappel period is now lost as also a work for the laity entitled *Loci communes rerum sacrarum ad Tuginos*. In the middle twenties,

[40] This author is convinced that Zwingli held to more than a mere commemorative view of the Lord's Supper.
[41] Published in *Unveröffentlichte Werke aus der Kappeler Zeit*, Theologisher Verlag Zürich, 1991. pp. 32-45. Bullinger sent Weingartner five works between 1524 and 1528.

Werner Steiner begged Bullinger to write a manual of advice for those wishing to take up theological studies. The result was Bullinger's *Studiorum ratio* which one would think came from the pen of a very experienced Christian and scholar but its author was only twenty-one years of age. Also at the age of 21, Bullinger authored his *Der Prophet*, explaining to the papist what the office of a true minister of Christ entailed.

The Romanists were quick to reply to Bullinger's *sacrifitio missae*. Frey had passed the work Bullinger had sent to him to Dominican monk Dr Johannes Burchard of Bremgarten who then wrote his *Gesprächbüchlein* in 1525 against it, using the pseudonym Theobald Perdutianus. Burchard's two arguments were that Bullinger should obey the authority of the pope and that youngsters of Bullinger's age should be seen and not heard. This forced Bullinger to take up his pen again and write his *De pane eucharistiae Declamationes* of 19 March, 1526 and his *Antwort an Johannes Burchard* in the winter of 1526/27. These works were written to be copied and distributed and were intended both to confute Burchard and help the Zug clergy to accept the Reformed position. This duel in words continued for several years, producing a number of works from each side. It raised a wide interest in the purpose and design of the Lord's Supper and ensured that both papists and Protestants became familiar with Henry Bullinger and his message. Burchard's main defence remained throughout the authority of the Roman Catholic Church, whereas Bullinger defended the Reformed position from Scripture, demonstrating that all the novelties and superstitions of Rome evolved from their idolatrous understanding of the mass. Rudolf Weingartner continued to solicit help from Bullinger who always replied with lengthy documents for general distribution such as his *Apologia ad librum Rod. Vuingarteri Tugini super eucharistiae negotio* of 1528. Sadly, Weingarten came out on the side of the papist Fünf Orte in the Kappel wars and served as a field-chaplain to the papist forces. It was Weingarten who gave the enemy troops the detailed information of the area, including hidden and secret paths, which they needed to surprise and defeat the Protestants.

By 1525, the Roman Catholic hierarchy was literally up in arms against Bullinger and he was repeatedly told, especially with reference to his *sacrifitio missae,* that he was a young hothead who had still the eggshell sticking to his head and he should leave theology to the wisdom of his elders and betters. Young papist hot-heads swore that should the Reformer cross the canton border to Zug, he would not live to return home. The Zug Council thus banned Bullinger from entering into Zug territory and the papists organised mass demonstrations against Bullinger before the houses of his friends in Zug. Bullinger replied that he was constantly reminded of his youth not only by the papists but also by older friends sympathetic to the Reformation who told him to wait until he was riper in years before he sought to reform his country. He added that all these advisers were already ripe in years themselves and still loved their peace and security instead of speaking out against popish idolatry. He confessed that he could not spend a life in silence but was called as a Christian to speak up, not because he thought he had any special, mature gifts but because he owed it to the Word of God and his calling as a Christian.

Young Bullinger's positive influence on the neighbouring clergy is illustrated by a letter dated 8 February, 1526 sent by Bullinger to Matthias von Seengen in Aargau. This minister was neglecting his flock and the Word of God and trying to stand with one foot in the papal system and one on the Reformed path. Twenty-one-year-old Bullinger, like a wise old apostle, lovingly explained to his friend what the difference was between a true shepherd and a hireling and outlined the Reformed doctrine of the Lord's Supper for him.[42] Bullinger's letter appears to have moved the man so much that in the 1528 Bern Disputation at which the Reformation was ushered into Bern, Matthias von Seengen bravely took the side of the Reformation. These early letters were passed from hand to hand by Bullinger's friends and enemies and copied in large numbers. They impressed and edified Ulrich Zwingli Junior, the son of the Reformer, so much that he had them printed with other hitherto

[42] The letter is given in Pestalozzi, pp. 31-35.

unpublished works shortly before his death in 1571. Thus he preserved important Reformed works just as Bullinger had printed hitherto unpublished works of Ulrich Zwingli Senior in the fifteen-forties. Bullinger's important educational works belong to those early works published by Zwingli's son but will be dealt with when we come to look at Bullinger the educator.[43] Bullinger had, by order of the Zürich Council, accompanied Zwingli to the Bernese Disputation and it was there that he first met Bucer, Capito, Farel, Blaurer and Oecolampadius.

In 1526, acting on Joner's and Bullinger's initiative, the city of Zürich took over the Kappel Reformed Latin school (*Schola Tigurina*)[44] and ministers' training college (*Prophezei*) so that what had been transformed from a Roman Catholic monastery to a centre of Christian further education by young Bullinger now became the official Reformed school and seminary for the entire canton and beyond to train those wishing to enter the ministry. Bullinger, of course, remained the headmaster of the school and the Principal of the seminary. In the document which Joner and Bullinger drew up to present the seminary to the city of Zürich, after the preamble concerning the function of such a college, the two Reformers stated that their gift to Zürich was under:

"the condition and request that instead of the misuse which has now ended, you will undertake a reformation which is fully according to God's Word. To this end, we shall assist all with advice and help and each of us is willing to take up those tasks for which God has gifted him in the sure and certain hope that you will all receive us in grace."[45]

Though the school and seminary were now 'under new management', Bullinger still did not receive a salary though his duties were greatly

---

[43] I am indebted to the work of Hans-Georg vom Berg for the details regarding Bullinger's works sent to Zug. See his Einleitung, *De sacrifitio missae*, Unveröfentlichte Weke aus der Kappeler Zeit.

[44] Büsser argues that not only Bullinger's *Prophezei* was the first Reformed training seminary in Switzerland but also he was the first to set up a Reformed Latin school, p. 29-30. He adds that Bullinger founded the *Prophezei* almost forty years before Calvin set up a similar institution.

[45] The full document is quoted in Pestalozzi, p. 49.

increased. The former abbey now became a full parish, including neighbouring villages where there were many poor but the school was now only allowed to give four poor scholars education, the rest having to pay according to their parents' income. Bullinger, however, soon found out a good way of helping the parish poor. The monks and clerics had worn good woven cloth of wool, silk, velvet, linen and cotton. As the monks had given up their robes and not even the clergy wore gowns, Bullinger had this material made up into shirts, skirts, trousers and jackets for a good many people who were too poor to provide themselves with adequate clothing. Much of the material was too 'fine' for the taste or usage of the poor so they were auctioned off and the poor received the money thus gained. The gold and silver ornaments in the church were melted down to be used as coins. This angered the papists the most as they thought making common coins out of the communion utensils was sacrilege as they had been consecrated to change bread and wine into the Lord! Others complained that they had seen 'holy' vestments sold at flea-markets and they were now worn by harlots! Zwingli merely replied to these protests with the calm statement that the garments had already been desecrated by their former priestly owners so they could hardly suffer a worse fate. Bullinger, always more tactful, explained that garments do not make Christians but hearts made pure by the presence of God. Furthermore, the gold and silver given to the church was originally not to enhance the fabric but to help spread the gospel amongst the needy. Being the historian and Christian he was, Bullinger gave his critics ample evidence from history to show that godly ministers such as Lactantius, Cyprian and Ambrose had always used church treasures, including the communion utensils to help ransom people in bondage and help the poor.

During the early years 1523-28 Bullinger was already eagerly sought by various parties for his wise advice and those who profited from his help urged the young teacher to put his views in print. These early printed works were mostly apologetic dealing with difficult points in Scripture such as whether Christ really descended into hell, the doctrine of Scripture, the Lord's Supper and baptism. These numerous productions drew the attention and admiration of Oecolampadius, Leo Jud and Ulrich

Zwingli. Indeed, parallel with these reforms at Kappel, Ulrich Zwingli was pressing ahead at Zürich in a similar way, though he was meeting more opposition, possibly because he lacked the tact and communication abilities that were so very much Bullinger's. Zwingli was also provoking the Fünf Orte (a union of five Roman Catholic districts) to war and had allied with Bern to cut off their supplies of food.[46] Actually, Zwingli had protested that Bern's aggressive policy did not go far enough and he was for an all-out war at once. The papists had not yet begun to persecute the Reformed people as it was left to the public vote which community should become Reformed or not. When the Roman Catholic powers eventually decided to put down the Reformation by force, it was not the cities of Bern and Zürich that they aimed to destroy first but the work of true Reformation at Kappel.

Anna Adlischwyler

Many of the Kappel monks, including Abbot Wolfgang Joner,[47] now married and these men assured Bullinger that a wife would be a great support to his ministry. In 1527, Joner gave Bullinger leave of absence from the school to find a bride. During this search, Bullinger visited the former Dominican nunnery at Oetenbach where the nuns had accepted the Reformed faith in 1525 and disbanded. Two ladies had remained to carry on a Christian witness. The elder of the two ladies, Justitia, was acquainted with Bullinger. The younger, Anna Adlischwyler, formerly of Zürich, who was a year younger than Bullinger, was the daughter of Hans Adlischwyler, who had served many leading citizens as cook and left a substantial fortune behind him at his death in 1512. Anna's mother was Elizabeth Adlischwyler, née Sadler. She had given Anne over to the Oetenbach nunnery when her husband died and boarded there herself so that she could be near her daughter. The Reformer recognised Anna as his future wife and wrote to her, asking her to be his bride. Bullinger's letter was as Scriptural and business-like as could be with a fine blend of

[46] Bern was more for the blockade than Zwingli who wanted nothing less than war. The compromise, however led to the war Zwingli wanted and in which he perished.

[47] Joner married in 1527.

seriousness and humour. He outlined all the advantages and disadvantages of the single life and then did the same regarding the married life. He confessed that he only received board and lodgings at the school and did not have a penny to his name. He admitted that he would have some little fortune to inherit at his father's death, but this would probably be in a very distant future.[48] Anne was perhaps no stranger to Bullinger as in this letter, he mentions that his parents and family were well-known to her.[49] Anna replied within a few days and her answer was 'Yes'. Bullinger returned to Oetenbach and, taking Anna to the Great Minster in Zürich where Zwingli ministered, proposed personally to her and was again accepted. They planned to be married, as the custom was, within two weeks of their engagement.

The two weeks were to become two years. Anna's widowed mother wanted her daughter to be her personal companion and only marry after her own death. She had thus agreed to the engagement which legally bound Anna to Henry but then refused to allow her daughter to marry him. In this way, selfish Mrs Adlischwyler bound her daughter to herself and made it impossible for Anna to marry anyone else. Anna continued to press her mother to allow her to marry but she said she would only relent if Anna found a rich man. Anna said that it would be Bullinger or nobody. Mrs Adlischwyler then said that it would have to be nobody. As public opinion was outraged at Mrs Adlischwyler's selfish act and put pressure on her, the lady looked for legal backing. Anna and Bullinger had become engaged before God but without a human witness and a new law passed in Zürich now ruled that no engagement was to take place without a witness. So now, Mrs Adlischwyler argued that her daughter had never been legally engaged. Happily, witnesses were called who had been privy to the written correspondence between the couple regarding their engagement and the court decided in the couple's favour. But still Mrs Adlischwyler refused to unbind her daughter. Even the personal intervention of Zwingli was no help. Henry and Anna left the matter in

[48] Henry inherited next to nothing from his father as all his money and property were confiscated by the Romanists after the Kappel War.
[49] The letter is reproduced in Cristoffel's *Bullinger und Seine Gattin*, pp. 21-34.

God's hands and almost two years later Mrs Adlischwyler died in her daughter's arms. The couple were speedily married on 17 August, 1529 at Birmenstorf, a two hours walk from Bremgarten where Johannes Bullinger, Henry's elder brother, was now pastor. Peter Simmler, the former Kappel prior, took the service. The marriage ceremony had been arranged at Birmenstorf because of the precarious situation at Bremgarten, so close to the Roman Catholics who could tolerate priestly concubines but not pastors' wives. Bullinger composed a special hymn for the occasion, calling Anna his Empress (min keyserin).[50] Meanwhile, Bullinger, as if he were now an expert on the fair sex, wrote a book which he entitled *Von weiblicher Zucht und wie eine Tochter ihr Wesen und Leben führen sollte*.[51] From this time on, Bullinger was often asked to write to the stewards of convents concerning whether the nuns should be encouraged to leave and find husbands. The Bullinger's first daughter Anna was born in the following May and Margareta was born in April 1531 before the couple were compelled to leave Bremgarten because of the war. From now on, Bullinger's favourite slogan was words he had used during the wedding celebration:

"Es hat mir g'stillt all Leid und Klag'
Im Augst der siebezehnt' Tag."[52]

Anna Bullinger must have been a woman of great strength and courage. When her husband was banned from Bremgarten by the papist troops, Anna was refused permission to leave the town to join her husband in Zürich. One night, she tried by stealth to leave the town via the Katzentor[53] which still stands, carrying her two babies with her. She was stopped by a guard at the town-gate and was commanded to return home. Anna overpowered the armed man, in spite of her burden, took the key from him, opened the gate and after a ten mile walk through the night

[50] Several verses from this hymn, which is more a Christian love poem, can be found in Pestalozzi's life of Bullinger, p. 60 and Cristoffel's *Bullinger und Seine Gattin*, p. 49.
[51] On female upbringing and how a daughter ought to lead her character and life.
[52] I was cured of all sorrow and complaint on August 17!
[53] Cat-Gate.

carrying the infants, she was reunited with her thankful husband. Bullinger had found lodgings at the home of Werner Steiner for whom he had written his *Studiorum ratio* some four years before. Steiner had been granted asylum by Bullinger in Kappel when he fled from Zug, so he was happy to be able to look after the Bullingers in the same way in Zürich.

Anna and Henry had eleven children. Anna and Margareta mentioned above were followed by Elizabeth (1532), Heinrich (1534), Johann (Hans) Rudolf (1536), Christoph (1537), Johannes (1538), Diethelm (1541), Veritas (1543), Dorothea (1545) and Felix (1547). Diethelm died as an infant but all the others lived to maturity which was quite an exception in those days. Christoph and Hans probably did not marry but the other brothers and sisters all married into the families of leading Reformers and Senators. It is said that all Bullinger's sons who survived childhood became pastors but Christopher also worked as a baker and a soldier in Landgrave Philip of Hessen's army. He disappointed his father by warring as a mercenary in France and Holland. Large as Anna's own household was, her wider family was much greater. Besides adopting several children after the Kappel wars had left many children orphans, the Bullingers also opened their home to Zwingli's widow and all his children. Furthermore, there was hardly ever a time when the Bullinger's Zürich house was not full of students boarding with them and an endless number of refugees, especially from England, France and Italy. Some such as Italian Secundo Curione and German Wolfgang Musculus, brought very large families with them. When the plague struck, the Bullingers did not flee as did a number of Reformers such as Zanchi but stayed to look after the sick. This led to a number of deaths in the Bullinger household, including that of Anna Bullinger herself.

Father and Son together in the faith

In February 1529, Heinrich Bullinger Sen., now sixty years of age, announced to his congregation that he had accepted the Reformed faith. His son recorded his very words in his diary:

"I have been your minister for 23 years and have preached and taught that which I believed was true and correct and have never striven to delude anyone. The times were, however, times of darkness so that I was blinded like many others and taught what I had received. I did not do this with evil intentions but because I was ignorant. I confess today my error before you and pray that God will forgive me. I am now determined with God Almighty's help to show you and lead you on the true and right way of blessedness through God's Word alone, that is the Holy Scriptures, in and through Jesus Christ our only Saviour."[54]

Most of the congregation took the news well but a few leading citizens such as the Honeggers left the church in protest on hearing Bullinger's words, complaining loudly of 'the old blind fool'. On 31 December, the pastor officially married his beloved wife of almost forty years according to the new Reformed rites.

As soon as Bullinger Sen. announced his conversion, the backing he received from his congregation failed to allay the fears of the city authorities who now believed that the security of the town was threatened in view of growing Roman Catholic protests against the Reformed movement. They thus had Bullinger ousted by armed force from Bremgarten but he immediately began to preach from village to village doing pioneer work for the Reformation in Roman Catholic communities. Zürich had been appealed to by Bullinger Sen. for support and so the city sent a delegation to Bremgarten to appeal to the council on his behalf. By a ruling going back to 1506, they demonstrated that the council could not dismiss Bullinger as he was appointed by a majority vote of the entire community. The Zürich men had to return home with their mission unaccomplished but they left the two factions in Bremgarten to carry on the debate. A papist priest, Hans Aal was set over the congregation but they soon grew tired of him, particularly as he refused to follow their wish and keep his sermons centred on the Word of God.

---

[54] *Merkwürdige Züge*, pp. 29-30.

Meanwhile, the Bremgarten congregation strove democratically to be given Reformed status and soon the Reformed faction in the council gained the majority. However, Henry's father was now pastoring a nearby parish, so the Bremgarten congregation called Zwingli's former assistant, Gervasius Schuler (1495-1563) of Strasburg, to be their pastor, hoping he would lead them from the papist system. Schuler, otherwise known as Scolasticus, was educated in Switzerland and became a deacon in Zürich in 1520. From 1525-1528 he served in Bischweiler in Alsace as pastor, a post he had been given through the direct influence of Zwingli. In 1529, he returned to Switzerland as Heinrich Bullinger the elder's successor and fled with the Bullingers to Zürich in the autumn of 1531 from where he travelled to Basle but only stayed two years there before obtaining a post in Memmingen. We gather from Bullinger's letters that Switzerland was going through a most nationalistic phase at the time in which foreigners were not welcome. However, Gervasius returned to Zürich for a short time in the late 1540s but became a minister in Lenzburg in 1550. He ministered there for thirteen years and died in 1563.

Though, according to Bullinger, Schuler was a pious and learned man, his Reformed manner was too slow for many of the parish so their thoughts now turned to one who was a more experienced Reformer, yet a citizen of their own town who could speak their own language. This was, of course, Henry Bullinger Jun., whom the Bremgarteners knew was hard at work at Kappel. They thus realised that it would not be easy to tempt such a well-known minister to their church. So, in May, 1529, Rudolf Gomann, a Bremgarten citizen, was appointed to visit Henry Bullinger Junior with a request that he should preach once and once only at their church. The Kappel teacher and newly ordained minister, promised to preach at Bremgarten on the following Whit-Sunday. So, on 16 May 1529, Bullinger now aged almost twenty-five, preached his first ever sermon at his home church before an enormous, attentive congregation. His subject was worshipping God in spirit and in truth. There was a tremendous spiritual reaction amongst the church-goers, and, after the service the images were torn down. On the day after, they were burnt in the church yard and the altar was demolished. Then the entire, united congregation dedicated themselves to God and the new faith and declared their intention to be a Reformed Church, come what may. On 18 May, the council formallly requested Bullinger to bring in the Reformation to the town. Bullinger, however, informed the people of Bremgarten that he was under oath to the Zürich council and could not take a step without their permission. Bremgarten then quickly despatched a representative to Kappel and one to Zürich to plead for Bullinger's release from his commitments there. Their arguments moved the Zürich council to allow Bullinger to take up the new post. Thus, on 22 May, the congregation called Bullinger by unanimous consent to be co-pastor with Schuler. As Joner and the ex-monks at Kappel, besides the Zürich clergy and councilmen had all given Bullinger their blessing and urged him to take up the call, he accepted the post with a good conscience. First, Bullinger went to say goodbye to all his colleagues and friends at Kappel and Zürich and entered his new calling on 1 June, 1529.

Besides Schuler's dedicated, but rather plodding ministry, the Bremgarten congregation heard Bullinger preach every Sunday afternoon and Monday, Tuesday and Wednesday mornings. He held a well-visited Bible Study every day at 3.00 pm. On 30 June, Bullinger began to organise the feeding and clothing of the poor, just as he had done at Kappel and started up a peripatetic ministry to the surrounding districts. He was joined by his wife Anna, on 17 August.

In the rather less than three years that Bullinger remained in Bremgarten, he preached through the entire New Testament during what was called the Spring Time of the Bremgarten Reformation. During this time Bullinger also translated thirty Psalms from the Hebrew into Latin and Swiss-German and wrote commentaries on both New Testament and Old Testament books. He also began his history of the Reformation in Switzerland which was to occupy him on and off for the next forty years. Meanwhile, Bullinger Senior's pioneer work in the Roman Catholic communities was being blessed so that soon Muri (1529) and Hermetschwil (1530) formally adopted the Reformed faith by the votes of the parish members. Bullinger Sen. was allowed back to Bremgarten around 1529-30 and became pastor at nearby Hermetschwil.

During this time of intense ministry and political anxiety, the Council at Zürich asked Bullinger to represent them at the 1529 Disputation at Marburg concerning the Lord's Supper. Few had written as much on the subject as Bullinger, so he was an ideal choice. However, he was so much involved with his parishioners, the poor and his writings that both the Bremgarten Council and the church said that they could not let him go. Most likely, Bullinger could have put his foot down and insisted on attending the Disputation but his heart was not in it. He wrote in his diary that he was sad that Luther had written against Zwingli and Oecolampadius so violently and knew that trying to argue with him would only deepen the bitterness on both sides and the gospel would lose out. Philip of Hessen was also shocked at the animosity shown by Luther which made him turn more and more to Melanchthon for help. Melanchthon, however, went to the other extreme on the one hand showing so much tolerance that one never knew where one stood with him and, on the other hand, formulating his *Augsburg Confession* prompted by the Swiss and Upper German side, which allowed for no alterations. Nevertheless, Philip called the Disputation at Marburg as a final effort to unite the Reformers over the question of the Lord's Supper. The Disputation divided more than it united, and one cannot help thinking how different the result would have been if, in Providence, Bullinger had attended. He, however, had more than enough to do where he was. He had come to the conclusion that his pastoral work was more important than arguing with so-called Reformed men who were still Roman in their sacramental and mystical thinking.

Life was far from easy at Bremgarten, situated as the town was on the very edge of the Roman Catholic Five Districts or Fünf Orte, the name given to Uri, Schwyz, Unterwalden, Lucerne and Zug who had sworn to keep "the old, true, right Christian faith". Only days after Bullinger settled down at his new post, Roman Catholic troops began controlling the borders and news came through of atrocities caused by their anti-Reformation hatred. Those Reformed preachers, such as Jakob Kaiser, pastor of Schwerzenbach, Canton Zürich, who dared cross the borders were quickly burnt to death. The Bern and Zürich army now occupied

Bremgarten and Muri and from 8 June on, Bullinger was required to act as pastor to the troops. A peace was arranged on 24 June which allowed each district to vote for or against the Reformation. However, the Zürich politicians, with Zwingli playing a leading role, began putting unbearable pressure on the Roman Catholics and even strove to starve them out.

Chapter 2

Taking Over from Zwingli

The Kappel Wars

By 1529 Zwingli had become convinced that the only way to spread the Reformation was by openly declaring war on the Fünf Orte which bordered on Zürich. He persuaded the Councils of Bern and Zürich to follow his advice, though they were very reluctant to do so. War was declared in 1529 but the Roman Catholics quickly sought for a peaceful agreement. This was totally against Zwingli's will who wished to see Roman Catholicism stamped out in the Five Districts. However, Bern and Zürich accepted the Roman Catholic plea and the First Peace of Kappel ensued, granting both parties rights to pursue their own religion. Bern had all along believed that they ought to starve the Roman Catholics out rather than risk a fight so they started a food-blockage and embargo on the Five Roman Catholic Districts with Zwingli still maintaining that the only way to gain freedom for the Reformed churches to expand into new Roman Catholic territories was by war. He forced the Roman Catholic cantons to break their allegiance with Austria and demanded large payments of money from them for alleged expenses of the Protestant forces in the short lived First Kappel War. It appears with hindsight that Zwingli was merely seeking another quarrel with the Fünf Orte to provoke another war. According to Ulrich Gäbler, as Zürich only backed Zwingli grudgingly, he handed in his resignation from his membership of the Zürich Greater Council in July, 1531.[1] Zwingli, who was only 47 years of age, then began to act as if he realised that his time of departure had come. This is the only explanation of the moving scene on 10 August, 1531 when he visited Bullinger's home at Bremgarten for secret talks with Jakob von Wattenwyl and Peter im Hag, ambassadors from Bern, which appear to have gone on through the night.[2] Early in the morning, Zwingli departed from the house and Bullinger accompanied him to the next village of Zufikon. The two men said farewell twice along the way but still walked on together. Then Zwingli burst into tears. He embraced his young friend for the third time and said "God's grace be upon thee, my dear Henry. May God preserve thee. Be true to our Lord Jesus Christ and His Church." Then he turned and departed, a very sad and troubled man. The two friends were never to meet again this side of Glory. On 11 October, 1531 Zwingli put on his armour and rode into one of the most senseless and useless wars in the history of mankind. Zwingli's cleaved helmet is still on display in Zürich to show how he died.

The background to this tragedy is quickly told. On 15 May, 1531, the Fünf Orte, goaded by the embargoes on food enforced on them by Protestant Bern and Zürich and Zwingli's boasting of military power, decided to use violence themselves.[3] Bullinger and Bremgarten protested at the un-Christian methods of the two Protestant Councils and when Bullinger was called to address both parties at the Diet (Tagsatzung) of Bremgarten, he denounced their warring politics from the pulpit. Realising that he was preaching to avoid a war, Bullinger argued that the matters under controversy were religious rather than political and religious debates were a matter for pastors and theologians and not armed soldiers. Neither side took any notice of Bullinger's pleas for peace between the confederates. Schulthess-Rechberg comments dryly that it

---

[1] *Huldrych Zwingli: His Life and Work*, pp. 152, 177. Gäbler is referring to original documents produced by Helmut Meyer. According to Gäbler a 'delegation of important councilmen' persuaded Zwingli to retain his post.

[2] This meeting took place during the *Eidgenössischen Tagungen* which were held on 14 and 20 June, 9 July, 10 August and 23 August 1531.

[3] Commentators are not of one mind concerning whether Zwingli backed the food embargoes. Büsser gives evidence to show that Zwingli was against them, pp. 65-66.

was obvious that Zwingli's aggressive plans did not meet Bullinger's approval.[4] This is an understatement indeed as Bullinger was fully opposed to them. He preached that there could not possibly be any spiritual Reform through warfare but only through the preaching of the gospel. Sadly, the Roman Catholics, whose representatives had heard Bullinger preach against the war, nevertheless placed the blame for Zwingli's merciless persecution on the true upholders of the Reformed faith at Bremgarten and not on the inane politics of the two cities. They realised that the driving force of the Reformers was in their gospel and not their politics. They knew where the centre of the Swiss Reformation was triumphing. Bern and Zürich quickly formed a large army, promising to defend Bremgarten. Faithful Christians, following Bullinger, told Zwingli that it was senseless to defend God's Word with chariots and horsemen. Bern and Zwingli took no heed and Bern placed Sebastian von Diesbach at the head of their forces. Rome laughed aloud. The pope had duped Zwingli and his military allies. Von Diesbach was an avowed opponent of the Reformation! When the Roman Catholic army approached Bremgarten on 11 October, von Diesbach withdrew his 'Reformed' soldiers to Lenzburg and left Zwingli with his smaller army of Zürich men to perish. Zwingli was struck down and handed over to the public executioner who had him drawn and quartered and then burnt to ashes. In a display of great diplomacy, the papists promised that each canton could follow the religion of their choice. Reformed Bremgarten was excluded from the Peace of Kappel treaty and the new masters in Bremgarten forced the town back under Rome's yoke and annulled Zwingli's *Burgrecht* (citizen's rights). As Zwingli had given the papists no rights, they felt that they were free to treat the Protestants with the same disdain. The once affluent Bullingers, now joined by Henry's brother Johannes, lost all their possessions and were now paupers, exiled from Bremgarten during the night of 20 November with Gervasius Schuler and his family. Most of the more well-off Bremgarten families were robbed of their goods or forced out of the town so that Bremgarten

[4] Heinrich Bullinger, p. 9.

became a poor town with hardly any commerce or trade. This poverty lasted until the nineteenth century when the spinning and silk weaving industries were established in the town. If Johannes Friedrich Franz is correct, Bullinger's father had much to be thankful for as he is said to have joined in the fighting so that he might receive Zürich citizenship.[5] The bulk of the Zürich ministers had been slaughtered by the papists but Bullinger's father was spared.

Sadly for Bullinger, in the storming of Kappel his close friend who had become his spiritual father, Wolfgang Joner, was also killed. Henry Bullinger was able to recover many books and household goods but all his parents' possessions were carried off by the plundering soldiers. This event in Bullinger's life must be borne in mind as scholars often argue that Bullinger was a member of the rich, land-owning class who were traditionally looked up to in Zürich. Wealth cannot have played a part in Bullinger's popularity as the Kappel War rendered him and his family penniless. He had never received a salary at Kappel and later at Zürich, his pastor's salary was hardly sufficient to pay for his children's education. Furthermore, Bullinger always refused generous personal gifts or gave them over to the Church who employed him.

The aftermath of the war in Zürich

Meanwhile, Zwingli's warring nature and Bern's inhuman politics had weakened the Protestant cause no end. Now, instead of the Protestant cantons led by Zürich starving out the Roman Catholic cantons, Zürich was virtually surrounded by papist states and the tables were turned. However, the papists did not give tit for tat and strive to starve out Zürich but they did pronounce woe on the Protestant who dared to step over the canton's border! The Five Districts also forced Zürich to give up her alliances with the other Reformed cantons. So too, the papists refused to allow wealthy towns such as Rapersweil, Gaster, Wesen, parts of St Gallen, Bremgarten and indeed, all the Freien Ämtern to find protection under the Peace of Kappel and felt free to plunder them as they wished.

---

[5] *Merkwürdige Züge*, p. 12.

Their Protestant citizens were forced either to attend Mass or forfeit life and goods. This was particularly tragic in the case of St Gallen which was the second city after Zürich to become Reformed. St Gallen had promoted the Reformation faithfully since 1527, but now this witness was seriously limited. Happily, Joachim von Watt, better known as Vadian by the English-speaking peoples, managed to keep up a stable witness in the Protestant enclave. That the papist forces did not take Zürich is a marvel nobody has been able to explain up to the present day, apart from it being the obvious will of God. However, this caused more problems for Zürich as the persecuted fled to the canton in masses from the areas conquered by the Roman Catholics. Though many in Zürich were for carrying on the war, the vast majority of the 60,000 inhabitants of the *Landschaft* urged the city to accept the papists' Peace of Kappel.

The Protestant clergy under criticism

Soon, there was a general cry of complaint in the city that it was the clergy who had got them into the mess by taking over the city's political leadership. Popular, ribald songs were quickly written and sung openly, lampooning the Reformation in general and Zwingli in particular. Haller in Bern was quick to answer in the same vein against the papists but subdued Zürich did not dare. However, a number of heartfelt serious hymns of lament and repentance were composed in Zürich by the faithful at this time.[6] Many in the city were heard to say that it was not the enemy outside (the Roman Catholics) who had weakened the city but the enemy inside (the Protestants). Numerous citizens who had merely professed to be Protestants for the sake of their livelihood, said that they could once again speak openly without persecution. Not a few Protestant leaders, including Leo Jud, went into hiding. It was even rumoured that some former Reformed pastors were seriously thinking of converting back to Rome or fleeing the city. Indeed Peter Füessli, a member of the Greater Council had already begun to re-attend mass at Einsiedeln and the Roman faction in the city was becoming stronger daily. Füsseli did not fear

[6] See Pestalozzi, pp. 85-88 for examples of these ditties and hymns.

criticism as the Council had begun to remove those councilmen who had voted for war. A letter is extant from King Ferdinand to his brother Emperor Charles V saying "this is the first of the victories which is predestined to revive the faith." He told Charles further, "Remember, you are the Head of Christianity and have never had a better opportunity to cover yourself in fame. The German sects are lost when the heretical Swiss can no longer support them."[7] Berchtold Haller, now greatly alarmed, wrote to Bullinger from Bern to hear if the rumour was true that Zürich was to reinstate the mass.[8] To make matters worse, the Senate had signed the Peace Treaty of 20 November which stipulated tolerance for the Reformed ministers but only after publicly acknowledging that the Roman Catholic cantons possessed the 'waren ungezwyfelten cristenlichen glouben', that is, 'the true, undoubted Christian faith'.[9] Not worrying about himself, Bullinger thought of Gervasius Schuler and his wife and two daughters who were German Protestants, especially hated by the Swiss papists. Bullinger wrote to his friend Ambrose Blaurer with whom he had been on good terms since the Bern Disputation. Blaurer was now a minister in Upper Germany and Bullinger asked him to take Gervasius on as a curate. Bullinger had no thoughts of fleeing himself but ended his letter to Blaurer with the words, "Farewell and pray for our poor Switzerland."[10]

Because of this dire situation, there was little agreement within the greatly weakened Zürich church and Council as to who should succeed Zwingli. No less than twenty-five pastors had died in the Kappel War together with nineteen members of the Greater Council and seven members of the Lesser Council. Of Zürich's leading citizens and merchants over a hundred had fallen in the battle. In all, in less than an hour, 512 Zürich citizens had been killed. Indeed, the problem for the few Reformed men left who were brave enough to speak up was how to convince Zürich that they needed another Protestant Superintendent of

---

[7] Quoted from *Heinrich Bullinger: Der Retter der Züricher Reformation*, p. 5.
[8] See Bächtold's detailed work *Heinrich Bullinger vor dem Rat* for more details concerning this period.
[9] Ibid, p. 13.
[10] Pestalozzi, p. 70.

their churches. Zwingli's motto had been, "Our peace is war" but after the horrifying experience at Kappel, the Council categorically said that they would not have another clergyman interfering and dominating in political affairs.

Oswald Myconius wrote from Zürich describing the scene:

"Here nothing but wailing and sorrows prevail. Our difficulties increase daily. More than the loss of Zwingli, more than the death of so many brave hearts, we are weighed down by the sorrow that the free word of the gospel has nigh perished, so that every comforting hope is denied us. The few men left who have received something of the gifts of grace do not dare raise their heads. The people are terrified by the continual threatenings of our enemies. How can the preachers of God's Word fulfil their office? So many intimidations surround them, so many daggers and swords, that they would need a power without equal, a veritable apostolic courage, to be like Paul who let nothing stop him from preaching the Lord Jesus and disciplining the Godless and depraved." [11]

Bullinger called to succeed Zwingli

It looked, at first, as if God would withhold such an apostle from the people of Zürich. Bullinger had received a call to lead the Church at Bern on 21 November, 1531 but when Oecolampadius of Basle died on 24 November that city, too, immediately asked Bullinger to take his place.[12] Then Appenzell asked Bullinger to lead their church. Bullinger's friends therefore took it for granted that he would soon leave Zürich. Bullinger, however, told his supporters that he was too young and inexperienced for a Superintendent's post and would seek a pastorate similar to Bremgarten, now sadly in the papists' hands.[13] Kaspar Megander and Hans Schmid were recommended as successors to Zwingli but these suggestions gained little backing. So the Zürich Church and Senate had only Leo Jud to turn

---

[11] Pestalozzi, pp. 71-72.

[12] Bullinger was officially called to Zürich on 9 December, 1531.

[13] Friends smarting under the papist yoke in Bremgarten urged Bullinger to accept the call to Bern.

to. But Jud had backed Zwingli in his plans for war and was judged too close to the Catabaptists and too politically minded for the Zürich councillors. Besides, he was going through a most depressed state and confessed that he was totally unfit for the task. Furthermore, Jud had rather erratic and extreme views, later modified through consultations with Bullinger, regarding an absolute separation of Church and state which would mean that the church would become a state within a state. The main pulpits in the city were now empty of their former ministers but young Bullinger, who had not lost his credentials as a Zürich minister, was asked to preach in the Great Minster on 23 November, 1531 which had been Zwingli's prerogative. Leo Jud, Erasmus Schmid and Heinrich Uttinger urged him to accept the invitation. Bullinger did so most reluctantly but Myconius records in a private letter what a tremendous impression Bullinger's preaching made on his downcast hearers. After outlining the misery of the city, he goes on to say, "then, last Sunday, Bullinger thundered out such a sermon that many believed that Zwingli was not dead but, like the Phoenix, has been again raised to life." Myconius added sadly that Bullinger was only a guest in Zürich for a limited period. The sermon had so awakened the city, however, that the Council begged Bullinger to preach again and on 9 December, 1531, he was unanimously called by both Church and Council to head the Zürich churches and receive the seat of the Great Minster. Bullinger, now twenty-seven years of age, accepted the call. Now Myconius realised that God had indeed sent the man of 'veritable apostolic courage' for whom he had prayed. Bullinger's supporters said they did not want a man who would build a state on supposedly Christian law but one who would bring in a time of grace. Thus it is said that Zwingli rescued a people from Rome but it was Bullinger who made them into a church. The Senate were still wary of Bullinger because of their experience of Zwingli and asked him to promise not to follow his predecessor's politics. This was a promise which Bullinger could gladly give. Bullinger was to superintend the Zürich churches for forty-four years until 17 September 1575, the date of his death.

As soon as Bullinger became leader of the Zürich church and took over Zwingli's former manse, he invited his parents and Zwingli's widow to join him and his wife and children. His father, Heinrich Bullinger died in his son's arms on 8 April, 1533 having reached the age of sixty-four. His last words were thanks to God for releasing him from Rome's yoke and placing him safely in the service of Christ. Bullinger's mother died in the arms of her son eight years later aged over seventy.

Combating false rumours

Before going on to outline Bullinger's future in Zürich as leader of the Reformation, it is necessary to compare Bullinger's character, calling, gifts and influence with that of Zwingli's, particularly as Bullinger is still often wrongly seen as the man who put 'Zwinglianism' into practice and whose fame merely lies in the fact that he followed meticulously in Zwingli's footsteps. This section aims to place such criticism in its correct perspective. During the early period of his ministry, Bullinger was kept busy warding off unjust criticism against his person and Zwingli from the Roman Catholic Fünf Orte. They had punished Bremgarten by denying them the rights of the Peace of Kappel which stipulated that each citizen might worship freely in his own religion. Strangely enough, however, though Zürich was the cause of the war against Bremgarten, the Roman Catholics had placed the city under the Peace of Kappel. They had banned Bullinger from his home and home church and now sought to prove that his leadership of the Zürich church was against the interests of the Peace on the grounds that he was following in Zwingli's footsteps and stirring up the Zürich citizens with anti-Roman Catholic preaching and rebellious words. Bullinger defended himself in writing by saying that the Fünf Orte had been ill-informed and as they had granted Zürich full religious freedom, he was keeping strictly to that agreement. However, what he had said against the mass must stand. The Reformed church at Zürich was required to keep to the Scriptures and the Scriptures said nothing about the Roman dogma of the mass. Furthermore, the Roman Catholic boast that they held to the old and therefore true Christian religion could not be substantiated from the Word. If the Roman

Catholics denied Zürich the freedom to believe this, it was they who were breaking the Peace. Bullinger sent his defence off to the Five Districts via the two Ambassadors Johannes Hab and Heinrich Rahn and nothing came of the papists' protest.[14]

Rescuing Zwingli's Good Work from Oblivion

One great problem for Bullinger was rescuing Zwingli's good Christian testimony from his more dubious reputation. A former student friend of Zwingli's, Johann Faber, had left his reforming, humanist background to make his career in the church of Rome and had become the favourite of Ferdinand of Austria who had him consecrated Bishop of Vienna. After Zwingli had been killed by the papist troops, Faber wrote with a pen of gall against both Zwingli and Zürich, saying that his former friend had led well over 6,000 of his fellow-Protestants to their deaths.[15] The fact that a Protestant minister was killed in battle was proof for Faber that Roman Catholicism was the true faith. Bullinger answered with his *tröstliche Verantwortung an alle die evangelische Wahrheit lieb haben Menschen* after making a detailed study of the fallen and published the 512 names of the true casualties. This lower number, however, is still relatively high when compared with the 80-100 of the Roman Catholics in the Fünf Orte who died in the battle. On Charles Day, 28 January 1532, the annual festival in memory of Charles the Great, Bullinger gave a speech to all the ministers, scholars and people in power which he entitled *The Office of a Prophet* (vom Amt eines Propheten) in which he outlined the duties of a faithful minister of the gospel. As his main example and one whom everyone knew from first hand experience, he chose to exhibit the positive side of Zwingli as preacher and pastor. He wished in so doing, to confute the commonly held opinion in Zürich that Zwingli could not have been a man of God, otherwise he would not have been slain in battle. Bullinger then went one by one through the great heroes of the Bible, showing how their lives were accompanied by many disappointments and defeats but they were nevertheless loved and used

[14] See Bächtold's *Heinrich Bullinger vor dem Rat*, p.22. ff. for documentation.
[15] Faber gives 5,000 men from Zürich, 700 from Berne and 500 drowned in the River Reuss.

by God. Indeed, in comparing Zwingli with Stephen, Bullinger almost made his death look like martyrdom. Bullinger, at this time of peril, wished to instil in his hearers' hearts the readiness to be faithful to the end and be prepared to die for their Lord and Saviour.

Differences between Bullinger and Zwingli

When describing the relationship of Bullinger with Zwingli, Carl Pestalozzi of the Zwingli Society says:

"Zwingli and Bullinger – what a difference! Zwingli's quick, fiery temper and Bullinger's calmness and relaxed nature; Zwingli's cutting, stinging wit and Bullinger's penetrating thoroughness; this explains Zwingli's brevity and Bullinger's comprehensiveness in almost all their works. How suitable they were for each other's advancement! This is why they developed, in spite of their age gap, a beautiful relationship of eager, happy exchange and mutual support."[16]

Distinctions between the work of Zwingli and Bullinger and their relevance to the Reformation are most important. Many church historians look on Bullinger wrongly as Zwingli's protégé. The historical fact is that Bullinger was Zwingli's equal if not superior in Reformation matters before the two men met. If Bullinger had not worked with Zwingli during his reforms and influenced him so much, and had he not taken the Reformation further after Zwingli's death, the Reformation in Zürich would have been a far smaller matter. This is why Johannes Suts sees Bullinger as the rescuer of the Zürich Reformation.[17] So too, Bullinger's views are often nearer those of his friend Oecolampadius than Zwingli's, especially in regards to the Lord's Supper. This relationship, touched on by Peter Opitz in his 2004 work on Bullinger's theology, needs further consideration.[18] So, too, the background of the two men was quite

[16] Pestalozzi, pp. 25-26.
[17] *Heinrich Bullinger: Der Retter der Züricher Reformation.* (Henry Bullinger: The Rescuer of the Zürich Reformation).
[18] Opitz, *Heinrich Bullinger als Theologe*, p. 224 ff.

different. Young Zwingli caused his parents a good deal of worry so that when his father received a letter from his son outlining his plans for his future which included "instruments, music and feasting" (Gastereien), he replied that he would rather have a philosopher for a son than a comedian.[19] Zwingli matriculated at Vienna University in 1498 but was quickly expelled. One source suggests he then lived in Paris under questionable circumstances and another says he studied at Tübingen. Zwingli matriculated again at Vienna two years later but soon broke off his studies again. History then loses sight of Zwingli for two years but in the summer of 1502, he matriculated at Basle and from then on stuck to his studies and his new conviction that he should become a Roman Catholic priest. Like Calvin, he was given a church living by an influential relation so that he could finance his studies without any church commitments. Zwingli took his *Baccalaureus* and proceeded to take his master's degree in 1506. With the help of the Bishop of Constance, Zwingli was given the lucrative parish of Glarus to minister though he had never preached and was not yet ordained. There was another candidate who had a claim on the living but Zwingli appealed to Rome and after paying 'over a hundred guilders' (guldinen), received the post. He immediately got himself into trouble when it was found out that he had already amassed two livings in Basle. Through good connections, he managed to hold on to these until 1511 when he was forced to give them up to avoid being put under a papal ban. The Bishop of Constance ordained Zwingli in September, 1506 after which he preached his first sermon ever and celebrated his first mass. Zwingli then entered fully into papist superstitions and even debauchery. From Glarus, Zwingli moved to Einsiedeln but on hearing in 1518 that a post was available at Zürich, he applied for the better position. During the examination to test Zwingli's eligibility for Zürich, his wild life was uncovered without his showing any repentance other than admitting the fact. Besides his love for a plurality of livings, he had had a secret affair with a very young woman during his recent ministry. He had tried to hide the matter from public

[19] Walther Köhler's *Huldrych Zwingli.*

notice by bribing the girl's father and his feeble and unmanly excuse for his conduct was that he was not the first lover the girl had had. This apparently spoke for Zwingli as ecclesiastical discipline was only strong in the case of robbing a girl of her virginity. The girl was now expecting a child but it was said that it was impossible to tell who the father was. The fact that Zwingli declared that he would not need the lucrative livings attached to the Zürich ministry also spoke for him in the eyes of both Church and council. A selection committee of twenty-four men sat to discuss Zwingli's application and as there were seventeen votes for him and only seven against him, he gained the post. Zwingli was still thoroughly papist at the time and his conversion must have occurred parallel to Bullinger's. In contrast, Bullinger had led an exemplary life before becoming a Christian and had never experienced being a minister under Rome's temptations and her double morals regarding ministers' chastity. Nor had Bullinger ever sought money but was content to serve the church for years merely receiving food, lodgings and an occasional change of clothing.

From 1523 on, Bullinger rode over to Zürich regularly to meet with Zwingli and Leo Jud. Bullinger attended the Disputations at Zürich on 29 January, 1523 on the subject of *Calling on the Saints*, but only as an observer. It was at this conference, attended by Zwingli's old student-friend Faber, now Vicar General to the Bishop of Constance that Zwingli revealed his 67 *Schlussreden* which have been compared to Luther's 95 thesis. The latter, however, were aimed at the novelties of the papal system which had corrupted the Church whereas Zwingli's theses proclaimed how one could build up the church-state of Zürich on the Word of God. Zwingli argued as a Christian statesman and therefore did not directly attack the Roman Catholic Church. He did, however, show that if a Christian was to be ruled by God's Word alone, letters of indulgences, pilgrimages, confessions, priestcraft and purgatory and all the additional means of 'earning' grace promoted by the papal power were merely hindrances along the way to God.

Zwingli showed that the gospel was not a new law but a means of being guided by the Holy Spirit to a personal saving knowledge of Christ.

Zwingli also argued that rule by the magistrate was also included in the gospel as the powers that be were set up to govern and discipline the state in which the Christian lived his earthly life. Republican Zwingli, however, made no secret of the fact that all rulers were only such when they had the mandate of the people and it was up to the people, not individuals, to make sure that tyrants were removed.

Although 600 attended the disputes, a discussion amongst academic or theological equals hardly took place. Both Zwingli and Faber, as the Bishop's representative, had their Hebrew and Greek Testaments open on their tables but even Faber said that he had not come to take part in the discussion but merely to observe what was going on and report on it. The discussion ended in an anti-climax. The Council affirmed that they agreed with Zwingli's position. The Reformation had crept into Zürich almost without being noticed by the Roman Catholic authorities. Their main reaction was to come some eight years later in the Kappel Wars. The first mark of the Zürich Reformation was the establishing of the Word of God. Then, in April 1523 ministers began to marry. It was not until September, however, that Zwingli began to reform church offices. Zürich was riddled with pluralities, sinecure posts and office-bearers whose salaries were enormous in comparison to the little work they did. As most of these office-bearers were elderly, Zwingli's policy was to wait until they died and then cancel the living, or bursary or whatever was financing the office-bearers. The money saved did not go into the pockets of the secular rulers as in the German states but was used for the welfare of the city, chiefly for charity and education, including, following Bullinger, a theological faculty. However, even at this stage, Zwingli had not broken fully with Rome and still had various sources of income from the papal system, including a direct pension from the pope himself.

However, by October of that year Bullinger was an official delegate at the Zürich Disputation on *Images and the Mass*. It was well-known that he had started up a seminary or *Prophezei* for training ministers and sending out Reformed preachers, so he was received as a fellow-Reformer of note. It took Zwingli another two years to establish such an institution for the instruction of the Zürich clergy. Bullinger first heard

Zwingli preach towards the end of 1523 and remarked, "I felt myself so much drawn to him as I had been a fiery follower of the same doctrines for almost four years but his strong, accurate and Biblical method of teaching served greatly to strengthen my convictions."[20] Thereafter, Zwingli and Bullinger became the very best of friends. Bullinger received little new from the older man but his mettle was sharpened by Zwingli's steel. Zwingli did not find a pupil or assistant in Bullinger but a worthy companion and fellow teacher in the faith. When, on 12 September, 1523, Bullinger told Zwingli he wished to publish his views on the Lord's Supper, Zwingli begged him not to because he was not ready himself. Bullinger warned Zwingli of the dangers of delay in not carrying out reform on this most controversial issue. Zwingli replied that if and when he was ready, he would publish on the subject and not Bullinger. The reason he gave was that the people were not yet ready for the change. This shows that Zwingli was already beginning to feel that Bullinger was not merely treading in his footsteps but overtaking him. Zwingli wavered long, slowly coming to a more commemorative view. However, in a letter written to Matthäus Alber[21] on 16 November, 1524, Zwingli did outline his views concerning the symbolic nature of the Eucharist albeit without going to any theological depth. Bullinger taught openly at this time that the Lord's real presence was to be experienced in the Supper because wherever two or three are gathered in His Name, He is there in their midst. Whereas Luther taught that Christ was to be found in the Supper, Bullinger believed that Christ was to be found in the believers. So Bullinger rejected transubstantiation and consubstantiation, indeed, any view that implied Christ's corporeal presence in the elements.

Zwingli's and Bullinger's debates on the Lord's Supper show how difficult it was for the Reformers to reach an exact agreement. Both Bullinger and Zwingli confessed that they agreed with the Waldensians on the matter of the Supper but they interpreted their agreement differently. Zwingli published his views on the Lord's Supper in opposition to Luther's position four years later but only after considerable

[20] Pestalozzi, p. 25.
[21] *Ad Matthaeum Alberum de coena dominica.*

consultations with Bullinger on the subject. Bullinger could not wait that long as his friends were pleading with him for pastoral advice on the subject. So, from November, 1524 on, Bullinger sent off no less than eleven works on the Lord's Supper to enquirers in the Zug district alone for general distribution whether to Reformed believers or papists, outlining the Reformed doctrine of the Lord's Supper. In June 1525 the awakened clergy and a number of lay people in Zug asked for a lengthier work and thus Bullinger sent Anna Schwiter and her friends his *Wider das Götzenbrot* (Against the Idol-Bread) in which he outlined what was true worship in the Lord's Supper and what was pagan idolatry. In this work, Bullinger did not merely dwell on the idolatrous nature of the papist mass but denounced the commercial enterprise Rome had made of it. This caused the Dominicans in Bremgarten to publish against Bullinger and his doctrines. In the middle twenties, Bullinger worked on his *De Origine Erroris in negotio Eucharistiae ac Missae* which he dedicated to Wolfgang Joner, Peter Simler and Andrew Curian. This work gained immediate popularity in manuscript form until published by Oecolampadius in 1527. The year after it was published at Heidelberg in German and went through a number of Latin and German editions, also being published in French in 1560. This work played a major part in establishing the Anglican doctrine of the Lord's Supper. Writing in February, 1567, Bishop Edmund Grindal said:

"There is no reason why you should so studiously thank me, for having so frequently, and with so much satisfaction, made honourable mention of you. For I do this on account of your merit, as well knowing how much you have benefited the church, as you still continue to do, both by your ministry and your writings. Besides, I owe this to you as an individual, that by the perusal of your Treatise on the 'Origin of Error', about twenty years since, I was first led to entertain a correct opinion respecting the Lord's Supper; whereas before that time I had adopted the sentiments of Luther on that subject. It is but just therefore that I should respect him from whom I have received so much benefit."[22]

The *Zürich Letters* editor adds an interesting footnote to Grindal's remarks concerning *De Origine Erroris*. A former monk, Montallinus who was later martyred for his faith at Rome, persuaded Jerome Zanchi to read the work adding that he would consider it a good bargain if he had to pluck out his right eye to pay for it and then read it with his left eye. Zanchi said that he soon purchased the book without losing an eye and it was a delight to his soul.

Thus, it is obvious that Bullinger was the major pioneer in teaching the Reformed doctrine of the Lord's Supper. Zwingli did produce a number of works between late 1524 and 1528 on the ordinance but these mostly arose in confrontation with Luther and the Lutherans on technical, scholarly points such as the meaning of 'is' in "This is my body" and they had little impact on the Swiss. Indeed, whilst Zwingli was busy debating on the Lord's Supper with the Lutherans, he was urging caution in carrying out reforms in his own churches. Such a further reformation was highly necessary as the Zwinglians were still surprising the Reformed in Bern and Basle by dropping to their knees every time the morning Mary bells were rung and crossing themselves devotedly. Zwingli had also still a number of problems to solve concerning his immoral life as a Roman Catholic priest. Unlike Heinrich Bullinger senior who had kept faithful to his dear common-law wife and married her as soon as he had accepted Reformation truths, Zwingli, had truly to alter his ways and though he saw the need for Reform from 1519 on, it was not until 1525 that he married his mistress, Anna Reinhard, but, as V. H. H. Green states in his *Renaissance and Reformation* (p. 161), "it was not so much an affair of the heart as an attempt to regularise a dubious relationship."[23]

For Luther the question of the Lord's Supper was the fulcrum of the Reformation. Those who did not accept his view of consubstantiation

---

[22] *Zürich Letters*, Vol. I, p. 182.

[23] As late as 1524, the pope still counted Zwingli as a loyal Roman Catholic. Adrian VI spoke highly of Zwingli and his successor Clement VII negotiated amiably with him for a time.

were immediately branded as *Schwärmer* or fanatics. Zwingli felt that the fulcrum of the Reformation was to be found in the preaching and not the ordinances. Once the preaching was Reformed, everything else would fall into place. Thus he envisaged a congregation ignoring all the rules, regulations and ceremonies imposed upon them by a church authority. Instead, they should merely listen to what the Bible says. Bullinger combined both these views. A right understanding of the ordinances, for him, was essential to true Reformation preaching. The Biblical teaching concerning the Person of Christ and God's covenant with His people was portrayed in baptism and the Lord's Supper. Thus not only right doctrines but the right use of the two ordinances must be defended. A preacher must preach against papist rites as a means of educating the congregation in the faith and not wait until the congregation has a perfect knowledge of doctrine before attacking them. Teaching the congregation to deal with Roman error was thus a necessary part of gospel preaching. If the ordinances as instituted by Christ to point to Himself and His Work were presented wrongly as in the case of Rome, then the basis of all gospel preaching would be removed.[24]

Professor Fritz Büsser of Zürich university, points out in his two volumed biography of Bullinger that much of what is called 'Zwingli's Zürich' or 'the Zwinglian Reformation' is fiction and that the hopes of Zwingli regarding his preaching proved to be an illusion.[25] Zwingli's preaching caused trouble and strife amongst the citizens until the Council began to enforce the Reformation under their own initiative by demands on the people and law-making rather than through evangelical preaching. Zwingli was quick to back the Council in this political form of the Reformation and spent much of his time away from pulpit and pastoral work, sitting on councils and committees in the Town Hall. At times, however, Zwingli's politics became one thing and his preaching another. He often urged his hearers to love their neighbours as themselves and

[24] See Ranke's Secession of Zürich from the Church of Rome in Book V, Chapter III of his *History of the Reformation in Germany* for a discussion of Zwingli's 'passive' view of combating Roman error.

[25] *Heinrich Bullinger: Leben, Werk und Wirkung*, Band 1, p. 85.

cried down the Swiss mercenary pride but did not hesitate to use military force in an attempt to convert Roman Catholics to the Reformed faith. What the formal Zürich Reformation still needed was a preacher who would put a spiritual heart of awakened flesh and blood into the rather stony, external Zürich Reformation and always practised what he preached.

Bullinger was this man and he made sure from the beginning that he would go his own way. He was neither influenced by Luther, nor Zwingli but gained his views through his independent studies of the Scriptures. For instance, it was Bullinger's interpretation of the Lord's Supper which became the standard Reformed view and not that of either Luther, Zwingli or Calvin. So, too, Zwingli cannot be said to have pioneered much in the way of creedal baptism. In his baptismal order of 1525, it is Jud's rather cursory presentation of his views between 1523-25 which is used. Bullinger was to formulate baptism in a creedal way in his comprehensive church order (*Gottesdienstordnung*) of 1535, the first of such orders ever used in Zürich. Thus scholars are becoming increasingly aware that what they have called 'Zwinglianism' for so long in order to describe the Reformation at Zürich should really be called 'Bullingerism'. Gottfried W. Locher in his book *Zwinglische Reformation and Huldrych Zwingli in Neuer Sicht*[26] wrote of 'late Zwinglianism' or 'the Zürich Reformation' to describe the four decades of Bullinger's work in Zürich and Joachim Staedtke in Ulrich Gäbler's and Endre Zsindely's *Bullinger-Tagung 1975*, asks the question *Bullinger's Theologie – eine Fortsetzung der Zwinglischen?* (Bullinger's Theology – a Continuation of Zwingli's?) in his title and concludes that 'Bullingerism' should be the correct expression to describe 'late Zwinglianism'. Indeed, it is far from incorrect to say that much of what today is called Calvinism might be called, with more right 'Bullingerism'.

Ulrich Gäbler in his book *Huldrych Zwingli: His Life and Work*, explains how difficult it is to present Bullinger as a different Reformer to Zwingli as Bullinger emphasised the importance of Zwingli whenever the

---

[26] A New Look at Ulrich Zwingli and the Zwinglian Reformation.

opportunity arose but kept a low profile on his own achievements. Thus, when referring to Bullinger's forty-year work, *Reformationsgeschichte* (History of the Reformation), first published in three volumes by the Vaterländisch-historischen Gesellschaft, Zürich in 1838-40, Gäbler comments that "His portrait of Zwingli's work is guided by veneration for his great predecessor and forms the basis for an emphatically 'Zürich' viewpoint." Though Gäbler obviously thinks that Bullinger has 'Bullingerised' Zwingli to make him conform more to the Zürich pattern,[27] he says "since the author frequently referred to original sources and quotes them literally, his work remains valuable." Nevertheless, Gäbler sums up:

"Zwinglianism changed under Bullinger. However, since Bullinger, in his more than forty years in office, never failed to proclaim his loyalty to his predecessor, and never uttered a word of criticism or correction, these changes were not obvious. His insistence that he was carrying on Zwingli's work was often believed, even though that is out of the question, since it was in fact Bullinger's interpretation of Zwingli that was being carried on. It was in this form that Zwingli's influence lived on."[28]

It was also in defence of Zwingli's memory that Bullinger made his strongest complaints against Luther who repeatedly heavily criticised Zwingli, and indirectly Bullinger for his association with him, as if they were worse than pagans. Indeed, it was Luther's stubbornness in not reading either Zwingli's or Bullinger's own works or giving them a fair hearing which convinced Bullinger during the thirties of the fallacy of seeking unity with the Lutherans via disputations. Such a unity was only sought by the Lutherans providing the other side became Lutherans.

---

[27] *Huldrych Zwingli: His Life and Work*, p. 171.

[28] Ibid, p. 153. When reading Zwingli experts such as Gäbler, Bächtold and Locher one cannot help but notice that they rely very much on Bullinger for their view of Zwingli. It is also plain to see that Bullinger, out of love for Zwingli, always presented the sunnier side of his fellow Reformer.

Writing to friends in Switzerland concerning Luther's obstinacy and his followers' conviction that his word was their rule, he said:

"When church unity merely means that nobody opens his mouth for the truth in opposition to Luther, we can dispense with it, because Luther is a man and not God. I am of the opinion that Luther is a man who can err and cause others to err so that he must be shown where error occurs and convicted of it. For theologians, the truth is more important than Luther."[29]

Zwingli was a Supralapsarian in his views of election, teaching that God elected some men to salvation and some to reprobation irrespective of the Fall. This caused Bullinger a number of problems as outsiders, invariably identified him with this doctrine, now known as Hyper-Calvinism, merely because he became Zwingli's successor. Calvin, who had taken over Zwingli's ultra-strict view, defended his Supralapsarian position before Bullinger by telling him that it was Zwingli's. Bullinger taught that God ordains some of sinful mankind to eternal life and some He passes by; that is, He allows their reprobation. Zwingli was never truly Reformed on the doctrine of imputation whereas Bullinger taught both the imputation of Adam's sin to all mankind and the imputation of Christ's righteousness to all the elect. Zwingli could not accept the book of Revelation as the Word of God but Bullinger not only accepted it but preached from it on numerous occasions. Zwingli held to a rigid church discipline and order as a mark of the true church, Bullinger emphasised experimental heart-religion. He believed that order and discipline should be flexible according to the church's situation. Bullinger was a man of peace and thus Zwingli often asked Bullinger to mediate in the difficult situations he often placed himself in. Bullinger disagreed with Zwingli concerning his involvement in the Kappel Wars and his trust in Bern's militant 'Reformation' policies. Indeed, whilst Zwingli was preaching war at Zürich, Bullinger was preaching how to maintain peace from his

---

[29] Schulthess-Rechberg, p. 53.

Bremgarten pulpit. Bullinger was almost alone in not joining in the Kappel war with the Zürich clergy. There is no evidence that Zwingli accompanied the troops as an army pastor as is so often claimed, though Zwingli had served as such in 1513 during the battle of Novara against the French led by the Duke of Milan.[30] Zwingli went fully armed into battle taking a large majority of the clergy with him ready to fight rather than preach. Leo Jud had called for war more vociferously than anyone but he apparently dodged the battle which he had promoted and suffered the shame until his dying day. As soon as the news of the ministers' and councilmen's death reached Zürich, Romanists and opportunists sought to take their places.

Bullinger was a man of the Church and not a politician. Zwingli had maintained a dominant role in the Zürich politics sitting on not only the Great Council but on most other political committees and advisory boards. Zwingli made many enemies because of this. Bullinger was far more diplomatic. He refused to hold political posts but was nearly always invited to advise the Council as an 'outsider' who had the welfare of the canton uppermost in his heart.

A student's education forms him for life and many of the differences between Luther and Bullinger on the one hand and Zwingli and Calvin on the other can be explained by the fact that both Luther and Bullinger were trained in the traditions of the so-called 'New School' with its emphasis on Humanism and a less dogmatic approach to learning, whereas Zwingli and Calvin had followed the 'Old School' with its emphasis on a scholastic approach based on Greek philosophy. However, both these schools met in their love for Augustine, a Church Father who influenced all four Reformers greatly. Another point of note is that Luther, Zwingli and Calvin were all ordained into the Roman Catholic ministry and had lived in deep superstition. Bullinger was ordained as a thoroughly Reformed man and had never taken part in the priestcraft of the Roman Catholic Church.

---

[30] See Gäbler's *Huldrych Zwingli: His Life and Work*, pp. 148-152 for a survey of Zwingli's Confessions and Politics (1529-1531).

Their harmony

Bullinger had developed much of his Reformed thinking before meeting Zwingli but when he read Zwingli's *Auslegung und Begründung der Schlussreden*[31] in the summer of 1523, he was highly impressed by Zwingli's testimony and confessed that *Auslegung und Begründung* had greatly strengthened his faith. Zwingli, who had been slowly turning towards Reformed views since 1519-20, soon became aware of Bullinger's extraordinary abilities. He thus asked Bullinger to take down the minutes of his debates with the Catabaptists Manz, Grebel and Röubli and encouraged him to publish his *Vergleichung der uralten Ketzereien und derjenigen unserer Zeit*, a comparison of ancient and modern heresies in 1525, albeit under the pseudonym of Octavius Florens. This rouse appears not to have been Bullinger's own decision but his older companions begged him to keep a low profile until he had a few more years on his back. In his *Vergleichung*, Bullinger lays the foundation stone for his later work in the *Decades* by both claiming and demonstrating that the boast of Rome and other erroneous systems that antiquity is on their side is an idle boast in comparison to those who show that they are on the side of Scripture. Thus Bullinger can say that there is no older faith than the Reformed faith which is planted by God in Christ and believed by the Patriarchs, Prophets and Apostles. Alluding to the names of Hussite, Waldensian and Wycliffite with which he was called, Bullinger shows how these older movements were far nearer the Scriptural norm than the excesses of the papists of his time. Thus for Bullinger, the Reformed faith was the old faith and his 1537 work on the Reformation was given the title *Der alt gloub*, that is, *The Old Faith.*

Bullinger challenged the weaklings in Rome who were most unhappy with the system they were in but cried "Heretics!" all the louder against those of the Reformed faith so that they would not come under suspicion themselves. Having already been threatened with death on several occasions by the papist clergy, Bullinger is obviously not theorising when

[31] Usually translated as *Analysis and Reasons for the Concluding Statements* but this work, Zwingli's longest, appeared in English under various titles and versions. Some 20 years later, for instance, *The Rekenynge and Declaration of the Fayth and Belefe of Huldrike Zwyngly*, 1543.

he cries, "How can you doctors, though you know that we teach the truth lead us poor sheep in such an inhuman way to the slaughter!" (Schlachtbank). When Vadian asked Zwingli what he thought of Florens, he replied that he was a young man but very learned both in secular and godly works, but he kept the secret of Bullinger's identity. Under the same pseudonym, Bullinger now brought out his *Anklage und ernstliches Ermahnen Gottes des Allmächtigen an die gesammelte Eidgenossenschaft, dass sie sich von ihren Sünden zu ihm Kehre* or *Summons and earnest admonition from God to the gathered Swiss confederacy that they turn from their sins to Him.* Now it was clear to both the papists and the would-be Reformers that they had a leader second to none in Bullinger, so Zwingli and his colleagues lifted their restrictions on their young friend and openly confessed that Florens was none other than Henry Bullinger.

In 1526 Zwingli requested Bullinger to publish a thesis, this time under his own name, on the relationship between state and church, especially in the field of jurisprudence. Zwingli requested the work as a gift to a leading Zürich politician. Bullinger responded with his *freundliche Ermahnung zur Gerechtigkeit* or *A Friendly Admonition to Justice* which became the basis for Zürich's church-state relationship.

It was through Zwingli that Bullinger gained the acquaintance of Konrad Kürsner, commonly called Pellican (1478-1556),[32] from whom he deepened his knowledge of Hebrew. Pellican, after the Kappel wars, was to write of Bullinger:

"Zwingli and many other fine scholars fell whilst defending their mother country, Church and the truth. Now the Church in Zürich stands firm and grows in faith, in virtue, in doctrine and public prosperity so that never before was hand and heart stronger. Through the grace of God, we received in Zwingli's place a youthful bishop, a choice (köstlich) man,

[32] Pellican is said by a number of authorities to have been of Swedish descent but like his Reformed Colleagues Leo Jud and Wolfgang Capito he was born in Alsace. The name Kürsner (mod. German Kürschner) means a furrier and perhaps refers to the family trade rather than the original family name.

pious, just, learned, faithful and dedicated, a preacher without an equal, who through his teaching at home and through his writings abroad in the whole of Christendom proves himself to be a man of God and full of gifts."[33]

Further new acquaintances at Zürich were Johannes Müller, commonly called Rhellikan,[34] Rudolf Collin (am Bühl) and Johann Jakob Ammann with whom Bullinger brushed up his Greek. In 1527, shortly after Zürich had taken over the work of the Kappel Abbey, Bullinger received permission from Joner to spend five months in Zürich. Bullinger requested that he should take his best student, Johannes Frey,[35] with him, to encourage him along the Reformation path. Bullinger himself wished to deepen his Old Testament studies. Thus from June to November of that year, Bullinger visited Zwingli's, Pellican's and Ammann's lectures. Bullinger had no money but the monastery owned a small inn on the outskirts of Zürich called the *Kappelerhof* where he and his student could live and be fed. The Zürich Senate became so impressed with Bullinger's learning that they asked him to join Zwingli in representing them at the 1528 Bern Disputation. This disputation was a gigantic get-together of all the leading Reformers, pastors and preachers in Upper Germany and Switzerland. The 60 man strong Zürich party was almost dwarfed by the 300 Bernese ministers who attended, albeit on home ground, but the Upper Germans arrived with a party of 100 from Strasburg, Memmingen, Ulm and Constance; Oecolampadius came with a party from Basle; Vadian brought a contingent from St Gallan and Farel came from Aigle with a small French speaking party. The Romanists sent parties from Freiburg, Zofingen and Appenzell to join the Bernese representatives of what they called The Old Faith.[36] The conference lasted twenty days and

---

[33] See Schulthess-Rechberg's *Heinrich Bullinger*, p. 1.

[34] Rhellikan was called such because he came from nearby Rellikon.

[35] Also spelt 'Frei' and also known as Liberianus. Frey succeeded Bullinger as Head of the Latin School at Kappel.

[36] This use of the term prompted Bullinger to write his early work *The Old Faith*, showing how the papists had introduced novelties never practised by the Old Faith which was believed by the Reformers.

there, Bullinger met many leading Reformers from both home and abroad and quickly became close friends with Berchtold Haller and Oecolampadius the Swiss Reformers; Ambrose Blaurer from Constance and Martin Bucer who had journeyed with Wolfgang Capito from Strasburg. Bucer, who was in turn influenced by Capito, was to prove greatly influential in the development of theology in the Reformed Church of Switzerland and the Reformed Church of England. Here, too, Bullinger met Farel who pioneered the Reformation at Neuchâtel and Geneva. In fact, when Bullinger drew up a list many years later of his seventeen closest friends, twelve of them had cemented friendships with him at the 1528 Bernese Disputation. Most of the delegates at the Disputation, like Zwingli, were several decades older than Bullinger. These men of the Bern Disputation have been greatly neglected in the history of our glorious Reformation. William Farel, for instance, can be truly said to be a greater pioneer of true Reform than Luther because though Luther confessed Christ in a Reformed context a few months before Farel, the German's works at this time still contained positive references to the adoration of the saints and to purgatory whereas Farel was by this time truly reformed.[37]

From now on, it became very evident that Zwingli had come to love his friend Bullinger as a younger brother, if not as a son, and he realised that he must decrease and Bullinger must increase. So we find Zwingli gradually writing to friends and, in 1531, even including in publications, that he was giving over his theological responsibilities to Bullinger. In 1528, the new Zürich Synod, set up and chaired by Zwingli and Jud, now requested Bullinger to take the oath of allegiance to the Zürich Church and ordained Bullinger as a preacher under their jurisdiction. Until this time, Bullinger had never preached from a church pulpit, limiting his public work to teaching and writing. Besides the headship of the school and the seminary, Bullinger was appointed to serve the local parish of Hausen am Albis, a mere half an hour's ride from Kappel. On 21 June, Bullinger preached his first sermon ever at the Hausen church. The Synod

[37] See Bevan's *The Life of William Farel*, pp. 52-54.

appointed Bullinger to represent the Zürich churches with Zwingli at the now famous Marburg Disputations of 1529 where he was requested to debate with Luther, Bucer and the other Continental Reformed leaders. This second major début on the international stage was not to be for reasons already given. Instead, Zwingli took Rudolf Collin from Zürich and Johannes Husgen, better known as Oecolampadius, from Basle [38]

Bullinger and the Catabaptists

One of the reasons why Bullinger did not travel to Marburg was that the Catabaptists were carrying out a steady proselytizing campaign in the surrounding provinces and had already invaded Bremgarten and the Zürich territories. Bullinger needed to be on his guard to protect his people. Zwingli had pulled Bullinger into the debate with the Catabaptists and now he was considered one of the major forces behind the opposition to the growing movement. Indeed, the success of Bullinger's debates with the Catabaptists which persuaded even prominent members such as Pfistermeyer to accept the Reformed faith was one of the many reasons why Zwingli realised that he should decrease but Bullinger increase. In his commentary on Jeremiah 34:14-17, Zwingli says that Bullinger "has taken the battle against the Catabaptists like a torch out of our hands. Thanks be to God!" Unlike Zwingli who had lost his patience and temper with the Catabaptists, Bullinger continued to enter into dialogue with them and by combating them in writing, strove to win them back into the orthodox fold. He had been closely involved with the development of the various movements since 16 January, 1525 when he took part in the first major disputation between the Reformed churches and the Catabaptists. In subsequent disputations held that year on 17 March, 20 March and 6-8 November, he had acted as secretary and clerk, taking down minutes of the debates. So, too, in January, 1531 Bullinger took part in a disputation with the Catabaptists on the topic of money gained through investment and banking. Now Bullinger entered into debate with the Catabaptists wherever he found them.

---

[38] McCrie, in Beza's *Icones* gives Oecolampadius the name Hausschein, both names meaning 'the light of the house'.

The term Catabaptist is thought to have been coined by Gregory of Nazianzus in the fourth century to tease those Christians who insisted on a sacramental understanding of the amount of water necessary for baptism by calling them 'submergers' or 'drowners'. Oecolampadius of Basle was the first of the Swiss Reformers to use the term and Zwingli took it over from him. Oecolampadius used the term in the derogatory sense of 'drowners' whereas Zwingli appears to have used the word to mean Counter-baptisers or Anti-baptisers in his 1527 work *Widerlegung der Ränke der Täuferzerzerstörer* (Against the Tricks of the Baptist-Destroyers). The word 'wider' in Swiss-German can mean 'again' or 'against', therefore Zwingli's 'widertouf' is ambiguous. Historically, Catabaptist was used before Anabaptist but the latter term has prevailed.[39]

Martin Luther rarely distinguished between the Catabaptists and the Zürich Reformed Christians, arguing that they were both a product of Switzerland and both rejecters of the true sacraments. He thus named them rather inappropriately *Sakramentierer* or Sacramentalists. His argument was that the Swiss controversy on baptism had left the country without true Christians and thus a true church. Bullinger allowed such rumours to be spread for many years but in 1560, he decided to turn the tables on the Lutherans and wrote his long planned major work *The Origin of the Catabaptists*. In this work, he showed how the same controversy regarding baptism began along the Saxon-Thuringian border in 1521 and was exported from there to Zürich in 1524-25. Bullinger points out that Thomas Münzer was then preaching along the Saxon-Thuringian border and that his correspondence with the later Swiss Catabaptists showed that they had looked to Münzer for guidance in setting up a Swiss movement along German lines.

As soon as Bremgarten became Protestant, the Catabaptists began to press for the acceptance of their new rites and beliefs by the newly Reformed church. Bullinger invited them into his church and to meet his people and debated openly with them concerning their extreme views in matters of state affairs and trust in external forms for their faith. At these

[39] See Harder's *The Sources of Swiss Anabaptism*, pp. 756-57 for a nigh exhaustive explanation of the term.

debates, the entire congregation was invited to air their views. In 1530 Catabaptist Hans Pfistermeyer of Aarau visited Bremgarten and drew crowds of well over 300 people to hear his preaching. Most of the crowd were merely curious and not Catabaptists themselves, but still, the fact that they showed interest and did not ignore Pfistermeyer was disturbing for Bullinger who wrote to Capito, telling him that he feared there would be a public uproar. This moved Bullinger to publish his four 'Books of Conversations' entitled *Von dem unverschämten Frevel der Wiedertäufer* (On the insolent Sacrilege of the Re-Baptisers).[40] In these works written in the vernacular, Bullinger teaches the less educated and uninformed about the errors of the Catabaptists. He emphasises the lack of the sense of a church in their theology and the fact that many of their preachers are self-appointed and self-sent. He also castigates the laziness of these preachers who shun the hard work needed to prepare a sermon and merely stand up and say they are the voice of the Spirit. Preaching, he argues, must be based first and foremost on the Word of God which is Spirit-breathed. Furthermore, ministers of the Word must be carefully called and chosen and fitted out for their service in the Word. The early Apostles were called and equipped miraculously at a time when there was no written New Testament or even Old Testament in ordinary people's hands. Now, however, only those who are prepared by their churches for the ministry and are diligent in their study of the Word and have a definite call can claim to be ministers or pastors. The Catabaptists, Bullinger argued, seek to hinder people from joining the true Church by non-spiritual means such as their teaching on private property, tithes, oaths, bank interests, government offices, etc. which contradict the teaching of Christ and the Apostles. They are not prepared to follow Christ's guidance in rendering to Caesar the things of Caesar and to God the things of God. So, too, Bullinger castigated the worldliness of these sects who strove to set up heaven on earth by a legal, carnal system of external strictures on what to do and what not to do.

---

[40] Written in the summer of 1530 but not published until the following year. The work's full title is, *Von dem unverschämpten fräfel, ergerlichem verwirren und unwahrhaften leeren der selbsgesandten Widertäufern vier gespräch Bücher, zu verwarnen den einfalten.*

Confusing Catabaptists with modern Baptists

These Catabaptists are often confused with present day Baptists but the similarities are far from compelling. Most Catabaptists were not even 'Dippers' at this time, as early 16th century usage of this term reveals that 'taufen' was by sprinkling or pouring. Indeed, of the numerous 16th century documents testifying to the practice of the *Wiedertäufer*, we find Grebel, Manz, Hut, Hubmeier, Münzer, Römer, Spitelmeier etc. using many different forms of baptism which had nothing to do with immersion. Some candidates had a wet hand placed on their heads, others were baptised with three drops of water signifying the Trinity, a number had a wet sign of the cross marked on their foreheads, and some had a skillet of water poured over them. One Catabaptist let the water drop below the eyes, another above the eyes. Some of these early *Wiedertäufer* evangelists adopted and adapted various forms to suit the acceptability of the people to whom they ministered at the time and also to keep on the legal side of the town authorities. They, however, added tiny extras so as to show that the *Wiedertäufer* were going their own way. It is quite certain that these early *Wiedertäufer* did not associate baptism with immersion but the water had a mere symbolic function to demonstrate what they called the 'inner' baptism of God's grace. Thus a number of early *Wiedertäufer* dispensed with water baptism entirely as they believed they had the inner baptism and thus no longer needed the outer sign. The custom of baptising amongst the *Wiedertäufer* developed so that the 'outer' baptism became more important as a badge to mark off the Baptists from others. Baptism thus became a denominational sign, not a Christian rite. Also, with the development of sacramental thinking and a love for the ceremonial, immersion gradually took over from sprinkling and pouring.[41] Some of the more militant *Wiedertäufer* such as Hans Römer used their various modes of baptism as a standard or rallying mark

[41] This is the view of Elsa Bernhofer-Pippert after consulting 400 early documents relating to the activities of the *Täufer* and 1,200 testimonies of early Baptists. See her *Täuferische Denkweisen und Lebensformen in Spiegel Oberdeutscher Täuferverhöre*, Reformationsgeschichtliche Studien und Texte.

for their extension of their Bauernkrieg and planned attacks on Reformation cities such as Erfurt. *Endzeit* (latter day) enthusiasts also gradually adopted a more demonstrative different mode of Baptism to mark them off from the established churches who they ruled were 'Antichrist' and the 'Great Whore of Babylon'. Soon, the mark of baptism overtook doctrine and Christian moral-living as that testimony or sign which separated them from the world. Sadly, a number of the *Wiedertäufer* dropped doctrine and Christian morals altogether and we find Hans Schmid, Fritz Striegel and Marx Meyer introducing the so called Inner Voice Baptists (*Innere Stimme Täufer*) who associated baptism with adulterous practices. This movement was outdone in perversity by the *Christerie Täufer* founded by Klaus Ludwig in Mülhausen who claimed that true baptism was the common fleshly union of the brothers and sisters. In this way, they demonstrated their 'freedom in Christ'.

Bullinger reckoned that within less than a decade the Catabaptists had split up into no less than thirteen different movements, some of whom went about well-armed and were extremely violent. In next to no time we see Catabaptist movements going by the names of Swiss, Sabbaths, Austerlitzers, Hoferists, Münsters, Hutterites, etc., treating one another as enemies of the truth. Balthaser Hubmeier, for instance, condemned Hans Hut for allegedly spreading sedition and political revolt and Hans Spittelmaier condemned the 'schismatics' from his young movement for refusing to carry weapons. He called them *Stäbler* or Staff-bearers in scorn. The Anabaptist sect of the sword bearers formed the *Schwertler Baptists*. Later Anabaptists looked on their Swiss fathers in the faith as 'misanthropes' and the Swiss Anabaptists looked upon the spiritual children they had fostered in other lands as 'false brethren'.[42]

Zwingli, fearing that the Catabaptists were plotting to overthrow the Zürich administration by armed force, became their persecutor. He had pulled Bullinger into the violent controversies by asking him to take part in his debates with the Catabaptists from 25 January, 1525 onwards and

[42] See Packull, Werner O., *Hutterite Beginnings*, John Hopkins University Press, 1995.

take down the minutes, some of which have been preserved. At first the town hall was used but as interest was so great, the debates were continued in the Great Minster. This was the time of the Bauernkrieg or Peasants' War in Germany and many Reformed men believed that this revolt against the establishment went hand in hand with Anabaptist tenets. A number of Reformed ministers, influenced primarily by Balthasar Hubmeier, who was influenced in turn by Thomas Münzer, went over to the Anabaptists. Amongst these, to Bullinger's lasting sorrow, was his cousin and constant companion Michael Wüst who gave up his pastorate in 1525, as it was deemed a dishonest occupation by the Anabaptists, and became a weaver. In the same year, Bullinger published his *von der Taufe und Kindertaufe* (On Baptism and Infant Baptism) in which he argued that baptism is like its Old Testament type, circumcision, a sign of the righteousness which is by faith. The Old Testament sign pointed forward to the shedding of Christ's blood which brought in the New Covenant in which Old Covenant saints such as Abraham had also trusted. Now the sign of Christianity is not the shedding of blood which wounds but the water of life which heals. Just as believers and their children were placed under the covenant promises of God in the Old Testament, so they are in the New. Baptism, like circumcision, is a badge pointing to the righteousness which is of faith given freely by Christ. It does not point back to works of faith performed by the believer. It is a sign signifying what Christ has done for his elect and not what man has done in order to appropriate Christ. Bullinger believed that Anabaptist parents disowned their children and robbed them of their birthright by not baptising them. The Anabaptist retorted that we nowhere find infant baptisms in the Scriptures but Bullinger replied that such distinctions as the Baptists make were not practised in New Testament times so it is no surprise that they are not to be seen. He pointed out that the Anabaptists rightly allow women to take part in the Lord's Supper, though there is nothing in the Scriptures which expressly says that they ought. The New Testament only knows household baptisms or the baptism of individuals such as Paul who had no family that we know of. Thus the Anabaptist argument from silence is contrary to the pan-Biblical evidence we have. After refuting the Anabaptists from Scripture, Bullinger also refutes the Anabaptist theory that the early church knew no baptisms of believers and their children, backing his argument by quoting the Church Fathers. Bullinger also rejects the Anabaptist claim that God would not allow the baptism of infants as they did not realise what was going on. Parents, Bullinger believes, have a God-given duty to bring their children up in the ways of the Lord and not wait until they might come to know of them by their own initiative. Besides, did not God command Abraham to circumcise his offspring? Must we presume that those tiny children knew what was happening to them? Finally, Bullinger attacks the Anabaptist proposition that baptism is solely a sign to show who truly believes from their hearts. The only such sign the Bible knows, says Bullinger, giving Romans 8:16 and 2 Corinthians 1:22, is the work of the Holy Spirit in their lives.

Differences between Zwingli and Bullinger in their approach to the Catabaptists

However, in spite of the many hundreds of letters extant between Bullinger and the Catabaptists and on the subject of baptism there is still much to be done before the full scope of Bullinger's understanding of the movement can be outlined. Heinold Fast, who has done tremendous work in this field,[43] believes that nobody has influenced an understanding of the history of the Baptists more than Bullinger. However, he compares this influence to a flaming torch which could give more light, but also be used to kindle the flames of persecution. That Bullinger did not kindle such flames becomes apparent when studying his leadership in Zürich until his death in 1575. During this period 40 Catabaptists were executed for their faith in Bern in spite of Haller's and Bullinger's protests but none were executed in Zürich.[44] Indeed, Bullinger surprised all by helping the Catabaptists legally to maintain their citizens' rights against discrimination. A number of debtors had, for instance, decided they could borrow from Catabaptists and need not pay them back as they were

[43] See, for instance, his *Heinrich Bullinger und die Täufer* and published by the Mennonite Historical Society in the Palatine (Pfalz, 1959).
[44] The four Catabaptists executed at Zürich were sentenced under Zwingli.

heretics! Bullinger refused to tolerate any kind of persecution in matters of faith where those who believed otherwise led a normal, inoffensive life. Such persecutions were incompatible, he argued, with an evangelical confession. A Christian had no right to persecute because faith is a free gift of God and cannot therefore be forced on anyone or forced from any one. Here we see the difference between Zwingli and Bullinger. The former insisted on usurping authority over the magistrates, whereas Bullinger strove, as far as his conscience allowed, not to interfere with their work. One possible exception was in the case of Servetus but Bullinger did not seek the death penalty for him because of religious error but because, in his opinion, he was a danger to public law and order, an enemy of mankind and a breaker of laws having authority in the Swiss states and her dependencies such as Geneva and the Pays de Vaud. He thus left the trial and punishment of Servetus to the secular authorities. Bullinger remained true to his anti-persecution stand all his life. When the shocking news of the Bartholomew's Day massacre of 1572 reached Zürich, Bullinger penned his *On the Persecution of the Holy Christian Church* outlining from Scripture all that awaited those who persecuted the Lord's people. The massacre was initiated by Catherine de Medici (1519-1589) quite in the tradition of her English cousin Mary.

Tolerant but also discerning

This does not mean that Bullinger was friendly to the Catabaptist cause. It only means that he kept in dialogue with them and, at times, lent them a sympathetic ear. He saw the difference between theirs and the Reformed way of thinking in their view of the Holy Spirit. The Catabaptist subordinated, in his opinion, the Scriptures under their understanding of the Holy Spirit as being in them and as being the one who opened the Scriptures to them. Bullinger argued that we cannot begin with the *a priori* view that we have the Spirit and then arbitrarily understand the Scriptures in this subjective light. The Scriptures are Spirit-breathed and we can only know the working of the Spirit through the Word's testimony concerning Him. Only then can we test our own lives to see if we are living spiritually. Bullinger also maintained that the

Catabaptist view of baptism was un-Biblical as it was purely centred in the, often very vague,[45] testimony of faith of the one to be re-baptised. Baptism, Bullinger argued, was the pictorial gospel of Christ's salvation offered to those of His covenant. It was a display of God's love to sinners and a means of calling the weary and heavy-laden to Him. In other words, the message of baptism was Christ's call to sinners and not the believer's reply after accepting the call. Baptism within the covenant promises of God includes the infant children of believers because God covenanted with those who said, "As for me and my house, we will serve the Lord". Besides, the Catabaptist idea that baptism is a testimony of election accomplished and not salvation offered, leaves the Catabaptists claiming that they know God's elect, a fact which only God knows. He believed that if the subjectivism of the Catabaptists were placed above the objective testimony of the Scriptures, there would be no standard of truth. Bullinger told the Catabaptists that they misused and misinterpreted the New Testament because they had lost sight of the unity of Scripture and the progression of revelation. They had rejected the Old Testament and thus severed the gospel branches from their roots in history and revelation. In his earliest letters after his conversion, Bullinger emphasised that the Old Testament is equally God's Word and we must view the New as a commentary on the Old. The Catabaptists retorted that the Old Testament was a by-gone dispensation and was a source of godly example at best but not a source of doctrine. They also rejected the Old Testament as part of God's everlasting covenant of grace with His people. This is why they could see no connection between the Passover and the Lord's Supper or circumcision and baptism. Their idea of baptism being of no avail if the baptiser did not live up to their standards moved Bullinger to argue that dissent was not the correct way to discipline worldly clergy and that the idea that baptism was only valid if the baptiser had a special spiritual standing before God smacked of Rome. The Catabaptists argued that sinners were not to be baptised but saints. Bullinger responded by teaching that all saints were sinners and the

[45] Often candidates were immediately baptised on their answering such question as 'Do you wish to live righteously?' or 'Do you wish to receive all God's blessings?' in the affirmative.

Catabaptist view of baptism for the pure only was against Scripture and common sense. The gospel call came to those who needed a physician, not to the already healthy. Furthermore, Catabaptist baptism re-introduced the old question of sins committed after baptism leaving, according to many Catabaptists, the sinner without salvation or providing a ground for a further baptism after further repentance. Bullinger avoided this confusion by teaching that baptism was God's gift to us and not our gift to God and that the rite demonstrated Christ's response to man's sin not man's response to Christ's salvation. He thus rejected the Anabaptist claim that only believers in their order should be baptised as no one knows who the elect are and the Anabaptists presumed that they could discern God's secret, electing will. For Bullinger, baptism was the enacted gospel for all who were under God's covenant and it was God's business to rule who was of the elect and who not and not man's. The Catabaptists accused Bullinger of confusing state with church but Bullinger argued that it was in the interest of common order that a democratic system was preserved. He pointed out that the Catabaptists held radically different views amongst themselves concerning taxation, government and church discipline and order and if they were all given a free rein, chaos would ensue. It was part of the Christian's testimony to be leaven in the world and not merely in a dissenting body of ever-splitting, temporary like-minded separatists.

Bullinger regarded the Catabaptists as most unstable citizens, and showed apparent harshness towards them by having them banned from ecclesiastical, military, administrative and legal posts. Actually, this was a concession to the Catabaptists as they strongly renounced such positions themselves. Thus Bullinger made their withdrawal from public life legal. He told the Senate right from the start of his ministry that he was against religious persecution and that no Anabaptist or Roman Catholic should be punished for not presenting his children for baptism or not attending the Lord's Supper himself. He was merely banned from holding a civic office, which, as far as the Anabaptist was concerned, he refused to hold anyway. Bullinger diplomatically disciplined the Catabaptists in the eyes of the magistrates but, in reality, allowed the Catabaptists to follow their consciences. He also refused to forbid the Catabaptists freedom of worship and it was not unusual at this time to find groups of Catabaptists gathered for worship in even remote country districts which numbered from two to three hundred. Bullinger was nevertheless convinced that the Catabaptists wished to establish a society of chaos and superstition, diametrically opposed to the rule of Scripture and Apostolic practice.

One outcome of the Catabaptist debate was that Bullinger turned to foreign countries for help in resolving the problems and found allies in Strasburg, Geneva and London. He was particularly influenced on the question of baptism by Martin Bucer of Strasburg who enabled many Catabaptists to return to the orthodox fold. Sadly, from Luther's side, apart from a short respite, he received only adverse criticism as Luther now ranked the Swiss Reformed churches with the Catabaptists, seeing little, if any, difference.

Anna Bullinger (née Adlischwyler)

Chapter 3

Establishing the Reformed Church in Switzerland

Settling down in Zürich

On 13 December, 1531, Bullinger appeared before the Council with his fellow ministers to give their 'freundliche Antwort' (friendly answer) to the Council's demand that the new superintendent and his ministers should swear their allegiance to the Zürich government. The clergy were also required to outline their views on the relationship between church and state. The Council had obviously expected the ceremony to be over in a matter of minutes with the ministers' brief affirmation that they would obey the secular powers. Bullinger, had, however, planned the 'Antwort' carefully so that the councilmen would be in no doubt where they stood in relationship to the Church. In Bullinger's introductory speech, he made it quite plain that his demands were serious and if the Council did not like them, they could choose another superintendent. Bullinger explained that the ministers neither believed in a state run by the church nor a church run by the state but they did view Zürich as a state ruled by Christian magistrates and expected them to live up to their Christian reputation. This would allow for Zürich to be governed under God with both Council and Church going about their duties with a Christian conscience. Each minister was thus prepared to take the following oath to show his allegiance to his call as a minister and his allegiance to the magistrates who were given secular rule over him:

"I swear according to the mandate imposed by my lords of Zürich to teach and preach the holy gospel and Word of God to which I am called, from the Old Testament and the New Testament, faithfully according to my rightful Christian understanding and ability, and not to meddle with any doubtful dogma or wayward, unauthorised teaching but follow the ruling of the general synod which is called twice yearly. Furthermore it is my duty and will to serve the Lord Mayors, Council and Citizens with faithfulness and a good disposition as my rulers and support the well-being and piety of the city and canton by preventing harm and providing admonition as much as lies in my power. I shall be obedient and true to them and their appointed constables and officials and to their commands and strictures in reverential and equitable matters and remain in attendance loyally and void of any menace."[1]

This rather shook the councilmen who had expected a quick ceremony with no initiative shown by the ministers. Bullinger and his fellow pastors were now ushered out and told that they would be received by the Council again after a short discussion and then would hear the Council's verdict. The councilmen then entered into a deep discussion concerning the ministers' demands which lasted for over five hours. Zwingli's example of overruling the Council with his political acumen caused many

---

[1] Pestalozzi, p. 76. Author's translation from the Swiss-German: "Ich schwöre, das heilige Evangelium und Wort Gottes, dazu ich berufen bin, treulich und nach rechtem christlichem Verstand, auch nach Vermög alten und neuen Testamentes, laut meiner Herren von Zürich erlassenen Mandates, zu lehren und zu predigen, und darunter kein Dogma oder Lehre, die zweifelhaft, noch nicht auf der Bahn und anerkannt wäre, mit einzumischen, sie sei denn zuvor der allgemeinen, ordentlichen Versammlung (Synode), die jährlich zweimal gehalten wird, angezeigt und von derselben anerkannt worden. Ueberdies soll und will ich einem Bürgermeister und Rath, auch den Bürgern, als meiner ordentlichen Obrigkeit treu und hold sein, gemeiner Stadt und Landes Zürich Nutz und Frommen fördern, ihren Schaden wenden und davor warnen, so weit ich's vermag, auch ihr und ihren bestellten Vögten und Amtleuten, ihre Geboten und Verboten, in geziemenden, billigen Sachen gehorsam und gewärtig sein, treulich und ohne alle Gefährde."

of the two hundred councilmen to argue that one should not allow the churches to bargain with the Council in any way. Others argued that the Reformation must be allowed to prosper. The argument that won the day was Bullinger's threat that if they believed they could put him into a pulpit with a muzzle on, they would have to find a new superintendent. They knew that Berchtold Haller was still urging Bullinger to leave Zürich for Bern and head the 189 parishes there. They also knew that the Bernese Council was prepared to give Bullinger total freedom to preach as he saw fit. Therefore after much arguing this way and that, the Council called Bullinger and his ministerial staff in and issued the following declaration:

"My lords the Mayors and both Councils are willing to commit the Divine Word of the Old and New Testaments to you as you request, free, unhindered, and without restrictions in the good hope that you will with all humility and earnestness use it fittingly in our full confidence that you will work for peace and equanimity."[2]

The church in Zürich was now free to carry on the Reformation as her Reformers, under God, saw fit without any let or hindrance from the government. Bullinger immediately wrote to Haller in Bern telling him that full freedom had been given him by the Zürich Council so he took this as a sign that he was duty-bound to stay and maintain the oath he had sworn to the Zürich Council in 1528. Another letter was sent off to Basle with Gervasius Schuler who was about to travel to Germany via Basle. However, in the letter, Bullinger recommended Schuler for the Basle post of Superintendent. Not being able to gain Bullinger, and finding Schuler unsuitable for the post, Basle now called Myconius to lead their Church.

Pamela Biel, in her excellent study of Bullinger's ecclesiastical reforms *Doorkeepers at the House of Righteousness: Heinrich Bullinger*

[2] Ibid, p. 77: "Meine Herren Bürgermeister und beide Räthe sind des Willens, euch das göttliche Wort des alten und neuen Testamentes, wie ihr begehrt, frei, ungehemmt und unbedingt zu lassen, guter Hoffnung, ihr werdet euch aller Bescheidenheit befleissen und es gebrauchen wie es sich gebührt, sowie in vollem Vertrauen, ihr werdet nach Frieden und Ruhe trachten."

and the Zürich Clergy 1535-1575, points out that though Bullinger did not enter into Zürich's political life as did Zwingli, his influence (and that of his fellow clergy) on the Council and the eight Lord Mayors under which he served during the period under study was enormous. Biel writes:

"Bullinger was, in the most literal sense, the main institutionalizer of Zürich's Reformation. Yet the institutions that he created, and the norms for the behaviour of the clergy that he established (and retroactively attributed to his predecessor), did not have the effect of rendering the clergy mute, uninfluential toadies of the civil government. Rather the synod and the *Fürtrag*[3] made sure that even those ministers who did not have Bullinger's background and connections could participate in the directing of the people of Zürich to the path of righteousness and were protected from being 'wise men whose advice is mute'. "[4]

It is a traditional belief amongst scholars that Bullinger always introduced reforms under the conviction that he was doing what Zwingli would have done in the circumstances. However, Bullinger's policy in relation to the Council was quite different to Zwingli's and, in the long run, far more successful. Furthermore, Bullinger was the first Reformed Zürich minister to be appointed Chief Pastor of the Church. Zwingli had never held this position and was appointed as one of three Leutpriester and had technically no more authority than his two colleagues. It is obvious that the major authority that Zwingli had was because of his political activities. It is equally obvious that the Zwingli image which is generally accepted today is chiefly because of the preeminence Bullinger gave him in his writings. Furthermore, Zwingli had combined his church and political offices with those of a university professor and Bullinger realized that he could not carry on this tradition so he arranged that Theodor Buchmann (c.1504-1564), commonly known as Bibliander, should take over the headship of the university. Bibliander is said to have

[3] Bullinger's reports to the Council.
[4] A quote from Bullinger's work *On the Office of a Prophet*.

mastered thirty languages. He studied under Pellican, Oecolampadius and Capito at Basle and, after teaching several years at Leugnitz, moved to Zürich where he taught Old Testament Exegesis, Hebrew and Islamic Studies. He also lectured on missionary strategy, especially to Muslims. The fact that Bibliander took over much of the work Zwingli had done, and also the fact that Bullinger never entered into politics, left Bullinger more free to devote himself to active Reformation and pastoral work.

A word here concerning the Zürich Council is perhaps necessary. The Greater Council in Zürich was made up of two Lord Majors (who received a mandate for six-months only), the forty-eight members of the Lesser Council, one-hundred and forty-four Zwölfer made up of twelve representatives from each of the twelve guilds and 18 Konstaffelherren (Constables) who were of nobler birth or people of independent means. The 212 councilmen were thus known as the Two-Hundred. The Lesser Council dealt with daily matters concerning local politics but the Greater Council sat when matters of pan-state concern were raised. During Zwingli's office as Superintendent, the Two-Hundred had insisted on maintaining the rule over the Church, which is probably one of the reasons why Zwingli combined his ministry with active council politics. Bullinger insisted that the Church should rule itself but left all secular administration, including punishments and fines, to the magistrates. Slowly but very surely, he gained privileges for the Church which Zwingli had never obtained. For instance, the Council ruled that the minimum church attendance should be doubled, they set up a charity fund for the poor, they allowed Bullinger to head the Synod which included councilmen and they gave Bullinger a free hand in organising the entire school system.

Bullinger the bishop of souls

Once established in his new calling, Bullinger preached at least once a day but often two or three times a day going first through the Gospel of John, then the Epistle to the Hebrews and then the Epistles of Peter. Looking back on the preaching ministry in Zürich between 1523-1574, Bullinger writes in his *Tiguriner Chronik* that from the beginning of the

Reformation to the time of writing, sermons were preached twelve times a week in the Great Minster; once on Mondays, Tuesdays and Fridays, twice on Wednesdays, Thursdays and Saturdays and three times on Sundays. During the initial ten year period of his ministry, Bullinger also published book after book in spite of the enormous work pressure preparing so many sermons. After Bullinger had spent a decade preaching intensively day by day, though helped out occasionally by two deacons, other local, national and international pastoral duties crowded so much upon him that the Council appointed Kaspar Megander to take over much of Bullinger's preaching. Even so, Bullinger found himself preaching three to six times a week for the rest of his life. 650 of these sermons were published in Bullinger's lifetime but 'a vast profusion'[5] of unpublished sermons are to be found in the Zürich archives, in particular in the Central Library. Fritz Büsser reckons that whilst Bullinger was Superintendent, 28,000 sermons were preached in the Great Minster.[6]

From the start of his ministry, Bullinger began to organise the eight parishes under his care, placing one or more preachers in each and deans to oversee the administration and discipline. He took the preachers to task for their laxness but he always spoke of 'our sins' and not 'your sins' when dealing with them. Zwingli, in his zeal to Reform the Zürich Church in 1528 had set up a synodal committee which met twice yearly to discuss matters of faith and order. All the clergy both in the city and the canton's provinces were called to attend these synods to which the Lord Mayor and various councillors were invited as observers. Bullinger continued to call such synods but on 22 October, 1532, he introduced a new order for preachers and members of the synod which emphasised the differences between the Biblical duties of the secular powers and those of the clergy in far more detail than in Zwingli's order. Bullinger's quite revolutionary work was accepted by the Council and remains to a large extent the basis for the synodal dealings of the Zürich Reformed Church today. The order is in three parts:

---

[5] "Eine ungeheuere Fülle", so Büsser, p. 166.
[6] Ibid, p. 166.

I. The election, mission and ordination (laying on of hands) of preachers (eleven articles).
II. The doctrines and manner of life of the preachers (eighteen articles).
III. The calling, discipline and organisation of the Zürich synod (ten articles).

This order served as a basis for the organisation of numerous other Reformed churches, especially in Swiss-German and German-speaking areas. The fact that both Church and state in Zürich lived in comparative harmony in contrast to the allied churches in French-speaking areas such as Geneva who witnessed many struggles is because both the Council and the ministers of Zürich had agreed, through Bullinger's initiative, to mark out the exact lines of their various tasks within the Reformed state. So, too, in October 1532, Bullinger introduced his first Order of Service which was based on various experimental forms Zwingli and Jud had used and which he was to expand to a more permanent and creedal form in 1535.[7] A copy of this hitherto unknown order or *Agenda*, written in Bullinger's hand and with continual additions was discovered by Leo Weiz in 1954 in the Zürich Central Library.

Zwingli had sat on most political committees and councils and the distinction between Church and state was almost lost in his thinking. As the synods had been one of Zwingli's means of mobilising the clergy to follow his politics, and public opinion was against them, the clergy were shy of continuing them in the weeks after the Kappel War. Bullinger, eager to reform the idea behind the synods to make them more pastoral and less political, commenced rallying the ministers together by sending them written bulletins and such works as his *The Prophets* concerning the true work of a pastor. Gradually, he won the clergy over to continuing the synods, in spite of fears regarding their 'Zwinglian' character, by outlining to them all the spiritual blessings for which they had to thank Zwingli. "He is the man", wrote Bullinger, "through whom God restored to us the glory of His Church." It is obvious in the many tributes that

[7] See Busser, p. 144 for a comparison chart of Zwingli's 1529 and Bullinger's 1532 and 1535 orders which show clearly Bullinger's development of basic ideas.

Bullinger paid to Zwingli that he is using his predecessor to emphasise his own ideals. This perhaps explains why Bullinger never criticised his older friend and always emphasised that he was continuing in the spirit of Zwingli. This was not duplicity on Bullinger's part but he wished to preserve Zwingli's strong pastoral witness at a time when both Church and state were more than ready to quarrel with Zwingli's political side.

Another reason for Bullinger's firmness in keeping regular synods was for reasons of internal discipline. The Roman Catholic clergy in Zürich had lost their livings in the Reformation and were now totally without any support. Zürich provided no pensions or compensation for them of the kind that ex-papist ministers and especially bishops received under Elizabeth I in England. Indeed, public pensions, to avoid misuse and to save Council money were very quickly banned in Zürich. This had caused many papist priests to profess that they were truly Reformed so that they might keep their homes and receive their accustomed salaries. The synods were ideal instruments for detecting who was truly Reformed and who was not so that measures could be taken to correct any misuse. Bullinger was very tolerant in such matters, seeking to coax, persuade and instruct the disguised papists before turning to sterner measures if needed. However, Bullinger had no great respect for church hierarchies and instructed the deacons to keep a constant eye on their pastors and report any obvious abuse of office to the synod. One of the first disciplinary cases to come up before the synod was that of Johannes Bullinger, Henry's own elder brother who had struck a member of his parish in anger. Another pastor was disciplined for his unseemly clothing and conversation and for carrying firearms. A number of ministers were corrected for carrying broadswords and other weapons to which they had accustomed themselves as warrior ministers in the Zwingli era. One minister was severely disciplined for quarrelling with his wife who had used filthy language and for being drunk and disorderly. To top this, the man had no books! The penitent minister promised to better himself and the synod replied that they did not want to hear pious promises but see concrete results – or else the minister would soon be an ex-minister. Pastors' wives who used unbecoming language or were evil gossips were sent to Wellenberg prison for a day or two. The prison was situated on a tiny island in the middle of Lake Zürich and the loquacious ladies were placed alone in damp and dark cells with only the walls to complain to. This does not mean that Bullinger acted as an all-righteous judge chastising his brethren. The synod was egalitarian in all things and did not hesitate to scold Bullinger when they thought he was being too mild or being lax in his criticism of the Zürich government.

Bullinger's main calling, however, was to the common man and his main instrument in reaching him was his preaching. He soon discovered that leading the Zürich churches was fraught with difficulties. Bern, realising what a strong leader of men Bullinger was, painted a bleak picture of Zürich in order to tempt him over to them. Letters are extant which tell Bullinger what difficulties he would have with the Zürich Council and how he would be better off in Bern. The Bernese underestimated Bullinger's diplomatic capacities and the Bernese Council often criticised their own Church's policies. A number of the Zürich magistrates, however, had become so used to the often heroic but equally often tactless stubbornness of Zwingli that they thought milder Bullinger was a second-best substitute. Furthermore, the Fünf Orte had been so stung by Zwingli's less than Christian statesmanship when representing Zürich's interests that they came close to re-declaring war on the city, thinking that Bullinger had taken up Zwingli's mantle rather than put on his own. This mistrust came to a head in 1532 when the Council demanded that Bullinger draw up a *Glaubensmandat* (Mandate of Faith) in the name of the city, proclaiming that the rumours that Zürich was opening her doors to Rome were entirely false, that the Reformation had come to stay and that Rome should be condemned in no uncertain terms. Bullinger questioned the magistrates' policy but complied. He thus composed a mandate affirming that the rumour that Zürich was about to re-introduce the mass in the city was evil slander, the mass had been abolished and all the laws of the canton would be adjusted to fit in with Reformed ethics and practice. Only if Roman Catholics sought by non-peaceful means to alter the situation, would they be fined or banned from the canton. The document advised all those who believed that the

Scriptures taught otherwise to inform the authorities peacefully of their position and they would be given a ready and tolerant ear. Sadly, the authorities thought Bullinger's resulting declaration was too mild and voted through a more militant version including a far stronger condemnation of the mass which the surrounding Roman Catholic districts viewed as not only a breach of the Kappel Peace Treaty but also a provocation to war. The Council's act was also timed to coincide with Charles V's Reichstag at Regensburg. Charles was striving to find some sort of mutual tolerance between Roman Catholics, Lutherans and Reformed and the *Glaubensmandat* appeared to threaten the Emperor's policy. Ennio Filonardi, the papal legate, demanded entry into Zürich in the name of the pope in late 1532 but was politely refused admittance. This caused him to promise the Swiss Roman Catholics help from Rome should war become inevitable. The Five Districts then asked Zürich to withdraw the mandate as it went beyond the Kappel Treaty which stated that each canton should democratically follow the religion of their choice but not interfere with other cantons. Bern, who had proved a dubious ally in the Kappel Wars, urged Zürich to maintain their militant position. Instead of aiming their anger at the Zürich Council, the Fünf Orte, thinking that Bullinger must have the politicians in his hand as Zwingli had, denounced him as enemy number one. The threat of war escalated as Zürich accused the Fünf Orte of breaking the Peace of Kappel by the Archbishop of Sankt Gallen's persecution of the Protestants in Rheintal. However, the Fünf Orte used the incident diplomatically to put further pressure on Zürich. You withdraw the mandate which denigrates our mass, they said and we shall show leniency to the Rheintal Protestants.

In May, 1533 Bullinger and his fellow pastors called a synod to work out a solution. Most of the pastors believed that their Council's mandate could be easily misused, allowing the Council to tell the churches what to preach. Bullinger was elected spokesman to tell the councillors that they could not prescribe for Roman Catholic ruled areas what they should believe and should allow the Zürich pastors to preach the Word of God and allow the Spirit to work as He will. They said that the mandate had been too bold, too negative and most un-diplomatic. Bullinger also made it clear that though the church would not tell the Council how to do their job, they reserved the right themselves to admonish from the pulpit those who lived and worked against the Word of God. Bullinger also told the Council in no uncertain terms that their task was to rule the city but not to play the pastor and tell his flock what to believe, or other cantons for that matter. The corporation withdrew the mandate and further war was eventually averted but not without a good deal of nervous plotting on both sides. Bullinger's position in the eyes of the Council was now strengthened and he was invited to appear regularly at the City Hall to meet the councilmen and inform them of the progress of the gospel in the canton so that a common Reformation policy could be worked out.

However, Ferdinand I and the papal legate still pressed for military action against the Protestants but Bullinger had many allies in Upper Germany both in the Lutheran states and amongst those cities who had accepted Bucer's *Tetrapolitana* Confession (Strasburg, Constance, Memmingen and Lindau) which had influenced the Swiss Reformers. Furthermore, the Lutheran princes had formed the Smalcald League in December 1530 to protect their territories from a Roman Catholic takeover by the Counter-Reformation and they were anxious to extend the League to include the Swiss. Bucer, the great mediator and diplomat wrote, thinking of Zürich:

"It would be contrary to brotherly love to pledge ourselves to show no favour to anyone who acknowledges the common Christ with us, even though he should not be at one with us in regard to some article, more in the letter than the spirit." [8]

Protestant Bern, however, as usual, thought that Zürich was not stern enough with the papists and a threatened breach with the city occurred over a triviality. Bern had no printing press so they approached Zürich printer Christopher Froschauer[9] (1490-1564), who served the English

[8] Quoted in Wilhelm Moeller's *History of the Christian Church*, Vol. III, p. 118 from Baumgarten, *Karl V. und die deutsche Reformation*, p. 65 ff.

[9] Also written 'Froschover'.

Reformers so well, requesting that he print a Bernese Protestant Declaration of Faith for them, illustrating it with Bern's symbol, a bear. The bear that Froschauer printed, however, had its claws withdrawn and looked quite amiable (or so the Bernese thought). Militant Bern took this as an affront to their pride and complained bitterly. Through contact with Berchtold Haller of Bern who was of a less fiery spirit than the city dignitaries, Bullinger prevented a major break between the two cantons, though Bern never dealt with Froschauer again. However, Froschauer's international reputation grew by leaps and bounds and his workshop became a central printing-press for the entire European Reformation, including the vast number of scientific works which the Reformation movement inspired. Nearly all the works of Italian Reformer Peter Martyr Vermigli (1500-1562) were published in Zürich by Froschauer, besides works on medicine, ornithology, botany and zoology. Added to these were 100 editions and versions of a single book, the Bible and, together with his nephew Christopher Froschauer (1532-1585), some 900 other separate works before 1575, the year of Bullinger's death. Also typical for Froschauer was that he printed scholarly works in the vernacular.

Difficulties with Leo Jud

Just as the Zürich churches were settling down to living in peace with Council and people, Leo Jud dropped something of a bombshell. He had been most influenced by Anabaptist and Moravian Brethren teaching and had begun to believe first that the Church should have no dealings with the state whatsoever but changed this gradually to a belief that all disciplinary action, previously undertaken by the Zürich's magistrates, should be taken over by members of the church elected for that office. These members were to form a kind of police force to control the movements and beliefs of each individual citizen with powers to discipline, exclude from the Lord's Table and excommunicate. It was obvious that Jud was reacting against the accusations of the Anabaptists that the Zürich church was too lax on church discipline. Jud's suggestions were not new as Oecolampadius had suggested similar reforms to Zwingli who had rejected them. Zwingli believed that it was the duty of the powers that be, i.e. the magistrates, to enforce discipline. Calvin was also to try in vain to introduce a church police force in order to discipline church members in Geneva. Now, in March, 1532, Jud wrote to Bullinger explaining that he thought the present crisis demanded a clear separation of Church and State and if the church had disciplined itself, it would not have fallen apart so easily when military defeat occurred. He also pointed out that there were a number of enemies of the Word of God and even papists on the Zürich Council. Jud assured Bullinger that he did not wish to return to monkish or Pharisaic ways like the Anabaptists but he believed that the Church should not tolerate vermin amongst them. At the end of his letter, Jud told Bullinger that he was enclosing a tract from the Moravian Brethren which would give him light on the subject.

Bullinger replied that he was as anxious for the purity of the Church as Jud but such a revolutionary change would cause another great upheaval at a time when the churches needed peace. Besides, he was not of the opinion that Church and State were totally different entities as the Christian was duty bound to honour the powers that be as they are appointed by God. Governments were thus in God's plan for His Church. The Church is not empty of the State and the State not empty of the Church. A statesman is also a servant of God and the idea of a Christian statesman is certainly not a contradiction in terms. It is furthermore, the Christian's duty to see that men are elected to the Council who will be able to enforce external public order. He also explained to Jud that the church is not fitted out to combat evil in the way the civil magistrates are who are appointed by God for that purpose. If the Church was to put law, order and discipline into the hands of a force elected from them, there were no greater guarantees that such discipline would work. Furthermore, he believed that Jud's idea of discipline regarding exclusion from the Lord's Supper and excommunication was too strict. All the disciples after they had celebrated the Passover with the Lord, proved unworthy and even Judas was not banned from the Lord's Table. To use the Eucharist as a means of reward and punishment could hardly be compatible with Christian witness. In 1534, Jud published his *Catechism* and his section on the church showed that he had taken Bullinger's advice to heart.

One might argue here that Jud had already dropped all idea of a separation of Church and State with his quite massive support of Zwingli in urging the Zürich Council to go to war against the papists. Also, now Jud was actually telling the State as much as the Church how to go about their duties of maintaining social order. Bullinger felt that he had no such calling to interfere in political matters in this way. He believed it was not his duty as Church Superintendent to change the political structure in Zürich, especially as things were now working well between Church and State. Furthermore, Bullinger was convinced that the Church should strive to be leaven in the State and the more the Church shut itself off from the State it should be evangelising, the more it would become an inward looking sect. Thus Bullinger sought to refrain from all interference with the Council's work, apart from using the freedom they, under God, had given him to admonish them from the Word. This practical position proved very practical as for the next forty years a peace reigned between Church and State in Zürich that was unrivalled elsewhere. So, too, the laws of Canton Zürich began to show a marked improvement in their Christian nature. This was made very evident from the early thirties on when the Council admonished their papist members such as Peter Füssil, without any threats of punishment whatsoever, to sit under the Reformed ministry. Füssil and his tiny party complied. Thus, the Council politicians, to a very large extent, followed Bullinger and allowed the ministers, under their oversight, to do what they felt was best for the canton. Diplomat Bullinger almost always managed to keep up a strong Christian testimony within the State system to the benefit of both State and Church.

The papists unfounded criticism against Bullinger

Still giving Bullinger the blame for the original severity of the *Glaubensmandat*, papist spies began to take notes during Bullinger's sermons in order to find anything in them which they could interpret as a breach of the Peace of Kappel. Delegates from the Fünf Orte, arranged a meeting at Baden, to discuss their fear of Bullinger and sent a Zürich observer back to Zürich with a document officially denouncing Bullinger for breaking the peace in a sermon preached on 16 June, 1532. He had, the delegates said, spoken in favour of going to war against the Roman Catholics and called the papists 'dung-beetles', and the mass 'blasphemous'. Bullinger and a number of his fellow ministers were immediately called before the Zürich Council to be disciplined. In his defence, Bullinger declared that the accusations had no basis in fact as his entire congregation were witnesses that he continually preached against military warfare, and the shedding of blood. He had, however, made it clear that the fact that the papists had won the war, did not mean that they were spiritually superior to the Protestants as they claimed. The Turks had put the Christians to flight in the battle of Mohacs in August, 1526 but that did not mean that Islam was superior to Christianity. Concerning the mass, Bullinger again pointed out that the Peace of Kappel allowed the Protestants to preach according to the Old and New Testaments and they could find no doctrine of the mass there. Once again, the Council asked Bullinger and the preachers who were with him to wait outside of the hall and, for the second time, the Council was obliged to sit for hours arguing what they should do. If they let off Bullinger without any sign of displeasure, another war might be the consequence. The rumour quickly spread amongst the citizens, who were awaiting the verdict outside the City Hall, that Bullinger would be dismissed from his post. After a long wait, the Council again called Bullinger in and told him that they accepted his defence but should he ever wish to preach on any subject which might involve the city and Council and the good name of the city, he had free access at all time to the Council to discuss this with them before preaching about it. He should continue to preach in keeping with what he believed was Scriptural, to the honour of God, and promoted liberty and peace. He should always have the salvation of his people in mind. Again, Bullinger had successfully defended his gospel before the Council and had gained more freedom for his church in doing so.

Jud causes further difficulties

On 24 June, Leo Jud preached a fiery sermon against the presence of papists in the city which caused a commotion both inside and outside the

Protestant fold. It was the festival of John the Baptist and Jud presented himself as a new John raising a lone voice in the wilderness. Leaving Bullinger's warnings to the four winds, he began an open attack on the Council for not driving a better bargain with the Roman Catholics on the latter's victory. He was particularly angry that the papists had forced the Council to accept their declaration that the Roman Catholic faith was the true faith. Jud's words reaped many an 'Amen', but others thought that Jud was causing an unnecessary commotion as the Council had made it quite clear that they were now sticking to a Reformed path. Brave as the sermon was, Jud, because of his past testimony, was not the man to preach it. The Council soon reminded Jud that the preachers had to share much of the blame for the war and the unsatisfactory outcome. It must have also been clear to Jud that very many of those pastors who had been killed or remained alive had been vociferous in promoting the war and very silent indeed in bargaining for a fair peace. Jud refused to retract a single word but Bullinger came to his rescue. He outlined to the Council how he had preached against war and for peace all the time and how the Council had accepted full responsibility for the war by enforcing the food embargo on the Five Roman Catholic States. So, the Council were not in a position to condemn the clergy en bloc or wash their own hands clean of responsibility for the war. Again, Bullinger won the day and also gained a further victory. He asked the Council why they could not trust the preachers to preach as their conscience led and accept that they must be stern with the people at times and mild at others. Bullinger must have been gifted with a golden tongue because from then on the Council refrained almost fully from striving to control what the preachers had to say from the pulpit.

The Five Districts' mandate against Zürich

All this did not go unobserved by the Five Orte who decided to outwit the Zürich Council. They openly broke the Peace of Kappel by issuing their own Mandate in September, 1532, denouncing Zürich's preachers. As they had expected, Zürich at once demanded that the mandate be withdrawn. Then the wily papists said they would be prepared to do so at once providing that the Zürich Council withdrew their Glaubensmandat of the previous May. Then, so the papists said, Zürich had spoken against the mass and thus they were the ones who had broken the Peace Treaty. Again Zürich was threatened with war if they did not respond positively. By this time Zürich realised that they could not rely on Bern to help them if war broke out and though Strasburg and Basle were supportive of Zürich's cause, they confessed that they were in no position to offer military assistance. Looking therefore for a peaceful alternative, the Zürich Council turned to Bullinger again and he now worked out a compromise and solicited Bern, Basle and Strasburg and even Hessen for support. These areas then promised Zürich every help possible should the papists not accept Bullinger's compromise. Bullinger's message was simple. He told the Fünf Orte that Zürich would stop complaining about them if they would stop complaining about Zürich and that each should allow the other to continue in mutual non-acceptance. Furthermore, the old confederacies in which there were now Protestants and Roman Catholics should be re-organised with due compensation given to cantons who would suffer by this. The Protestant states should join each other in a new confederacy if they so wished and the Roman Catholic states should also ally as they wished. Though this was more or less acceptable by the papists, Bern had many an objection as they claimed huge areas where Roman Catholics were in the majority. The papists had already planned to make two new cantons out of the Bernese Roman Catholic areas whatever compromise was reached. St Gallen had also a number of Roman Catholic enclaves which would demand independence, indeed it was the Abbot of St Gallen who had organised much of the protest against Bullinger. The Zürich Superintendent argued diplomatically that to give up what is already in the hands of the papists was but a small price for Protestant freedom.

Meanwhile, the churches in Zürich, in face of the danger of being attacked any day but with a pastor such as Bullinger amongst them, now grew amazingly strong in faith and witness. Ambrose Blaurer wrote to Bullinger from Constance, saying, "Salvation be to you! Under the heavy cross which you are carrying, Zürich's Church has become much stronger and the strength of the Lord radiates through your weakness brighter than ever before." On 16 March, 1533, the Reichtstag sat at Einsiedeln and the papists made a formal complaint that the Protestants had broken the Peace of Kappel. The Zürich delegates rejected such accusations strongly and again there was talk of war. Both Haller from Bern and Capito from Strasburg said they were preparing for military action. Bullinger urged Zürich to adopt his plan and at last the Protestant city sued for peace by promising to withdraw their mandate of May, 1532 in support of Bullinger's compromise. They also promised not to undertake anything which was aimed at insulting their Roman Catholic confederates. The delegates thus all agreed to keep their disagreements to themselves. The papists would continue to say that theirs was the original faith but Zürich was free to maintain that they wished to go their own way without condemning other districts who disagreed.

Though the Zürich Council accepted Bullinger's new mandate, they had great difficulty in persuading the canton that they had done the right thing. The papists took Bullinger's compromise as a sign that they had gained another victory over the Protestants and made much of Johann Faber's claim that the defeat at Kappel was because the Protestants had forsaken the true church. German-born Faber was now Bishop of Vienna. Bullinger counteracted this rumour by writing his *Auff Johansen Wyenischen Bischoffs trostbüchlein* in 1532. Faber was initially friendly to the Reformation but after a visit to Rome and rapid promotion including becoming Ferdinand I's confessor and chaplain, he became known as 'the Hammer of the Heretics' and burned many a saint in Hungary and Austria. During this period, Bullinger was busy writing his commentary on Hebrews which was published in 1532. In this work Bullinger showed how the papacy strove to inflict a new Jewry onto the churches. This was the work that had drawn Gervasius Schuler, then at Basle, to become more thoroughly Reformed. However, so great was Zürich's fear of Faber that they supposed he would organise Austrian troops to invade Zürich.

In May, 1533, the half-yearly Synod sat to discuss the new situation and Lord Mayor Walder begged the ministers to be of one mind in urging peace. Martin Bucer was on a visit to Zürich at the time and he was invited to join in the transactions. Bullinger led the Synod and declared that if the Council had not taken upon itself to speak for the Church and use the Lord's Supper as a political argument, the papist districts would not have been angered. The gist of Bullinger's speech was that the church should remain free to preach the Word of God and to point out the un-Biblical nature of the popish novelties but the politicians should live according to the Word themselves and not issue Mandates which would give the enemy grounds for protest.

Zürich was still at loggerheads with Bern over their weakness in assisting the Zürich forces at Kappel so Bullinger and Haller of Bern now made great efforts to try and bring the Protestant cantons closer together so that they could keep up a joint witness against Rome. However, Bern had become half-hearted in her relationships with her French-speaking protectorates due to a great extent to the constant unrest in the church, ministers' conference and council at Geneva. Bullinger was looked to from both sides to mediate in these disputes which demanded a great deal of his time and work. He was gifted, however, with great strength and patience and his preaching, pastoral and written work do not appear to have suffered.

Bullinger's skill in introducing new policies

Bullinger's diplomatic and strategic acumen is clearly seen in the way he kept ordinances and policies which Zwingli had founded but filled them with new content, thus enabling him to both lean on Zürich traditions and practices but at the same time making sure that they bore his individual mark. Just as Bullinger filled Zwingli's idea of a joint Church-State synod with a more pastoral function, so he took over Zwingli's orders of service from the late twenties and reformed and expanded them further. In 1535, he introduced the Zürich Order of Service which was Zürich's first official comprehensive order concerning preaching, prayer and supplication, confession of faith, the reading of Scripture and the celebrating of the ordinances.

This order was to remain binding on the Zürich Church throughout Bullinger's life time.[10] A lengthy foreword to the Agenda shows that Bullinger intended the work not merely as a form of worship but also as a clear statement of the Reformed faith. Here, however, Bullinger was not merely building on Zwingli's earlier statements but also on his own works of 1528-9 which strongly emphasised the need for a sound order of worship. To this end, he wrote his *On the Origin of Error in the Eucharist and Mass*[11] and his *On the Origin of the Cult of Saints and Images*.[12] These works were expanded and reprinted in 1538 and 1569.

Like Zwingli, Bullinger strove to make his order of service as least like the old Roman Catholic mass as possible without discarding genuine Biblical forms of worship. The mass had been idolatrous but the Reformed Christian form of worship must be true adoration of God with the emphasis on preaching, prayer and praise. Sung worship played a very minor role in the church service as both Zwingli and Bullinger felt that sung liturgies and instrumentalised worship were relics of Rome and her Old Testament shadowy understanding of doctrines which were fulfilled and transformed in the New Testament. Such music also reminded Zwingli of his own embarrassing past as a tavern entertainer. Bullinger pointed out that one never finds Christ singing words set to tunes in his ministry and showed how the few words for 'singing' used in the New Testament really meant speaking or declaring.[13] However, Bullinger did not forbid singing, but pointed out its historical misuse. Bullinger's most positive statement regarding singing is perhaps to be found in his Second Helvetic Confession in which he says in Article XXIII:

"Likewise moderation is to be exercised where singing is used in a meeting for worship. That song which they call the Gregorian Chant has

---

[10] Zwingli had published forms of church order in 1525 and 1529 but they were of limited form. Jud had also suggested various forms of liturgy since 1523. Büsser has a fine section on the development of the 1535 Church Order in his biography 'Die Zürcher Gottesdienstordnung von 1535', pp. 142-147.

[11] *Vom Ursprung des Irrtums in Eucharistie und Messe.*

[12] *Vom Ursprung des Heligen- und Bilder-Kults.*

[13] See Bullinger's *Decades*, Book V, Fifth Sermon on praying, singing and thanksgiving for an understanding of his views on hymn singing.

many foolish things in it; hence it is rightly rejected by many of our churches. If there are churches which have a true and proper sermon (oratorium) but no singing, they ought not to be condemned. For all churches do not have the advantage of singing. And it is well known from testimonies of antiquity that the custom of singing is very old in the Eastern Churches whereas it was late when it was at length accepted in the West."[14]

One interesting feature which was to cause friction between the Reformed churches of Bern and Zürich was that in Bullinger's church service, he still included the reciting of Luke 1:28, better known to the papists as *Ave Maria*. Another was that the ministers whilst officiating in the pulpit and at the Lord's Table were to wear ordinary but decent clothing and not *Schauspielerkleidun*g, i.e. the clothing of actors. This distinguished the Zürich Church from that of several of her neighbouring cantons but also the Church of Geneva, the Church of England and the Lutheran churches. Büsser points out[15] that though Bullinger removed all superficial decorations from the churches, the Reformation was accompanied by a church-building boom and the churches were very well-kept. This contrasts with the situation in Geneva where many of the church buildings were derelict and ministers even complained of having to preach in churches which had become roofless and no help was in sight.

Internationally renowned as an educator

Shortly after Bullinger had established himself at Zürich, his friend and colleague Conrad Pellican, Professor of Hebrew at the Zürich *skola*, wrote:

"Zwingli and many fine and scholarly men fell whilst defending their country, their Church and the truth. Now the Zürich Church stands firm and is growing in faith, in virtue, in doctrine and in public prosperity so

[14] Taken from *Reformed Confessions of the 16th Century*, Arthur Cochrane, pp. 290-293.
[15] *Heinrich Bullinger*, p. 149.

that never were hand and heart stronger. By the grace of God, we received in place of Zwingli, a youthful Bishop, an exquisite man, pious, upright, learned, faithful and devoted, a preacher with no equal, who, through his teaching at home and his writings abroad in the whole of Christendom has shown himself to be a man of God, full of talents."[16]

Zürich soon had ample opportunity to experience the truth of Pellican's words. After the Kappel Wars, Zürich was left with immense debts and the public gave the Church the blame arguing that it was Zwingli who had driven them to war. As the Church was the cause of the trouble, they maintained, so she should pay off the city's debts. To this end, in July, 1533 the Council appointed an *Obmannamt*[17] to administer church funds as the Council saw fit. This meant that not only Bullinger's plans for church extensions would be thwarted but also his ambitious plans for founding new schools and seminaries. Bullinger did not protest much against this new venture but merely persuaded the Council that preaching and education were the two means of preserving and strengthening a Protestant state and that he did not expect the Council to be so short-sighted as to ignore their importance. He then worked out a more efficient financing plan thus pacifying all sides. Instead of handing over church surpluses to the Council, money was raised by the ministers who canvassed generous giving in order to provide for schools and training institutions which would be a benefit to the entire canton and beyond. Bullinger then authored a church constitution which defined exactly what relationship the Church had to the state[18] and this, too, was accepted by the Senate. He trained and recruited many new teachers and authored curricula and examination regulations. Bullinger organised regular examinations and by careful drilling speeded up the time students needed for studies. Abandoned abbeys, nunneries and cloisters were turned into schools and sound educationalists such as Professor Rhellikan were appointed as inspectors. Teachers of international renown like

[16] *Konrad Pellikan Chronikon von 1544*, ed. E. Riggenbach, pp. 124-125.
[17] An Obmann is an umpire, chairman or overseer.
[18] *Pradikanten- und Synodalordnung.*

Theodor Bibliander, Conrad Gessner (1516-1564), Josias Simler and, at a later date, Peter Martyr, were given the task of training the Zürich youth. Soon, Bullinger's school reforms spread to neighbouring cantons and associate states such as Graubünden and the Italian-speaking districts. Bullinger's educational policies quickly found international acclaim, especially in England and Poland. The English during the reigns of Henry VIII, Edward VI, Mary I and Elizabeth I willingly sent their young people to be trained by Bullinger and King Sigismund of Poland, one of Bullinger's many royal correspondents sent students to sit under his tuition and that of Bibliander and Pellican. These foreign students told their congregations, children and grandchildren of the heavenly times sitting at Bullinger's feet in his private home, listening to Bullinger expounding Isaiah and the other prophets. Indeed, one of the most important reasons why Bullinger became so popular in England during the reign of Elizabeth was that many of the exiles had found great hospitality and good teaching under Zürich roofs when driven from their home country by Mary.

Zürich: an exegetical, linguistic and scientific centre of learning

Bullinger built a new college at Zürich and introduced through Bibliander, Conrad Gessner and other experts in Islam and linguistics, a careful study of the Koran and the Semitic languages with a view to spreading the gospel in Turkey and the Arab states and protecting Christians from Islamic proselytising. To this end, Bibliander produced a book in 1542 giving Christians advice on how to witness to Mohammedans and a year later, he produced a Latin version of the Koran. Bibliander's and Gessner's linguistic studies were virtually centuries before their time and were not rivalled in their depth and scope until the Applied Linguistics of the 1960s arrived with the Transformative and Generative Grammar of Noam Chomsky. Studies were carried out into the origin and development of languages and in the common attributes all languages have with one another. Bibliander and his team went beyond languages to study the thought processes that gave rise to them. These studies opened academic doors to the truths of the language confusion at Babel described in the Bible and, coupled with Biblical exegesis, pointed a way back to the original language of mankind. Here we have the seeds of the modern linguistic method of working out the surface and deep structures of language indicating a common thought process amongst human beings. The results of such studies convinced the Zürich Reformers of how closely associated languages were with religion and that all the world's religions had a common source in the earliest Biblical writings and the ancient works used by Moses. Gessner, who was amongst his many qualifications a trained doctor, botanist and geologist, carried his linguistic studies into the medical sciences and produced works on human health, veterinary diseases, botany, ornithology and geology (fossils). Besides Gessner, Pellican, Bibliander and Martyr, further internationally renowned scholars who held chairs at the Zürich College during Bullinger's superintendentship were Josias Simler (1530-1576), Johannes Wolf (1521-1571), Johann Wilhelm Stucki (1542-1607) and Johann Jako Fries (1505-1565). Leo Jud (1482-1542), the Bible translator, Rudolf Gualter (1519-1586), Johannes Stumpf (1500-1577), Peter Colin (?-1542), Conrad Klausner (1515-1567) and Ludwig Lavater (1527-1586) also served as lecturers in the college with other Zürich ministers.

Opening up Zürich to the nations

Bullinger's pioneer work in education, particularly in training boys and students for the ministry, for which he wrote some ten text books, has not been fully appreciated in the definitive accounts of the Reformation. He had set up institutions for the training of evangelical, reformed pastors in the early fifteen twenties - long before reformers in other countries even attempted the same. England had to wait until the late 40s, German universities such as Heidelberg the late 50s and Calvin was first able to set up his Geneva Academy in 1559. In his reforming and fund-saving measures, Bullinger reduced the number of prebendaries and abolished pluralities, using canonry funds to pay the wages of teachers and pastors and provide grants for students in order to relieve the city treasury. By 1532, he had already worked out and published his *Prädikanten- und*

Synodalordnung regulating theological studies, church order and administration. In October of the same year, when the Council officially appointed Bullinger *Schulherr* or minister for schools, he drew up a *Schulordnung* (Regulations for Education) for studies at the Minster School which were in Swiss-German, Latin and Greek. Then he set up a rigorous system of church visitations to see that pastor's salaries were fixed and paid and church buildings kept in repair. Again, we can compare this affluent state of the Church positively to that of Geneva where Calvin complained that the ministers lived on a beggar's income and ministers complained to the Council that they had to preach in roofless churches. In 1538, Bullinger opened up a boarding school in Zürich to replace the schools in Kappel and Rüti in the aftermath of the Second Kappel War and provided free board and accommodation for poor students in a former nunnery. A system of looking after the poor and the sick was drawn up and Bullinger wrote handbooks as guides for their care. Though traditionally only higher education was placed under the Church's administration, Bullinger used Church money to set up general elementary schooling for all children. Students who made themselves notable through high academic and spiritual attainments were also sent on grants to other cantons, the German, Dutch and Belgian states and to Britain where Richard Cox and later Edmund Grindal took care of them. Cox called Bullinger 'the pillar of the Church of Christ'[19] and 'a second Elijah'. The English students, thrilled by their studies under Bullinger, Bibliander and Pellican, on returning home, not only distributed Bullinger's and Zwingli's works published by him throughout England but arranged for British businessmen to do business with the Zürich Senate. This gave the Zürich traders less cause to accuse the church of spending money rather than earning it for the good of the canton. For instance, wood from the Zürich area was in great demand in England as it was most suitable for making bows and staves. This led John Butler and his close friends to initiate transactions which proved lucrative for the Senate and helpful for England. Butler also helped finance Zürich

[19] *Zürich Letters*, First Series, pp. 286 and 317. Repeatedly in his letters Cox also refers to Bullinger as a 'most solid pillar of the Church'.

students abroad as, for instance, Rudolf Gualter at Marburg. It was through Gualter that Bullinger heard of Marburg's Landgrave Philip of Hessen's bigamy which was supported both by the pope and Lutheran leaders. Calvin was thrilled with the way Bullinger was improving the education of the canton and wrote to him on 7 November, 1542, congratulating him on his success but informing him that though he would love to do likewise in Geneva, they had not the finances to implement such reforms. The truth was that they had no one like Bullinger to set such reforms in motion both in the means of raising money and of spending it wisely.

Sending out ambassadors of learning throughout Europe

After the Kappel wars Zürich was far poorer than Geneva but Bullinger and his circle had the initiative and know-how to raise funds when needed.[20] When Bullinger's students visited foreign universities, Bullinger demanded that they should keep a regular account of their expenses and be prepared to stand before Bullinger on completing their studies to tell him all they knew about the history, traditions, cultures, religions and politics of their host countries. In this way, Bullinger could add to his various chronicles and publications on history and European politics. So, too, these students were informed that they were ambassadors for the truth in foreign parts and were expected to keep up a faithful Reformed witness and work hard, keeping up a good testimony, in their studies. All this activity on Bullinger's part made Zürich the religious and cultural capital of a wide area, including a number of Southern German states. Ulm, Lindau and especially Memmingen where Gervasius Schuler was now pastor, looked to Bullinger for help and leadership. Even Augsburg, which one might have thought was a Lutheran stronghold, had very close ties with Zürich through Bullinger. The city appealed to Zürich, not Wittenberg, to send them Reformed pastors and Bullinger's young friend and protégé Johannes Haller was sent to strengthen the Augsburg churches until he was forced out by the

[20] Geneva became almost bankrupt some 15-20 years later.

Emperor. Württemberg, too, appealed to Bullinger to send them a good man and his answer was Reformer Ambrose Blaurer. Similar calls came from Alsace and Mülhausen. When Jan Laski (John à Lasco) began establishing churches in Friesland, Laski chose Zürich student Martin Micronius to serve the new congregations and Bullinger assisted him greatly in his disputations with the Anabaptist Menno Simons and the militant Lutherans. Friedrich III of the Palatine turned to Bullinger when he left Lutheranism for the Reformed path and the result was that the former Zürich students Olevanus and Ursinus went to Friedrich's assistance and authored the Heidelberg Catechism. This catechism is still regularly in print and widely used in Germany's churches and schools. It reflects Bullinger's Helvetic Confession in word and contents. This is hardly surprising as Friedrich made Bullinger's work the new confession of the Palatine Church. Heidelberg became a centre of Reformed religion after the Zürich pattern, influenced by the Palatine Reformers Olevanus and Ursinus and printed Bullinger's works. The city became gradually more Genevan orientated when Olevanus introduced harsher forms of church government which were not in the Zürich tradition. Ursinus, however, kept more to the Bullinger line. Philip of Hessen remained close to Bullinger who used all his diplomacy in attempting to have Philip freed from the imperial prisons. Almost needless to say, Philip sent his son to sit under Bullinger's tuition and Bullinger's third son Christoph entered the Landgrave's services, was knighted by him and given a *Rittergut* (knight's mansion). Christoph was killed serving Philip in France. When Zürich opened her homes to refugees from Saxony and Constance and other Protestant areas during the Smalcaldian Wars and the so-called Peace of Augsburg, Zürich's influence spread throughout entire Germany, an influence which did not please the Lutheran leadership.

Bullinger's importance for the Hungarian Reformation

Modern Hungarian scholars such as Mihály Bucsay, István Schlégl, Barnábas Nagy and Endre Zsindely have reminded the Reformed world of the enormous influence Bullinger's teaching had on the Hungarian Reformation. Hungarian Reformers such as Petrus Juhász Melius, Josef

Macarius, János Fejérthóys, Gál Huzár and Kaspar Heltai[21] had approached Bullinger either personally or by letter with a view to publishing his works in Hungary in German, Latin and Hungarian and Bucsay writes that though Luther, Melanchthon and Calvin also influenced the Hungarian Protestants, Bullinger "left all the others behind" in particular through the spreading of his Second Helvetic Confession which was accepted in Hungary as a doctrinal standard. Bucsay goes on to argue, however, that this confession did not merely link the Hungarian believers to Switzerland but also to those in the whole world.[22] So, too, after the devastations caused by the Turkish wars and the enslaving of thousands of the cream of Hungary by the victorious Turks, the country needed a new pattern for both state and Church structures for which they appealed to Zürich. One of the major problems was the care of families left in Hungary after parents, mothers or fathers were taken into captivity never to return. Also the problem of re-marriage became acute as neither those left nor those transported had much chance of being re-united. The ministers' training academy at Zürich specialised in bringing the gospel to Islamic states and it is to be noted that the Swiss Reformation spread the quickest in areas of Hungary which were occupied by the Turks. Bucsay believes that Bullinger was so popular because he was clear and unambiguous in his writings and he wrote so that even people with little education could understand him. As the Hungarians had no time for mysticism, abstractions and sentimentality, Bullinger's matter-of-fact and sober arguments from Scripture appealed to them as also his comprehensive overview of doctrine, presenting theology in its wholeness. The fact that Bullinger presented God as the loving Father, rather than the abstract, impersonal God also drew the Hungarians to his teaching. Bucsay challenges the usual 'Calvinistic' doctrine that God created man solely for His own honour and, like Bullinger, emphasises that God created man in the form that His Son

[21] The names of twenty-seven of Bullinger's Hungarian correspondents and visitors have been preserved.

[22] *Gesammelte Aufsätze zum 400. Todestag*, Leitgedanken der Theologie Bullingers bei Petrus Melius. Ein Beitrag zur Ausstrahlung des Züricher Reformators nach Ungarn, pp. 197-214.

adopted as a means of fellowshipping with man in Christ. In other words, when the Father said of the Son that He was well-pleased with Him, he included also those who were placed in Christ, too. So, too, the view of predestination in the theology of such as Melius was consequent, scriptural Bullingerism rather than inconsequent Calvinism. He followed Bullinger in teaching that Adam was created so that he could have withstood sin and that God is not the source of sin but Bucsay relates how Calvin told the Genevan Council on 6 October, 1552 "However, I am free to confess, that I have stated that God not only has foreseen, but also foreordained, the fall of Adam, which I maintain to be true, not without good grounds and evidences from holy writ." Here Calvin is defending his 1551 edition of the *Institutes* which Jean Trolliet had criticised for its alleged teaching that God ordained sin. Trolliet was dismissed from the ministry by the Genevan secular authorities but his criticism still illustrates the weakness of Calvin's position at this time. In the 1551 version of the *Institutes*, Calvin is certainly striving to eat his cake and keep it, arguing both that Adam was created to fall for the glory of God's Name but that he was also damned because of his own (God given?) perversity. Indeed, here it appears that in arguing for the latter point, Calvin is also suggesting that God condemned Adam for what he foresaw he would do, though he otherwise argues that election was because of foreordination and not fore-knowledge.[23] Both Bolsec and Trolliet, or anybody else, can hardly be condemned for misunderstanding Calvin here. The final triumph of the Reformation under Bullinger's leadership in Hungary came on 24 February, 1567, three years after Calvin's death, when the Hungarians called the Council of Debrecen and ruled that Bullinger's doctrinal works should become the confessions of their faith and doctrines. These works also became the basis for Hungary's state-Church relationships for several hundred years to come. The Zürich superintendent's ministry in Hungary, however, was to spread still further

[23] "Although that by the eternal Providence of God man has been created for that state of misery in which he is, yet notwithstanding he has deserved the cause of that misery for himself, and not from God. For he perishes only because of his having through perversity, degenerated from the pure nature which God had given him." See Calvin's address before the Council and the editor's quotes from the 1551 *Institutes* in the Ages Ultimate Library, Letter 301, p. 371 ff..

as the Trinitarian Controversy broke out and Bullinger was relied on by the Hungarians to defend Orthodoxy in their country. Correspondence between the two countries became so brisk that Bullinger had to appoint Ludwig Lavater (1527-1586), Josias Simler, Conrad Gessner and Johannes Wolf (1521-1571) to help him with his witness to Hungary and Poland.

Bullinger's influence amongst the Italian refugees and those persecuted in their home-country

Peter Martyr, the Florentine Reformer is indelibly associated with the Zürich Reformation as it was through the teaching of Zwingli and Bullinger that he first received new life in Christ and it was in Zürich where he was cared for by Bullinger, that he ended his earthly days. Martyr was first brought to rethink his position on Roman Catholicism through reading Zwingli's *Commentars von der wahren und falschen Religion*[24] and then proceeded to read Bullinger's works. For some time afterwards whilst he was Prior of S. Petri ad Aram in Naples and S. Frediano in Lucca, Martyr automatically began to practice the Reformed faith though still within the Roman system. Then, in 1542, the inquisition under Cardinal Caraffa, pope Paul IV and Loyola's Jesuits raised its ugly head in Italy and Martyr fled to Zürich and was received as a brother by Bullinger and his wife who soon became Martyr's close friends. Martyr lodged with Bullinger until his Swiss friend found a post in Strasburg for him. Another Italian who sought asylum under Bullinger's roof was Bernardino Ochino of Siena, a close friend of Martyr's and an expert in Latin and Greek. A further refugee from Italy, albeit a Frenchman, who had been won for the Reformed faith by reading Bullinger's books in Naples was Hieronymus Bolsec who had served in the monastery headed by Ochino. Bolsec stayed a month as Bullinger's guest and his host found him eager to learn concerning the Reformed faith and otherwise 'learned and without fault' (gelehrt und sonst unklagbar). Then Bullinger gave Bolsec a sum of money for his travelling expenses and sent him to Chur

[24] *Comments on the True and False Religion.*

with recommendations to the brethren. As no post was available there, Bolsec settled down on the banks of Lake Geneva and opened up a doctor's surgery. There he was received most unfriendlily by Calvin. Bolsec was quickly followed by Celio Secondo Curione of Piedmont with a large following, mostly composed of family members. Curione brought with him a letter of reference from Bullinger's Italian correspondent Countess Renata von Ferrara who was striving to support her fellow Reformed countrymen. Bullinger quickly found a post for Curione as rector in the newly founded academy in Lausanne. Curone was followed by Girolamo Mariano and then by Isabella Menrica de Bresegna, the wife of a Cardinal and a number of Venetian believers. Soon Bullinger found himself finding posts for Italians all over Switzerland, Geneva, Upper Germany and England. No wonder that an English bookseller wrote to Bullinger from Venice in 1547 to tell him that his commentaries were read by the Italian believers more than any other books.[25]

In two letters of thanks to Bullinger written in 1544, Curione writes:

"My fellow-countryman Girolamo Mariano cannot tell me enough about the loving reception he received at your hands and about your hospitality. He has not told me anything new. I know all about that from my own experience. How lovingly you have so often received me, how graciously you have looked after us and helped us further on our way. Yes, I know my Bullinger's godliness and his burning heart ever eager to support the persecuted brethren."

"Your friendliness and Christian care towards us whilst we stayed with you demands my most hearty thanks. Greet your wife from my wife, too, with our friendly and cordial respects. She cared for us so well and showed her love for us so clearly. Our greetings also to your children who were so tender, gracious and so ready to serve us. I belong totally to you because I am in debt to you for everything that I am."[26]

[25] *Bullinger und Seine Gattin*, p. 264.
[26] Quoted at greater length in Christoffel's *Bullinger und seine Gattin*, pp 104-5.

Outstanding in his services for the Reformation and a great friend of Bullinger's was Petrus Paulus Vergerius (1498-1565). Vergerius (Vergerio) was made Roman Catholic Bishop of his hometown Capo d'Istria in 1536. He was sent to Worms in 1541 to argue against the Protestants but, after studying the Reformers' writings carefully in order to refute them, he was persuaded of the correctness of the Reformed position. Vergerio became an ardent supporter of Bullinger but also a fine Reformer in his own right doing pioneer work in Poland and Bohemia. He eventually settled down to a writing ministry in Tübingen where he died in 1565. Though contempories viewed Vergerio as one of the key figures of the Reformation, he is sadly almost unknown today.

The Locarno Church moves *en bloc* to Zürich

One of Bullinger's labours of love which endeared him most to the Italian-speaking Christians was his care of the refugees from Locarno. The city on the banks of the Lago Maggiore[27] and most of present day Tessin had been placed under the jurisdiction of the Confederacy of Twelve (*Alteidgenossenschaft*) formed by Zürich, Bern, Clarus, Basle and Schaffhausen who had become Reformed, and Luzern, Uri, Schwyz, Unterwalden, Zug, Freiburg and Solothurn who were still papist. The Eidgenossen had been given Locarno in 1512 for their services in the North Italian wars prior to the Reformation. The cantons took it in turns to send governors or *Landvögte* to rule Locarno, each governor serving a two years' period of office. Socially, financially and morally, however, the province suffered from lack of direct control. Thanks to the evangelistic work of Giovanni Beccaria, a Reformed church of some 200 was established in the tiny city-state and under the care of the two friends Landvogt Joachim Wäldi from Clarus and Bullinger in Zürich, the believers were supplied with Bibles and Christian literature. The Church evangelised the dukedom of Milan which bordered on their territory and opened their hearts and doors to the needs of the Italian refugees. When the Swiss and Italian papists realised what was happening in this former

[27] Also called Langensee.

Roman Catholic enclave, they flooded Locarno with officials and preaching priests who began to persecute the Protestants and threaten the Protestant Swiss cantons within the *Eidgenossenschaft* with war. Bullinger's and other Reformers' books were banned. The papist cantons, who were in the majority, exiled Beccaria, who fled to Bullinger in Zürich, and ordered the Locarno Protestants to either convert back to Rome or leave the city. The congregation remained true to their faith so, on 24 November, 1554 the papist cantons, directly urged on by the pope, proclaimed that Locarno must keep the 'old faith', i.e. adhere to their popish novelties. As the staunch Protestants were familiar with Bullinger's criticisms of the 'new faith' of the papists which they presented falsely as the 'old faith', they stuck to the faith as taught by the Scriptures and were ordered to leave Locarno on 3 March, 1556 and cross the Alps to one of the Protestant cantons. One of the major accusations against the Reformed believers was that they were Anabaptists, a term Rome gave to anyone who baptised outside of their institution. Bullinger had foreseen these events as early as 1549 and had gained the support of the Council in offering Locarno every assistance. He had also contacted the churches in Bern, Basle and Schaffhausen, urging them to support the Reformed believers in Locarno. On the same day as the Locarno Christians were outlawed, Bullinger wrote to Calvin, asking his prayers for the protection of the refugees who had a long, torturous journey ahead. As the Protestants left their homes, they were accompanied for a short way by their jeering and laughing neighbours. The Locarnians' first thought had been to settle down in the Graubünden valley of Misocco but the papists barred the route and put pressure on the small Reformed Church there not to cooperate with their exiled brethren. Soon, it became apparent that there was only one place of refugee available to the exiles and that was Zürich which was already bursting its seams with refugees from all over Europe. Bullinger sent a warm hearted invitation to the pilgrims to come to Zürich. So, already weary, the Locarnians began to climb the steep, snow-filled paths of Mount St Bernard on their way to their new home from home. From 12 May onwards, a steady stream of refugees arrived in Zürich, some on foot, some on horseback and some in wagons. They numbered one hundred and twenty grown-ups and eighty children. The town had already organised quarters and collected bedding, clothing and other necessities of life for the two hundred refugees. As the city was already full of 'guests', food prices had risen enormously so the city opened up their corn reserves for free distribution to the weary travellers. At the insistence of Bullinger, places of worship were set up for the Italian-speakers and the Locarno people were placed under their own pastors who were financed by Zürich.

Bullinger and his wife worked out a scheme for financing the refugees until they found work and permanent accommodation and collected money from ready givers whose pockets were already strained. Bullinger wrote to Calvin, informing him of the sound character of the Locarno Christians but the most famous of the teachers who Bullinger set over them disgraced the Locarno Church. This was Bernardino Ochino who, in his old age, began to challenge the Trinity, Christian morals and monogamy and thus had to be expelled from his post and the city by the Zürich Council who had shown him so much benevolence. Ochino toured Poland and Moravia with his poisonous teaching and loose living until he died of the plague in 1564.

The common father of the afflicted

The relatively large number of children left without parents by the Kappel wars and the plague was a strain on public funds so Bullinger encouraged his colleagues to adopt the orphans. Though Bullinger and his wife had a large family themselves, they set an example by taking in several youngsters such as Zwingli's children Regula and Ulrich[28] and Rudolf Gualter, who had been Bullinger's pupil at Kappel. Bullinger enabled Gualter to study in Basle, Strasburg, Lausanne and Marburg. Gualter eventually married Zwingli's daughter, Regula, and became first Jud's successor at St Peter's and then Bullinger's successor at the Great Minster. Bullinger also took in Heinrich Lavater so that he could attend school in Zürich. Bullinger and his fellow ministers also opened their

[28] Zwingli's son Wilhelm was taken care of by Lienhard Tremp in Bern and mentored by Berchtold Haller.

homes to the English persecuted under Henry VIII and Mary the Bloody. Extant is a letter written by James Pilkington who had stayed at the Bullingers' and was now visiting Geneva on his way to the largest church of British exiles on the Continent at Frankfurt. The letter is addressed to Bullinger's protégé Rudolf Gualter and says:

"Whom can we English salute with greater reason than you, our good masters at Zürich, by whom we have been regarded as brethren? And to whom else can I especially, whom you have so liberally entertained far beyond my other friends, wish grace and life in my frequent and affectionate letters, rather than to yourself?" Pilkington continues, "Let this my letter, I pray you, salute as affectionately as possible that common father of the afflicted, master Bullinger, to whom, as he so richly deserves, I wish every happiness; and since the Lord has made you witnesses of my affliction, go on, as you have begun, to love me, to help me by your counsel, and entreat the Lord for me in your prayers, that I may again be restored to you, when it shall seem him good."[29]

The clergy supported Bullinger almost without question and welcomed all his reforms which were also supported, after initial doubts, by the entire Council. Here again, we see the difference between Zürich and Geneva where inner strife robbed both Church and state of their peace until the late fifteen fifties. The letters of Pellican in the Zürich city archives reveal this great unity amongst the Zürich clergy. The Hebrew scholar writes to friends of the Reformation:

"During the nineteen years in which I have served the Zürich Church, there has never been a quarrel regarding doctrine amongst our clergy … Bullinger, the Superintendent of the Church and Bibliander the teacher of theology understood each other perfectly and in the most beautiful harmony ruled the Church."[30]

---

[29] *Original Letters*, Vol. I, pp. 134-136.
[30] See Schulthess-Rechberg, p. 50.

An exchange student testifies

In 1548, John ab Ulmis, born in Thurgau and a descendent of a long line of Swabian gentry, left his studies under Bullinger to matriculate at Oxford where he proceeded to take his MA and eventually became a Fellow of St. John's College. A large number of letters addressed to 'the faithful patron of all students', and signed "your most attached pupil" have been preserved and show how avidly Bullinger sought news of the English situation and how eagerly Ulmis told him of all that was happening amongst the Reformers. Judging by the many greetings Ulmis sent from leading churchmen, there must have been few men and women of the English Reformation who did not think it important to be on good terms with Bullinger. Thanks to his position in society, the fact that he was closely related to the Blaurers and other Reformed friends of England abroad and his close relationship to Bullinger, all doors were opened for Ulmis by both Church and state during his four years at Oxford. Writing soon after his arrival in England, Ulmis tells Bullinger:

"You must know then that England, which I have entered under favourable auspices, but not without very great pecuniary expense, is adorned and enlightened by the word of God; and that the number of the faithful is daily increasing in vast multitudes more and more. The mass, that darling of the papists, is shaken, and in many places its condition corresponds with its name; that is, by the best of rights, namely, a divine right, it is condemned, and with a safe conscience entirely abolished. The images too are extirpated root and branch in every part of England; nor is there left the least trace which can afford a hope or handle to the papists for confirming their error respecting images, and for leading away the people from our Saviour. Holy wedlock, too, is now free to the clergy and sanctioned by the king himself. It has been proved by Peter Martyr to the great satisfaction [of his hearers], both from the writings of the orthodox, as well as from the holy scriptures, that there is no other purgatory than the cross to which we wretched beings are exposed in this life. He has also maintained in like manner the cause of the eucharist and holy supper of the Lord, namely, that it is a remembrance of Christ, and a solemn setting forth of his death, and not a sacrifice. Meanwhile, however, he speaks with caution and prudence (if indeed it can be called such) with respect to the real presence, so as not to seem to incline either to your opinion, or to that of Luther. But the public preachers for the most part openly and candidly confute, according to their ability, the notion of a carnal partaking [of the Lord's supper], and have brought over a considerable number to this their opinion. The Capernaites, papists, and this class of sarcophagists, are not sleeping, by whose weapons the truth is attacked; but, by the grace of God, it is never wounded; nay, rather they themselves are perishing miserably and pierced through by their own swords and sophisms."[31]

Ulmis[32] wrote in Latin and his pun on the mass's condition corresponding to its name is not directly translatable into English. The term 'missa', apart from meaning the mass, can also mean 'dismissed'. Concerning university life at Oxford, Ulmis writes "it everywhere abounds with excellent and most agreeable writers, and is adorned with great numbers of men who are most distinguished in every kind of learning; and as to myself; that I can enjoy in this place to my heart's content both sacred and profane studies, with the entire liberty of a most delightful and honourable leisure." Foremost in Ulmis' praise of his teachers is Richard Cox the university Chancellor whom he finds Reformed in every single doctrine. It is easy to read between the lines and see that Cox is especially favouring Ulmis because of their mutual love and respect for Bullinger. Indeed, if we are to believe Ulmis, and he supports all he says with a good deal of evidence, Bullinger was looked on at Oxford as being absent in the body but everywhere present in the spirit. Ulmis also testifies to the fact that Bullinger's books were being rapidly translated into English. Concerning Hooper, who studied several years under Bullinger, Ulmis says that he never heard or saw anyone who spoke more piously and with greater kindness respecting Switzerland, and especially Bullinger's Church. When Ulmis comes to praise Peter Martyr,

[31] *Original Letters*, Vol, II, p. 377-8.
[32] Ab Ulmis' son of the same name took on the name of Ulmer. He, too, studied at Oxford.

then a Professor at Oxford,[33] it almost seems as if he is giving himself a little too much importance as he writes to Bullinger:

"I must tell you that I am most intimate with Peter Martyr, not as a pupil, but as a son; for as I delight to hear him, so I ardently love his peculiar suavity. I pass whole hours with him, so that I have henceforth no occasion for any introduction. If you desire to read any of the lectures or disputations of Peter Martyr, I will send them to you; for I have them all written out, and with Martyr's own corrections."[34]

Further influence of Bullinger's educational policies abroad

Sadly, a number of French students who trained under Bullinger left Zürich in the 1550s to fall into the hands of French King Henry II's inquisitors who quickly had them burnt at the stake. Then Bullinger heard similar threats from Italy and that the pope's legate had publicly damned him and had his books burnt in public. Even Bullinger's Dutch students were told that they were not welcome in the Dutch states and, under pressure from Emperor Charles V, Bullinger's books were burnt at Löwe. The Hungarian, Romanian and Bulgarian students were in particular danger as Protestants were attacked on the one flank by the pope and on the other by the Turks. Here, Bullinger's influence became great and through his teaching and writing he was able to help build a church there which covered a vast area. He also carried out a written ministry to the Hungarian prisoners in Turkish camps in Thrace and along the Aegean coast. Here he was supported by Hungary's ambassadors abroad such as Johannes Féjertóy who was a Hungarian diplomat in Vienna. Sandwiched between Rome and the Turks, the Hungarians asked Bullinger whether they should flee the country or not but Bullinger urged them to keep up their witness in Hungary. To build them up in the faith, he sent them a 'letter' of 50 chapters covering the faith, hope and love necessary in

---

[33] Martyr had to leave Strasburg in 1548 because of pressure from Charles V and became Regius Professor of Hebrew at Oxford in that year. He had to flee Oxford during the Marian persecutions and eventually returned to Strasburg before taking up a post in Zürich where he spent the last few years of his life.

[34] Ibid, p. 410.

Christian witness. This document became the Confession of Faith of the Hungarian Church and was the forerunner of the Second Helvetic Confession.

The Bullingers' house in Zürich

Chapter 4

Bullinger, Calvin and the Reformation in Geneva

Geneva and the Eidgenossenschaft

What is today called French-Switzerland was mostly a foreign country seen from the point of view of the Swiss political confederacies at the beginning of the Reformation. The largest French-speaking cities, Geneva and Neuchâtel (Neuenburg) and the entire Pays de Vaud (Waadt) were under the jurisdiction and administration of Savoy and traditionally looked to France and Italy for their culture and political alliances. The city of Geneva had been under the direct rule of the Roman Catholic Church for almost two hundred years and for the past century a series of prince-bishops of the House of Savoy had kept the city isolated from the political and religious improvements enjoyed by their neighbours the Swiss Germans. Bern, after accepting the Reformation and in defiance of Charles of Savoy, had cleared French-speaking Geneva of his troops and papal influence by the fifteen thirties and now dominated the city's politics, culture and religion. Bern, however, was not the originator of the Genevan Reformation, though they supported it in their special way. Gottfried W. Locher in his re-estimation of the development of the Swiss

Reformation sees the work of the gospel in Geneva as developing gradually amongst ordinary people. He therefore writes:

"The city of Geneva became Protestant (evangelisch) through the influence of Zwinglian, Lutheran and Erasmian writings and disputing refugees long before Calvin appeared. This was purely a lay movement. The man-in-the-street finally forced the Episcopal hierarchy against its will to enter into these disputations."[1]

Early disagreements between Bern and Calvin

Antony Froment and William Farel were encouraged by Bern to minister to the budding Reformation's needs in Geneva, but both Bern's council and clergy rarely agreed with the way the Reformation progressed in the city-state once Calvin entered Geneva. This is certainly one of the main reasons why Bern's occupation of Geneva was half-hearted, and the city-state neglected to strive for a lasting agreement with Savoy until 1564, the year of Calvin's death. This half-heartedness almost led to a break between Bern and Geneva in 1543 concerning the borders of the former Genevan Lord-Bishop's domains. This would have certainly meant that the Savoy would have striven to regain Geneva and Bullinger feared that the Emperor, whose presence was rarely felt in the Vaud, would claim Geneva for his own and then hand her administration back to the Savoy Lords. Happily, Bullinger's diplomacy came to the rescue. The Zürich Superintendent had a canny knowledge of the ins and outs of international politics and pressed both Bern and Geneva to meet for arbitration so that the two cities' problems could be solved in the Reformed camp. Bullinger's enormous prestige and influence won the day and the two cities decided to keep their status quo through fear of a papist takeover of Geneva. At this time the Bernese were being infiltrated by Lutheranism but Bullinger managed when vacancies occurred in the Bernese clergy to have fully Reformed men put in their stead and thus, by 1548, the tide had turned. It is of note that Calvin also tried to have one of

[1] *Huldrych Zwingli in neuer Sicht*, p. 21.

his closest followers, Franz Hotman, placed strategically in Bern in 1549 but this was thwarted by the Bernese, according to Calvin, because of their personal animosity to him.[2] It was Hotman, from his position in Basle who suggested to Calvin, after reading Sebastian Castellio's notes to his Latin translation of the New Testament, that Castellio was writing against Calvin personally, though Calvin's name was nowhere mentioned. Another example of Bullinger's influence in placing the right man in the right place at the right time was when Melanchthon's protégé, Simon Sulzer, once an influential Bernese church leader[3] was compelled to leave Bern but given a chair in Hebrew at Basle, Bullinger had his own protégé and son of Zürich, Johannes Haller, take his place and he became the Bernese Superintendent although still in his twenties. Basle's church, too, was in the hands of Bullinger's close friend Myconius, formerly of Zürich who had also gained his position through Bullinger's intervention. Here, it is of note that Calvin allied with Lutheran-minded Sulzer from time to time at Bern in an effort to gain a hearing in the city and when Sulzer moved to Basle, Calvin more or less dropped canvassing Myconius with his views and concentrated on finding a foothold for them in Basle through Sulzer.[4] This did not improve the two cities' opinion of Calvin. Haller was initially antagonistic towards Calvin, but was won over by Bullinger to a more moderate opinion. Both Haller and Myconius, however, had a difficult time in their churches as there was not the same harmony between Church and state as in Zürich. When Myconius died in 1552, Wittenberg's man in Switzerland Sulzer took over the leadership of the Church and immediately caused Bullinger and Zürich problems.

Though Bullinger exercised a great personal influence on Geneva for thirty years and Zürich served as a diplomatic buffer between Bern and Geneva, Zürich only entered into a confederacy with Geneva in 1584, nine years after Bullinger's death and twenty years after Calvin's. By this

---

[2] Letter to Haller dated 26 November 1549, Ages Ultimate Library CD.

[3] The Lutherans had trained Sulzer at Wittenberg in the hope that he would return to Bern and lead the canton into Lutheranism. See Melanchthon in Europe, pp. 50 and 80.

[4] See Uwe Plath's *Calvin und Basle in den Jahren 1552-1556*, p. 26 ff. and passim for information concerning the often-changing friendship of Sulzer and Calvin.

time, Geneva had been almost emptied of its former ruling classes and had been flooded with French refugees. This caused great friction and rivalry in the city at first because of the fierce patriotism of the Genevans and their fear of a French takeover. It was the patriots called the *Eidguenots* or *Eidgenossen* (Companions of the Oath) who had appealed to Bern to drive out the Mamelukes, or Savoy party and once they were gone, they fought for a Geneva for the Genevans. The hated occupiers were called Mamelukes (Arabic: mamlūk = slave) because of parallels seen with the action of the Caucasian slaves who seized the throne of Egypt in 1254 and subdued the city. This explains why Calvin, a Frenchman, was as hated by the patriots as he was by Bern and his success as a Reformer grew with the gallicizing of the city and the Pays de Vaud so that Geneva only began to experience inner political and religious stability in the late fifteen-fifties when many of the leading Geneva families who had opposed Calvin for various reasons had either fled, were banished or had been executed. This fact underlines the main differences between Bullinger and Calvin. The former was the organiser, keeper and counsellor of a local church which longed for a full Reformation. Bullinger had few if any, internal critics and most of the Reforms he turned his hand too prospered. Once other churches, such as that of England saw the success of Bullinger's action, they, too, were willing to be influenced by him. Calvin was a hard-pressed man who lived in a city going through hard, revolutionary times. His Geneva was challenged both politically and spiritually by many an enemy. His sojourn of a little over a quarter of a century in Geneva was a hard struggle from beginning to end. Through this experience, he became the spokesman of many a foreign and especially French church that was going through persecution. Where peace reigned both for State and Church in other countries such as England, he became the most unwilling spokesman of the revolutionary and separatist parties who sadly isolated his revolutionary ideas from much of his pastoral and exegetical teaching and followed the former more than the latter. Thus Calvin's present reputation in England is that of a strict, dogmatic and philosophical critic of the status quo whereas Bullinger is remembered for his conservative, peaceful approach which leads even serious scholars to believe that he was far too peace-loving and mild in his theology to clearly reflect the just sovereignty of God. Both these pictures deviate from the historical figures of Calvin and Bullinger. They serve to explain, however, why Bullinger's reputation in Cromwellian and post-Cromwellian England dwindled, whereas Calvin's revolutionary side became a standard which still holds sway amongst Presbyterians and Congregationalists and has left the Church of England all the weaker for their separation. It is thus high time that the real Calvin and the real Bullinger of history should be known. It is this author's sad experience that the little the English-speaking world knows about Bullinger and the great deal that is professed to be known concerning Calvin is more of the stuff that dreams are made of than a knowledge of sheer, historical, balanced fact.

The theological and literary background to Calvin's *Institutes*

Dating Calvin's conversion is not easy but it appears that he must have renounced Rome shortly before 1534.[5] After publishing on Seneca's *De Clementia* and writing a small work against soul-sleep called *Psychopannychia* aimed at the Anabaptists, Calvin's first Reformed work was published in 1536.[6] This was a "wee booklet" as Calvin called it, measuring approximately two and a half inches by four and a half inches of type per page and composed of six chapters and entitled *Christianae Religionis Institutio*. The letter to Francis I of France which preceded the work is dated 23 August, 1535 in the name of the persecuted Protestants of France but the systematic work appended was published after the drawing up of the First Helvetic Confession in Basle in March, 1536. This work has received such a wide acclamation amongst modern Calvinists as a pioneer work in systematic theology that it is often forgotten that Calvin's contemporaries were not only easily abreast of the Frenchman in their reforming theology but had preceded him in similar

[5] See François Wendel's *Calvin* for a lengthy discussion concerning Calvin's conversion.
[6] Concerning Calvin's two publications before his *Institutes* Principal Tulloch writes: "They are ... more like the exercitations of a student than the productions of a mind strongly moved by religious reforming zeal." *Luther and the Leaders of the Reformation*, p. 188.

works. Calvin's enormous dependence on Martin Bucer (1491-1551) for the contents of his *Institutes*, especially the editions after 1539, has been outlined in Lang's *The Sources of Calvin's Institutes*, Evangelical Quarterly, 1936 and Wendel's *Calvin*, 1963. We are also indebted to Ford Lewis Battles' *Analysis of the Institutes of the Christian Religion*, for information showing Bucer's influence on Calvin regarding prayer and predestination and further ideas for his *Institutes*. It is clear that Calvin leaned heavily on Bucer's theological presentations, including even his sections and subsections, in authoring subsequent editions of the *Institutes*. Thus older writers such as Gustav Anrich claim that it was Bucer who was the father of Calvinism and not Calvin.[7] Sadly Martin Bucer's great reforming theology is as lost today as is Bullinger's.

Richard A. Miller in his *Ordo docendi: Melanchthon and the Organisation of Calvin's Institutes, 1536-1543*, [8] argues that though Calvin's name and reputation are inseparably joined to his *Institutes*, the main idea behind Calvin's work was supplied by Philip Melanchthon in the 1535 edition of his *Loci communes theologici* and in his work on the theology of Paul's letter to the Romans. Melanchthon's *Loci* was indeed the pioneer Reformed systematic theology and was used as a standard by generations of systematic theologians up to modern times. However, it is equally obvious that much in Calvin's brief work, published in Basle, reflects the influence of Zwingli who had sent a similar letter to Francis I in 1525, and an exposition of Christian doctrine to the French King in 1531, shortly before Zwingli's death. The view that Calvin was very much dependent on Zwingli has been developing in recent years. In 1966 Alexandre Ganoczy presented his view to a surprised readership that Calvin had relied heavily on Zwingli's *Commentarius de vera et falsa religione* in composing his 1536 Institutes. Sadly, this work did not reach the English speaking public until over twenty years later. Ganoczy draws up a long list of parallels between the two works starting with the same

---

[7] *Martin Bucer*, Strasburg, 1914, pp. 143-144.

[8] Found in *Melanchthon in Europe: His Work and Influence beyond Europe*. Miller is thinking primarily of Calvin's recasting of his 1536 edition in his 1539 edition which became the true basis for further editions.

thoughts expressed in each and going on to show verbatim borrowings. Ernst Saxer in his *Calvin's reformatorisches Anliegen* published in 1970 shows how many terms used in a particular way by Zwingli were taken over and given the same connotations by Calvin. In 1986, Fritz Büsser presented his *Elements of Zwingli's Thought in Calvin's Institutes* at the International Calvin Symposium at McGill University and elaborated on and extended his findings in his *Die Prophezei* of 1994 in his chapter "Grundgedanken Zwingli's in Calvin's 'Institutio'". Since then, scholars on both sides of the Atlantic have begun to reconsider radically the long-held opinion that the *Institutes* were unique to Calvin and his personal pioneering genius.

In February, 1536, whilst Bullinger was working on the Helvetic Confession, he met Calvin for the first time. At this theological workshop, Bullinger announced that the First Helvetic Confession should be a continuation of the Swiss Reformation as expressed in Zwingli's *In Expositionem Fidei ad Regem Christianum Expositio* of 1531 which was re-published parallel with the Confession. This work was a systematic presentation of the Christian faith which Zwingli had given to Francis I. Bullinger's aim was to show that Luther's wild criticism that Zwingli was a heretic and an Anabaptist had no grounds whatsoever. It was merely because Luther was ignorant of Zwingli's written works and confessed that he could not understand his spoken words and was basically very prejudiced. In his foreword to the *Expositio*, Bullinger said that he was reprinting it as "an answer to all slanderers of the evangelical faith and evangelical preaching and to give them an *apologeticum quondam absolutum*. So as to bring the work up to date on Reformation issues, Bullinger added a treatise on the Protestant Lord's Supper and the Roman Mass and a liturgy to be used at the communion service.[9] Without needing to speculate as to whether Calvin's work was, as Ford Lewis Battles says of Calvin's Seneca Commentary, a 'learned parroting of various classical views',[10] it does appear that Calvin wanted to do for

[9] See Rudolf Pfister's Introduction to the *Expositio* in Vol. 11 of Zwingli Hauptschriften, Zwingli Verlag, Zürich, pp. 297-299.
[10] *Institutes of the Christian Religion: 1536 Edition*, p. xxv.

French readers what had already been done for readers of the various German dialects between 1520 and 1536. Calvin's action is most untypical of the Reformers, however, in that his *Institutes* gives few sources and Calvin does not acknowledge his obvious enormous reliance on the works of other, first generation, Reformers. It was as if, in seeking to support and teach the second generation of Protestants in France, Calvin wished to be seen as going entirely his own way.

It is interesting to note how scholars, in writing on one subject as a notable event, tend to close their eyes to others which occurred at the same time, and which would make their subject less remarkable. M. Howard Reinstra, Director of the H. H. Meeter Center for Calvin Studies in his Preface to Ford Lewis Battles' edition of the 1536 *Institutes* says, "1536 was not a particularly memorable year", and he goes on to say of Basle, "In that year, in that city, an aging scholar died, and a younger scholar published the first edition of his 'little book', as he affectionately called it." This reference to the death of Erasmus and the debut of Calvin as a systematic theologian leaves out the historical fact that the *First Helvetic Confession* was drawn up at Basle early in 1536, thus paving the way for the Reformed Church which Calvin was to join thirteen years later at the signing of the *Consensus Tigurinus*. It also fails to see the historical and theological importance of the drawing up of the Helvetic Confession in which the leading Swiss-German Reformers distanced themselves from the popish teaching which they saw in Luther's attitude to the sacraments. Furthermore, it fails to appreciate the lasting importance of Bullinger's extended publication of Zwingli's *Expositio*, a work which is still highly favoured amongst Reformed scholars and still in print and which outlined long before 1536 elements of Reformed teaching on the Lord's Supper which Calvin was not to acknowledge tentatively until 1549.

The *Institutes* as a compilation of contemporary Reformed thought

Though many scholars have emphasised Calvin's dependence on Melanchthon, Zwingli and Bucer, few have compared Calvin's *Institutes* with Bullinger's works. Walter Hollweg in his *Heinrich Bullingers*

Hausbuch written in 1956 devotes an entire chapter to Bullinger's enormous influence on Calvin's *Institutes*, in particular the 1550 version.[11] He states that Calvin is not guilty of plagiarism but leaves the impression that Calvin avoids the charge merely by rewording Bullinger in the numerous passages taken from him. Hollweg points out that Calvin not only included Bullinger's themes and Scriptural proofs but even the examples Bullinger gives to illustrate them. Gillian Lewis, writing in 1986 has obviously little to say about Bullinger's influence as Calvin is his subject. However, soon after writing of Calvin's death, Lewis turns her gaze on Bullinger and, not surprisingly, but rather critically, says that Bullinger sat like a spider in the centre of the web of the Reformation.[12] When we turn to evidence given in the recent works of Fritz Büsser, especially his *Die Prophezei* of 1994 in which he compares Calvin closely with Bullinger, we find there is just cause to question the idea that is so dominant in today's Reformed churches that Calvin, under God, was the rock on which the Reformed faith was built.

As one studies the growth of Calvin's *Institutes* from the six chapters of the first 1536 edition to the eighty chapters of the last 1559 edition one is amazed at the industry of the author. However, it is a compendium of Wittenburg, Strasburg and Zürich theology with very little new thought in it. Indeed, the doctrines which are outlined in it were fixed Reformed doctrines long before the major editions of the *Institutes* were written. Thus any influence this work has had on the theological development of other countries such as Holland, England, Scotland and the New World, is because of the thorough-going Reforms of Saxony, Pomerania, Hessen, the Palatine and the Swiss and Upper German states which had already produced enough spiritual giants to transform Protestant world theology. Though Calvin's name alone is on the title page, its contents proudly proclaim the names of Zwingli, Melanchthon, Bucer, Capito and Bullinger besides Calvin's own. This goes also for Calvin's church order which is built solidly on the Strasburg orders. The one big difference

[11] See Chapter 3, Der Einfluss des Buches auf die Institutio Calvins und den Heidelberger Katechismus.
[12] *International Calvinism*, p. 67.

between the French-speaking Reformation and the Swiss-German Reformation is that the former viewed the ordinances of baptism and the Lord's Supper as methods of establishing church discipline whereas the latter saw them as modes of preaching the gospel to all who would receive it. Unlike Calvin, Zwingli and Bullinger never sought to discipline their people by threats of exclusion from the privileges of sitting under the gospel.

The Sixteenth Century Demand for Bullinger's and Calvin's works

Calvin did not reach the international eye until the 1540s. Even then and as late as 1550, Calvin had published little, especially on sermons and preaching, whereas people were reading literally hundreds of Bullinger's sermons and doctrinal works in several languages. So, too, it is important to note that Bullinger outlived Calvin by twelve years throughout which he published many works and gained in international recognition. Bullinger's 124 major theses, not counting his thousands of tracts and letters, were initially in far greater demand than Calvin's, though Calvin's popularity grew in the early 17th century almost solely through the impact of his *Institutes*, and Bullinger's waned throughout the period of the Great Rebellion. He had allied himself too much with the Church of England in the opinion of many Presbyterians, Independents and Dissenters who then traditionally turned to Calvin rather than Bullinger, falsely believing Calvin had a more Congregational and Separatist church order. However, the doctrines first re-introduced by Bullinger after popish dogmas had plagued the nations for centuries have remained fundamental to the Puritan cause though they have lived on under the inappropriate name of 'Calvinism'. This is especially the case regarding Bullinger's teaching on the Word of God, the Covenant and the Sabbath. What Bullinger has to say about the covenant is of special importance in the development of the Reformed faith as from it, he developed his doctrine of predestination, salvation, sanctification and justification, which became hallmarks of the Reformation. So, too, Bullinger developed his teaching on the covenant and predestination in relation to his Christology rather than to the arbitrary, philosophical *fiat* of many later 'Calvinistic' Puritans.

Immanuel Leuschner relates in his *Bullinger's Wirken in Zürich* how neither Zwingli's nor Luther's nor Calvin's teaching concerning the covenant is as central to their theology as it is to Bullinger's. Yet it is Bullinger's covenant teaching which has survived as the basis of Reformed theology.[13] It must also be remembered that Bullinger's works were widely circulated in England some thirty to thirty-five years before Calvin's[14] and during the 16th century there were well over fifty European printers turning out hundreds of editions of Bullinger's reforming works in at least five languages. Within a hundred years, at least 400 editions of Bullinger's works had been printed in Switzerland alone and some 230 editions in other countries, including England. Throughout the 16th century, Bullinger was easily the most read Continental Reformer in England so that by the 1550s, he was invariably referred to as 'that famouse clerke' as if everybody would know who was meant.

French reception of Bullinger's pioneer work in the Reformation

Calvin has rightly gained recognition for his interest in the development of the Reformation in his own country of France but Bullinger's influence in France is far less known. Bullinger kept an observant eye on all that was happening in Calvin's home-country and reckoned several French diplomats, ambassadors and churchmen amongst his many correspondents, such as d'Aubespine, the Abbot of Bassefontaine and John de Fresse, the Bishop of Bayonne. Bullinger told de Fresse, "I love France because she has produced so many martyrs and more true believers than any other country."[15] His interest became all the more acute when Henry II of France waged war with the Emperor in Italy and both sides canvassed for support amongst the German-speaking nations. So, too, Switzerland was automatically drawn into French politics especially at this time because of the French demand for Swiss mercenaries. Several letters are extant of Bullinger's correspondence with

[13] See Blanke and Leuschner, *Heinrich Bullinger: Vater der Reformierten Kirche*, p. 279 and extensive footnote on p. 323.

[14] See Benjamin Warfield's fine essay entitled *On the Literary History of the Institutes* for Calvin's reception in England, Works, Vol. V, *Calvin and Calvinism*.

[15] Pestalozzi, p. 437.

Henry II whom he sought to win for the Reformation as also his letters to influential men and women in England concerning English support for the war-torn French Protestants. In 1551, Bullinger addressed his *von des Christen Vollkommenheit*[16] to Henry II, pleading for tolerance for the French Protestants. Bullinger reminded the King of the old French Royal slogan, "Christ is victorious, Christ reigns and Christ commands". Bullinger published the work in Latin and German but Beza translated it into French and Peter Vergerio into Italian.

Bullinger's influence in France was greatly strengthened through his connections with Theodore Beza (1519-1605), which began long before Beza joined Calvin in Geneva and continued over a decade after Calvin's death. Beza had come to accept the Reformed faith round 1535 chiefly through reading Bullinger's earlier work *De origine erroris in Divorum ac simulachorum cultus* of 1529 on the origin of error which went through several Genevan printings in the 1540s. Beza wrote to Bullinger on 18 August, 1568 to tell him:

"Granted that I know Christ today, that is that I live, I owe this to a great extent to your book. Through this book, especially in that part where you reject the lies of Jerome, the Lord opened my eyes so that I could see the light of truth. From this source, I began to owe to you the agency and instrument of my eternal salvation."[17]

Beza became one of Bullinger's most faithful correspondents and no less than 275 of Beza's letters to Bullinger are extant compared to 115 from Calvin. Very many of these letters are taken up with the Reformation in France in which Beza solicits advice from Bullinger as to how to proceed. When Beza, for instance, heard of the terrible massacre of Protestants on Bartholomew's Day, 1572, it was to Bullinger, that he first confessed his sorrow and fears and asked his Swiss friend for his

---

[16] *On the Christian's Perfection.* The work is not about the subjective perfection of the Christian but the fact that Christ becomes All-in-All to him.

[17] Translated from Büsser's account of Bullinger and Beza in Vol. 2 of his Bullinger biography, pp., 137-138.

prayers and requested him to use his international influence to help his persecuted countrymen. Beza felt the loneliness of his position greatly in Geneva and thus confessed to Bullinger that he had become his father with whom he could discuss all things. In May 1552, Bullinger was again active in defence of the French Church when five French students returned to Lyon from their theological training in Lausanne and were immediately arrested as 'heretics'. Bullinger heard of the case through Beza and immediately used his right to stand before the Council to beg them to use all the diplomacy in their powers to prevent the students' threatened execution. The Zürich ambassador at the French court was then commanded to bring the matter up before King Henry. Sadly, the ambassador merely received insults from the King for representing 'a country of rebels and wicked people' and the young martyrs were burnt at the stake. Bullinger wrote to moderate French ambassador Abbot d'Aubespine, soon to become the Bishop of Limoges concerning the five young martyrs, saying:

"Those men of faith were not Anabaptists nor were they influenced by any other heresy but enjoyed the true faith to which the Swiss also profess. In both ancient and modern times God's punishment never failed to reach the persecutors of the Christians. It is a terrible, terrible thing to fall into the hands of the living God!"[18]

In another letter to the ambassador he told him that his king would come to a miserable end for allowing 'blood-men' to rule his country and begged him to do all in his power to persuade the King to have mercy on the innocent Protestants.

On hearing how the perverse act had brought gloom over the French Church, Bullinger wrote to Calvin to encourage him to battle on:

"Let us turn with still more fervour to God. He is still alive who delivered His people out of Egypt. He is still alive who brought back the

[18] *Bullinger und Seine Gattin*, p.115.

prisoners out of Babel. He is still alive who dethrones Emperors, Kings and Dukes but protects His Church. We must go through much tribulation in entering the Kingdom of God. But woe be to them who harm the apple of God's eye! We shall continue to be steadfast in expounding God's Word, in preaching the gospel of Christ and, in doing so, keep our gaze with all the saints fixed heavenwards. He will not forsake us who has promised, 'Lo, I am with you always, even unto the end of the world. In the world ye shall have tribulation: but be of good cheer; I have overcome the world.' Christ will preserve us and His Church!"[19]

When Henry II died in 1559 and sixteen-year-old Francis II (the husband of Mary Stuart) came to the throne, Bullinger immediately sent the new king a copy of his *Unterweisung in der Christlichen Religion* (Instruction in the Christian Religion). By 1572, Bullinger felt himself too old and frail to take up his pen to write a major theological work but when he heard of the terrible slaughter of Protestants on Bartholomew's Night, 1572, he quickly wrote and published, though then crippled with pain and weakness, his *On the Persecutions of the Church* (Von der Verfolgungen der Kirche).

Most analysts of Bullinger's works have come from the German and Dutch-speaking nations but though Calvin's works were rarely printed in Zürich and it took several decades before they were translated into German, the Genevan printing houses were industrious in publishing Bullinger's works in French. In 1939 André Bouvier published his masterly work of 593 pages entitled *Henri Bullinger: réformateur et conseiller oecuménique*. The work was printed in Paris and Neuchâtel in 1940 and reprinted in Geneva in 1979. Bouvier whose mother Mathilde Ott, was a descendent of both Zwingli and Bullinger, provides us with a most refreshing French look at our subject, and outlines his immense importance in the French-speaking world, especially in strengthening the Huguenots and introducing the French humanists to a sound Christian faith. Naturally, in an area which most non-French-speaking Reformers

[19] Ibid, p. 113.

appear to believe was reformed principally by Calvin's influence, whatever Bouvier has to tell us of Bullinger and the French is of great interest and importance. However, Bouvier's work is a formidable obstacle for any reader as the author obviously believes that those who read him are as gifted linguistically as he is himself and he turns from French to German, then to Swiss German and Latin without ever a hint of a translation. This is the genius of Swiss theologians who, because of their multi-lingual nation, all seem to have at least three languages given them in their cradles.[20] When comparing Bullinger with the other great men of the Continental Reformation, Bouvier claims that Luther was the prophet, Zwingli was the civic, Calvin was the scholar-teacher and Bullinger was the pastor, historian and exegete. He maintains that whereas Calvin was the greater logician, Bullinger was the better psychologist, especially in expounding the doctrines of grace. He also makes it clear that though Calvin was a great moralist, it was Bullinger who was more able to reveal the loving side of God to the sinner rather than the moral judge. Bullinger, educated in Germany, knew no French and he was only known in the French-speaking world through his Latin works and translations, yet Bouvier shows how Bullinger was able to capture the French spirit and one gains the impression that Bouvier, who in his own background merges German and French culture, feels that Bullinger was more traditionally 'French' in his conduct and Calvin more traditionally 'German'. On reading Bouvier's summing up of his position regarding Bullinger, he obviously believes that if strangers to the Reformed churches wish to open a door of understanding to the Reformed faith, it is Bullinger and not Calvin who can best provide that door. He reasons that Bullinger has the edge on Calvin because of the way he deals with God's grace, and the gospel and above all in the way he places Christ at the centre of his theology. Calvin, to Bouvier is the theoretician whereas Bullinger is the practitioner.

---

[20] This is also true of Peter Opitz's great work on Bullinger published in 2004 *Heinrich Bullinger als Theologe: Eine Studie zu den 'Dekaden'*, in which the Swiss author writes in a multi-lingual style with copious footnotes which would baffle anyone not familiar with at least three languages and as many German and Swiss-German dialects.

We gain an insight into the Genevan respect for Bullinger in the *Registres du Conseil* which records Beza's nomination as Calvin's successor on 18 August, 1564. In discussing what powers Beza should have, the Council ruled that he should become a minister under the same conditions as the ministry held by Bullinger, Bucer, Oecolampadius and Calvin. In the context, the order of the names is obviously of major importance.[21] We must note, too, that when the Genevan authorities gave permission for the *Institutes* to be printed in Geneva, they ruled that they were to be published alongside doctrinal works of Bullinger for the sake of a comprehensive balance. At least a dozen major works from Bullinger's pen appeared in various French editions from the Genevan Press. During the years 1550-1565, according to Büsser,[22] his sermons on the Apocalypse in French ran into no less than 11 Genevan editions and his *Summa* reached 13 editions under the title *Résolution de tous les points de la religion chrestiens*. If we compare this with the French versions of Calvin's *Institutes*, printed at Geneva over the same period, according to the table provided by Alister McGrath,[23] two editions had appeared before 1550 but only eight editions followed between 1550-1565. This means that during Calvin's ministry in Geneva, the printers there were more industrious in making Bullinger known than in promoting Calvin's major work. Geneva, however, was not the end target of Bullinger's works in French but he used the city-state as an agent in distributing his works throughout French-speaking regions. Thus Bouvier, Hollweg and Büsser all quote Frenchman Franz Hotman who in a letter dated 1 February, 1572, congratulating Bullinger on his fortieth anniversary as Superintendent of the Zürich Church, told him that he was no less popular in France than in Switzerland and that his sermons on Revelation had been a major factor in turning Frenchmen from the tyranny of Antichrist.[24] It is interesting to note that most of Bullinger's

---

[21] See Choisy's *L'état Chrétien Calviniste à Genève*, Chapters 1-2.
[22] Büsser's *Büllinger* biography, Vol. 2. p. 187.
[23] *John Calvin: Eine Biographie*, pp. 187-188.
[24] Bouvier, p. 367, Hollweg, p. 78 and note 16, Büsser, Vol. 2, pp. 186-187.

French works printed in Geneva bore the official imprint of the Genevan Council and Consistorium with their '*cum privilegio*' stamp.

Bullinger's strong influence over Calvin is well observed by Gustav von Schulthess-Rechberg who was appointed by the Zwingli Society to write a biography of Bullinger in 1904, four hundred years after the Reformer's birth. This Swiss pastor at Zürich, on comparing the two stalwarts, says:

"Calvin and Bullinger were by nature, and because of their subsequent development, quite different men. They stood equally firm for almost four decades in a mutual relationship of respect and trust which was not disturbed by temporary upsets. The Genevan Reformer surpassed the Head of the Zürich Church as a thinker and writer but Bullinger had the greater influence over him. Bullinger had developed his theology in its main traits before Calvin approached him and he found no necessity in adopting any portion of Calvin's thought-world and writings. On the other hand the irritable, often imprudent Frenchman was not unwilling to let himself be calmed, advised, admonished and comforted by the prudent and more eminent Swiss-German. Bullinger recognised Calvin's great value and was tireless in such pastoral service."[25]

W. Kolfhaus, pastor in Eberfelt and a co-author of the 1909 Leipzig *Calvinstudien*, says in his *Der Verkehr Calvin's mit Bullinger*,[26] "Calvin scarcely won any serious battle without Bullinger's more or less intensive participation; hardly any heavy burden was laid on Calvin's shoulders without his friend's comforting support in carrying it."[27]

Bullinger's first encounters with Calvin

Bullinger first met Calvin in Basle in February, 1536 when he was sent there by the Zürich Church with Leo Jud to help draw up the *First Helvetic Confession* with the German speaking churches of Strasburg,

[25] *Heinrich Bullinger der Nachfolger Zwinglis*, pp. 56-57.
[26] Calvin's Association with Bullinger.
[27] Op. cit. p. 27.

Constance and Switzerland. Calvin, then almost unknown to the German-speaking churches, had recently fled from France and found asylum in Basle where he lived for about a year under the assumed name of Martinus Lucianus. Through Bern's and Freiburg's influence William Farel, Antony Froment and Peter Viret began to evangelise Geneva and on 21 May, 1536, the Citizens' Assembly[28] declared Geneva to be Protestant though there had hardly been an official papist presence in the city for two years. In October of that year, Farel and Viret took Calvin with them to the Lausanne Disputation and eventually persuaded him sometime between late 1536 and early 1537 to settle in Geneva to help continue their reforming work. Bullinger's correspondence with Calvin dates from this time and was to continue until Calvin's death. 162 extant letters from Bullinger to Calvin and 115 letters from Calvin to Bullinger still testify to this enormous mutual correspondence. In order to encourage Calvin at Geneva, Bullinger sent a number of sound men over to help Calvin gain a footing in the Swiss churches and also help him become better known in other countries. Amongst the English intellectuals and Reformers whom Bullinger introduced to Calvin were John Butler, Nicolas Partridge, Nicolas Eliot and Bartholomew Traheron who were furthering their education at Zürich. These fine, godly men were able to link up Calvin with the budding Swiss and English Reformations. For a time, Bartholomew Traheron became a follower of Calvin's more radical Supralapsarianism and urged Bullinger to be more like Calvin. However, he became more critical of Calvin when he realised that Calvin was not at all eager to be considered a revolutionary hardliner.

Calvin's first Genevan controversy and appeal to Bullinger for help

As soon as Calvin moved to Geneva he entered into a controversy over the Trinity with the Bernese Reformation in general and Peter Caroli, whom he had met at Basle, in particular. This led to Calvin having

[28] At this time, Geneva was ruled by three councils: the Petit Conseil, the Council of Two Hundred and the General Citizens' Council. Laws were passed, for instance concerning the adoption of the Reformation, only when the three councils were in agreement. For simplicity's sake, I merely refer to these councils as 'the council'.

to defend himself before the Court of Arbitration of the Bernese Church. Caroli demanded that Calvin should confess his allegiance to the Athanasian Creed pointing out that the creed claimed that those who could not accept it, could not be saved. Calvin, said this was the very reason why he would not sign it, not because he rejected it but because it would be tyranny to impose such a statement on the churches and call everybody a heretic who would not sign it. He had sworn belief in the one God and not in the formulas of Athanasius which could never have been accepted by a true Christian church.[29] The Bernese did not forget such statements as Calvin, contrary to his position on the Athanasian Creed, had begun to insist that the Genevans should adhere to the letter of his own creeds and catechisms or otherwise be punished severely. So, too, Calvin went on to support Melanchthon in drawing up his *Augsburg Confession* and even professed his thorough agreement with joint statements of faith coming from the Lutherans and papists. Megander complained to Bullinger on 8 March, 1537 that Calvin was causing bother. He had just received a letter from Calvin defending his attitude to Caroli when he visited the Genevan Church. Calvin began his letter by saying that Caroli believed in aiding the dead by prayer "so that they may be raised up as expeditiously as possible". Calvin's language in debunking Caroli was, however, as exaggerated as his interpretations of Caroli's character. He goes on to say:

"That he (Caroli) might therefore, appear to have got the better of us in something or other, he accused the whole meeting of Arianism. I rose up immediately and brought forward the confession of our Catechism, which is repeated in our public letter to your college. Even this did not quiet him, but he declared that we would be suspect in this matter, until we subscribed the creed of Athanasius. I replied, that it was not my practice to approve anything as the words of God, unless upon due consideration. Here observe the rabid fury of the little ass. Thereupon he cried out, that it was an expression unbecoming a Christian man."[30]

[29] See Kolfhaus' *Der Verkehr Calvins mit Bullinger*, p. 30.
[30] John Calvin Collection, Ages Christian Library CD.

On 20 May, 1537, Myconius, senior pastor at Basle,[31] wrote to Bullinger, asking him to intervene in Basle's controversy with Calvin on the grounds that he and Farel were suspected of being Arians and even supporters of Servetus. Whilst at Berne, Calvin had written a long letter to Simon Grynaeus of Basle, denouncing Caroli in fierce tones but again hardly ridding himself of the suspicion that he could not accept the Athanasian Creed himself. Of Caroli's attitude to Athanasius, Calvin wrote, enclosing his own Confession of Faith:

"Though, indeed, for a season, the fellow may try to set out his wares to the best advantage under the sign of Athanasius, as if we were suffering in defence of the faith, there does not, however, appear to be any great danger that the world will esteem as an Athanasius a person who is sacrilegious, a whoremonger, a homicide steeped in the blood of many saints."[32]

Calvin provides no evidence to back up his terrible accusations but maintained that the Athanasian Creed "was never approved by any legitimate church".[33] As the Athanasian Creed was used as a standard for almost a thousand years by orthodox Christianity, Calvin was certainly risking his neck in his own defence. On 9 July, Myconius again wrote to Bullinger, informing him of Calvin's fierce attacks on Caroli, stating that he believed Calvin was unorthodox on the Trinity. His reasons were that Calvin had refused to use the words 'Trinity' and 'Person' concerning God at the Lausanne Synod of October, 1536. Actually, the Lausanne Articles for the French-speaking churches under Bern's protection are so brief that they do not include an Article on the Godhead at all. The main work leading to them was done by Viret and Farel who proposed them to the synod. The opening sermon was delivered by Farel, and Calvin only

---

[31] Called *Antistes* in Swiss-German.

[32] Written May, 1537, John Calvin Collection, Ages Christian Library CD.

[33] See Ganoczy, p. 114 and entire chapter entitled Calvin in Geneva, 1536-1538. See above letter to Grynaeus of May, 1537 and Calvin's letter to Megander dated February 15, 1537, Ages Christian Library.

spoke briefly in the public debate on the Lord's Supper.[34] Bullinger replied to Myconius, on 23 July, saying how terrible it would be for the churches if, in their present weak state, they would be now burdened with a controversy over the Godhead. He advised his Basle friend to keep out of such debates and simply expound God's Word to the people on the attributes and Work of God. Calvin and Farel then drew up a Confession of Faith which they presented to the Swiss-Germans for approval. On reading it, Bullinger argued that Bern's and Caroli's interpretation of Calvin's doctrine of the Trinity could only be supported by over-academic hair-splitting and they should drop the quarrel. Myconius insisted that this was not possible as the churches must be warned against Calvin's Arianism. In June, 1537, Bullinger wrote to Myconius saying:

"I think it is more important to approach these mysteries worshipfully and with the heart and to believe them according to the Word in which they are anchored in Scripture than strive with academic sharp-sightedness to force an entry into this holy place. We shall see to it that in this matter no disputation over mere words shall arise."[35]

On 13 August, Calvin wrote to Bullinger personally, appealing for help. He denied the charges levelled against him, and argued that his controversy with Caroli was necessary so that he could rid himself of the charge of Arianism. On 1 November, Bullinger replied, urging Calvin and Farel to be careful in their controversy with Bern and Basle but he nevertheless assured them of his support against Caroli whom he believed had himself departed from the Reformed path. Myconius was never fully reconciled to Calvin and believed that Calvin had merely wormed his way out of suspicion by denigrating Caroli's character.[36]

The Caroli affair happened when Bullinger was having great success in reducing the tensions between Bern and Zürich caused by the Kappel

[34] See Arthur Cochran's *Reformed Confessions of the Sixteenth Century*, pp. 112-116.
[35] Letter written to Myconius on 23 June, 1537.
[36] See Professor D.P. Werle's fine study of the Calvin-Myconius relationship in his *Calvin und Basle bis zum Tode des Myconius 1535-1552*.

wars and as Bern still controlled Geneva, he had to tread warily. This was made more difficult by Calvin's doctrine of the Lord's Supper which also antagonised the Bernese Reformers. There was a minority of Lutherans amongst them whom they managed to force out and even banned from the Canton. In their eagerness to purge the canton of all sacramentalism, the influential Bernese pastors Peter Kunz and Jodokus Kilchmeyer now accused Calvin of being one of the hated Lutherans.

Calvin never succeeded in entirely ridding himself of accusations of unorthodoxy regarding the Trinity and from time to time Calvinists have striven to present a more acceptable view of the Reformer's thinking. Calvin obviously, in rejecting the ancient creeds on the subject, strove to go his own way and present what he regarded as a more Biblical and evangelistic approach. Rather than emphasise the permanent nature of the Godhead in their attributes and eternal relationships, he sought his definitions in God's distinctive roles in His redemptive activities. Calvin leaves us thus with a somewhat artificial and speculative sharp distinction in the roles of the Triune God which are at times more speculative than Scriptural and he leaves out such passages in the Scriptures as 1 Corinthians 1:24; 2 Corinthians 12:9; Acts 6:3 and Ephesians 1:17 which do not allow for such sharply-cut distinctions. This difficulty in understanding Calvin on the Trinity was highlighted recently[37] in lectures given by Professor of Philosophy Paul Helm, a popular writer for the Banner of Truth Magazine, and the former Warden of Latimer House, Oxford, R. T. Beckwith. Prof. Helm, a professing 'Calvinist', speaking on the subject of 'Cautious Trinitarianism' at the London Theological Seminary, censured Calvin by claiming that his doctrine of the Trinity was 'obscure and unilluminating'. He strove thus to clear up the difficulties in Calvin's teaching by stressing more strongly that the differences within the Godhead are to be understood solely within the order of redemption and not in the eternal properties of the Father, Son and Holy Ghost. Though Prof. Helm stated that he wished to avoid a speculative approach to the Trinity, in questioning Biblical accounts of

[37] February and October, 2001.

the essential, eternal relationships within the Godhead, he is throwing the doors of speculation wide open concerning whether or not there are essential differences within the Trinity at all. Is he saying that God was merely One before redemption but then took on a Triune form merely for redemption's sake? Are the Son and the Spirit thus only temporary manifestations? Whereas Calvin left the matter of God's eternal nature open, for others to speculate on, Helm seems to be saying that we know nothing whatsoever about the eternal being of God. This would mean that we cannot possibly think in terms of a Trinity of three Persons in One. Thus Dr Beckwith concludes in his Protestant Reformation Society reply to Helm, "So, if the error into which Calvin's theory of the Trinity risked falling was Tritheism, the error into which Professor Helm's theology of the Trinity runs much greater risk of falling is the opposite one of Sabellianism."[38] It would appear then that though Calvin had a rather stunted view of the Trinity, those using his name for their theology, have abandoned the traditional theology of the Athanasian and Nicene Creeds altogether. Dr Beckwith also accuses Prof. Helm of 'playing down' important Biblical evidence[39] which, one would think, clearly disproves his radical theory. Beckwith quotes freely from Scripture to show that there is no distinction between the Trinity in eternity and the Trinity working in redemption, saying, "The work of the divine Persons in the world is consistent with their eternal relationships, and the willingness of the apostles to speak in these ways is bound to cast some degree of doubt on Calvin's proposal. So perhaps the Creeds are being more faithful to Scripture in declining to distinguish the Persons except by their personal relationships as Father, Son and Spirit."[40] Beckwith concludes by bemoaning the fact that modern professors of Calvinism seem intent on belittling the eternal relationships within the Trinity, believing that Helm's reductionist approach is 'a rather extreme example' of this trend. That this trend is sadly moving on to a blatant Tritheism is evident judging by recent Banner of Truth authors such as John Murray, Iain

[38] *The Calvinist Doctrine of the Trinity*, p. 8.
[39] Given by Dr Beckwith on pages 8-9.
[40] Ibid, p. 6.

Murray and David Gay who ignore the unifying relationships within the Trinity and stress a supposed disunifying clash of wills in the work of redemption. David Gay even argues that Christ had a different will to His Father's,[41] totally ignoring the grand pan-Scriptural evidence that Christ voluntarily made Himself our Saviour in full unity with the joint will of the entire Godhead.[42]

Calvin and Farel flee to Zürich from Geneva

Whilst Bullinger was still mediating in the Caroli affair and dealing with anti-Lutheran accusations, Calvin entered head over heels into another controversy. He raised the ire of many citizens by demanding that Genevan citizenship should be linked with the acceptance of the Reformed faith in the form he prescribed. Though he was a foreigner himself in Geneva and did not receive citizenship for many years to come and technically merely lecturer in Holy Scripture and a junior partner to William Farel,[43] he demanded that the political authorities should follow his leadership. He even claimed that all who would not accept his still immature theology on oath should be exiled from the city state. Calvin then authored a catechism which he entitled *Instruction et confession de foy dont on use en l'église Genève*. This catechism was the most severe theological document Calvin ever penned and it out-did Zwingli with its Supralapsarian, harsh teaching on predestination and reprobation. Those who diverted from his catechism in the least, he maintained, would have to undergo severe penalties. He then proposed the setting up of an ecclesiastical police-force to control the morals of the citizens and enforce

---

[41] See John Murray's *Free Offer of the Gospel*; Iain Murray's *Spurgeon v. Hyper-Calvinism*; K. W. Stebbins *Christ Freely Offered*; Erroll Hulse's *The Free Offer*; Hulse's *The Great Invitation*; David Gay's *The Gospel Offer is Free* and his two BOT essays *Preaching the Gospel to Sinners* (Issues 370/371-2; David Silversides *The Free Offer; Biblical and Reformed*; Philip R. Johnson's A Primer on Hyper-Calvinism, (*Sword and Trowel* March, 2002) and Malcolm Watts' *The Free Offer of the Gospel* (Emmanuel Church, Salisbury, 2001-2002). All these works under a pretence of preaching a fuller gospel, are industrious in the undermining of Trinitarian thought and the promoting of a Trinity of three wills in the name of 'Calvinism'. This is, however, not Calvin's Calvinism.

[42] Psalm 40:8; Matthew 26:39; Ephesians 1:5 ff., etc..

[43] See Wilcox's *The Lectures of John Calvin and the Nature of his Audience, 1555-1564* for background material and sources.

discipline. At every communion service, the names of the outcasts were to be read out publicly. Calvin complained against the Council's wish to accept the Bernese Reformation in the city, rather than his own, and denounced his Bernese Reformed brethren publicly in a lecture as 'councils of the devil'.[44] The Bernese had protested against the Genevan Church's early action, to which Calvin, according to Beza had agreed, in removing all the baptismal fonts from the Genevan Churches. To quote from Beza's account, the Genevans "considered them unnecessary for performing the office of baptism". Beza adds that the Genevan Reformers had also "abolished all festivals except Sunday".[45] These measures were radically opposed to the agreement drawn up at the Synod of Lausanne in October, 1536. Beza relates that Calvin appealed to Bullinger's Zürich to hold a synod to reverse the Lausanne ruling but does not go into further details. Such a synod on the topic does not appear to have been called.

The Genevan Council, by nature suspicious of the French and frustrated by the foreigner to whom they had given asylum, alms and clothing, strove at first to ignore Calvin, merely referring to him as 'that Frenchman'. Indeed, the Council at Bern also called Calvin derogatorily 'that man', apparently to emphasise that Calvin was a nobody in their eyes. However, the Council at Geneva had become so suspicious of French claims on their republic that they stopped granting citizenship with voting rights and privileges of holding office to those from outside Geneva, and limited citizenship to those born in the city-state. Calvin was neither born in Geneva nor had Genevan citizenship so his presence was no longer wanted. Richard Hörsik writes thus in his essay *John Calvin in Geneva, 1536-38*, "the Genevans could not accept the dictates of a couple of French refugees, who were not even bourgeois."[46] By the Spring of 1538, the newly elected Council of Two Hundred forbade Calvin and Farel to interfere in the politics of the city.

Soon the general opposition against Calvin became intense and church, people and Senate took to the streets in anti-Calvin

[44] See Crisis in Geneva and Exile to Strasbourg in Ganoczy's *The Young Calvin*, p. 120 ff..
[45] See Beza's biography of Calvin in *Ages Ultimate Christian Library*, p. 11.
[46] *Calvinus Sacrae Scripturae Professor*, p. 163.

demonstrations. By September, 1537 whole districts had rejected Calvin's ecclesiastical and, indeed, political tyranny. Instead of striving to work out a temporary compromise so that he could peacefully instruct his hearers further as had been Zwingli's practice and also that of Bucer and Bullinger, Calvin would not budge an inch. As a result at Easter, 1538, the Council banned Calvin and Farel from Geneva giving them seventy-two hours in which to set their affairs in order. They were threatened with grave consequences should they not leave within the specified time. Bullinger had always been against using the ordinance for disciplinary and political purposes and had blamed the Zürich Senate for such abuses. Thus, when Calvin appealed to him for help, he could not back Calvin in his enterprise but he appealed to the Bern Council to show lenience to Calvin and Farel because of their obvious gifts.

Nevertheless, Calvin now fled to Zürich with Farel, hoping to find asylum under Bullinger's care. At the time, Bullinger was leading a conference at Zürich from 29 April to 4 May. Its aim was to discuss problems arising from Luther's opposition to the Swiss Reformation. Bucer of Strasburg, who was trying to mediate between Luther and Bullinger was also there. As Luther was again calling Bullinger an Anabaptist, and had begun again to confuse his theology with that of Zwingli, which he also misunderstood, his dealings with Zürich were often carried on via Strasburg and vice versa. However, in his honest zeal to help, and probably because of severe language difficulties, Bucer tended to exaggerate the similarities between the Lutherans and the Bullingerians which caused both contenders to protest that Bucer had not adequately presented their positions. Furthermore, when one compares Bucer's writing and style with that of Luther and Bullinger, one finds the latter's letters outstanding in their perspicuity and elegant, though colloquial, style. On the other hand, Bucer's writing is extremely difficult to read and his language and syntax highly complicated. Furthermore, Swiss German differed highly from Strasburg's Upper German dialect and even more from Luther's East German mother tongue. Even when they wrote or spoke Latin, their words were liable to be misunderstood. More than once, Bucer had stood up to speak at Zürich and had soon tired out his hearers who, rather unkindly asked him to stop speaking on the grounds that they did not know what he was talking about.

Calvin and Farel were asked to give an account of their experiences in Geneva and presented the assembled theologians with a list of 14 articles concerning what they were prepared to modify and what they could not give up. These were more designed to pacify the Bernese Council rather than the Genevan Church but because the assembled divines did not share Calvin's view of church discipline, they could not accept the articles. The two exiles' defence was made more difficult as Calvin knew no German and Bullinger and his friends knew no French so matters were discussed in Latin and through an interpreter. Calvin was adamant that he was fully in the right and insisted that the synod should help him force Geneva to conform to his pattern of orthodoxy. Bullinger, however, counselled Calvin to be more moderate and the synod suggested that Bullinger and Calvin should work out a milder form of church government and discipline for the French-speaking city together. It was also decided that Bullinger should both write to the Council at Geneva and recommend that they accepted Calvin back with the less severe church order and then contact Bern and ask them to have their representatives in the city put in a word for Calvin and Farel so that they might return. Bullinger's letter to Nikolaus von Wattenwyl, a leading Councillor in Bern is extant and shows Bullinger doing his diplomatic best in a cause which was not his own. He told von Wattenwyl that Calvin and Farel were "learned, pious men who must be forgiven much" and are possessed by "too great a zeal". He nevertheless asked the Bernese Council to put in a good word for the two ministers because of their outstanding qualifications. At first, it looked as though Bullinger would have his way but then certain Bernese at Geneva who leaned more to the Lutheran system, spoke against Calvin and Farel, so the Council refused to lift their ban.[47] Calvin himself rather complicated procedures by informing Bern that Zürich

[47] In the next decade, the Reformation at Bern was to suffer greatly as Lutherans, Calvinists and Bullingerians began to quarrel over what, for others, were minor details.

accepted his 'reforms' in Geneva, which was, to put it mildly, a great exaggeration.[48] Kolfhaus comments:

"When Calvin claimed that the Zürich Synod of 1538 had agreed to his articles, he was confusing the synod's general consent to his endeavours with agreement with his specific points. Especially his main point (excommunication) met up with a very cool reception if not absolute rejection on Bullinger's and his circle's part."[49]

Calvin is given asylum at Strasburg

Calvin had formerly been extremely critical of Martin Bucer, but now Bucer, a most difficult man to fall out with, took pity on the exiles and offered them posts in Strasburg. Calvin took advantage of the offer, whereas Farel moved to Neuchâtel (Neuenburg). Farel quickly made himself unpopular in Neuchâtel by striving to force on the church the hard disciplinary measures he had striven to introduce in Geneva with such dire consequences. When the story reached Bullinger's ears, he wrote to Farel saying, "If we wished to pursue such a foolish course as to question each person concerning his faith before allowing him to partake of the Lord's Supper, what difference would this be to paving the way for the aural confessions of the pope? We must beware honoured Farel that we do not take to popish paths after we hitherto have done everything according to the rules of the Apostles."[50] Calvin, under Bucer's careful eye, did not strive to introduce measures in Strasburg which had failed in Geneva and modified his views quite radically on the Strasburg pattern. Indeed, Cornelis Augustijn writes of Calvin making 'a swing of 180 degrees' in his attitude to both the Strasburg and Wittenburg Reformations.[51] Instead of speaking of 'us' i.e. Calvin and Farel and 'them' i.e. Bucer and Luther, Calvin now speaks of 'us' i.e. the Germans

---

[48] Calvin even wrote to Bullinger on 20 May, 1538 complaining that Bern had not taken into consideration the fact that Zürich was 'in general' in agreement with him.

[49] *Der Verkehr Calvins mit Bullinger*, p. 39.

[50] Translated from the German found in W. Kolhaus' *Der Verkehr Calvins mit Bullinger*, p. 37.

[51] Calvin in Strasbourg, *Calvinus Sacrae Scripturae Professor*, p. 171.

and 'them', the Swiss Reformers.[52] One thing marred Calvin's stay in Strasburg. Bucer showed the same friendliness to Caroli that he did to Calvin which enraged the latter.

Bullinger campaigns to have Calvin re-instated at Geneva

After a two-year period of inner strife, many of the Christians and Councilmen in Geneva now saw that the Reformed Church was falling apart in the city state and they began openly to say that it was a grave misunderstanding that had caused Calvin to leave Geneva. Bullinger, supported by his friend Johannes Zwick in Constance, used all his diplomatic skills to open Bern's and Geneva's eyes to Calvin's usefulness for the Reformation. Soon even Bern began to reconsider their action in banning Calvin from Geneva. The Bernese Council's secretary (*Ratschreiber*) Eberhard von Rumlang asked Bullinger to use his influence on Calvin to come to an agreement on the Lord's Supper as the Frenchman was too valuable to be ignored. Leo Jud did his best to support Calvin by translating two of his tracts into German. He sent copies to Zwick who introduced Jud's translation of Calvin's *de Christiani hominis officio in sacerdotiis papalis ecclesiae vel administrandis vel abiciendis* to the Lutherans and sought to have it published in Augsburg.

However, Calvin was now very happy in Strasburg. Capito and Bucer were two of Germany's leading theologians and they soon introduced their young friend to all the great Continental Reformers, moving from disputation to disputation with him throughout most of Germany. Indeed, Calvin was elated with his new life amongst the leaders of the German Reformation and was now determined to defend Bucer against all criticism. Calvin, however, was never much of a diplomat and we find him actually playing Bucer against Bullinger in an attempt to show his closeness to the former. Calvin thus wrote to Bullinger, telling him how much at home he was in Strasburg but that he thought there was some 'coldness' between his Swiss friend and Bucer. He suggested that

[52] Ibid, p. 172.

Bullinger must have angered Bucer as the latter had not written to him for a year and a half. Such 'coldness' was most unlike both Bucer and Bullinger, and it is most difficult to understand what Calvin was aiming at. However, from then on, Calvin was to occasionally remind Bullinger that all was not well between him and Bucer. What makes Calvin's statement seem hollow is the fact that Calvin wrote to Bullinger on 12 March, 1539 to apologise for not writing to him for *a year and a half* on the grounds that he had often thought of his Swiss friend but had been too busy to write! However, when Bullinger did not answer Calvin's letters at the very earliest possible opportunity, Calvin rebuked his patient friend strongly.

The only real historical evidence for such a coldness is Calvin's feeling that he now had some influence on both Bucer and Bullinger and could 'mediate' as their advisor. Furthermore, friends of Bullinger's such as Grynäus at Basle were urging Calvin not to neglect his own correspondence with Bullinger because he needed the Zürich Superintendent's support. As Bullinger was working hard behind the scenes to have Calvin leave Strasburg and returned to Geneva at this time (1540-41), and as this was obviously against Calvin's own wish, perhaps Calvin presumed that this had nothing to do with himself and the good of the church at Geneva but to some kind of animosity Bullinger might have against Bucer and Strasburg. Furthermore, Bucer travelled widely between 1539 and 1541, often taking Calvin with him in his enormous efforts to unite the Protestant churches in Germany, so he had little time for private correspondence. When Bullinger wrote to Strasburg early in 1541, for instance, Bucer was at Regensburg. On the other hand, Bullinger felt strongly that pastoral duties were more important than permanent ministers' conferences and often told Bucer to let Luther go his way and the Swiss churches go their way instead of entering into endless arguments with each other at great neglect of other matters appertaining to the gospel. Nevertheless, before Bucer had started on the Leipzig-Regensburg three-year marathon of disputations, he had been busy writing letters of over thirty pages to Bullinger and when Calvin returned to Geneva, Bucer corresponded with Bullinger at the rate of up to two letters per month. Besides, even during the 1539-40 period mentioned by Calvin, much of Luther's correspondence was copied, answered and passed on regularly between Bucer and Bullinger. By this time, Bullinger was influencing and even monitoring the entire process of reinstating a very unwilling Calvin back in Geneva. Having been appealed to both by the Geneva Council and the Genevan Church, Bullinger sent letters to Bern and Strasburg, arguing for a quick return of Calvin to the church he had so quickly been forced to leave.

So too, whilst Calvin was grumbling about the lack of correspondence between Bullinger and Bucer, we must remember that this was the terrible time of the 1540-1541 plague in Zürich during which Bullinger's mother, one of his sons and his right-hand-man Leo Jud died[53] before he could complete his gigantic work on the *Biblia Tigurina.*[54] Bullinger himself was struck down and wrote, "The plague has struck us. We are awaiting what God has in store for us. I am troubled by dizziness and almost unbearable headaches." A year later, he was still in the grip of the plague and wrote, "I am still alive by the grace of God. The plague has not yet spent itself. Those who die leave us in great faith and truly blessed so that their families who are left behind praise God and each day finds them with less fear."[55] Bullinger tells Vadian that he is so ill that he cannot work. However, in spite of his illness, Bullinger's greatly reduced number of letters for this year shows that he is still well abreast of European affairs.

In short, Bullinger had more than enough to do and under the worst conditions during Calvin's almost holiday-like sojourn in Strasburg. Furthermore, Calvin was soon to experience that his own correspondence with Bullinger was to undergo various breaks of a year or so, not so much because letters were not sent but because the couriers chosen were robbed on the way or even opened the letters themselves and had them copied so that many people knew of their contents before they reached their original

[53] Grynäus and Capito died about the same time.
[54] Zürich Bible. Jud died on 9 June, 1542. Theodore Bibliander and Conrad Pellican continued the work.
[55] Letters to Vadian dated 2 June, 1540 and 1 October, 1541.

destination through much delay. Once, in January, 1549 when Bullinger and Calvin were putting the finishing touches to their agreement on the Lord's Supper, Bullinger gave his comments on Calvin's views on the Supper to Beatus Comes, a close friend of Calvin's and Farel's, and asked him to take the letter speedily to Geneva. Comes, however, carried the letter to his private house and apparently forgot all about it. Many weeks later, another friend of Calvin's visited Comes, looking for a lost letter from John Hooper that had been sent to him. In his search, he came across Bullinger's letter to Calvin and then made sure that it reached its destination. Haller also complained that letters either were not reaching Calvin or were intercepted and copied on the way. Most of the German and Swiss Reformers made similar complaints about post sent to them.

Calvin refused to return to Geneva

When Calvin found out that efforts were being made throughout Switzerland and Upper Germany, to have him returned to Geneva, he refused even to consider the idea and was supported in his conviction by the Germans. Indeed, it appears that if Calvin had only written a letter of goodwill to the Genevan Council, he might have been restored. Some commentators, indeed, argue that Calvin was prepared to confess his mistakes and they quote Calvin when writing to Farel, "Before God and his people let us confess that partly by our inexperience, carelessness, negligence, and errors the Church committed to us has so sadly declined"[56] This statement, however must be carefully studied in its full context which is that Calvin refused to take on any of the blame before the Council for what had happened. The words were merely written to theorize what Calvin might have acknowledged if the matter was between him, God and the Church but not before the Council. Concerning the letter of goodwill requested from Calvin, the exile actually says:

"But suppose that might be hoped for, at what point could we begin? Shall we, as though we were authors of the scandal, study to conciliate

[56] See, for instance, Hörcsik's John Calvin in Geneva, Calvinus Sacrae Scripturae Professor, p. 164.

them? And that we may not blink that consideration, shall we consider, also, what method should be observed for the reparation of the offence? I am not of the opinion that past negligences are so far about to be amended, nor do I perceive any provision about to be made for the future. We may indeed acknowledge before God and his people, that it is in some measure owing to our unskilfulness, indolence, negligence, and error, that the Church committed to our care has fallen into such a sad state of collapse; but it is also our duty to assert our innocence and our purity against those who, by their fraud, malignity, knavery, and wickedness, have assuredly brought about this ruin."[57]

Calvin goes on to write that should he write the letter of goodwill to the Council, he would be exposed to scorn and mockery and the cry would go up that he had only written the letter so that he might be restored to his former position in Geneva.

As if to sever all ties with Geneva, Calvin now took out Strasburg citizenship. He was now a Burger of Alsace. Even when the Geneva Council wrote officially to Calvin inviting him back, Calvin thus declined. He argued that the new ministers who had taken his and Farel's places, and with whom he would have to work in future, were already intent on ruining his reputation. He called them 'iniquitous' and 'slanderous' and the bulk of the citizens of Geneva 'dregs of humanity'. Calvin writes as if Geneva were next door to hell but William Naphy[58] shows how in Calvin's absence, Geneva went through something of a moral and spiritual renewal, enforcing measures that must have been dear to Calvin's heart. So, too, Viret, who had pioneered the Reformation in Geneva with Froment and Farel was again working in Geneva during Calvin's absence and he was one of the greatest French-speaking Reformers. Calvin criticised him, however, for not sticking to the order and discipline which had caused Calvin to be banned from the city.

---

[57] Letter to Farel dated September 1538, Ages Christian Library.

[58] Calvin's Letters. Reflections on their usefulness in Studying Genevan History, *Archiv für Reformationsgeschichte*, Jahrgang 86, pp. 67-89.

Bullinger's letter to the Strasburg ministers is extant and illustrates his great eagerness that Calvin should be able to return to Geneva:

"The Geneva church is situated directly on the borders to Germany, France and Italy. From such a position a man like Calvin who is so well endowed with extraordinary gifts can more than anywhere else be of great use to several countries in extending the Kingdom of Christ."

Bullinger added that only Strasburg could now save Geneva from ruin. He also wrote that if Bucer and Capito were not prepared to let Calvin go or did not encourage him to leave if he wished to stay, the Reformation in Geneva would suffer greatly.[59] Bullinger also pressed Basle's ministers to write to Strasburg's pastors and councillors to explain how urgently Calvin was needed at Geneva. In a letter written in April 1541, he warned Calvin against listening to the voice of his flesh so intently that he might not hear God's call. At the time, Calvin was with Bucer in Regensburg and Strasburg informed Bullinger that they would discuss the matter with Calvin as soon as he returned. Bullinger's letter to Calvin, however, was forwarded to Regensburg and he replied on 31 May, 1541 that if his Strasburg church advised him to return, and the Geneva Council so wished, he would be prepared to comply with their wishes. Bullinger had also written, "We need not provide evidence to show you that God is calling you. Your conscience is telling you this."[60] Bullinger's letter, however, was not the only appeal to Calvin's conscience. Towards the end of February, 1541, Farel had written to Calvin at Regensburg what Prof. Wernle of Basle University calls one of his 'terrible thunder-letters', telling his friend that if he did not return to Geneva, he would have nothing more to do with him.[61] At Bullinger's prompting, the Zürich Council appealed to Strasburg on 7 June to let Calvin go and the Basle Council followed with the same request on 11 June.

---

[59] Quoted from Pestalozzi, p. 246.
[60] Letter sent 4 April, 1541.
[61] Calvin und Basle bis zum Tode des Myconius, p. 32.

Calvin finally persuaded to return to Geneva

Meanwhile, in Geneva, the so-called Artichauts who had opposed Calvin and ruled Geneva were deposed and Jean Philippe, their leader, was executed.[62] Now revolutionary Ami Perrin, who had supported Calvin, was asked by the new council to find ways of inducing Calvin to return. He travelled personally to Strasburg to discuss the matter with Calvin. By this time Bullinger had managed to gain a measure of co-operation between Bern and Geneva and as Bern now also gave the 'all clear' and Strasburg was willing to let Calvin depart, Calvin was persuaded to return to his former brief ministry on 13 September, 1541. Nevertheless, the troubles in Geneva were not over by any means, and would not be for some time.

As soon as Calvin reached Geneva, he made it quite clear that he regarded himself as being in sole charge of the church and quickly fell out with those leading citizens such as the Perrins[63] who had supported him in 1538 and enabled his return in 1541. He wasted no time in complaining that his colleagues were 'rude and self-conceited', and had 'no zeal and less learning' and were 'profane spirits'.

Calvin's claims for his own grandeur at this time are most exaggerated and Naphy remarks, "This is not to imply that Calvin was intentionally misleading, rather, that, because of his personal beliefs and presuppositions, Calvin's perceptions might differ radically from the reality of a situation." and, a page later, regarding Calvin's boast to Myconius that he could have dismissed the lot but kept them on to humour them, Naphy comments, "For the reader today, and perhaps for Myconius at the time, it is difficult to decide which is the more incredible assertion, that Calvin decided to keep such men when he did not have to, or that the magistrates might actually have been willing to reduce the city's ministerial staff to Calvin alone."[64]

---

[62] 10 June, 1540.

[63] See Calvin's letter of 15 June, 1555 to Bullinger (Ages Library) denouncing Ami Perrin in the strongest terms.

[64] Naphy, William G., *Calvin's Letters*. The latter quotes are from pp. 72-73. Calvin's letter to Myconius, dated 14 March, 1542 is reproduced in full under the title 'Establishing the new regime' in Calvinism in Europe 1540-1610, pp. 25-28 in a new translation.

Calvin has to work with those he claimed were 'iniquitous'

Bullinger now wrote to Calvin to use his influence in the city to bring about peace between Bern and Geneva. He explained that Roman Catholic Emperor Charles V was planning to take matters into his own hands and if peace was not established at Geneva, Charles would claim the city back for Rome. Perhaps this was Bullinger's strategy to calm Calvin because after this letter, Calvin began to say that he could now work well with the ministers whom he had formerly labelled as 'iniquitous'. Charles' policy was to allow Protestant states to remain Protestant if they so wished but if their governments or Lords became Roman Catholic, they had to go over to Rome. On the other hand, if the government of a Roman Catholic province became Protestant, their province had to remain within Rome's fold. The Swiss method of each canton becoming either Protestant or Roman Catholic by majority vote was thus to be preferred. Calvin now took the initiative by addressing Roman Catholic Emperor Charles directly concerning the need for a Reformed Church in Geneva. This caused Bullinger to admire Calvin's courage but to tell him that it was a waste of energy talking to Charles, because "If God gives him the victory, he would misuse it to persecute the Name of the Lord! Because his heart is hardened."

Calvin had learnt much from the Strasburg pastors and now sought to guide his flock in a more pastoral way, building his doctrines and order of service on Strasburg models. Cornelis Augustijn comments, "The Calvin who returns to Geneva is a different person."[65] On arriving at Geneva, this time without Farel who stayed in Neuchâtel, Calvin submitted his *Ordonnances ecclésiastiques* to the Council who altered a little for form's sake and on 20 November, 1541, Calvin took up his new preaching and pastoral duties, greatly humbled. He was, however, still struggling for a better understanding of the Lord's Supper and the doctrine of predestination. Calvin's powers were now strongly reduced. He was not allowed to sit on any of the councils and repeatedly refused Genevan

[65] *Calvinus Sacrae Scripturae Professor*, p. 176.

citizenship until 1559, eighteen years after returning from Strasburg and only five years before his death. Calvin had now a long struggle before him because of opposition from the Favre and Perrin clans, with whom he had formerly sided. This opposition lasted until they were exiled from Geneva in 1555 and several of their supporters executed. Kasper von Greyerz comments, "This marked the ultimate victory of Calvin's reform".[66]

Trying to understand Calvin on predestination

When we compare Calvin's *Catechismus Genevensis* of 1545, written after the trouble his *Instruction et confession* had caused him in 1537-38, we can clearly see how Calvin learnt from his mistakes. But this was a most difficult process. Calvin's 1545 edition of this catechism does not even have a separate article on predestination and Calvin embeds it in his doctrine of the church, thus now approaching Bullinger's position. However, it is clear that when Calvin was under pressure to be more ecumenical, he saw predestination as derived from the doctrine of the church, and where he found he could safely go his own way, as after the Servetus controversy, he resorted to subordinating the doctrine of election and the church to a double predestination.[67] However, a number of modern scholars, both from the Reformed and Arminian schools, tend to argue that Calvin never believed in an absolute double predestination. Thus even where Calvin is at his sternest in making predestination and reprobation the start of his gospel, Eva-Maria Faber gives three reasons for believing that Calvin the preacher was more warm-hearted than Calvin the systematic theologian. The first is that Calvin sees history from the point of view of a time for the sinner to decide and not the eternal decree; the second is Calvin's view of the relationship between the time of decision, the covenant of Grace and the vicarious work of Christ and the third is Calvin's doctrine of a temporary and not final reprobation

---

[66] *The Reformation in National Context* (eds Bob Scribner et al), CUP, Chapter 2, Switzerland, p. 38.

[67] See Eva-Maria Faber's helpful article *Zur Frage der Prädistinationslehre in der Theologie Johannes Calvin's.*

as in the case of the Jews. Ingenious and probable as Dr Faber's hypothesis might be, her way of talking Calvin out of his absolute predestination mechanism, apart from the complicated new nature she gives it, leaves us with a Calvin who was never of one mind with himself over any longer period of time. In stark contrast to this, Bullinger held to a milder, more plausible, more God-honouring and more obviously Biblical approach to predestination than Calvin, which he never felt the need to vary. Indeed, nowhere more than in his doctrine of predestination does Calvin show that he is a second generation Reformer who has parted from the position of earlier Reformers such as Tyndale, the Edwardian Anglicans and Bullinger. Thus, though Calvin is more the systematic theologian and lecturer and Bullinger more the preacher and evangelist, Calvin is demonstrably less systematic on predestination than Bullinger.

Coming to a consensus on the Lord's Supper at Zürich

Since 1539, Calvin had strongly criticised other Reformers' views of the Lord's Supper, including Bullinger's, before he came to any stable interpretation himself. His signing of the Lutheran Confessions showed that he stood nearer Luther than Bullinger. He complained that though the Swiss Germans had cleansed the ordinance from superstition, they had not really stated just what the true power of the rite was. In criticising them, he was also criticising himself as his own pronouncements on the Eucharist up to this time were far more nebulous than either Bullinger's or Zwingli's. Indeed, he had angered the Bernese Church by at times appearing to support views of the Lutherans in Saxony and at times claiming agreement with Bullinger who had by the early forties lost all hope of coming to an agreement with Luther.

Bullinger had striven time and time again to come to terms with the Saxon Reformer who would go into uncontrolled tantrums when he heard the name of Zürich. Every time Luther called the Zürich Church 'Anabaptists', 'Enthusiasts', 'heretics', 'the lost' or 'poisoners of the faith', Bullinger either responded politely in a God-honouring way or sent Luther an exegetical work to demonstrate his adherence to Scriptural truths. By the time of Luther's letter of 1543 to Froschauer refusing to have any fellowship whatsoever with the Reformed churches unless they became Lutheran, Bullinger realised that unity with the German Lutherans was impossible. He thus turned more and more to Calvin who had been corresponding with him throughout the forties on the subject of the Lord's Supper and had come to a measure of agreement with him. Calvin was Bullinger's last hope of finding some form of consensus within the Reformed churches as he was daily faced with popish criticism ridiculing the Protestants for merely being united against Rome but disunited among themselves. This fraternising with Calvin did not please many of Bullinger's friends who warned him against the Frenchman's alleged fickleness. Gerhard ter Camp (Kampius) wrote from the Emden Church on 31 August, 1545 to tell Bullinger that Calvin had sent them his new catechism with new teaching on the Supper. He confessed to Bullinger that Calvin's old teaching on the Supper had suited him best but they wished that Calvin would write so that ordinary people could understand him. Leopold Fry wrote from Biel complaining that Calvin paradoxically believed that Christ's body was in Heaven but nevertheless trusted that believers encountered Christ's real flesh and blood in the Sacrament.

In spite of such warnings, Bullinger continued his correspondence with Calvin on the ordinance and sent him the manuscript of his *Absoluta de Christi Domini et catholicae eius ecclesiae sacramentis tractatio*, asking for his comments. Calvin decided to share Bullinger's manuscript with Farel and wrote to him:

"If you could come here, it would be worth your while. But come soon, I have something in my hand which I must return soon. I would like to discuss it with you and you will see that my request was not without reason."[68]

[68] Kolfhaus, p. 55 and Ages collection of Calvin's letters. My translations are often from the German as the John Calvin Collection in the Ages Library often lacks material included in German collections.

Calvin frightened of coming too much under Bullinger's influence

Calvin was very anxious to shake off his reputation of being a Lutheran rather than a Reformed theologian and was thus eager to take up Bullinger's invitations to find agreement on the Lord's Supper. He also urgently wanted to ally himself with Zürich to give him support against Bern. A third reason was that Geneva needed stronger ties with Switzerland because the Roman Catholic forces were talking of annexing Geneva. However, Calvin did not wish to lose his independence as leader of the Genevan church. His position was delicate enough as matters stood. He knew that Bullinger would not move from his own position on the Lord's Supper and wrote to Viret, saying, "Here you have Bullinger's letter in which you will observe an astonishing obstinacy. I said to you once that the Zürich people always sing the same tune."[69] This was rather undiplomatic of Calvin as Viret himself was coming under fire from Bern and Viret was looking to Bullinger for help. Indeed, Calvin and Farel journeyed to Zürich early in 1548 especially to solicit support from Bullinger for Viret but also to continue to discuss the Lord's Supper issue. Calvin was disappointed with the way the talks went but was pleased to meet Bullinger's former student Johannes Haller who had been called to Bern to help heal the quarrels in the Church there. Haller, who was at first suspicious of Calvin, became his correspondent during 1548-49 and, as Bullinger kept him informed of his own correspondence with the Frenchman, Haller was able to assist in finding a mutual agreement with Calvin on the Supper. However, Haller became disappointed with Calvin when the French Reformer made a secret visit to Zürich in order to discuss the matter with Bullinger without informing Haller of his plans.

Meanwhile, Bullinger corresponded patiently with Calvin although the latter complained that Bullinger always put too much emphasis on his words. He also sought to assure Bullinger that he did not speak with two voices and that what he said in Zürich was the same as he said in Geneva. So too, he denied that what he said in his commentaries contradicted his personal testimony to Bullinger. A mutual 'friend' had informed him that

[69] *Der Verkehr Calvins mit Bullinger*, p. 56.

this was commonly believed.[70] Bullinger collected together all Calvin's arguments and dealt with them one by one and sent them to Calvin in November, 1548. Bullinger also sent a copy of this letter and one written shortly after to Calvin, to Haller. Because of the negligence of the courier, Beatus Comes, the letter did not reach Calvin until the following January. In this long letter, which Calvin calls 'a packet', Bullinger strove to rid Calvin's ambiguous terms from any trace of Lutheranism. He rejected in particular Calvin's repeated statement that the elect actually received what the sacrament symbolised in the partaking of it. Again, Calvin replied that it was Bullinger's prejudice that made him misread his letters and that Bullinger was more interested in getting the language right than the truth it was supposed to convey. Calvin also felt it unfair that Bullinger was always pressing him to alter his wording but did not make such gestures himself. In short, he felt himself greatly misunderstood by Bullinger and complained:

"You are perplexed in regard to many points which present difficulty, simply because you put upon the majority of my statements a different construction from what you have any ground for doing. A preconceived opinion regarding me leads you to imagine and attribute to me what never occurred to my mind."[71]

Calvin and Bullinger begin to understand each other better

Nevertheless, Calvin filed away again at the detailed wording of his views on the Supper and sent them on to Bullinger with his letter of 21 January. Meanwhile, Haller had made a visit to Geneva to attend a synod of the Berne and Pays de Vaud ministers and took the opportunity to inform Calvin of the Bernese Council's attitude to him. His comment to Bullinger on Calvin's character was brief but comprehensive,

---

[70] Calvin's letters to Bullinger of 1 March, and 26 June, 1548, John Calvin Collection, Ages Library CD. Kolfhaus gives excerpts from a letter dated 20 February, 1547, p. 57, not found in the Ages Library collection,.

[71] Letter from 21 January, 1549, John Calvin Collection, Ages Library CD.

"He is a pious and learned man who is valued much in France, but he is of a very unsettled spirit. We can, it appears, best deal with him when we tell him directly what we like and dislike about him and how far we agree with him and how far we do not. He is friendly in his demeanour and approachable."[72]

On 15 March, 1549, Bullinger wrote a most conciliatory letter to Calvin confessing that they were nearing each other at last. He told his friend:

"With your last answer, you have brought me a great step towards you. I now understand your latest letters better than I formerly did. Do not marvel that I wrote to you so bluntly. Today, we have highly educated men who change their opinions more than is good for them. I do not say that you belong to these, but I wanted to hear from you where you stood in plain words. By the way, I have not a bad opinion of you so please excuse my bluntness. I strive to formulate my opinions only in so much as they are true and you do not say that they are false. You say yourself that your disagreement with us is not a disagreement of heart and disposition. I cannot understand why you differ from us at all. When you have read my answer, you will, I trust, find no more disagreements. ... I am satisfied that you love us sincerely. May we cease from provoking each other and love each other heartily to the edifying of our churches."[73]

In his comments on Calvin's remarks Bullinger suggested that they could find unity of faith in the formula, "In the communion service, the Lord works internally through the power of the Spirit that which he externally seals through the symbol. He gives Himself to us to nourish him in our hearts and renews and strengthens our fellowship with him."[74]

---

[72] Der Verkehr Calvins mit Bullinger, p. 64.
[73] Ibid, p. 65.
[74] Ibid, p. 65.

Calvin leaves off discussions with Zürich and turns to Bern

Before Calvin received the above positive letter from Bullinger, he had sent the formulas which he and Bullinger had worked out to a meeting of the Bernese synod in March, 1549 as his own suggestions for church unity with the Bernese. The synod had been called to rid the Bernese church of the last elements of Lutheranism and Calvin, who had a reputation in Bern for being more a Lutheran than Reformed, had chosen the worst of times for his action. Haller was chosen to preside over the synod and Calvin's move did not please him. Haller had been party to most of the correspondence between Bullinger and Calvin on the issue of the Lord's Supper and knew that it was really Bullinger's and Calvin's joint work that Calvin had sent in the name of his own Church. The twenty articles that Calvin sent, however, did not contain Bullinger's final proposals and Haller immediately realised that there were still points of difference between the two parties. He therefore refused to lay the document before the Synod and wrote to Calvin saying that there were still ambiguous and confusing statements in it which could not be a basis for union. Haller was sensible enough to realise that Calvin was wanting to win for Geneva the privilege of being the first to gain concord with the Swiss-Germans through Bern. This meant that Calvin had turned his back on Bullinger whose hard work of many years was behind Calvin's attempt at a consensus with Bern. Calvin's ruse also meant that he was prepared to throw overboard the leadership of Bullinger and the Zürich church in a union of Swiss-German and Genevan churches. Obviously, he had imagined himself as that leader as his subsequent action proved.

Calvin again turns to Bullinger

Haller's and Bern's rebuff made Calvin more eager than ever to gain some sort of agreement with the Swiss-Germans and maintain some sort of leadership amongst the Swiss. However, instead of looking to himself for reasons behind the Bernese fiasco, when he wrote to Johannes Haller on 26 November, 1549, he told him that Satan had too much influence on those that regarded themselves as ministers in Bern.[75] Thus Satan was to blame for the lack of agreement, but not John Calvin! Meanwhile, he turned again to Bullinger on 7 May, albeit without mentioning Bern, thanking him for his heartfelt condolences on the death of his wife Idelette and confessing that after Bullinger's last suggestions for unity he could say, "I am very glad that hardly anything – or at least very little – hinders us from agreeing now even in words." Calvin mentions almost by the way that he would like Bullinger to visit Geneva and work out the final details with him.[76] Bullinger, who had scarcely ever left German-speaking Switzerland after taking over the Zürich church, replied that such a journey was not necessary and they could finish off the final particulars by correspondence. Before this letter reached Geneva, however, Calvin had decided he could not wait for a reply and dashed off to Zürich without informing anyone, not even his close friend Viret, of what he intended to do. Later, he told Myconius in November, 1549 that he had made up his mind to travel to Zürich only two days before starting the journey.

On 20 May, 1549, Calvin therefore asked the Genevan Council for permission to visit Zürich on a diplomatic mission concerning the needs of the Protestants of France. This was what might be called a white lie showing the circumlocutions of Calvin's thoughts. Pro-France Calvin felt that Switzerland, England and France should ally with one another. Thus the English under Edward VI could help curb the persecutions in France and if the French-speaking Protestants of Geneva and the Pays de Vaud were allied with the Protestant Swiss-Germans, this would make France more open to the Protestant cause and thus help relieve the persecuted Protestants in France. However, Bern and Zürich were fundamentally opposed to such a plan as far as the Swiss-German churches were concerned. Behind the French King loomed the long shadow of the Emperor and they did not want to give him the chance of meddling in Protestant affairs. Furthermore, France was using Swiss mercenaries against the French Protestants and any close alliance with France would

[75] John Calvin Collection: Ages Ultimate Christian Library CD.
[76] John Calvin Collection: Ages Ultimate Library CD.

make enrolment of mercenaries easier for them. Thus Calvin led the Genevan Council to believe that he was visiting Zürich on a purely diplomatic mission but Calvin had concealed his real reason, though his own private interpretation was that a consensus with the Swiss-Germans on the Lord's Supper would strengthen Geneva's bargaining power with France. None of this was in Bullinger's interest. Indeed, on 21 May, 1549 Bullinger wrote to Calvin, telling him not to make his proposed journey to Zürich. His reasons were perfectly clear. He told Calvin:

"We have hitherto understood each other better via correspondence than through an oral for and against discussion. Everything has progressed well with our written correspondence. So there is no need for you to leave your church and come to me at great expense and tire yourself out with a journey."[77]

This was typical Bullinger who never wasted money travelling and would never leave his pastoral duties for the sake of a heated argument which could be better solved in the peace and quiet of homely, pastoral life. Carl Pestalozzi sees the matter in a different light. He believes that Bullinger was not prepared to meet Calvin on Genevan soil at all because he feared becoming entangled in one of Calvin's political discussions concerning a treaty with France which Bullinger felt was not in the interest of the Reformed churches. Indeed, Bullinger told Calvin firmly in his reply that Zürich was not interested in such a treaty.[78] However, by the time that this letter was on its way to Calvin, Calvin was on his way to Bullinger under an assumed diplomatic mission.

Though Calvin must have passed through or close to Bern on his journey to Zürich, he did not inform Haller of his intention, though Haller had now become a fixed partner in the discussions. This was obviously clever strategy on the part of Calvin as he had informed Viret on 7 May that Haller had 'a great many unimportant and trivial points' to add. However, Calvin called on Farel at Neuchâtel, asking him to journey with

[77] Translated from the German quoted by Pestalozzi, p. 381.
[78] Ibid, pp 381-382.

him as an advisor and supporter. Indeed, in a letter written to Myconius in Basle on 26 November, 1549, Calvin said that the whole idea had been Farel's and not his own and he had at first rejected the idea because of his pessimistic nature.[79] Thus, when Calvin and Farel arrived at Zürich, they took Bullinger totally by surprise.

Full agreement within two hours discussion

According to Calvin, full agreement was reached within two hours. Bullinger quickly called together his fellow ministers and with them read through his joint correspondence with Calvin on the Lord's Supper and reduced them to 24 Articles, leaving out points which they found unacceptable and adding those which they felt represented the fullness of the Reformed doctrine. This time, Calvin found the Zürich ministers more critical than their Superintendent. Bullinger then asked Calvin if he could use this formulation as a basis for union. Calvin replied in the affirmative, asking leave to make a couple of minor alterations. Judging from what he told Bucer in June 1549, he added two paragraphs which Bucer had maintained Bullinger would never accept. However, Bullinger agreed with a calmness that surprised Calvin. The Frenchman told Bucer later that had all been of Bullinger's opinion, he would have gained more concessions. Yet, Calvin complained to Viret on 22 July concerning supposed 'absurdities' in Bullinger's Prefix to the Consensus and of his 'over-scrupulousness'. Nevertheless, during Calvin's surprise visit, Farel, Calvin and Bullinger put all disagreements aside and drew up their *Consensus Tigurinus*.[80]

A critical look at the traditional 'Calvinist' view of the Consensus

The traditional 'Calvinist' view is that in the *Consensus Tigurinus*, Genevan theology triumphed over the Zürich Reformation. The typical Lutheran view is that Calvin's Lutheran position, witnessed by his signing the *Consensus* triumphed over Bullinger's Reformed position. Neither of these views meets the facts. Concerning the idea that Calvin's

---

[79] Ibid. p. 67.

[80] Tiguria was also the English name for Zürich at the time.

views triumphed over Bullinger's, this could only be said if we, like so many writers on this period, leave Bullinger totally out and think as Imbart de la Tour in his *Calvin: Der Mensch-Die Kirche-Die Zeit* that the *Consensus Tigurinus* was a battle between the extremes of Zwingli's alleged memorial view of the Supper on the one hand and Calvin's more Lutheran view concerning the physical presence of Christ on the other. These two extremes had been balanced out in the theology of Henry Bullinger early in his youth and the winds of change had been blowing for 18 years in Zürich but de la Tour writes as if neither he nor Calvin had noticed it. So the same author tells us that Calvin came as 'a herald of peace' but nevertheless with the view of "defending Luther against the heavy accusations of the Zwinglians." If it had been Calvin's aim to defend Luther at Zürich, nothing of such a defence is seen in the *Consensus*, so such an aim came to nothing. Here it must be explained that the idea that Zwingli celebrated communion merely as a memorial rite of mere symbolic nature is certainly one of the many myths surrounding this man of whom we still know so little. As early as 1525 in his first Reformed Church Order, Zwingli showed that he had a far more developed and spiritual view of the Lord's Supper. Bullinger on several occasions had to tell Calvin that he had put Zwingli in the wrong drawer. Furthermore, shortly before his death, Zwingli said in his 1531 Appendix to his Order, "We believe, that Christ truly (wahrlich/*vere*) is present in the Lord's Supper; Yes, we believe that it cannot possibly be a Lord's Supper if the Lord is not present there."

The plain fact of the *Consensus* is that Bullinger, as foretold by Calvin, gave up nothing and took over nothing. All the changes were from Calvin's more Lutheran ideas to Bullinger's view of a real spiritual presence but not a presence in physical substance. Thus, though de la Tour believes that the victory was Calvin's because the *Consensus Tigurinus* is not according to his conception of Zwinglianism, he is forced to add, "Viewed theologically, it was a very mediocre victory for Calvin. His own doctrine took a back seat. He had to drop the term 'substance'."[81] The agreement reached was that the worshipper 'fed on Christ by faith and the power of His Spirit' which had been Bullinger's view since his student days and his early debates with Zwingli and the view anchored in the 1536 First Helvetic Confession, drawn up on Bullinger's initiative. Indeed, Calvin complained in letter after letter up to the *Consensus Tigurinus* taking place that Bullinger maintained his own opinion to the very last, whereas, he, Calvin, continually had had to accommodate his to Bullinger's.[82] So, too, Bullinger never visited Calvin in Geneva to discuss the Lord's Supper but Calvin made the difficult journey to Zürich in 1545, 1547, 1548 and 1549, twice with Farel, to consult Bullinger. Lindsay, a staunch free church Presbyterian, preserves what he feels is Calvin's fingerprint on the *Consensus* by arguing that the theology in the *Consensus Tigurinus* is still Calvin's, though it is expressed in 'Zwinglian' terms.[83] As the language of the *Consensus* clearly explains the theology behind it and Calvin's view of the Supper is not spelt out, it is safer to conclude that both the language and the theology are Bullinger's. Indeed, as Wilhelm A. Schulze in his anniversary article *Bullingers Stellung zum Luthertum* points out, "(Bullinger) first met Zwingli in 1523. Then, precocious Bullinger had developed an independent doctrine of the Lord's Supper which in no way was identical to that of Zwingli and Oecolampadius."[84] Thus, although Calvin put his signature to the consensus, in his analysis of Bullinger's and Calvin's doctrine of the sacraments and the Christology, ecclesiology and teaching on the atonement that goes with it, Gottfried W. Locher speaks only of the *Dissensus Tigurinus*.[85]

Paul E. Rorem in his *Calvinus Sacrae Scripturae Professor* essay entitled 'The Consensus Tigurinus (1549): Did Calvin Compromise?' argues that, in fact, both Calvin and Bullinger compromised in reaching an agreement. Rorem begins his study with Calvin's 1541 work entitled *A Short Treatise on the Lord's Supper* which strives, he argues, to find a

[81] De la Tour's *Calvin*, pp. 96-97.
[82] See, for instance, Calvin's letter to Bullinger 21 January. 1549, Ages Ultimate Library CD.
[83] *History of the Reformation*, Vol. II, p. 60.
[84] *Gesammelte Aufsätze zum 4000*. Todestag, Band 2, p. 287.
[85] *Bullinger und Calvin*, p. 3 ff.

middle way between the teaching of Wittenberg and Zürich. In this treatise, Calvin defines transubstantiation as an invention of the devil and the idea of the ubiquity of Christ incarnate, so rigidly held to by the Lutherans, as a pernicious fancy. When dealing with Zwingli and Oecolampadius, leaving Bullinger quite out of the debate, Calvin charges them with forgetting 'to define what is the presence of Christ in the Supper in which one ought to believe, and what communication of his body and his blood one there received.'[86] So he concludes that both Luther and Zwingli erred. However, at this time, Calvin had read little of Zwingli so that Bullinger had to point out to him in their discussions leading up to the *Consensus* that he had taken over Luther's mistaken idea of Zwingli concerning the Lord's Supper as a mere symbolic feast of remembrance without checking Zwingli's works. So, too, Calvin's own emphasis in concluding his treatise that the bread and wine "are such signs that the reality is joined to them," and that the faithful "are truly made partakers of the real substance of the body and blood of Jesus Christ",[87] shows that Calvin was nearer the Lutherans if not the Roman Catholics, in their understanding of the Supper than he was to the Reformers at Zürich. This emphasis is quite missing in the *Consensus Tigurinus*. So Rorem sees the litmus test of whether Calvin compromised or not in the question "Is the sacrament ever called an 'instrument' 'through' which 'we are truly offered what it signifies?' He finds that this idea is absent in the *Consensus*, or at least not expressed in the words Calvin normally used, so that we can speak of a compromise on Calvin's part. Concerning Bullinger, Rorem sees a possible compromise regarding Calvin's instrumentalism in Article 19 which states that 'Christ communicates himself to us in the Supper'. He admits, however, that Bullinger most likely did not take *in coena* (in the Supper) to mean 'by means of the Supper' but merely 'during the Supper'. So too, there is a possible compromise on Bullinger's part, according to Rorem when he substitutes 'instrument' for 'implement' or 'aid', but again, this need not imply instrumentalism but merely that the Supper is a help to faith but not

[86] *Treatise on the Lord's Supper*, Library of Christian Classics, Volume XXII, p. 165.
[87] Ibid, p. 166.

an instrument which conveys it. Rorem's conclusion, based on such scanty evidence, is, however, very daring but it echoes the rightly suspicious thoughts of Bern and Basle when they heard how much Calvin had given up in striving to reach a Swiss-Genevan agreement with Bullinger. It was widely agreed that the *Consensus* would not be Calvin's final position. In this spirit, Rorem affirms:

"The basic difference in sacramental theology between Calvin and Bullinger endured beyond these negotiations and their agreement on a text. Although alternative interpretations are possible, the most coherent assessment of the overall process is that they achieved a consensus statement principally because Calvin agreed to omit a crucial component of his position, to omit it for the moment but not for long." [88]

He goes on to argue that, in reality, there was no lasting compromise on Calvin's part because he immediately reverted back to his pre-consensus theology. Thus two different views of the Lord's Supper lived on side by side in Reformed theology. However, the Reformed view of the Supper as a spiritual partaking of Christ which exists today within those churches who hold to the text of the Thirty-Nine Articles, the Canons of Dort and the Westminster Confession is certainly that of Bullinger rather than Calvin. Oddly enough, however, this is commonly called 'Calvinism' today.

Rorem's evidence of a mutual compromise, however slight on Bullinger's part, is open to question. He begins with Calvin's 1541 work, which he admits was more Lutheran than Zwinglian. However, Calvin had been corresponding with Bullinger on the subject since at least 1538 and had also corresponded with Farel concerning Bullinger's views. Thus Bullinger's position on the Supper was quite familiar to him when he drew up his 1541 *Short Treatise*. However, in this work he put forward his views in relation to Luther and Zwingli but left Bullinger, the Superintendent of the Zürich Church and the major writer on the Lord's

[88] *The Consensus Tigurinus (1549): Did Calvin Compromise?*, p. 90.

Supper of the time out of his argument as if Bullinger had taken no part whatsoever in the debates. Yet Bullinger had been producing one work after another on the subject since around 1524 and had, according to Rorem, taken an individual line on the Lord's Supper since 1521. Furthermore, Rorem claims that Calvin's twenty articles that he sent to Bern in March 1549 composed the 'parent text' of the *Consensus Tigurinus*,[89] suggesting that thus Calvin's work was used as a basis for the discussions at Zürich. This is misleading as the twenty articles Calvin sent to Bern were the result of intensive communications with Bullinger who had filed and, at times, hammered them into shape and was hoping for a speedy agreement with Calvin. Again, however, Calvin left Bullinger out of his attempt to influence Bern his way and placed his compromise with Bullinger in the hands of the Bernese as if the articles were his very own. Furthermore, as explained above, Bern was still far from pleased with the theology represented in the articles and it took further work on Bullinger's part to bring them into line with Zürich's, i.e. Reformed, thought. Thus, as has been described above, we see Bullinger's major influence on the *Consensus Tigurinus* almost from Calvin's earliest days as a writer on doctrine and church order and worship. By the time the *Consensus* was agreed on, Calvin had become familiar with several of Bullinger's lengthier works on the Lord's Supper, including his Latin *De Sacramentis* of 1545 which was, according to Rorem, especially written not as "a polemic response to Luther but an irenical statement shared with Calvin." This work was originally merely for private help in the Bullinger-Calvin debates but was published as the sixth and seventh sermon in Book Five of the *Decades*.[90]

In all, there are three Calvinian-Lutheran[91] elements missing from the *Consensus Tigurinus* which are otherwise found in Calvin's Genevan publications, especially his Catechism: 1. the emphasis that the substance of Christ is present in the elements; 2. the resurrection of the body seen as

---

[89] Ibid, p. 85.
[90] Ibid, pp. 77-78.
[91] Nowadays Reformed writers use (or misuse) the term 'Calvinian' to mean part Calvinist and part Arminian. The term actually means merely 'appertaining to Calvin and his teaching' as 'Lutheran' means 'appertaining to Luther and the Church which bears his name.'

a surety given in the partaking of the elements and 3. the lack of emphasis on the spiritual eating of the bread and wine. These obvious facts led Justus Heer in his brief sketch of Bullinger's life in *Schriften des Vereins für Reformationsgeschichte*[92] to declare, "Only ignorance could lead to the idea that in the *Consensus Tigurinus*, German Switzerland accepted Calvin's teaching on the Lord's Supper." However, one looks in vain for Bullinger's name in the lengthy title that Bullinger placed at its head, though Calvin's name is there. This is typical of Bullinger's great humility and absolute aversion to making himself known by name. He gave the *Consensus* the title, *A Mutual Agreement Concerning the Sacraments between the Servants of the Church at Zürich and John Calvin, Servant of the Church at Geneva.*

Bruce Gordon, joint-editor with Emidio Campi of *Architect of Reformation: An Introduction to Heinrich Bullinger, 1504-1575*, concludes concerning the *Consensus*:

"Too much has been made of this agreement, which was, for the most part, a practical arrangement which suited both men. It was a partnership which worked well: Bullinger supported Calvin both openly and tacitly, agreeing not to disagree in public, and together they formed a common front against Lutheran opponents, such as Joachim Westphal, who wrote against the Swiss in the mid 1550s."[93]

The point is, however, in Bullinger's case the public stand he took was also his private stand but in the case of Calvin, his public support of the *Consensus Tigurinus* was often betrayed by his private utterances and works proceeding from Geneva solely in his own name.

The results of the Consensus

The *Consensus Tigurinus* allowed for joint-participation of the Lord's Supper between Zürich and Geneva. Happily, all the Protestant districts and cities joined Zürich and Geneva, led by Neuchâtel, Sankt Gallen,

[92] Vol. XXII, p. 89 ff.
[93] Op. cit. p. 20.

Biel, Schaffausen and Basle and finally, with a great deal of dilly-dallying, Bern, in signing the Zürich agreement. Haller of Bern was angry that he had been left out of the final drawing up of the consensus document, which did not improve his attitude towards Calvin. Peter Martyr wrote from England to congratulate Bullinger, saying:

"I congratulate also your churches upon the agreement among your ministers; and I beg and implore God to make it perpetual, whereby we may at length see one spirit, one faith, one baptism, as there is one Lord, and ought to be one body, the church."[94]

The signing of the consensus was a major step in Calvin's personal development as he was thus placed in fellowship with the major Swiss Reformers and internationally accepted as a Reformer of note himself. Ulrich Gäbler comments, "The Zürich Consensus brought a rapprochement between the Geneva and Zürich churches and allowed Calvin to find his place within the Swiss Reformed Church."[95] In this and other ways, Bullinger led and encouraged Calvin. One notable outcome of the Zürich conference was that the term 'Reformierte Kirche'[96] came into being to describe the Swiss Protestant churches and the Genevan Church so distinguishing them from the Roman Catholic system and Lutheranism. This is why Blanke and Leuschner call Bullinger 'Vater der Reformierten Kirche'[97] in their joint biography of the Reformer.[98] A. G. Dickens comments, "By the Zürich Agreement of 1549 on the Lord's Supper and by the Second Helvetic Confession of 1566, Bullinger united the forces of Zwinglianism and Calvinism into one Reformed religion, a faith able to conquer lands which Zwingli never knew."[99]

---

[94] Letter dated Oxford, 27 January, 1550, *Original Letters*, II, p. 279.

[95] *Huldrych Zwingli: His Life and Work*, Fortress Press, 1986, p. 159.

[96] Reformed Church.

[97] Father of the Reformed Church.

[98] Blanke's work on the young Bullinger was first published in 1942 and this life was completed by Leuschner in 1990 by his adding the story of Bullinger's life in Zürich.

[99] *Reformation and Society*, p. 124.

Critical reactions in Geneva and Germany to the Consensus

Many of Bullinger's and Calvin's friends were not at all pleased when the two Reformers signed the *Consensus Tigurinus*. Beza, who joined Calvin at this time, reacted at once in writing. He believed that Geneva should now lead the Swiss churches and the Waldensians and speak not merely with them but for them. He thus penned a new declaration concerning the Lord's Supper which approximated the Lutheran position that Calvin had given up in Zürich and soft-pedalled on the points of difference. This, he claimed, was the true teaching of the Swiss and Genevans. Thus, no sooner was a consensus gained than it was rejected by the very person who was to be Calvin's successor. Bullinger, Haller and Peter Martyr protested at once and the matter remained a great embarrassment for Calvin who was too indebted to Bullinger and their joint aim of uniting the Swiss churches to go it alone. No sooner was Calvin dead, however, than Beza once again emphasised the partaking of the substance of Christ in the Lord's Supper.[100] This led Lutheran Reformers to attack Bullinger's *Decades* on the grounds that his teaching on the Supper was at variance with Beza's which they recommended.[101] The ministers of Bern maintained that as Calvin was so ambiguous in his theological terms, the probability was that he would interpret the consensus in a way foreign to the exact wording. Myconius of Basle hesitated long before signing the document. He had always been suspicious of Calvin's doctrine of the Trinity and was also angry that he had not been invited to take part in the final discussion. The truth is that Zürich and Geneva never succeeded in keeping to exactly the same path on more than just the Lord's Supper. This is often explained by the French mentality of Geneva and the German mentality of Zürich. This theory does not fit the facts. Calvin leaned heavily on German-speaking Zwingli regarding predestination and was nearer German Luther sporadically on the Lord's Supper than Swiss-German-speaking Zürich

---

[100] "La participation à la substance de Jésus-Christ en la Cène," Choisy, p. 76. Choisy says that this caused a temporary discord between Bullinger and Beza which is rather an understatement.

[101] See Hollweg's discussion of this problem in Chapter 4 of his book *Heinrich Bullinger's Hausbuch.*

had ever been since their papist past. The fact that Calvin's church and ministerial colleagues were rarely one hundred percent behind him often bound his hands where Bullinger was quite free to lead. We know also from Calvin's letters that he would have willingly incorporated a number of the English reforms such as Confirmation, the laying on of hands and taking the Lord's Supper to the sick but his church would not allow him. Indeed, John Whitgift's major defence of the Reformed Church of England against the criticisms of Thomas Cartwright who claimed to be a 'Calvinist' was that Calvin stood far closer to the Church of England than Cartwright who rejected a number of Calvin's views. Not only Cartwright had difficulty in understanding Calvin. Carter Lindberg points out that Calvin was so often misunderstood by second-generation Lutherans because they invariably interpreted his moves towards Luther as signs that he was actually moving towards Zwingli.[102]

The Predestination Issue

Even whilst Bullinger and Calvin were discussing a way to bring about a consensus of faith regarding the Lord's Supper, the Pays de Vaud and Bern entered into a further controversy. Lausanne was led by Viret, who was perhaps even more of a thorn in the flesh to Bern than Calvin and who insisted on working closer with Geneva than with Bern. The quarrels between the stronger Bern and the 'protected' Pays de Vaud were not only over theological differences but also because Bern always felt that as they had rescued the Vaud from papal aggression, the Vaud should not strive to be too independent of Bern. The problem became so acute that both Haller in Bern and Viret in Lausanne asked Bullinger to mediate. Calvin joined their pleas from Geneva as his strictures on some of the controversies were behind Lausanne's stance. Bullinger took up his mediator role most unwillingly as both sides kept chopping and changing their opinions and thus Bullinger, whose doctrines remained constant, found himself criticised by jealous contenders when he appeared to side

[102] See also Horton Davies on *The Worship of the English Puritans* for further sources on this subject as also the Parker Society's volumes of Whitgift's works, Lindberg's *The European Reformations*, and my own *The Troublemakers at Frankfurt*.

with either one or the other contestants from time to time. In all, the controversy between Bern and Viret lasted from 1551 to 1559 when Viret gave up the fight and moved to Geneva, leaving his church behind him. Although the initial controversy was because of a false rumour that Calvin was once again planning to abolish the Christian holy days and make Sunday the sixth day of the week, it soon developed into a fierce discussion concerning predestination.

Chapter 5

Ridding Geneva of Heresy

Hieronymus Bolsec (d. 1585)

Amongst the many French refugees who sought asylum in Geneva was Hieronymus Bolsec, a former Carmelite monk and doctor. On 16 October, 1551, Bolsec accused Calvin of adding elements to his teaching on predestination which were not Biblical such as his presentation of God as the author of sin and the fall and double predestination.[1] Indeed, Bolsec's criticism was not so much concerned with predestination itself but it was because he felt that Calvin's idea of God was based on the classical Greek view of God as an arbitrary tyrant and not on the God of love revealed by Christ in the Scriptures. Predestination must be viewed according to the believer's standing in Christ rather than through a mere act of God's will irrespective of reasons apart from that will.[2] Bolsec argued that Calvin's doctrine of a double predestination as a mere arbitrary act of God was thus unscriptural and was derived from a faulty view of God. Scholars are basically agreed that this controversy did not trouble the Reformation until 1551 when Calvin is seen as the originator of it. Thus J. Wayne Baker writes in Chapter Two of his *Henry Bullinger*

[1] The teaching that God decreed not only the faith of the elect but also decreed the reprobation of some irrespective of the Fall.

[2] See Büsser, Vol. 2, pp. 119-121 for further thoughts on the Calvin-Bolsec controversy.

and the Covenant in the section entitled 'Predestination and Covenant in Bullinger's Thought':

"Predestination, insomuch as it was incipient in sola gratia, was a generally accepted doctrine from the very beginning of the Reformation, although it was not a source of contention in the early years. The importance of the teaching grew, however, until after mid-century, absolute double predestination increasingly became the test of orthodoxy in Reformed circles. But this did not happen without a struggle. Calvin himself was the author of the controversy, particularly in his argument with Bolsec in the early 1550s."

Calvin was highly insulted by the attack on his doctrine of double predestination, especially coming from Bolsec who had given up his original calling as a Roman Catholic priest on accepting Reformed doctrines to take up medicine. In his anger when criticising Bolsec for becoming a doctor as if this were tantamount to becoming a renegade, Calvin obviously forgot that many who were clerics under Rome had been forced to take on secular professions after they had left her. This was especially the case in France where many former ministers were now part of the underground church and had taken on secular professions. Bolsec's accusation resulted in his being arrested by the pro-Calvin faction and brought, not before a church tribunal or the Synod but before the Council. Bolsec, however, pleaded that he held to the evangelical faith and that it was Calvin who had brought in heresy. As most Protestants in Switzerland and her protectorates in those days, it was customary for them to either claim that Bullinger was on their side or look to him for arbitration. Bolsec, therefore, appealed to Bullinger. He also appealed to Melanchthon and Johann Brenz (Brentius) whom one would think had quite opposite views on the subject. The city's preachers did not back Calvin but asked the Council not to proceed with the trial until they had consulted Bullinger and the Zürich ministers. Calvin immediately wrote to Bullinger, informing him that Bolsec was a liar and had merely mentioned Bullinger to save his skin. Calvin then pleaded with Bullinger to write to the Council in support of Calvin's position on predestination.[3] Bullinger, who rarely agreed with Calvin concerning his severe methods of church discipline, replied personally saying that his agreement with Calvin on predestination was already clearly stated in Article XVI of the *Consensus Tigurinus* and this had already been declared publicly. This answer did not satisfy Calvin as Bolsec had challenged him on the special issue of predestination to reprobation which was not emphasised in the *Consensus*. So Bullinger, eager to put an end to the controversy, met with his fellow-ministers to draw up a formal reply for the Genevan Council. On 27 November, 1551, the Zürich ministers composed a clear, detailed statement of faith in Divine predestination and election according to the Infralapsarian understanding and forwarded it to the Genevan Council. In this statement, they also stressed that the sinner is responsible for his own fall and not God and that he could not give God the blame for Adam's or any man's sin but was without excuse.[4] This formal, orthodox statement angered Calvin as it left out the harshness of his own position which he wanted Bullinger to defend and therefore give it legitimacy. He felt that the statement from Zürich merely preached down to him and told him what to believe. He wanted Bullinger personally to condemn Bolsec outright so that they could get on with the trial. Beza intervened and explained to Bullinger that Calvin needed a personal favour from Bullinger and begged him to write something privately to Calvin for his comfort and in his defence, touching more closely on Calvin's problem and at more at length on the subject of Bolsec's criticism. Bullinger thus wrote again privately to Calvin in December, 1551 giving him his Reformed views concerning a personal predestination. Obviously such a letter was more in Calvin's favour than Bolsec's if the rumour that Bolsec rejected personal predestination and election altogether were true. It was said that Bolsec argued backwards from the acceptance of the gospel against the background of a common election for all who believed. Nevertheless, Bullinger pleaded for mildness on Calvin's part, saying, "If Hieronymus

[3] Sehe Hollwegs Buch, p. 295 für Quellenangaben.
[4] Ibid, p. 296.

attributes our entire salvation to the grace of God and nothing to our powers, and if he cannot come to a conclusion regarding reprobation but friendlily censures others, who also ascribe everything to God's grace, so he must, in my opinion, by means of wise admonition from you, so that he might maintain a balanced position, be prevented from falling." Thus Bullinger appealed to Calvin's pastoral duties rather than his disciplinary judgment. Bullinger also told Calvin that his dogmatism was out of place as his own doctrine of predestination was badly grounded in Scripture. On being informed of Bullinger's opinion, the Genevan Council freed Bolsec, saying that they had no case against him. Patronising Bern scolded Geneva for bringing Bolsec to trial in the first place and granted him asylum. Some years later, Bolsec revenged himself on Calvin by writing a very negative biography of his life and that of Beza.

Calvin was now very angry with Bullinger. As soon as he read what the Zürich ministers in general and Bullinger in particular had to say, he took their wise words as a personal attack on his integrity and honour. He told Farel in a most exaggerated way, "I can hardly express to you, my dear Farel, how much I am annoyed by their rudeness. There is less humanity among us than among wild beasts." He added, "Should you be displeased with the general letter of the men of Zürich, let me tell you, that Bullinger's private letter to me was not a whit better."[5] Exaggerating even further, Calvin told Farel that Bullinger's words showed 'supreme contempt' for his Genevan friend. Calvin fretted over the Zürich letters for some time but in January of the following year, he decided to write to Bullinger and give him a piece of his mind. He told his friend that he was 'grieved beyond measure' asked him if he did not realize that Bolsec was 'a worthless wretch'. The entire relatively long letter is one of complaint, self-pity and enmity without one of Bullinger's scriptural points being taken up. Calvin closes with the rather hollow, haughty and ill-placed words, "Although you disappoint my expectations, I nevertheless gladly offer you our fellowship."

---

[5] Letter written 8 December, 1551.

Bullinger replied on 20 February, 1552 explaining to Calvin that he gave the impression of teaching that God had not only foreseen Adam's fall but predestinated and activated it so that He is made the author of sin. Such a teaching would only scare people away from listening to the gospel, Bullinger added. This was exactly the point Bolsec had made against Calvin. Bern, greatly angered by Calvin's attitude, used all their political power to curb him and forbade the people of the Vaud to go to neighbouring Geneva and take communion there. Again, Calvin turned to Bullinger and begged him to mediate. Bullinger saw that the Bernese Council were now going to extremes themselves and told them that their reaction was too extreme. As a result of Bullinger's mediation, Bern lifted the Lord's Supper embargo on Geneva. One would now have thought that Calvin, in turn and out of thankfulness for Bullinger's mediation, would show some flexibility himself as the Bernese Reformers had shown in his own case. He, however, remained inflexible and continued to demand punishment for Bolsec.

After the Bolsec scandal had died down, Bullinger became seriously ill and did not correspond with Calvin for several months. Mutual 'friends' told Bullinger that Calvin had taken this amiss and was now openly stating that Bullinger had become his enemy. Bullinger thus wrote to his easily insulted friend, saying, "If any one has told you that Bullinger has become Calvin's enemy, then he has spread an evil rumour. Though in the matter of Bolsec, I did not share your views in all respects, this does not mean that I am no longer your friend. I told you then why we could not fully support you."[6] Calvin replied that he would not give up his trust in Bullinger and his fellow ministers with the exception of Bibliander of whom he had heard that he was writing a book against his doctrine of predestination. Bibliander was the senior professor at Zürich's *Prophezei*, appointed by Bullinger and one of his very closest friends. This very statement of Calvin's showed his sensitivity in listening to and believing evil reports. Bullinger replied;

[6] *Der Vekehr Calvins mit Bullinger*, p. 84.

"I do not think that our Professor Bibliander, without doubt a pious and learned man, is your enemy, although not all your views please him. Every thing that the Ancients (Church Fathers) say does not please me without me suddenly calling them enemies. You wrote yourself that we did not meet your expectations in your quarrel with Bolsec but the cords of unity and love have not been cut. Also, I do not believe that our Bibliander is writing a book against you."[7]

Calvin was soon forced to forget the accusations he had made against the Zürich ministers as his troubles with Servetus were now starting and he needed all the support he could obtain from his Zürich friends. However, he remained increasingly critical of Bibliander, always listening to rumours that this most peaceful-minded man was going to produce some work or other denigrating the Genevan minister. This remained a phobia with Calvin up to 1564, the year both Bibliander and Calvin died.

Michael Servetus (1511-1553)

The brutal execution of the Anti-trinitarian and Anabaptist Spaniard Michael Servetus has been traditionally used by Rome, who paradoxically condemned Servetus to death themselves, and a number of anti-Reformed churches, to denigrate the entire Reformation movement. In particular, Calvin has been universally branded as the church tyrant of tyrants who burnt Servetus to death. As Bullinger took a much stronger line against Servetus than Calvin, and was in a more authoritative position to send Servetus to the scaffold, it is necessary to look more carefully into this matter, allowing history to speak for itself.

Servetus had fled from his home country to avoid persecution as a young man and had hoped to settle down in Basle. There, in 1530, he published his Arian work *De Trinitatis erroribus*, arguing that there was no basis for the doctrine of the Trinity. Oecolampadius, the Superintendent of the Basle Church, immediately accused Servetus of

---

[7] Ibid, p. 85.

blasphemy, calling his book, *liber terque quaterque blasphemus ac impius* and had him banned from the city. Shortly afterwards, Servetus began to correspond with the young Calvin, a fact that was later used as evidence against Calvin when he was accused of Arianism by Bern and Basle. Servetus now moved from place to place, greatly restricted in his movements by enemies on both the Roman Catholic and Reformed sides. Whilst in Vienna, Servetus was betrayed to the papist and political authorities, imprisoned and sentenced to death by burning. According to Johannes Friedrich Franz of St Gallen, it was John Calvin who disclosed Servetus' whereabouts to the Roman Catholics.[8] This would be one factor explaining Servetus extreme hatred of Calvin which was reciprocated. Another was that Servetus strove to discredit Calvin and Christianity in general, in his *De Christianismi Restitutio*. It was this work which caused the papists to condemn Servetus to be burnt. Even in the papist prison in Vienna, however, Servetus denounced Calvin in the strongest terms, calling him a dealer in magic and a sycophant. He even demanded that the Geneva Council, amongst whom he had close friends, should punish Calvin to the uttermost. Servetus managed to escape from prison and was invited to Geneva by very influential citizens such as Perrin and Berthelier who were former supporters of Calvin but now looked to Servetus and wished to set him up in Geneva against Calvin whom they now detested, chiefly for his turn-coat attitude to them.

Geneva's policy with heretics and blasphemer's had always been severe before ever Calvin had any authority whatsoever in the city. Indeed, the party responsible for banishing Calvin from Geneva in 1538 did not hesitate to torture and behead those who left the paths of their church. According to the city records, however, there seems to have been no set punishments for particular 'crimes' as one blasphemer was only given a jail sentence on 4 June, 1539 and people caught dancing on the Sabbath were merely let off with a warning on 20 February, 1539.[9] Furthermore, it must be said that there was not a country or state in

[8] *Merkwürdige Züge aus dem Leben des Zürcherischen Antistes Heinrich Bullinger*, pp. iii-iv.
[9] See lists produced by William, G. Naphy in his *Calvin's Letters: Reflections on their Usefulness in Studying Genevan History*.

Europe at the time in which the denial of the Trinity and blasphemy were not capital crimes. German Lutheran Melanchthon, for instance, urged the Swiss not to show any leniency whatsoever regarding Servetus; he must be put to death. Furthermore, the major blame given to Calvin for the burning of Servetus has no historical backing. Actually, Calvin had neither the power, nor the opportunity, nor the wish to burn Servetus. The Geneva magistrates had initially asked Calvin to give his opinion of Servetus because they were under great pressure from Bern and Basle to undertake action against the blasphemer. Calvin had replied mildly that he had little hope of bringing Servetus to his senses and that he needed to learn humility. This was hardly a view which would help the Council condemn anyone to death.

Calvin was ignored in the Servetus trial

Anyone reading such standard Reformed works as William Cunningham's *The Reformers and the Theology of the Reformation* and who have been brought up on the eulogies concerning Calvin contained therein will be moved into thinking that the Frenchman's 'commanding influence' was so prevalent in his day that the Genevan church and secular authorities were unanimous in acclaiming him to be the greatest Christian and the most influential hero short of the New Testament Apostles themselves. It appears that he had only to speak in Geneva and all were automatically at his beck and call save for the ne'er-do-wells and papists.[10] It is thus commonly thought in certain 'Reformed' circles that Calvin had full control over the Geneva magistrates. This was by no means the case. Calvin was not unanimously supported by any means either by the Council or by the Church and he was constantly in danger of being re-expelled after his 1538-41 expulsion. On several occasions between 1541 and 1553, he had thought of fleeing from the city because of his own lack of acceptance amongst his fellow ministers and the Genevan Council. Both the Council and opposition wanted more state and less church but Calvin's doctrine of State-Church relationships went

[10] See especially his chapter 'John Calvin'.

through various extremes but he tended gradually to prefer more Church to less State and campaigned for a Church which would take over many responsibilities formerly held by the State. Geneva never found the balance which proved so successful in Zürich. During the period of Servetus' influence in Geneva, Calvin was again threatened with expulsion as we know from his correspondence with Bullinger who begged him to remain firm and keep up his witness in spite of the anti-Calvin riots in the city. Such happenings caused August Lang to write in his *Zwingli und Calvin* "The years 1552 and 1553 were the most bitter and saddening in Calvin's turbulent life. He experienced disparagement and even contempt."[11]

On hearing of Servetus' criticisms of Calvin and the city authorities suspicion of him, Bullinger assured Calvin of his support, remarking that Servetus was no common heretic but a dangerous deceiver of men who was beyond correction and the Geneva magistrates ought to deal with him under the full power of their laws. Bullinger also told Calvin that the Zürich Council believed that Geneva should "put a stop to this pestilence", that is, put Servetus on trial and pronounce the death penalty.[12] It is obvious from the context that Bullinger was in full agreement with his Council. As Calvin was seriously considering leaving Geneva himself, whatever the magistrates decided, Bullinger quoted Acts 18:9-10 to him "Be not afraid, but speak, and hold not thy peace: For I am with thee, and no man shall set on thee: for I have much people in the city," and begged Calvin not to give up the good work he had begun at Geneva. Bullinger reminded Calvin of his calling to protect the French Protestant refugees, pointing out that this work would collapse if Calvin left his post at Geneva. It is, however, at this moment of weakness on Calvin's part, and at a time when he was in as much danger as Servetus of reaping the anger of the magistrates, that some commentators would have us believe that Calvin ruled Geneva!

After fleeing from Vienna and spending some time in Italy, Servetus, thinking that he would be safe in Geneva, sought asylum there. On 13

[11] Bielefeld und Leipzig, 1913, p. 127.
[12] *Original Letters*, Vol. II., p. 742.

August, 1553, Servetus was recognised in Geneva by several citizens who applied for his arrest. Actually, thinking himself secure, Servetus had sat in the congregation of Magdalena Church where Calvin was scheduled to preach! He was quickly put on trial but the magistrates became nervous because of the pro-Servetus lobby. Calvin wrote to Farel on 20 August 1553:

"We have now new business in hand with Servetus. He intended perhaps passing through this city; for it is not yet known with what design he came. But after he had been recognised, I thought that he should be detained. My friend Nicolas summoned him on a capital charge, offering himself as security according to the *lex talionis*. On the following day he adduced against him forty written charges. He at first sought to evade them. Accordingly we were summoned. He immediately reviled me, just as if he regarded me as obnoxious to him. I answered him as he deserved. At length the Senate pronounced all the charges proven … I hope that sentence of death will at least be passed upon him; but I desire that the severity of the punishment may be mitigated."[13]

As usual in his letters to Farel, Bucer, etc., Calvin seeks to show himself as the one being in control of the situation but this letter, especially the words, "He intended perhaps passing through this city', actually shows that Calvin did not really know what was happening. So, too, his words "I thought that he should be detained" are very ambiguous. Does this mean that Calvin is describing a private thought, or was it a thought publicly aired or does it mean that Calvin had Servetus arrested as believed by those who say that Calvin controlled Geneva? Actually, the trial did not run at all as smoothly as Calvin claims. The Director of Public Prosecutions, Rigot, was a member of the opposition party and an avowed opponent of Calvin. Indeed, Calvin's opinions were of no interest to the court but the majority also refused to be put under pressure by the influential minority who supported Servetus. Not daring to judge Servetus

[13] John Calvin Colletion, Ages Library CD.

alone, they gave up their responsibility as an independent court and told Servetus that they would hand him over to the Roman Catholic authorities who had already condemned him to death. Servetus begged in tears to remain in Geneva. Then the Geneva Senate suggested appealing to all the Protestant cantons, promising they would abide by their decision. Servetus and his defenders agreed at once. Calvin protested against this move but the Senate ignored him completely. He thus wrote to Bullinger on 7 September, 1553:

"Our Council will, on an early day, send the opinions of Servetus to your city, to obtain your judgment regarding them. Indeed, they cause you this trouble, despite our remonstrances, but they have reached such a pitch of folly and madness, that they regard with suspicion whatever we say to them. So much so, that were I to allege that it is clear at mid-day, they would forthwith begin to doubt of it."[14]

Protestant Switzerland unanimous in demanding the death penalty for Servetus

Basle told Geneva that if Servetus did not repent, they must use the powers that God has given them to rid the world of one who was so dangerous to the Church. Bern, who was always critical of Calvin's policies, told Geneva to eradicate the plague which had settled down amongst them and burn Servetus at the stake. Haller wrote to Bullinger, "The man is an arch-heretic and has deserved that the Church should be freed from him"[15] Bullinger's Zürich reply was, "No severity is too great to punish this outrage". The other cantons gave similar judgements. Bullinger wrote to Theodore Beza privately on 30 August, 1553 saying, "But what is your most honourable senate of Geneva going to do with that blasphemous wretch Servetus? If they are wise, and do their duty, they will put him to death, that all the world may perceive that Geneva desires the glory of Christ to be maintained inviolate."[16] It must be noted

---

[14] Ibid.
[15] *Der Verkehr Calvins mit Bullinger*, p. 86.
[16] Ibid, Vol. II, pp. 741-42.

here that Bullinger did not seek the death penalty for Servetus as a heretic but as a blasphemer of God, one who wished to destroy the democracy that the Swiss people loved. He believed Servetus was not only a plague to the churches but his system aimed to overthrow civilized society. Calvin told Farel of the Swiss-German reaction on 26 October, writing:

"The messenger has returned from the Swiss Churches. They are unanimous in pronouncing that Servetus has now renewed those impious errors with which Satan formerly disturbed the Church, and that he is a monster not to be borne. Those of Basle were judicious. The Zürichers were the most vehement of all; for they not only animadverted in severe terms on the atrocity of his impieties, but also exhorted our Senate to severity. They of Schaffhausen will agree. Also to an appropriate letter from the Bernese is added one from the Senate, in which they stimulate ours not a little … He will be led forth to punishment tomorrow. We endeavored to alter the mode of his death, but in vain. Why we did not succeed I defer for narration until I see you."[17]

The Senate thus sentenced Servetus to death by burning. Calvin's plea that the sentence should be changed to death by beheading, which was thought more merciful was ignored. Once again the rumour spread around Bern that Calvin would resign. Even Bullinger, whose friendship with Calvin was stable, could not help telling his Geneva friend that he had made a mess of things and had not spoken up against Servetus when he should have done. Referring to Calvin's belated written refutation of Servetus in late 1553 in which Calvin had quoted a private letter from Bullinger without asking his permission, Bullinger tells Calvin that he fears that his book will make little impact because of its brevity and obscurity and the weightiness of the subject. He also tells Calvin that his style is too perplexing, and adds, "I know that you will kindly take this freedom of mine; for I love you from my heart."[18]

---

[17] John Calvin Collection, Ages Library CD.

[18] Ibid, Vol. II, pp.743-47. See also Calvin's letter to Bullinger dated 30 December, 1553 in which Calvin tells Bullinger of his anti-Servetus work.

Calvin replied in April, 1554 saying:

"In my little treatise, I have been under a constant apprehension lest my brevity should occasion some obscurity. This, however, I have not been able to guard against, nay with deliberate intention and induced by other reasons, I have not even sought to guard against it. For what I had not only principally but I may say singly proposed to myself, was to make manifest the detestable impiety of Servetus. But an eloquent treatise on the matters in question would have seemed a feat of cunning, and by the pomp of its style, not to refute tenets so impious. In my style, I do not perceive that stateliness which you speak of, on the contrary, I made it my endeavour, so far as it was possible, to give, even to the unlettered reader, a clear notion of the perplexing sophisms of Servetus, without any troublesome deduction or laboured explication. However, it does not escape me that though I am concise in all my writings, in this one I have been more than usually succinct. But let it only appear that with sincere faith and upright zeal, I have been the advocate of sound doctrine, and this single consideration will have more weight with me than that I should repent of the work I have undertaken. You yourself, from your affection towards me, and the natural candour and equity of your temper, judge with indulgence. Others animadvert on me with greater harshness, even a master of cruelty and atrocity — that I now mangle with my pen the dead man who perished by my hands. There are also some not malevolently disposed, who could wish that I had never touched on the question of the punishment of heretics. For they say that all the others, in order to avoid odium, have expressly held their tongues. But it is well that I have you for the partner of my fault, if fault indeed there is, since you were my prompter and exhorter. Look then that you get ready for the contest."[19]

This stance was sadly all too typical of Calvin. He praises his own steadfastness but is always ready to hand over the responsibility to others

[19] *Calvinism in Europe 1540-1610*, p. 39.

if things do not turn out to his satisfaction. However, it is obvious that the Swiss Protestant cantons, with Bullinger to the fore, were unanimous in condemning Servetus for his blasphemy and godless religion. On the other hand, it was Geneva that showed the most uncertainty as how to proceed. This was because the position held by Calvin was not shared by an influential group in both council and Church and there was not that unity of mind in Church and state that flourished in Bern, Basle and especially Zürich. Calvin always gave his critics the blame, saying "Because the godless know that I am short-tempered, they seek by all means to irritate me and to tire my patience."[20] Of the Reformers, Calvin was certainly not the most vigorous in condemning Servetus, possibly because he was in no position to say much in the city about him at all. Indeed, Bullinger's position in Zürich was far stronger than Calvin's ever was in Geneva. He was also most likely able to view the matter more objectively, not being directly and personally involved in the controversy as was Calvin. If any one man can be given the responsibility of Servetus death, it must be Bullinger who strongly influenced the other cantons in his antagonism to Servetus. Thus, the idea that it was Calvin's iron rule of the Genevans which forced them to burn Servetus, a myth both critics of the Reformation and even some Reformed writers affirm, is without any historical backing whatsoever. Old prejudices die hard and though, for instance, August Lang says that Calvin's influence in Geneva at this time was the lowest that it had ever been, and it had had many ups and downs, he still gives Calvin full responsibility for Servetus' burning. He accuses Calvin of not being man enough to confess that he was behind Servetus' arrest and execution but he brings no evidence whatsoever to support his theory.[21] One thing is, however, certain. After Servetus' execution, Calvin's star began once again to ascend in Geneva. It was, however, Bullinger's strong testimony against Servetus which put off many a writer such as Professor Felix Nüscheler mentioned above, from attempting to write a biography of him.

---

[20] *Der Verkehr Calvins mit Bullinger*, p. 88.
[21] *Zwingli und Calvin*, pp. 130-131.

Sebastian Castellio (1515-1563)

This was not the last time by far that Calvin was compelled to look to Bullinger for support in a difficult situation. As soon as the problem of Servetus was out of the way, Calvin was caught up in controversies over his church order and discipline and thus wrote to Bullinger on 26 November, 1553 with a new request for help:

"Here is another new labour for you. Those desirous of living a life of licentiousness have not ceased for the past seven years to oppose the discipline of the Church, which is in a tolerable state of efficiency here. We would not, however, have been so much annoyed by loose-living men among the common people, if there had not been leaders who wished to convert this license into a means of power. It has now come to this, that whatever church order has hitherto flourished will be rooted up if you cannot afford us a remedy. And it is on this account that our very excellent brother, M. de Bude, has not scrupled to undertake a journey to you, at this trying season of the year, in order to acquaint you with the whole business .... However, things will be better in a short time, I trust, if you will come to our assistance."[22]

It soon became obvious that what was worrying Calvin was a controversy in his church concerning the disciplining of heretics. Now, having supreme confidence in his good friend and knowing his own weaknesses, he thus wrote to Bullinger assuming that he would be able to clear up the matter quickly in his usual way. Calvin told Bullinger on 28 March, 1554, "A short time ago a book was also published clandestinely at Basle, in which under feigned names Castalio and N... argue that heretics ought not to be repressed by the sword. Would that the pastors of that church at length, though late, aroused themselves to prevent the evil from spreading wider." Actually the treatise Calvin referred to *De non Puniendis Gladio Haereticis* appeared under the name Martinus Bellius which gave the impression of its being a pseudonym. In this work, Calvin

[22] John Calvin Collection, Ages Library CD.

was castigated for insisting that church discipline including the death penalty should be enforced by the Council. So the next controversy Calvin had on his hands was with Sebastian Chatillon, commonly called Castellio,[23] the famous Bible translator and educator and Calvin's close friend from his Strasburg days. Castellio argued that the death penalty had been too severe for Servetus' heresy, so Calvin placed him in the group of Anti-Trinitarians that Servetus represented. However, sufficient proof is still lacking to show beyond reasonable doubt that Castellio was either the author or part author of this and other small works published anonymously or under pseudonyms[24] in French and Latin which attacked Calvin for his ruthlessness in using the secular arm to force citizens to obey Calvin's church orders. These writings also accused Calvin of teaching that God was the author of sin and that God had two wills in salvation. The accusations of Castellio (if Castellio were truly their author) are of great interest in the modern debate as those who hold that God is the author of sin on the Hyper-Calvinist side and those who hold that God has two wills amongst those who call themselves 'Moderate Calvinists' are now divided into two militant camps both of whom insist that they are interpreting Calvin aright. Calvin replied with at least two works. The first is now lost, but his *Brief Reply in refutation of the calumnies of a certain worthless person* has been preserved and is available in a number of languages.[25] Although, Bullinger criticized Calvin for dealing with predestination outside of the believer's union with Christ, and warned him that he was actually accusing God of being the author of sin, he did not receive a fraction of the abuse that Calvin poured on Castellio. However, if Castellio were indeed the author of the anti-Calvin works mentioned (which is doubtful for reasons given below), he appears to have believed that God did not determine human actions in any way at all. When Bullinger was asked to help Calvin, he warned his

[23] Also spelt 'Castallio' and 'Chateillon'.

[24] Anti-Calvin tracts were authored by a Georg Kleinberg and Basilius Montford and were thought by Calvin to be pseudonyms for Castellio. Calvin also accused Celio Secondo Curione of writing against him under a pseudonym but Curione denied this.

[25] See J.K.S. Reid's Introduction to Calvin's *Brief Reply in refutation of the calumnies of a certain worthless person, Calvin*: Theological Treatises, p. 331-332.

Genevan friend against condemning people on flimsy evidence and not to claim that he knew who had written the offending tracts when he had no idea. Bullinger thought the tracts had most likely an origin amongst the Italian Anti-trinitarians and this is very much the stance Professor Uwe Plath takes, giving detailed evidence, in his *Calvin und Basle in den Jahren 1552-1556* published by Basle University in 1974.[26]

Calvin has been strongly criticised for his treatment of Sebastian Castellio. Writers coming mainly from the Methodist schools have painted Calvin in very dark colours for combating Castellio's alleged doctrine of universal predestination and election according to conditions to be performed by man. Reformed writers have, however, praised Calvin for his strong-armed tactics against the 'heretic'. Actually, it is difficult to work out what Castellio actually taught and what is merely attributed to him from various sides who wish to use Castellio as a banner for their particular views. So, too, when one reads Calvin's anti-Castellio writings both in book and letter form, the dualism in Calvin's view of God becomes apparent so that the reader finds Calvin both affirming that God appointed Adam to sin and denying it in the same work. So in Calvin's *Brief Reply*, he argues that nothing ever happens unless by the will of God but that God is not implicated in the vice of men.[27] So, too, in his *Articles concerning Predestination* Calvin affirms:

"Before the first man was created, God in his eternal counsel had determined what he willed to be done with the whole human race.

In the hidden counsel of God it was determined that Adam should fall from the unimpaired condition of his nature, and by his defection should involve all his posterity in sentence of eternal death.

Upon the same decree depends the distinction between elect and reprobate: as he adopted some for himself for salvation, he destined others for eternal ruin. While the reprobate are the vessels of the just wrath of God, and the elect vessels of his compassion, the ground of the distinction

[26] *Basler Beiträge zur Geschichtswissenschaft*, Basle und Stuttgart, see especially pp. 29 ff; 79 ff; 154 ff..

[27] *Brief Reply*, *Calvin Theological Treatises*, p. 333.

is to be sought in the pure will of God alone, which is the supreme rule of justice.

While the elect receive the grace of adoption by faith, their election does not depend on faith but is prior in time and order. As the beginning of faith and perseverance in it arises from the gratuitous election of God, none are truly illuminated with faith, and none granted the spirit of regeneration, except those whom God elects. But it is necessary that the reprobate remain in their blindness or be deprived of such portion of faith as is in them.

While we are elected in Christ, nevertheless that God reckons us among his own is prior in order to his making us members of Christ.

While the will of God is the supreme and primary cause of all things, and God holds the devil and the godless subject to his will, nevertheless God cannot be called the cause of sin, nor the author of evil, nor the subject of any guilt."

Such statements puzzled more than Castellio and Bullinger, especially the idea of election in Christ prior to being made a member of Christ. For Bullinger, election was, by definition, being placed in Christ. Yet Calvin could write his major treatise *Concerning the eternal Predestination of God* and *Concerning Free will* against Pighius without giving as much as a hint that predestination and election were 'in Christ'.

Bullinger's importance in the Castellio controversy

Here, again, the enormous influence of Bullinger on the entire Castellio controversy is often ignored. Castellio, a native of St Martin-du-Fresne in the Savoyan district of Bugey, met Calvin when both were exiles in Strasburg. The two men apparently concurred in their opinions as Calvin subsequently nominated Castellio as rector of the de la Rive city high school at Geneva, which Castellio accepted. Indeed, Castellio professed to have been awakened to the Reformation by reading Calvin's *Institutes*. The school at Geneva was to prepare pupils for either the ministry or civil administration and government. It soon became apparent, however, that Castellio and Calvin not only disagreed on the treatment of heretics which Castellio thought was solely a matter for inner-church counsel and discipline but they also disagreed on predestination. Castellio also castigated Calvin for his book against Servetus which, as we have seen, did not impress Bullinger too much either. Bullinger, however, also earned Castellio's wrath for apparently aiding and abetting Calvin in his attitude to heretics. Castellio believed in taking Titus 3:10[28] literally, which was the usual Reformed way of approaching the passage. He thus felt that Bullinger had departed fully from the spirit of Scripture by interpreting 'reject' as 'put to death'. However, to be fair to Bullinger who was thinking more politically here than perhaps pastorally, he condemned Servetus formally as an enemy of the state and did not seek the death penalty for a 'heretic', though, according to the most comprehensive of Christian standards, Servetus was a heretic of heretics. Another point of difference between Calvin and Castellio which has since been greatly exaggerated by Calvin's defenders was that in 1543 when Castellio applied to become a preacher and had to give a public statement of his faith, he spoke critically of the Song of Songs as a canonical work and professed that he took Christ's descent into Hell literally. Castellio followed the older theological schools in linking 1 Peter 3:19 to the 'descent into Hades mentioned in the Apostles Creed. In his interpretation of Christ's death, Calvin also differed from the traditional interpretation. He had maintained since his early work *Psychopannychia* (1534) that 1 Peter 3:19 had nothing to do with the creedal statement. Bullinger saw a connection between the two but argued that the efficacious work of Christ's death embraced all the dead in Christ and served to damn the 'disobedient'. He added that there is no Scripture which refers to the dead elect being imprisoned but that they are referred to as being in Abraham's bosom or in Paradise.[29] Castellio followed Luther in his interpretation of the canon, believing that all the books were not equally inspired and that one should search for the Spirit in them rather than merely believe them because a church council had compiled them. This caused Calvin to reject Castellio's application and he also refused to back Castellio in his work on a French New Testament. In spite of strong protests from the Bernese

[28] 'A man that is a heretic after the first and second admonition reject.'
[29] See Locher's *Bullinger und Calvin*, p. 15 for a wider discussion with sources given.

Council, Calvin had Castellio deprived of his post at the school and threatened with 'punishment'. Castellio fled to Basle where he lived under most difficult financial circumstances before managing to publish his Latin translation of the Bible after which he gained a chair as Professor of Greek. Calvin could have found other, more diplomatic and pastoral, methods of ridding Geneva of Castellio as he was under strong criticism himself for distinguishing between the Word of God and the canon and going to extremes concerning the doctrine of predestination. Indeed, at that time the Reformed cantons of Bern and Basle thought Calvin was a more dangerous challenge to orthodoxy than Castellio. Calvin's rejection of Revelation was hardly less radical than Castellio's view of the Song of Songs. Furthermore, Castellio's successors lacked his educational and organisational abilities and the school that he had set up as the pride of Europe went through a ten-year period of acute deterioration. Calvin could find no one of Castellio's academic stature to take his place. Bernard Riggenbach, whilst commenting on Castellio's Bible work says:

"After living there (Basle) for several years in great poverty, he published, in 1551, his Latin translation of the Bible, dedicated to Edward VI of England; and in the following year he was made professor of Greek. In 1555 appeared his French translation of the Bible, dedicated to Henry II of France. The Latin Bible of Castellio, the last edition of which appeared in 1756, may be characterised as the Bible of the Humanists. The powerful realism of the original text is often weakened by the elegant forms of the translation. But the violent attacks of Calvin and Beza find their explanation, not so much in the faults of the work as in the connection in which Castellio stood to certain anonymous treatises against Calvin's doctrine of predestination, and to Martinus Bellius's *De non Puniendis Gladio Haereticis*."[30]

---

[30] *Schaff-Herzog Encyclopaedia*, Vol. I, p. 414.

Sadly, disillusioned by what he felt was unjust and un-Christian treatment at the hands of Calvin, Castellio became one of his staunchest critics and both Bern and Basle denounced Calvin as a radical extremist. Calvin kept Bullinger informed of his troubles both inside and outside of Geneva. On 18 September, 1554, he wrote to his Zürich mentor:

"Of the state of our affairs, I write to you nothing, except that we are still floating in suspense, that through our sluggishness, the profligate are allowed to make game of us with as much sauciness as impunity. Meanwhile, I am more than atrociously outraged by our neighbors. For the preachers of the Bernese territory denounce me from the pulpit for a heretic, worse than all the Papists put together, and the more snappishly each one falls foul of me, the surer he is of meeting with encouragement and protection. Because I had sufficiently experienced that nothing was to be hoped for from our own brethren, whom these injuries, however, ought to affect, I maintain as profound a silence as if I were dumb. The wicked may be satiated and the envious glut themselves to their heart's content, for any obstacle that I throw in their way. In the mean time the Lord will look down from heaven and will be avenged."[31]

Bullinger immediately got in touch with Haller at Bern who assured his friend that there was not a single person in Bern who called Calvin a heretic but added, "He is, however, more or less hated by a number of us because of being a busybody, but we strive as much as we can to tone down their inclemency and teach them to give more honour to such great men." So, once again, Calvin's sensitive spirit had caused him to exaggerate the strength of the opposition against him. Nevertheless, many Reformed leaders at Basle and Bern supported Castellio in his protests at Geneva and sought to gain advancements for him. Even Haller, the mildest of the Bernese, was soon comparing the situation in Geneva with that of darkest Africa. When the insurrection of 15-16 May, 1555 occurred in which the Genevans strove to oust the French, Calvin again

[31] John Calvin Collection, Ages Library CD.

came under suspicion and it was commonly felt that Calvin would do anything to separate Geneva from Bern. Haller wrote to Bullinger, "We hate Calvin. Letters from him to friends … have increased this hatred." He then described the situation in Geneva as "a wild sea of troubles and toils" for the Bernese protectors. Franz Hotman, Calvin's close associate, wrote to Bullinger around the same time, informing him that at Basle "Most are so loyal to Castillio and attached to him so that one might well believe that religion and piety are supported by him as the Heavens are by Atlas … Calvin, however, has here no better name than he has in Paris. For whenever a cursing or unbridled person is convicted, he is rebuked by calling him a Calvinist."[32]

The tide turns in Calvin's favour

Another plot was formed to have Calvin ejected from Geneva because it appeared that Calvin's pro-France politics would bring religious disaster to the city. It appeared, too, that Calvin was finding backing in Geneva for a Geneva independent of Bernese control. Such an independence, however, would make a possible membership of the Swiss confederacies for Geneva impossible. The German-Swiss were against any extension of Roman Catholic France's powers and knew that Geneva would not remain independent if Calvin's plan of an alliance with France materialised. Calvin turned to Bullinger for help but Bullinger wrote to his troubled friend outlining for him the obvious disadvantages should Geneva go it alone against the German-Swiss. The Savoy, France or Rome could then step in at any moment, not as an ally but as a master and the Reformation would be lost. The independence faction in Geneva did manage to annul the pact with Bern for a short time but Bullinger and his Swiss-German friends were able to have it re-established and hindered a Savoyan take-over by means of diplomacy.[33] Calvin appeared to have

---

[32] Author's translation. See Hollweg's Heinrich Bullinger's Hausbuch, pp. 288-289.

[33] In 1526 Bern and Geneva entered into a union which was to last 25 years, after which it would be subject to revision. In 1551 the treaty was renewed but only for 5 years. This terminated in 1556 but many Genevans who looked for union with France, protested against a renewal of the treaty. One other reason for Geneva's opposition which soon broke was that Geneva wished to keep the Basle obmann who traditionally chaired conferences between Bern and Geneva but

little idea of such political diplomacy and in the midst of criticism from all sides, he began to campaign again for the right of the Church to excommunicate its members. When Calvin wrote to Bullinger concerning the 'good-for-nothings' and 'wretched people' in his church, Bullinger pointed out to him that the pure church would be gathered in Heaven and that even the Church in New Testament times[34] was a 'mixed' body of more-or-less believers. Thus a pastor must be very careful how he deals with those of little faith. However, the tide was definitely turning for Calvin in Geneva. As the bulk of the French immigrants were behind him and as more and more refugees from France settled down in Geneva and as the old Genevan families such as the Perrins and Bertheliers lost their powers or their lives or were forced into exile, Calvin found that he could gain concession after concession through his new alliance with new councilmen. In the elections of February, 1555, Calvin's new friends gained power and immediately allowed the French refugees to receive Genevan citizenship. Oddly enough, Calvin still did not receive Genevan citizenship himself.

As a result of this policy, however, the cleft within the Genevan Church widened considerably. Any alleged friends of Castellio's were treated with great suspicion by the pro-Calvin party even to the extent of ministers refusing to marry and accept into membership those who did not accept the doctrine of predestination. This strife within the Protestant churches escalated when the Genevan Church issued strictures against Basle for protecting Castellio. Those who had signed the Basle Reformed Confession of 1534 were now refused permission to marry in certain Protestant churches true to Calvin's policies such as the Reformed Church at Lyon, France. The vague reason given was that the Basle Confession was not precise enough. As usual, all sides turned to Bullinger. The Consistoire at Lyon and a number of non-Swiss

---

Bern demanded that the treaty with Basle should be abolished and an obmann should be found in Roman Catholic Schwyz. Here it seemed that Bern was going against their own Reformed convictions. Bullinger, of course, suggested that Zürich and Basle should appoint the obmann. Through Bullinger's diplomacy, a compromise was reached which pleased all sides and the treatise was renewed.

[34] See, for instance, Pestalozzi, p. 423 ff.

Reformers, including Peter Martyr looked to Bullinger to condemn Castellio and his influence.[35] However, the families who now found they were not allowed to marry or were refused church membership also appealed to Bullinger. When, in 1562, Castellio was appointed to a Lausanne teaching post by the Bernese Council without asking either the Bernese Church, or the Lausanne Church for advice, these churches also turned to Bullinger and asked him for help.

Bullinger's dilemma

This was the most difficult position Bullinger had ever been in. The fact that Bullinger had a ready ear to listen to the troubles of all those who sought his aid, often led the most conflicting parties to believe that Bullinger must be on their side. Nevertheless, Bullinger had made it very clear in a number of essays, sermons and letters that he believed in predestination and election from eternity and though God was benevolent to all in Providence, he nevertheless restricted his salvation to the sinful elect. What Bullinger could not accept was the extreme view that God reprobated certain sinners irrespective of their sins. He believed that God saved sinners irrespective of their sins but any lost sinner was not lost irrespective of his sins and personal responsibility but because of them. He thus wrote to Calvin in 1553 complaining of the 'plague-bringing spirits at Geneva' which scholars believe is an allusion to Castellio and his more humanistic friends. Bullinger protested to the Bernese council and wrote to his friend Haller advising him to draw up a new confession of faith and request Castellio and his supporters to make a clear statement of belief regarding the Trinity, free will, election and whether they believed that all men without exception were elected to salvation or not. Castellio, however, thought that such a move against him broke the spirit of tolerance. This led Bullinger to support Calvin in preventing Castellio from obtaining any teaching office in the Swiss Reformed confederacies and dependencies, especially in those French-speaking areas which stood close to Calvin. Thus, when Castellio was called to take up a

---

[35] The Consistoire had originally planned to appeal to Bullinger, Gualter and Beza but those under suspicion appealed solely and directly to Bullinger, a course the Consistoire then followed.

professorship in Lausanne, Bullinger told the city that he would fight their move with hands, feet and every part of his body and added, "Beware, Beware, Beware!"[36] To be fair to Castellio, he himself believed, according to Walter Hollweg[37] in fines, excommunication and exile in certain cases of heresy but he was against the death penalty as such. Castellio was obviously before his time on these matters. To the relief of Geneva and Zürich, Castellio turned the call to Lausanne down. Nowadays, most of Castellio's doctrines would be considered either 'Wesleyan' or 'moderate Calvinism', but few would call them 'heretical'. Indeed, with the many fine appraisals of Wesley's work which have appeared in the once anti-Wesley press recently, and the widespread rejection of five-point Calvinism in the once High Calvinist para-church Reformed institutions who now plead for Amyraldianism and 'Moderate Calvinism', it appears that the beliefs of Castellio have become 'orthodox' again![38]

Striving to keep a balance

Bullinger rarely, if ever, forgot his balanced position when lending Calvin a helping hand. Though he principally supported Calvin in his doctrinal differences with Castellio, Bullinger certainly leaned more to Castellio's side regarding church order and discipline. In 1553, the Genevan Council became suspicious of Calvin's demands for excommunication and wrote to Bullinger asking for advice. Bullinger replied to both the council and Calvin requesting them to forgo the strict practice suggested by Calvin so that the weaker vessels in the churches might not suffer. Diplomatic as always, Bullinger said that it would be folly for Zürich to impose its views on Geneva as each church and state must come to an agreement amongst themselves concerning how to administer discipline as the situation and local conditions were different

---

[36] Cave, Cave, Cave.

[37] Heinrich Bullinger's Hausbuch, p. 292.

[38] See, for instance, Iain Murray's *Wesley and Men Who Followed* for an about-turn estimation of Wesley by a former critic of the man and his methods.

in each case. Concerning Bullinger's views on excommunication, Bruce Gordon says:

"Bullinger rejected all attempts by men to judge the souls of others; he was adamant that the authority of the magistrates had to be upheld, and that both believers and non-believers had to be punished when they transgressed the laws of the state, but his attitude towards the sacraments and church discipline revealed the depth of his abhorrence of the arrogance of presumption. For Bullinger, this meant that excommunication could have no role in the life of the church. Unlike Calvin, Bullinger did not believe that the Lord's Table was to be protected from unbelievers, because it was not up to humans to discern the identity of the elect. This was at the heart of the distinction between the private and the public."[39]

Nevertheless, the myth still survives, particularly in works defending Calvin's harsh views of church discipline and the function of the public magistrates, that Bullinger was two-sided in his approach. They argue that though Bullinger taught that excommunication was not to be practiced by the church, the public magistrates were within their God-given rights to excommunicate those who offended their Christian brethren and departed from the orthodox path. Thus Alister E. McGrath in his Calvin study *The Life of John Calvin: A Study in the Shaping of Western Culture*[40] when speaking of the Genevan disciplinary Consistorium which he argues was set up during Calvin's exile from the city on the Zürich pattern, argues that Bullinger taught that excommunication was a matter for the civil magistrate. McGrath, after seemingly 'proving' that excommunication by the secular arm was part of the Zürich-Geneva disciplinary pattern, goes on to deal with Calvin on excommunication.[41] McGrath's evidence for such a Bullingerite practice is most unsatisfactory. In a source footnote, instead of referring the reader

[39] Architect of Reformation, p. 28.
[40] This author is using the German edition published in 1991 by Benzinger.
[41] See Das Konsortium, pp. 149, *Johann Calvin.*

to a work of Bullinger's, he cites pages 55-140 of J. Wayne Baker's work, *Heinrich Bullinger and the Covenant*, stating that this topic is discussed at length in the great number of pages cited. This is not only not the case, but where Baker briefly comments on Bullinger's views on excommunication, amongst many other subjects,[42] he makes it quite clear by numerous quotes that Bullinger rejected the idea of excommunication both by the church and by the state. Baker points out that Bullinger maintained that excommunication was unheard of in the Apostolic church and first came into being, in conjunction with the Lord's Supper, when bad popes imitated bad emperors in the third century. The Church was to take care of spiritual matters and the magistrates' task was to prevent and prosecute public crimes. Baker thus concludes that "Bullinger, in fact, opposed the entire concept of exclusion, either from the church assembly or from the Supper," and that "Excommunication, a papal invention and a tool of tyranny, had no place in the Christian commonwealth."[43]

Mixed reactions to Bullinger's policies

Bullinger's replies to Geneva received general acceptance amongst the Reformed churches. Soon German states such as the Palatine and various dukedoms were writing to Bullinger concerning how best to practice church discipline in a Reformed manner. The Genevan Council did not see eye to eye with Calvin until 1555 after a revolt occurred in the city-state which threatened not only the life of Calvin but that of the French refugees. Peace was soon concluded but at the expense of many lives. June, July and August, 1555 were taken up with the execution or exiling of those who wished to keep Geneva for the old Genevans and purge the city-state of foreign influence. Again Bern gave Calvin much of the blame for these violent disturbances and again Bullinger was required by both sides to mediate.

Later generations have had ever-varying views on church discipline and the 16th century debate is of great importance in discerning why Bullinger's reputation waned and Calvin's waxed after the Council of

[42] See pp. 90 and 118 in Baker's work, *Heinrich Bullinger and the Covenant*.
[43] Ibid, pp. 90 and 118.

Dort. For a number of years the Reformed Church at Heidelberg who used Bullinger's Second Helvetic Confession became a centre of the Protestant Counter-Reformation, emphasising a stricter form of church discipline in the name of Geneva. English Precisians and critics of the English Reformation such as Thomas Cartwright thus made Heidelberg the centre of their revolutionary activities and a form of Ultra-Calvinism based on disciplinary externals reigned there for a few years which became most critical of Bullinger's policy that church discipline was to better Christians and not to punish and even destroy them. Later, these disciplinarians were mistakenly associated with the Heidelberg Confession and thus with orthodoxy. Bullinger's influence behind the Heidelberg Confession was large but Olivanus, one of its authors joined the Heidelberg extremists. Ursinus, the other author of the Confession remained the friend and correspondent of Bullinger. A further issue amongst the Precisians was their strong, fatalistic doctrine of predestination which became for many the epitome of their false Calvinism. One of the families who complained to Bullinger of persecution due to their being followers of Castellio was the Bauhins of Bern who argued that their views were based on their studies of Bullinger, Gualter and Melanchthon. Jean Bauhin the younger, a doctor, thus composed and published a compendium of quotes from the works of these theologians allegedly criticising the Reformed doctrine of predestination and election. Though Bullinger taught predestination, election and perseverance as firmly as any Reformer, the rumour remained amongst Pelagians and Arminians that Bullinger was one with them. This was also the view of the Ultra, Supralapsarian Calvinists at Dort, thinking of Traheron's and the English Precisians' correspondence with Bullinger, and forgetting their later strife with Calvin. Thus both extreme sides at Dort claimed that Bullinger was Arminian. Though neither side brought evidence either for or against the hypothesis and although Bullinger had denied time and time again that all men are created to be saved if they only will, the rumour has persisted that Bullinger was a Castellioite on predestination.

Mixed opinions about Calvin's view of Church and State

With the popularity of Calvin growing amongst the French, the name of Calvin became more and more hated amongst the Protestant Swiss. He was given the blame for all the atrocities that had occurred in the revolt of the old Genevan regime against the new pro-French (if not actually pro-France) insurrection and it was rumoured that Calvin had even assisted in the torturing of the old Genevan clans who had supported him in his early, equally turbulent days at Geneva. One after the other, the leading men of Bern and Basle wrote to Bullinger asking him to intervene. Simon Sulzer, a friend of Calvin's though with many ups and downs, wrote on 3 September, 1555 warning him that Bern was about to leave Geneva to her own fate. Five days later, Wolfgang Musculus urged Bullinger to use his influence over Calvin for the cause of peace. The German exile who had made a name for himself as a Reformer in Bern, appealed to his friend as the spokesman of Zürich's policy:

"I think it necessary, to appeal to your prudence as the situation in Geneva grows daily worse. We fear that the quarrel between the two cities will spark off a fire which you and our other neighbours must quench. The hate against our beloved brother in the Lord Calvin is growing through the evil intentions of others, so that I fear that when an open conflict comes, he will be given all the blame. Thus he must, according to my opinion, be advised with all zeal to prevent our two cities from drifting apart. I am convinced that if he could persuade his side to accommodate themselves with the Bernese, he would be successful. He must realise that he and his Frenchmen will be doubtless held responsible if the alliance between the two cities ends."[44]

Haller urges Bullinger to intensify his mediation

Haller found the situation so threatening that he travelled to Zürich on 26 September, 1555, to urge Bullinger to act. Bullinger had, however, already started using his enormous behind-the-scenes diplomatic skills

---

[44] *Der Verkehr Calvins mit Bullinger*, p. 97.

and had also written to Calvin explaining the seriousness of his situation to him. Bullinger, added, however, that he could believe none of the tales that Calvin had suddenly become an Inquisitor. Bullinger explained to Calvin how the Church in Geneva had grown through the alliance with Bern and how Geneva had become a home for Europe's persecuted Christians. Furthermore, Geneva had become the voice of the gospel of the Lord Jesus Christ to French-speaking states.[45] All this, Bullinger felt, could easily be lost if Geneva severed ties with her Protestant allies.

The problem of Swiss mercenaries

One of Bullinger's major sorrows in seeing Geneva drift into French hands through the erratic politics of Calvin was the problem of mercenaries. Bullinger, from the beginning of his ministry, had fought against the Swiss confederacies and Geneva accepting any revenues from France with a view to promoting France's army. The high standard of the military forces in Switzerland had caused other countries to recruit mercenaries amongst the Swiss and this exporting of men trained to kill had become a lucrative method of financing the cantons. Most families in Switzerland could tell tales of sons lost or corrupted through being traded to other countries, especially France as *Kanonenfutter* (canon-fodder). Bullinger's family had also suffered from this trade in human flesh during the last three generations. Five family members had been killed and one left an invalid but all had suffered in their characters through serving for money in other countries, chiefly France. At the beginning of Bullinger's ministry in Zürich it was estimated that 12,000 Swiss mercenaries from Roman Catholic cantons were serving in France alone and were being used to eliminate Protestant citizens. The massacre of the Waldensians in 1545 after Francis I occupied the Savoy was sadly due to the use of Swiss mercenaries. Indeed, the pope regarded the Swiss hirelings as part of his personal army against the Reformation. Even today, the pope's bodyguard and private army is composed almost entirely of Swiss mercenaries. The French King pushed the Swiss into the fiercest battles,

[45] Ibid, p. 98.

not caring about their lives as they were merely regarded as imported commodities. For instance, of the 10,000 sent out to serve the French King in 1570, 6,000 soon lost their lives. Switzerland was thus losing the bulk of her young men. Bullinger protested to the cantons supplying the troops and to the French King and his ambassadors but not only was he not listened to, but the pope placed a bull on him, the Emperor Charles V declared him to be a *persona non gratia* and the French King told Bullinger that he had no business to interfere with French policy. This was because Bullinger had dared to inform them that "It is not just for a man to let himself to hire, to kill those who have done him no injury." The main reason that Canton Zug offered so much resistance to the Reformation pioneered by Bullinger's Zürich was that the council and churches were all deeply involved in trading mercenaries.

Needless to say, Bullinger moved the Zürich magistrates to forbid the exporting of mercenaries from the city and its rural districts and happily, as usual, the Protestant cantons followed Zürich's move. The Roman Catholics then filled the breach, thus making even more money but ruining the future of their own dear country. When Francis II, husband of Mary Queen of Scots, came to the French throne at the age of 16, Bullinger sent him a statement of faith, outlining what the French Protestants believed and how they were law-abiding citizens but the carnage continued with the Swiss mercenaries to the fore. This was the only part of Bullinger's service to his Master in which he gained merely a part triumph. Bullinger was thus horrified to think that Switzerland could be drawn into a union with France which would enable the French King to plunder Switzerland's youth for his popish military campaigns.

Calvin made one of his many political about-turns and put Bern's and Bullinger's fears at rest and rather surprisingly, given the circumstances, told Bullinger that he only wished that the Bernese were as faithful to the alliance as he was and appeared to feel himself innocent of any pro-French intrigues against the Swiss-Germans. Bullinger immediately sent this report to Bern and then urged Calvin to persuade the Genevan Council to write a detailed report about the riots and rebellion that had occurred and send it to Zürich before the counter-reports of the Perrins and other rebels could be distributed. This reflected Bullinger's strong spirit of diplomacy. He knew that Bern wished to have an alliance with Geneva against France whereas Calvin hoped for an alliance with Bern that was pro-France. Bullinger merely concentrated on both Bern's and Geneva's wish for an alliance with each other, leaving aside the fact that both sides wished for an alliance for a different purpose. Thus began two years of intense diplomacy on the part of Bullinger. Even in January 1556 when Bern actually refused Geneva the right to continue the alliance and rejected Bullinger's mediation, he did not give up. As matters worsened, Bern was forced once again to listen to Bullinger who was now assisted by Basle and Schaffhausen. Then, on 25 November 1557, Haller was able to write to Bullinger concerning Geneva saying, "Last Sunday, by the grace of God, the alliance with Bern was renewed not just for a few years but for ever." The fact that Geneva eventually became an equal member of the Swiss *Eidgenossenschaft* is, to a great extent, due to the mediatory work of Henry Bullinger. If left to Calvin, Geneva would have been swallowed by Roman Catholic France and the Reformation outlawed. When Geneva was eventually permitted to be viewed as an integral part of Switzerland, independent of Savoyan and French claims in 1564, Bishop Robert Horne wrote to Rudolf Gualter, congratulating Zürich on their stance against France, saying:

"In the treaty between France and Switzerland, I commend the clear-sightedness of Zürich, in having detected the artifices of the French, disguised under the pretence of religion; and I hope that your neighbours, the Bernese, will, after your example, withhold their concurrence in so dishonourable a league."[46]

W. Kolfhaus, in his collection of correspondence between Bullinger and Calvin, closes this most important period in the spread of the Reformed faith and the political growth of Switzerland with the words:

---

[46] *Zürich Letters*, First Series, p. 141

"Throughout this long quarrel, Bullinger was not the mentor of his fiery, irascible friend in vain. He had protected him not only externally with the shield of his prestige, but also by holding him back from taking over-hasty steps and exhorting him in the most desperate situations to act patiently and sensibly without demanding of him that he should give up his idea of a Geneva independent of Bern"[47]

[47] *Der Verkehr Calvins mit Bullinger*, p. 101.

Heinrich Bullinger (1469–1533) – Henry Bullinger's father

Chapter 6

Wittenberg versus Zürich
The Continuing Reformation

Luther's tragic break with the Swiss Reformers

Luther's criticism of Bullinger whom he accused scathingly of merely standing on Zwingli's shoulders is sad, indeed tragic. Bullinger was most impressed by Luther's works, especially his *Babylonian Captivity of the Church*, his *Freedom of the Christian* and *Treatise on Good Works* and he recognised Luther as the greatest pioneer of the Continental Reformation. However, he felt that Luther had stopped the Reforming process prematurely and, by 1523 Bullinger had set out on the path of a continuing Reformation including ecclesiastical renewal. However, it was the Waldensian teaching on the Lord's Supper that helped him gain an understanding of the ordinance which was quite different from Luther's. Bullinger, at this early date, had optimistically believed that what he had experienced would be the lot of the Lutherans, too as they progressed along the Reformed path. After the Disputation of Marburg between Zwingli and Luther which the Bremgarten magistrates forbade Bullinger to attend, the Lutherans hardened in their doctrine of Consubstantiation. Rather than acknowledge that their doctrine was more Roman than Reformed, they accused Bullinger and Zwingli of being betrayers of

Christ's sacrament and enemies of the Reformation. In 1534, Bullinger drew up a statement regarding the Supper which emphasised the real presence of Christ in the celebration but that the elements were symbols, signs and witnesses of the Lord's presence with believers. He offered the Lutherans the right hand of fellowship but told them that he could not accept the idea that Christ's actual flesh and blood were in the elements but one fed on Christ in a spiritual manner through faith. Yet Bullinger argued that Lutherans and Reformed could celebrate the Lord's Supper together, each understanding the ordinance as his heart led. Luther rejected this offer of fellowship in several writings.

In January, 1536, Bullinger, accompanied by Leo Jud represented Zürich at a conference of all the Swiss Protestant churches at Basle. Here, Bullinger, assisted chiefly by Myconius and Grynäus, drew up the *First Helvetic Confession* which was sent to Luther as a peace treaty, again pleading for fellowship around the Lord's Table for all Protestants. This time, Luther responded in June, 1538 with a friendly letter congratulating the Swiss on their efforts to bring unity and concord to the churches. After this Bullinger and Luther corresponded friendlily on the issue of church unity for some time. This correspondence was suddenly broken off by Luther who could not get rid of his hate for Zwingli and his suspicion that Bullinger and his friends were all Zwinglis in disguise. As an excuse for breaking fellowship with the Swiss, he complained that Zwingli was responsible for the Turkish menace which was threatening Europe. In his commentary on Genesis, published in 1544, he called Zwingli the most inappropriate negative name as if he had been one of the greatest heretics the churches had ever seen. Luther was also rattled because Bullinger, unlike more Lutheran-minded Calvin, had refused to sign the Wittenberg Concord, arguing that if the First Helvetic Confession had pleased Luther, any more agreements were unnecessary. Bullinger replied to Luther's criticism of Zwingli, and thus Bullinger by association, by reprinting Zwingli's works so that the world could see that Luther was fighting windmills. This caused Luther to attack Zürich more violently than ever in his writings. The positive outcome of this controversy for the Reformation was that Calvin, who had leaned heavily towards Luther on the Eucharist, was now moved to approach Bullinger in November, 1544 in order to come to a better understanding of the Lord's Supper with him. This mutual endeavour eventually gave rise to the Zürich Consensus of 1549.

Sadly, Luther had picked up every bit of the exaggerated papal protests against the Zürich Reformation and Zwingli's war-faring position and accepted them as the truth and a sign that Zwingli's theology was as objectionable as his behaviour. He even claimed that Zwingli was an Enthusiast (*Schwärmer*) and a Catabaptist and had sinned against the Holy Ghost. Now Bullinger who had been against Zwingli's militant policy and represented a more mature theology had both the papists and Lutherans against him. Bullinger soon found out that Luther and other critics of Zwingli knew little of Zwingli's overall pioneering theological position and even less concerning the Kappel Wars, so he wrote a systematic account of his predecessor's faith and a history of the wars which helped to allay much criticism, though not Luther's. The German Reformer reacted by advising Markgraf Duke Albrecht von Brandenburg to ban all those holding the Zürich faith from his realms. Thus one Protestant became the persecutor of other Protestants and Rome looked smugly on.

Bullinger had never accepted Luther's view of the Lord's Supper

There is thus no doubt that the works of Luther and Melanchthon which led gradually to the Reformation in Lower Germany, also assisted Bullinger in his break with Rome. Bullinger's 1525 lectures at Kappel am Albis on the Epistle to the Romans alone provide abundant evidence that Bullinger was not only familiar with Luther's and Melanchthon's Wittenberg works but he also showed a high degree of agreement with them in his own exegesis.[1] However, we also find Bullinger affirming in his written debates with Burchard at this time that trying to insult him with the epithets 'Hussite' or 'Lutheran' was quite pointless as he had

[1] In Hans-Georg vom Berg's and Susanna Hausammann's edition of Bullinger's Exegetische Schriften aus den Jahren 1525-1527 we find over fifty signs of dependency on or agreement with Luther's works and over forty with Melanchthon's.

chosen his own path.[2] Indeed, Bullinger rejected both the papist transubstantiation and the Lutheran consubstantiation after reading Luther's *De captivitate Babylonica* in 1521-22. There is also an entry in Bullinger's diary for 12 September, 1524 in which he affirms that it was the Waldensians and Augustine besides intensive study of the Scriptures which had led him to his own Reformed view of the Lord's Supper. So Bullinger, in his first major works *De Scripturae negatio* (1523), *De sacrifitio missae* (1524), *Wider das Götzenbrot* (1525) and *Von dem Touff* (1525) testifies that his doctrine of the Lord's Supper, which differed from both Luther's and Zwingli's view, is derived from 'listening to the Scriptures', especially 1 Corinthians 11:23ff.. Bullinger, out of respect for Luther, seldom mentions his name in the early development of his theology but on such early occasions as when expounding 1 Corinthians 11:24; Hebrews 9:12ff and 10:12 in his *Wider das Götzenbrot*, Bullinger stresses that Christ's body is sacrificed and His blood shed but once for all time and eternity and in the cup there is never anything else but wine. It is thus clear that Bullinger rejected both the papist transubstantiation and the Lutheran consubstantiation very early in his Christian life.

Though privately when talking to family members and friends, Bullinger was very critical of the Lutherans, he remained on good relationship with Melanchthon and even with Luther whose angry criticisms of the Swiss often astonished Bullinger.

Luther's final break with the Reformed churches

The last straw occurred in 1543. At Bullinger's request Froschauer had sent Luther a complimentary copy of the newly translated Zürich Bible in 1542. This was a most scholarly and accurate work at which Jud, Bibliander and Pellican had laboured for many years. Luther answered a year later in what can only be described as a fit of rage. After thanking Froschauer formally, Luther goes on to write:

---

[2] See *Unveröffentlichte Werke aus der Kappeler Zeit*, p. 163.

"It is a work of your preachers, with whom according to the Church of God I can have no fellowship. I am sorry that they have worked so hard on it in vain and are lost to boot. They have been warned enough to depart from their error and not to take the poor people so piteously to hell with themselves. But no warning helps so I must let it be as it is. Therefore, you must stop sending me or giving me anything that they produce or work on. I will have no part in their damnation and blasphemous teaching and remain innocent but I shall pray and teach against them until my death. May God convert some of them and help the poor Church to get rid of such false, seductive preachers, Amen. They might laugh at this but one day they will cry when they find the doom of Zwingli whom they follow. May God protect you and all innocent hearts from their poison."[3]

Bullinger wrote to Melanchthon on 22 July, 1544 concerning the incident, saying:

"Never did the pope thunder against us in this manner; amongst us are many who hold onto Christ in true faith, in true religion, love and honour Him with an upright life and hate the Antichrist, superstition and all forms of godlessness. What a vexation it would be if many thought of us like Luther! The right hand does not need the left hand as much as the Church needs unity. That such a great man can forget himself in this manner and so dishonour himself! We continue to seek concord."[4]

Bullinger asked Melanchthon to use his influence to see that works sent from Zürich should be examined carefully by the Wittenberg scholars before being condemned unseen. Luther answered Bullinger's pleas for mutual respect with his *A Short Confession concerning the Holy Sacrament* in which he called the Zürich Christians 'heretics' and told them that they had no part in the true Church. Bullinger replied in 1545

[3] Letter dated 31 August, 1543, *Martin Luther Briefe: Eine Auswahl*, Leipzig, pp. 285-286.
[4] Schulthess-Rechberg, p. 83.

with his *The True Confession of the Servant of the Church at Zürich*[5] in which he explains the Reformed teaching on the Lord's Supper. Typical of Bullinger, he did not attack Luther personally. When the news of Luther's death reached Zürich the following year, Hooper wrote to Martin Bucer, telling him of Zürich's response to the fact that the pioneer of the Wittenberg Reformation was no more. He also waved aside Bucer's fears through evil rumours which kept coming to him that he was not respected at Zürich. These rumours obviously came from both Saxon and Genevan sources. Hooper wrote:

"My master, I pray you in Christ Jesus, not to pay too much regard to envious and slanderous calumniators. You are not ignorant that the malevolence of envy is ever wont to tear most persons in pieces; that detractors invent many falsehoods, and that brotherly love is disturbed by envy and detraction. Away with the persons who would sow dissension between yourself and those men. This I promise you, that they very frequently make mention of you in friendly and honourable terms. And although they may dissent from your opinion in the matter of the eucharist, as I do myself, yet they do not make any breach in Christian love, much less regard you with hostility, but are anxious to aid by their prayers both yourself and those whom the Lord has entrusted to you in his church; and they earnestly hope that, on your part, you will do the same for them. For Christ's sake therefore, who by his own blood hath triumphed on the cross over all enemies, hell, and sin, be ye not at variance through strife and emulation, that ye may neither quarrel any more with your tongue, nor give ear to those persons who are deficient in nothing but religion and virtue. Let controversy be settled by the authority of the word. Let no one defend his opinion with obstinacy; but let us rather return unto the way of truth, and humbly acknowledge our errors, than continue always to go on in error without repentance, lest we should seem to have been in the wrong. Let us bear in mind that we were made for friendship and concord, that in this most miserable age we may, by

[5] *Wahrhaftes Bekenntnis der Diener der Kirche zu Zürich.*

our mutual kindness, relieve the distresses of each other, and at last reign together with Christ in everlasting happiness. For what frenzy is it, what folly or madness, to pursue with hostility here on earth that individual, who, should he die in Christ, will pass from death unto life, (whither I also, Christ being my guide, hope to flee away after this darkness,) and with whom we shall be united in perpetual love and everlasting joy! I entreat you, my master, not to say or write any thing against charity or godliness for the sake of Luther, or burden the consciences of men with his words on the holy supper. Although I readily acknowledge with thankfulness the gifts of God in him who is now no more, yet he was not without his faults. I do not say this by way of reproach of the departed individual, because I know that no living man is without blame, and that we all stand in need of the grace of God. After the dispute with Zwinglius and Oecolampadius respecting the [Lord's] supper had begun to grow warm, he did violence to many passages of scripture, such for instance as the following, 'He ascended that he might fill all things';[6] 'I am with you alway even unto the end of the world';[7] and 'we are flesh of his flesh, and bone of his bones';[8] that he might establish the corporal presence of the body of Christ in the bread; but how mistakenly, is declared by the very nature of the passages. Did we not at this present time stand in need of consolation rather than of controversy, I could easily prove to the satisfaction of every one, that these places cannot properly be brought forward in confirmation of his opinion. Every one too is aware, with what calumnies and reproaches he attacked even the dead. Christ taught his disciples another doctrine. He rebuked James and John, who wished that fire might fall from heaven to consume the people of Samaria. And he has commanded us to do good to our enemies, and bless them that curse us. He, my good sir, who knoweth the secrets of the heart, may judge what spirit occasioned so much wrath to be kindled among the ministers of the word of God. Nevertheless all the ministers of this church were grieved at his death, not as if they had lost an adversary or a detractor; but rather an

[6] Ephesians 4:10.
[7] Matthew 28:20.
[8] Ephesians 5:30.

ally and partner in their glorious work. These things are, in my mind, great and real evidences of kindness and charity. I do not write thus by way of reproach of a most learned man, but that no one may swear by his opinions, as if whatever he wrote were an oracle of Apollo, or a leaf of the Sibyl."[9]

Bucer had obviously mentioned something averse coming from Calvin but Hooper tactfully replied, "I do not rightly understand what you write respecting Calvin. I had never any intention of using my pen either against him or Farel, although his commentaries on the first epistle to the Corinthians displeased me exceedingly." Hooper left Zürich in March, 1549 and journeyed to Strasburg via Basle and was just in time to dine with Bucer before his departure from the city by order of the popish Emperor on 31 March, 1549. Bucer told Hooper that the Reformed people of Strasburg were greatly delighted at the concord of the Swiss churches.[10] He found that Fagius had already left the city for an as yet secret destination. Bucer also kept his destination secret but Hooper told Bullinger that he had received invitations from England, Poland and Saxony. Bucer and Fagius eventually journeyed to England where they received professors' chairs at Cambridge.

When Bullinger first received the uncertain rumour that Luther had died early in 1546, he wrote:

"If Luther is dead, I trust that he died happily as there is much about him that the best people rightly admire and praise. Even the greatest men in the Church in the early days had their failings and so had Luther so that in God's Providence they would not make a god of him, too."[11]

No sooner was Luther buried than a number of prominent German theologians, scholars and politicians wrote to Bullinger, asking him to

---

[9] *Original Letters* I, pp. 45-47.
[10] *Original Letters* I, pp. 50-51.
[11] Pestalozzi, p. 237.

take up the dialogue where Luther had broken it off. The Lord Major of Augsburg wrote encouraging Bullinger to take up correspondence with Melanchthon again, and Philip of Hessen encouraged Bullinger to write and explain to the Saxons how much he and Zürich had been misrepresented. Bullinger had not written much to Melanchthon solely because he did not wish to have Luther's anger fall on the one Luther regarded as his closest friend. So Bullinger now wrote a long letter of condolence to Melanchthon in which he said:

"It affects me very much that we have lost this man whose advice and help in our mutual religious endeavours would be so beneficial to us. Though he had weaknesses of human nature, we must acknowledge his great measure of steadfastness. Brave and persevering, he clove to the pure evangelical doctrine against the papists, refusing to make any concessions one way or the other. With his typically penetrating eye, he recognised that such opponents were dishonest, even malicious in their efforts so that from them there was little or nothing good to expect. He viewed them as Paul when he said. 'They are people of a depraved spirit and reprehensible in their faith. Turn from them.'[12]

Melanchthon and Bullinger a brief comparison

After Luther's death, Europe, including Britain looked for a new father figure for the Reformation. The choice was between Bullinger and Melanchthon. The Swiss Reformed Church and the churches of England, Poland, Italy, Hungary, France, Romania, Holland and Belgium were mostly united in looking to Bullinger for leadership as a Reformer but the Lutheran states were now severely divided concerning their allegiance to Melanchthon. Summing up the situation, Schulthess-Rechberg says:

"One looks in vain at Melanchthon for a life's work of equal unity and organic development. He appears from the very start to have had

[12] Sie sind Menschen von verdorbenem Gemüth, verwerflich im Glauben, wende dich von ihnen. I have been unable to trace the exact passage in Scripture to which Bullinger is referring but the sentiments are those of 1 Timothy 6:5.

affinities with so many different currents of thought that this made it impossible for him to concentrate on one main subject. His public life is a chain of compromises in which he gave up so much without gaining anything in return, and, above all, without winning the peace which was his main aim. One has, not without good reason, regretted his lack of personal strength of character. But could Bullinger, who was in these matters so much superior to Melanchthon have built up such a spiritual monument as Melanchthon did?"[13]

Schulthess-Rechberg answers his own question in the negative, explaining how it was not Bullinger's aim to erect an organisational or ecclesiastical monument such as Melanchthon had erected around Luther's memory. Bullinger's task was not to found a movement called Zwinglianism or even Bullingerism. His entire calling was to be a good and faithful pastor and serve his church to the best of his abilities. He had no other ambitions. Bullinger could have become a rich man. Though his family's fortune was lost in the Kappel Wars, Bullinger was presented with many large grants of money and pensions from the countries of Europe which were forever in his debt. These Bullinger merely returned with a brief note to say that the government of Zürich did not allow such gifts and pensions from foreign powers. He added that the reputation of Switzerland had been marred by foreign gifts for political purposes and for the promotion of mercenaries and he did not want to cultivate such an impression. Luther's and Melanchthon's authority were given them by great lords who also assisted in the financing and organisation of their work. They thus held their positions as ministers of the gospel more through their dependence on the nobility rather than the people. Bullinger remained in office from 1531 until his death in 1575 because of his people's love for him. This explains why Bullinger omitted references to himself as a major church figure in his various historical works of great people, church leaders and the institutions of the Reformation, but wrote very much about the faith and Christian practice of his beloved fellow-

[13] *Heinrich Bullinger*, p. 87.

citizens and church members. This self-effacing grace gave Bullinger his lasting greatness, leaving men such as Luther, Melanchthon and Calvin far behind him, though their fame has lasted longer than Bullinger's. But this, by God's grace, can quickly change and there are encouraging signs in the awareness of today's Christians that Bullinger's great contribution to Church History and the spread of the gospel are being given the acknowledgement they deserve and Bullinger is once more being recognised as one of the noblest figures in the history of the Church.

Bullinger and Calvin versus the Gnesio-Lutherans

Sadly, partly due to the uncertain tones that came increasingly from Melanchthon, the Lutherans split up into two different movements as far apart as the Sunnis and Shiites in Islam. The so-called Philippists sought for tolerance but they scarcely knew what they were supposed to tolerate as Melanchthon changed his mind, theology and view of the church so often. The so-called Gnesio-Lutherans under Joachim Westphal, the Lutheran fiery spirit and Pastor in Hamburg, could not stomach Melanchthon's brand of Lutheranism and fought for external conformity so fiercely that they soon left off defending any vestiges of sound doctrine and battled on over mere externals and different terms. Calvin had constantly claimed that Melanchthon was on his side and urged him for the sake of unity to confess that he was one with Calvin. Melanchthon remained silent on the matter in public but denied the charges in private.[14] This led to further misunderstandings so Westphal called Melanchthon a Crypto-Calvinist. Calvin's claims concerning Melanchthon turned many Lutherans against the author of the *Augsburg Confession*, thus weakening their position but Melanchthon argued that Westphal confused the issue concerning the Eucharist because of his insistence on coining new terms to describe it and that Calvin's language was ambiguous.[15]

Such controversialists as Joachim Westphal and Johann Brenz (1499-1570) outdid outspoken Luther in their hatred of their Reformed brethren.

[14] See Karin Maag's *Melanchthon in Europe*, p. 39 for further comments and sources.
[15] Ibid, Chapter 1 by Timothy Wengert, "We Will Feast Together in Heaven Forever: The Epistolary Friendship of John Calvin and Philip Melanchthon."

During the early years of these inner turmoils, whilst Luther was still alive, he kept out of the limelight, rarely attending disputations unless ordered by the Emperor or Electors and left the theologising and systematising to others. Now and then, when things within the Lutheran churches were getting gravely out of hand, Luther let his voice be heard. Such an occasion was when Karlstadt, Zwilling, the Zwickau Prophets and the Spiritists were striving to set up a church without the Word of God in Wittenberg during his absence at the Wartburg. Luther gave up his voluntary exile and returned to his pulpit to thunder against the troublemakers. Peace was restored at once.

Fearing the popularity of the *Consensus Tigurinus*

Westphal, followed somewhat later by Brenz, now played an indirect part in spreading the reputations of the Swiss Reformers and their Genevan allies, Calvin and Beza. He seemed to fear the Swiss Reformers more than all the papist cardinals put together and began to campaign from around 1552 against what he called the *Sakramentschwärmer* or *Sakramentirer.*[16] He became especially alarmed when Melanchthon and other Lutherans showed an eagerness to sign the *Consensus Tigurinus* and realised that the states supporting Martin Bucer's more Reformed views were moving away from Lutheranism towards a 'Zürich' interpretation.[17] The ultra-Lutherans thus regarded Bullinger and Calvin as their major opponents, simply because they were the fathers of the *Consensus Tigurinus* which they regarded for reasons best known to themselves as 'blasphemous'.[18] For the Lutherans, their faith was summed up in their doctrine of consubstantiation whereas the Reformed Church looked on consubstantiation as being a half-way house to Rome. The Gnesio-Lutherans' aggressive methods of preserving Lutheranism

---

[16] Sacrament visionaries or enthusiasts, sacramentalists.

[17] Actually, it was Bucer who radically influenced Genevan order and discipline but I am stating the case as Westphal saw it. Westphal's theological understanding was strictly limited, for instance, he thought Calvin was a pupil of Zwingli's whereas, as François Wendel says in his Calvin, p. 136, Calvin ridiculed Zwingli's prestige and "Zwingli must have remained completely foreign to Calvin."

[18] See Pestalozzi, Section 105, *Bullinger und Calvin gegenüber den Angriffen Westphals und Andere.*

against Reformed encroachments, however, served only to split up the Lutheran movement. Combating Westphal's errors and acute intolerance took up much of Bullinger's precious time from 1554-1564. From 1561 to 1571, he was busy combating Brenz. These debates became not only international but also brought in Italian and Savoyan Anti-trinitarians such as Francesco Stancari (1501-1574), Georgio Blandrata (1515-c.1585) and Bernardino Ochino (1487-1564), who had little in common with Westphal and Brenz but were pleased to join them in attacking the Reformed position. When the Italian Anti-trinitarians fled to Poland, Lithuania, Transylvania and Hungary, these parties continued to attack the Reformed churches side by side with the Lutherans. Especially Westphal persecuted the Reformed Christians with the fervour of Mary I of England. Indeed, when the English Reformers and members of the various Stranger Churches fled from England to the Continent on Mary's coming to the throne, Westphal moved the authorities all along the German and Danish coasts to refuse them anchorage in the middle of winter storms, hoping they would either be wrecked at sea or starve. He was particularly merciless to Jan Laski and the faithful band of English and Continental believers whom he led to seek asylum in Continental Europe. Westphal's excuse for this extreme behaviour was that the Reformed members of the Church of England who suffered and lost their lives under Mary were 'the devil's martyrs'. As Westphal's influence over the King of Denmark grew, Bullinger dedicated his *über die allein durch den Glauben an Christum uns rechtfertigende Gnade* (On Justifying Grace Solely through Faith in Christ), written in 1554, to the sovereign. Bullinger wrote to Utenhoven in Emden expressing fears that the Lutherans would not pass on a copy such a *Schwärmer* as himself had sent the King and added, "May God forgive them and give them a spirit of prudence and charity."[19] On hearing that Countess Anne of Oldenburg had given the refugees from England and France asylum in spite of the threats of Westphal and Charles V, Bullinger wrote to her thanking her in the name of the Reformed churches and encouraging her to be steadfast.

[19] Pestalozzi, p. 388.

Concerning their Lutheran and Roman enemies, Bullinger expounded James 2:13-16 for the Countess.

Brenz strove to make the sojourn of the English, Dutch, Belgian and French Reformed refugees who gathered at Wesel, Frankfurt and Strasburg as difficult as possible. Indeed the opposition of Westphal and Brenz against the Reformed faith was far greater than that of Charles V. The Emperor gave the refugees from the Reformed Church of England and the Strangers' churches the freedom of Frankfurt and the Roman Catholics in the city gave them the use of at least two churches in which they could meet for worship.[20] This shocked Westphal so much that he wrote to the Senate at Frankfurt urging them to cast out the 'heretics'. He was particularly enraged when he heard that Anglican refugees from the Marian persecutions who travelled via Duisburg, Wesel, Emden and Strasburg on their way to Frankfurt had introduced the Reformed Lord's Supper in the towns and districts through which they travelled. Thus towns such as Duisburg and Wesel on the western frontier of Germany first heard of the Reformation (as opposed to Lutheranism) from the Anglicans.

Bullinger's and Calvin's first engagement with Westphal

Westphal[21] and Brenz wrote work after work against the Swiss Reformers, answered ably by Bullinger and Calvin, but it was Laski who first drew their attention to early Gnesio-Lutheran opposition. Laski had written to Bullinger on 3 March, 1554, enclosing a copy of Westphal's *Recta fide*,[22] saying:

"A Hamburg pastor, Joachim Westphal, has written a book against us all which is full of lies and evil speech without saying anything which has not been said better by others. I am sending it to you in case any of you would be interested in answering it. I have not the time at present. I

[20] The Weissfrauenkirche and the Katherinenkirche.
[21] Westphal had been informed of the *Consensus* by Alexander Bruchsal, then in Antwerp.
[22] At the same time, Laski sent a copy to Calvin.

would like very much for someone to answer him; not for his sake but for the sake of the people who listen to him."[23]

Bullinger replied on 17 March, saying that a reply would come from Zürich via Bibliander on behalf of his fellow-ministers and that Calvin had already asked Bullinger if he thought he should reply to which Bullinger had replied in the affirmative. Bullinger then answered in his own way without personalising the debate by reprinting his *Vom heiligen Nachtmahl* which he had published in both German and Latin in the previous year,[24] and issuing his *Vom Heil der Gläubigen.*[25] When he heard how Calvin was approaching the subject in a very personal, vindictive way, he advised him against writing. Calvin was going through a time of extreme dogmatism on the predestination issue and using extreme language. Bullinger feared that he would react equally intemperately to Westphal, leaving out the main subject, the Lord's Supper, and merely giving Westphal a piece of his mind. Bullinger told his friend at Geneva that he should stick to the *Consensus Tigurinus* they had both signed for their theological formulas and begged him "not to present the teaching of predestination so that you cancel all grace and make yourself more hated than before. You must beware of such turns of speech such as 'Adam was so created that he was incapable of not sinning and he who sins commits sin according to God's plan." Bullinger continued, "I remind you of this, not to instruct you but to advise you so that you will be very careful in this matter concerning what you say so that a bigger fire might not be made out of predestination than was made out of the Lord's Supper."[26] This letter made Calvin ask Viret to take up the task for him. Indeed, Haller had already suggested that Viret was the man to reply on behalf of the French-speaking Protestants rather than

---

[23] *Der Verkehr Calvins mit Bullinger*, p. 102.

[24] On the Holy Supper of our Lord Jesus Christ: how, in what form and why He inaugurated it. The Latin title is *De sacro Sancta Coena.*

[25] On the salvation of believers. Here, Bullinger deals with the relationship of the preached Word and the sacraments.

[26] 4 Privatbriefe an Calvin von 1552-1555, Walser's *Die Prädestination bei Heinrich Bullinger*, VI., 4, pp. 180-181.

Calvin. Now sure that someone amongst the French ought to write, Bullinger put together a number of points which he felt should be in any reply to Westphal and sent them to Beza as a guide. Beza passed these on to Calvin who said that he would work on them and then send his results to Bullinger for approval and comment. Bullinger answered, "May the Lord give you His Holy Spirit so that the enterprise will be to His honour and a blessing to many. I await your answer with longing." The answer to Westphal came on 6 October, but Bullinger and the Zürich ministers were not happy with it. They thought it too mild by far in judging the Lutheran position on the Lord's Supper and its attitude to the Augsburg Confession. On the other hand, it was a most aggressive attack on the integrity of the Gnesio-Lutherans without any real analysis of their position. Furthermore, the ministers complained that Calvin's language was unclear in formulating the Reformed position. Bullinger had the hard task of writing to Calvin to inform him of their comments. He told his friend:

"It appears to us, dear Calvin, that you proceed far too roughly against our opponents. Three or four times, you call them 'good-for-nothing' and you reproach them because of the cows of their country and their nearness to the polar seas and you call Westphal 'a beast'. Well, we admit freely that they deserve such harsh treatment but – not from you and not from us. It will be more to our favour to remain charitable. It was exactly invectives like this in Luther's writings which put off many sincere people. Your written response therefore, should be, in our opinion, thoroughly moderate in tone, so that one will in every respect appreciate that the author simply aims at the upkeep and defence of the truth. He retains his Christian dignity and leniency in spite of these stormy and violent times. We wish, as far as is possible, to give Westphal, this verbose and belligerent man, no further opportunity to squabble. In Saxony and northwards to the Baltic Sea there are many thousands of well-meaning people whose friendship, as you mention, we should cultivate. Perhaps, however, exactly these people would feel insulted by your offensive statements. As you use general terms of abuse concerning cold and icy people, beasts and ne'er-do-wells, it would be better to strike them out and name the renewer of the sacrament controversy by his correct name, Westphal, so that everyone will know that we are proceeding against him."[27]

Calvin had no first-hand knowledge of Luther on the Lord's Supper

Bullinger not only corrected Calvin's language but also his doctrine. He told his friend that he had taken a position near to Luther's which would give Westphal the opportunity to accuse Calvin of duplicity. He also criticised as totally exaggerated Calvin's claim that if Luther were still alive, he would have accepted the *Consensus Tigurinus*. Bullinger put this down to the fact that Calvin had no first hand knowledge of Luther's harsh criticisms of the Reformed position and Luther's own works on the Lord's Supper, mainly because he could not read German. Bullinger offered to send Calvin a collection of Luther's works on the sacrament that he might inform himself of what Luther actually believed.

Calvin took the criticism remarkably well and altered his work accordingly. We would, he promised, in his reply to Bullinger and the Zürich ministers on 13 November, 1554, not call Westphal 'a stupid ass' in his defence, though he could not bring himself to address Westphal by his own name. Calvin admitted, however, that in spite of writing in defence of the *Consensus* against Westphal, he still differed from Bullinger regarding the value of the *Augsburg Confession*, the 'Variata' form of which he had personally signed in Frankfurt in 1536 and which was approved by Luther. When the corrected version was sent back to Zürich, Bullinger was delighted with the result and advised Calvin to go to print at once. Bullinger did not mind it bearing Calvin's name only.

Bullinger persuades the Genevan Council to sanction Calvin's work against Westphal

However, neither Calvin nor Bullinger had reckoned with the Genevan Council who were not willing to give Calvin a *carte blanche* on

[27] Translated by author from the German version given by Pestalozzii, p. 389.

such a delicate diplomatic mission and demanded that they, as Calvin's employers, had the right to edit the work. Now Calvin lost his temper and threatened to throw the work into the fire. He told the Council that even if he lived in the city for another 1,000 years, he would never publish there again. He then returned the work to Bullinger, begging him to use his influence in obtaining its acceptance in the Protestant Swiss-German and Geneva. Bullinger immediately used his vast powers of persuasion to move the pan-Swiss, French and Italian churches and to pacify the Genevan Council. Soon Geneva capitulated to Bullinger's diplomacy and the work was printed simultaneously in Zürich by Christopher Froschauer and in Geneva by Robert Stephanus. Bullinger added an epilogue in which he emphasised that Geneva and Zürich were determined to continue to defend the Reformed faith together against the wiles and whims of Westphal.

Westphal response and further replies from the Zürich-Geneva alliance

Almost as soon as the joint-work was off the press, Laski wrote saying that Westphal was ready with his printed response. Westphal could outdo Calvin in harsh words and Calvin, on reading Westphal's new work, was cut to the quick and took the matter most personally. Perhaps Calvin was rather upset to find that in spite of his being more sturdy in tone against Westphal than Bullinger, Westphal still believed that Calvin was only writing under Bullinger's authority, and it was the Swiss-German who was the true initiator of the works against him. He thus called Calvin the 'Genevan Calf', whereas he called Bullinger 'the Bull of Zürich". Bullinger, Farel, Peter Martyr (now at Strasburg) and other friends told Calvin that if he replied, he should write nothing personal and not even mention Westphal's name but defend the Reformed doctrine of the Lord's Supper. However, Calvin replied with great bitterness. On being challenged about this, he confessed that he could not understand himself as he had planned to be mild but as soon as he began to write his temper ran away with him. Bullinger now strove to smooth the waves by bringing out his *Apologetica exposition* in 1556, in which he kept strictly to the subject without being polemic or personal. Nevertheless, he felt bound to scold Calvin gently by saying, "I unite myself with you in the battle, not with the same strength but with all my heart. However, I fight so as not to make peace impossible."[28] During these debates, Bullinger's works on the Lord's Supper, his *Compendium of the Christian Religion*, his *Apology* and numerous sermons were printed in French at Geneva and in several unnamed printing houses in France.

Meanwhile, Peter Martyr had been having a hard time at Strasburg. The Gnesio-Lutherans were putting great pressure on the theological academy there and threatening to undo all Bucer's, Capito's and Martyr's good work. Again, it was the Reformed teaching of the Lord's Supper that angered them and especially Martyr's taunt that the so-called ubiquity of Christ's human nature was a novelty so ridiculous that even Rome could not be so un-Scriptural as to think it out. In 1556, Conrad Pellican, one of Europe's foremost Hebrew scholars and a beloved member of the Zürich Council died. The ministers were unanimous in requesting that Martyr should be called to take on Pellican's vacant teaching posts. At first the Council were determined to appoint a Zürich citizen but they soon discovered that they had no one to recommend who came anywhere near Martyr in ability, walk of life and international renown and thus agreed to Martyr's call. The Italian Reformer accepted the invitation at once as the Eucharist controversy was raging so fiercely that it was making normal, academic and pastoral work impossible. Now, too, Bullinger had a formidable foe of the Lutherans as his ally and colleague as Martyr was not only gifted in Latin, Greek and Hebrew, besides several modern languages but was also a first class apologist, debater and preacher. He was both a scholar and a very practical man. Bullinger, the Zürich ministers and the Council promised Martyr that he would have full liberty in Zürich to exercise his talents and calling as he felt fit.[29] Bullinger kept his word, even though Martyr did not get on with

[28] *Der Verkehr Calvins mit Bullinger*, p. 107.

[29] Martyr's inaugural speech to the Zürich college is extant in which he explained in detail why he had answered the call to Zürich. See *Inaugural Oration Delivered at Zürich When He Took the Place of Doctor Konrad Pellikan*, The Peter Martyr Library, Vol. 5, pp. 321-334.

the senior professor at Zürich, Theodor Bibliander, one of Bullinger's closest friends, and was mostly responsible with Calvin for Bibliander's resignation so as to keep the peace.

Martyr was overjoyed to be given such a welcome in Zürich as he had long wished to join the staff there since his flight from Italy in 1542 but there had been no vacancy at the time. After staying a few days in Zürich, Martyr was called to Strasburg to replace Wolfgang Capito, also a Hebraist, who had died in 1541. Now, fifteen years later, Martyr was given a cherished and important chair in Zürich.

Beza's compromising attempt to seek union with the Lutherans

Beza tried to intervene in securing a consensus with the Lutherans between 1556 and 1558 by taking up a suggestion of Laski's to attend disputations in Germany on the subject of the Lord's Supper. His misguided and misplaced efforts, however, led to a worsening of the situation. Bullinger warned the Genevans not to be deceived by such ideas. All the Germans wanted them to do was to accept the *Augsburg Confession* and no peace would be offered on any other terms. Beza made three visits to Germany, professing to speak on behalf of the Swiss but departing gravely from the *Consensus Tigurinus*. He declared that he could accept the *Augsburg Confession* on all but one point (Article 10) but added that a mutual understanding of that article, too, seemed possible. Beza and Farel then drew up a joint statement which they called the *Confession of the French Church* in which they declared that the Supper was not only a sign to them but that Christ is present who makes us his members through faith. The Germans found this statement "somewhat obscurely set forth" but accepted it as a step in their direction.[30] For some time Beza kept Geneva's go-it-alone action from Bullinger but Westphal began to boast that Beza's signature under the French confession was proof that the Swiss-Germans and the French Genevans were divided. So Bullinger soon found out what had happened and told Beza and Farel in no uncertain terms that they had betrayed the

[30] See Moeller's *History of the Christian Church*, Vol. III, Reformation to 1648, pp. 185-187 for a detailed discussion of these events.

Reformed consensus of 1549 and that the Lutherans would only use the 'French' declaration as a weapon against the Swiss churches. This was a great embarrassment to Calvin, chiefly because of Bern's, Basle's and Zürich's negative reaction so, according to Wilhelm Moeller, he withdrew Beza from active participation in further discussions by placing him at the head of the newly founded *Academy of Geneva*.[31] When the Beza scandal became public, Beza rushed to Zürich with the men who had accompanied him to Germany like anxious students who wished to keep on good terms with their professor. Bullinger wrote to Calvin on 26 September, 1557 saying, "We discussed the (Beza's) Confession in a friendly way. They promised in future to avoid such action and to argue their case clearer and in more detail should the Saxons wish to continue the debates on the basis of that Confession. We parted in cordial unity."[32]

Beza's efforts to find a more Lutheran formula to that of the *Consensus Tigurinus* resulted in the Germans renewing their criticism of Bullinger's *Decades*, hitherto the only fully comprehensive work on Christian doctrine available in German. In 1557, Heidelberg, who had already published a German edition of the *Decades*, now translated and published Beza's *Confession of the Christian Faith* in 34 brief Articles, claiming that this came much nearer the Lutheran view than the *Decades* and the *Consensus Tigurinus*. The work was re-printed in 1562 and 1563. Over the next few years, the Lutherans strove without success to convince their German Swiss neighbours that they should drop the *Decades* for Beza's *Confession*. In March 1569, we still find such Lutheran ministers as Johannes Sylvanus writing to Bullinger's relative and fellow minister Johannes Wolf at the *Frauenmünster* in Zürich, telling him:

"Here we are fighting against Bullinger's *Decades* because of three errors in them: their teaching on predestination, on the descent into Hell and the sacraments because Bullinger will not acknowledge the sacrament as a *vis justificandi* (justifying power or force). They prevent the people

[31] Ibid, p. 186.
[32] *Der Verkehr Calvins mit Bullinger*, p. 113.

from buying and reading the *Decades* and tell them to read Beza's *Confession* which does not contain these errors."[33]

Bullinger's friend Erastus wrote on 22 May of the same year, warning him that the Lutherans were emphasising the difference between the Reformed theology of the Swiss Germans and the alleged more Lutheran theology of Geneva which was leading to a suppression of the *Decades*. However, even the most bigoted of Lutherans soon realised that Beza's brief work could not compete with Bullinger's multi-volumed work on Christian doctrine and so they decided to translate Calvin's *Institutes* into German. This proved a long and expensive business, mostly handicapped by the lack of general interest amongst the clergy for such a work. The translation work was finished in 1572; eight years after Calvin's death and over twenty years after Bullinger's *Decades* were published in German. The *Institutes*, called *Unterricht in der christlichen Religion* (Instruction in the Christian Religion) in German went into a second edition in 1582 and a third in 1608. That Bullinger corresponded with Erastus convinced the Lutherans, for some unclear reason that Bullinger, for all the good work he had done for the gospel, must have been all along a heretic or had recently become one. Thomas Erastus (1524-1583), Swiss doctor to the Elector of the Palatine and Professor of Medicine at Heidelberg was said by the hardliners to be weak on church discipline and Bullinger, by association, was condemned with him. In 1580 Erastus was forced to leave his post through pressure placed on him by the party led by Kaspar Olevianus who was for the Genevan method of discipline including separation from the Lord's Table. Erastus then received a chair in medicine at Basle. Erastus held to a rather complicated doctrine of church-state relationships which influenced both English Anglicanism and Presbyterianism[34] strongly. Erastus' teaching that church members should be disciplined by their office-bearers and not the civil magistrates caused the Genevans and especially Beza to condemn him. Erastianism is

---

[33] See Hollweg's, *Heinrich Bullinger's Hausbuch*, pp. 163-264.

[34] See Hooper for Anglicanism and Selden, Lightfoot, Coleman and Whitelocke for Presbyterianism.

used nowadays to depict a system whereby the state maintains supremacy in all matters of religion. This teaching has little to do with Thomas Erastus.

Peter Dathen (Petrus Dathenus) of Ypres, now chaplain to Friedrich III in German Palatine wrote to tell Bullinger in 1570 of how his star had allegedly fallen in Germany and Belgium, accusing him of damning the church discipline of Christ and the Apostles and going back on his own word and rejecting the teaching of Zwingli, Oecolampadius, Bucer and Martyr and thus losing all his authority gained over the years and assisting to bring in atheism.[35] As Hollweg comments, "Truly, that was no beautiful and honourable letter!" The truth was that the men Dathen mentioned did not always agree on church discipline but they believed in fellowshipping with one another in spite of this. Dathen himself, unlike Bullinger, had departed from such tolerance. His ridiculous accusation that Bullinger's more pastoral and ecclesiastical view of church discipline *led to* atheism merely reveals how bitter the debate was at the time. One wonders how using the secular arm to enforce severe penalties on wayward church members could *prevent* atheism. One letter from Bullinger to Dathen put all things right and in their correct perspective and Dathen cooled down for a time as quickly as he had flared up. However, his exaggerated, unfounded reaction shows how precarious was the theological situation in Germany and how strong was the opposition to Reformed doctrines amongst supposedly Reformed Lutherans and Genevans. To use Hollweg's words, Dathen's criticism hit Bullinger like a stroke of lightning. The trouble was that tolerance amongst the Lutherans and Genevans had become a lost item and they were striving more and more to enforce their own beliefs through censorship and public slander. Thus Beza's words sound somewhat hollow when, in spite of his strong support for the rigid Calvinistic discipline, he wrote to Zürich saying, "In the old days, one could be of a different opinion on various issues without harming anyone's friendship. It is the calamity of our day

[35] See Hollweg's *Heinrich Bullinger's Hausbuch,* p. 266 ff. for a detailed account of Dathen's and Bullinger's correspondence.

that one cannot tolerate other opinions."[36] It must be noted that the severest disciplinarians on the Lutheran and especially the Genevan side were angry young men in their twenties who, in their fervor to make a most legalistic Calvinism work, rejected the pastoral, loving care for back-sliding sinners of the older generation. They were for a rule with an iron hand, or as Bullinger told Beza, the Genevans tended to sweep with an iron broom. These fiery spirits made their headquarters in Heidelberg, where young legalists from the various Reformed churches gathered to work out ever stricter and more rigid forms of keeping outward observance as an enforced indicator of inner godliness. Several young Englishmen went thither to hear of the new piety. Bishop Sandys, who had had enough of religious persecution himself and was to suffer further under the criminal energies of the disciplinarians, wrote to Gualter in August, 1574 expressing great concern regarding the extraordinary new love of severe discipline on the Continent which was uniting the Lutherans and Genevans where doctrine had seemingly failed. Sandys continues:

"Our innovators, who have been striving to strike out for us a new form of a church, are not doing us much harm; nor is the new fabric of theirs making much progress as they expected. Our nobility are at last sensible of the object to which this novel fabrication is tending. The author of these novelties, and after Beza the first inventor, is a young Englishman, by name Thomas Cartwright, who, they say, is now sojourning at Heidelberg. He has lately written from thence a treatise in Latin, in defence of this new discipline which he wishes to obtrude upon us. I have not seen the book, but I hear that it is printed, and has been brought over to us. As soon as it shall come into my hands, I will take care it shall be sent to you."[37]

From this time on, Bullinger had to take second place behind Beza and Calvin in Germany, chiefly for his criticism of consubstantiation and his

[36] Quoted in Hollweg, p. 278.
[37] *Zürich Letters*, First Series, pp. 312-313.

rejection of extreme church discipline for cases of concern where Christian love, understanding and right teaching ought to prevail. So great was the hatred of Bullinger amongst the anti-Zürich party that the letters of German leading Reformers and Statesmen to Bullinger were intercepted, opened, read and their most private contents spread abroad with the lie that it was Bullinger himself who had been indiscreet. This gained for Bullinger especially the animosity of Friedrich III of the once Zürich-minded Palatine. Friedrich had confided in Bullinger only to find his most intimate thoughts spread abroad by evil-doers who blamed Bullinger for the leakage. The Elector reacted by practicing a more severe church discipline. However, in Geneva, during this time, thanks to a sympathetic Council, the *Decades* quickly went through three French editions sanctioned and further editions were being printed elsewhere in Latin, German and Dutch. Indeed, it had been the popularity of the *Decades* in Germany owing to the Heidelberg edition and the spread of the *Decades* in both French and Flemish-speaking Belgium that had made the Lutheran and Genevan clergy so fanatically anti-Bullinger. Soon after Dathen's harsh letter to Bullinger, Ursinus had written from the Palatine to tell Bullinger that dialogue with the Lutherans had become impossible and it would serve the Reformed cause in Germany better not to get caught up in useless debates but merely keep quiet until a better time came. Sadly, Dathen, for all the good work for the gospel he had done in Germany, Belgium and Holland, went from extreme to extreme and even began to dabble in alchemy and allied with Baptist John David Joris who became notorious for his abnormal ecstatic piety and unbridled sensuality and for driving his followers into martyrdom, though keeping clear of such danger himself. Towards the end of his life, Dathen confessed that he had been a blind leader of the blind. In his lengthy comment on Dathen, Hollweg concludes, "Such was the man who warned Bullinger against stepping into atheism!"[38] Sadly the Lutheran persecutions grew and Augustus, Elector of Saxony, began to persecute those of Bullinger's persuasion, throwing some into prison, banishing others and using the

[38] See Hollweg's *Heinrich Bullinger's Hausbuch*, pp. 260, 266-272, 274 f., 277.

public magistrates in an attempt to force the Reformed men to take up Lutheranism. Richard Cox wrote to Zürich from England some time in 1575:

"I am exceedingly grieved at the persecutions that have lately taken place in Saxony: that Lutheran party is very cruel. May the Lord vouchsafe to aid those who are sincerely pleading his cause! Oh, the enemy of mankind, who, whenever the good seed is sown, ceases not to sow tares among them! Meanwhile by the grace of God we must do our best, and leave the issue to the Lord our God. The Lord hitherto by his favour preserves us at peace. The papists are grumbling, and nursing I know not what monstrosity. But may God himself destroy the wicked, and long preserve you in safety to his church!" [39]

Calvin's visit to Germany also caused more problems than it solved

Calvin, however, had already placed the Reformed position in jeopardy himself by journeying to Frankfurt in the late summer of 1556, where the Reformed pastor Valerand Poullain was to face a combined church and city tribunal for allegedly causing strife. In Frankfurt very stiff punishments were meted out to all those who broke the peace of the city and John Knox had already been banned from the city after similar complaints had been made. Calvin was invited to mediate in the matter and discuss plans for unity with the Reformed (Waloon-French, Dutch and English) and Lutheran churches in Frankfurt. Poullain was pastor of the Franco-Belgian Church and a man who stood close to the Strasburg, Zürich and Genevan Reformations. Poullain, had taken over Calvin's church at Strasburg in 1541, but he and his church had been driven from Strasburg by the Emperor and had found asylum in Edward VI's England where Poullain had assisted in drawing up various Reformed orders of service including work on the Church of England Prayer Book. When Mary came to the throne Poullain and his church were compelled to flee again and settled down in Frankfurt, sharing a building with English and

---

[39] *Zürich Letters*, First Series, pp. 315-316.

Dutch worshippers. Poullain had lived at peace in Frankfurt until newcomers, friends of Calvin's, came in who immediately demanded that Poullain should go and that a plurality of pastors should be set up. Poullain thought that this was some Genevan plot and criticised Genevan interference in his church. Poullain, however, made the mistake of answering criticism by taking the same disciplinary measures that Calvin had taken in Geneva before being exiled. He forbade the troublemakers the right to partake of the Lord's Supper.

On his way to Frankfurt, Calvin called in at his old church in Strasburg but the pro-Poullain church refused him permission to enter the pulpit. The background to this was probably the enmity Calvin had shown Poullain in 1547 regarding a court case involving Isabella Hamericourt, for whom Calvin was looking for a suitable husband and who had broken off an engagement to Poullain, obviously under pressure from her influential relatives. Poullain claimed that Lord de Falais, Miss Hamericourt's guardian, had given his permission for him to marry Miss Hamericourt who had accepted his engagement ring. De Falais, a friend of Calvin's who employed Poullain at the time, later denied that he had given the couple his blessing and though Poullain asked for the matter to be settled before the church, de Falais took the issue to the secular marriage court at Basle, arguing that Miss Hamericourt had been promised to another. John Hooper, the English martyr and Poullain's brother-in-law was also indirectly involved in the controversy and supported Poullain, as did Bucer and Ochino.[40] Hooper's servant had chaperoned a journey to Basle which Poullain and Miss Hamericourt had made at de Falais' request and could confirm what Poullain said. The maid had then returned to Zürich[41] where she was requested to appear as a witness for the defence. Calvin, who hoped that de Falais would found a church for the French refugees in Basle, joined him in denouncing Poullain in the strongest terms, sending Viret and others to advise de

[40] Hooper's wife, Anne, eventually joined Poullain and his church when her husband was imprisoned by Mary. When the English church was formed at Frankfurt, she joined the family's friends there.

[41] The Hoopers were guests of Bullinger in Zürich.

Falais against Poullain and his alleged betrothed. However, the court, in spite of de Falais' pressure put on them, was unable (or afraid) to come to a final verdict, though they admitted that Poullain's version was the most credible. Each party had to pay his own costs. Many criticised Poullain for being impertinent enough to contradict a nobleman in court. This was also Calvin's argument as he always looked on the gentry as having rightful privileges over ordinary people. Indeed, Calvin wrote to Poullain telling him that his vision was not blinded by the splendour of rank, but nevertheless he must castigate Poullain for having been presumptuous enough to contest such a noble family. He wrote a number of letters to de Falais, poisoning his mind against the couple by referring to the fact that both had been rejected by others formerly as if this were a spot on their characters. De Falais thus responded by calling Poullain openly a whoremonger and adulterer. In Calvin's rather servile letters to de Falais he accused Poullain of being a venomous animal, a man of low reputation and one who writes letters in a drunken stupor, seeing double.[42] Such language was sadly typical of Calvin in controversy.

Poullain's backing from the Reformed corner was large but many also backed him merely because they thought him courageous for speaking up against a nobleman. Others criticised him for contesting the word of a member of the gentry. Strasburg, for instance, remained true to Poullain but Basle was divided. Prof. Werle comments that Calvin took de Falais' side 'with fire and flame' and did not care what weapon he used to place his fellow preacher at a disadvantage.[43] Poullain came out of the controversy with two enemies who had formerly been his friends, the powerful nobleman de Falais and his predecessor at Strasburg, John Calvin who now used every opportunity to harm his Reformed colleague. After the debacle, Calvin strove to find Miss Hamericourt a 'better' husband; a task in which he believed he was successful. Nobody, except Poullain, seemed to be interested in what Miss Hamericourt herself

[42] See Calvin's letters to de Falais and Poullain during the year 1547, Calvin Collection, Ages CD Library.

[43] See *Calvin und Basle bis zum Tode des Myconius*, p. 60 ff. for a detailed account of the controversy.

thought and the poor lady was married off without any regard to her own feelings at all.

The rebuff in Strasburg did not help to improve Calvin's temper on his way to meet the Frankfurt Senate. Nor did his experience improve the opinion of Poullain he had formed ten years previously. When Calvin arrived at Frankfurt, he found that the Magistrates had set up a formal *Schiedsgericht* (Court of Arbitration) which Calvin was to chair. He was dismayed to find that Robert Horne, the pastor of the English Church, and Jan Laski, who was representing the Dutch Church he had established, supported Poullain. However, Calvin insisted on a secret trial from which Horne and Laski were excluded. He then insisted that Poullain should be reprimanded and removed from his church, maintaining even that 'no punishment was too severe for him'.[44] Poullain had begged Calvin not to reach a decision before consulting Laski and the other pastors in the city but Calvin refused to have his decision influenced by any other man. He had been given the Chair by the Senate and his word was final. The church majority were for keeping their beloved pastor but, out of respect for Calvin, the Lutheran Senate, who were hoping for some sort of concord with Geneva, ruled that Poullain had to go. He was divested of all his rights as a citizen but refused a passport and permission to travel. When the news of Calvin's action leaked out, there was an enormous protest amongst the city's pastors. The act was also seen as a blow against Strasburg who had so cordially given Calvin asylum in 1538. To make amends for their clumsy strategy, the Senate invited the pastors to debate the matter with Calvin, but they took this as a further insult and refused to meet with him. Poullain died soon afterwards at the age of forty, a broken man.

Whilst in Frankfurt, Calvin won Laski over to the idea that he, Melanchthon and Laski should meet together in Frankfurt in September 1557 to discuss the Lord's Supper. Laski, on leaving Frankfurt for Poland, called on Melanchthon who said he was willing to join the discussions at Frankfurt. This caused Calvin to emphasise in his debates

---

[44] See Bauer's *Valerand Poullain*, p. 256 for Calvin's letter to Musculus explaining his attitude to Poullain. Also my *The Troublemakers at Frankfurt*, pp. 234-237.

with Westphal that Melanchthon was his ally, whereas Melanchthon was keeping quiet on the matter regarding Westphal so as not to rock the Lutheran boat. Westphal now turned on Melanchthon with more aggression than ever. Calvin wrote at least three letters to Melanchthon, urging him to come out openly on Calvin's side, but Melanchthon did not reply. On 3 August, 1557, Calvin demanded to know why Melanchthon refused to answer his letters, whereupon Melanchthon sent him a short testimony of friendship without giving him any theological details. About the same time, Calvin published his *Ultima ratio* against Westphal, and, leaving all discretion aside, he emphasised strongly Melanchthon's alleged sympathy with his own position. After this, Melanchthon never wrote to Calvin again and the conference Calvin had planned at Frankfurt never materialised. Wilhelm Neuser in his essay commemorating the four-hundredth anniversary of Bullinger's death, argues that Calvin's *Ultima ratio* was the cause of Melanchthon's final break with Calvin.[45] Calvin's anti-Poullain act had angered the churches in Frankfurt and as he had now angered Melanchthon through his lack of tact and diplomacy. Calvin returned empty-handed to continue his battle with Westphal from Geneva, still arguing that his views were not in conflict with Melanchthon and the *Augsburg Confession*.

Bullinger holds to Calvin in spite of his lack of diplomacy and balance

Calvin now told Farel that he could not write as if Westphal was a brother in Christ as he held him to be the worst of heretics. When Calvin received wide criticism for his bad temper, he told Bullinger that he knew that he was a much hated man but it would comfort him to know that Bullinger at least thought that he was of some service to the cause. Bullinger gave Calvin a friendly and pastoral reply void of criticism. However, the Gnesio storm was still raging in 1560, especially because Lutheran Palatine went over to the Reformed cause. Bullinger told his

[45] Die Versuche Bullingers, Calvins und der Strassburger, Melanchthon zum Fortgang von Wittenberg zu Bewegen, *Heinrich Bullinger 1504-1575, Gesammelte Aufsätze zum 400. Todestag*, p. 49.

friends concerning the continued controversy, "I have better things to do in my free time than to refute such childishness." Bullinger had hit on the correct course. He now persuaded the Swiss-Germans and Genevans to ignore Westphal, arguing that if the Reformed churches did not argue with Westphal, the Gnesio-Lutheran would have nothing to write about.[46] Bullinger had come to the opinion that as he did not have Geneva behind him, it would be folly to present a divided front against Westphal.

Brenz enters the fray

Now Brenz began to persecute those of the Reformed faith in the Württemberg area (now Baden-Württemberg), especially in Stuttgart, and closed down the Reformed churches of Reichenweiher and Mömpelgard. He forced on the churches a most strict form of his teaching on Christ's ubiquity. Picking out Bullinger as his main target, he wrote three Latin works against him on the question of whether Christ in His human body could be in Heaven and everywhere on earth at the same time. His 1661 Tübingen work *On the Personal Union of the Two Natures in Christ* showed that Brenz believed that Christ's presence in the Lord's Supper was carnal but at the same time ubiquitous.[47] Bullinger maintained that ubiquity does not belong to the human but to the divine and that Christ's presence in the Lord's Supper is to be understood spiritually and not corporally. Peter Martyr now came to Bullinger's assistance and wrote his famous *Dialogue* on the two natures of Christ. This ran into five Latin editions and was also published in French and English.

The Church of England, now ruled by a good number of Reformed bishops, followed Bullinger's and Martyr's witness to the Hyper-Lutherans with great interest. Bishop Parkhurst wrote on 1 September, 1561:

"I wish the Ubiquitarians a better mind, if indeed they have a mind at all; being both out of their mind and without a mind; and persons over whom you and Martyr will gain an easy conquest. But I well know the

---

[46] Ibid, condensed from, p. 108.
[47] Ubiquitarians believe in the omnipresence of Christ's human body.

nature of these boasters. They will not yield even when conquered; but unless they repent, Christ will overcome them and Satan bind them. May the Lord strengthen with his Spirit and long preserve in safety the Palatine of the Rhine and the Hessian."[48]

Shortly afterwards, Martyr became seriously ill and could not continue the debate so Bullinger was left to combat Brenz alone. He replied with six works between 1561 and 1571, probably the most important and most widely read books being his *Fundamentum firmum* (Sure Foundation) which first appeared in both Latin and Swiss-German. This was followed by Bullinger's *Repetitio et explication* (Repetitions and Explanations) on the dual nature of Christ as God and Man. Bullinger saw Brenz' teaching on the humanity of Christ as a virtual denial of that humanity or rather a deification of it. He therefore argued that the resurrection of Christ as perfect Man is the believer's guarantee of his own resurrection as a restored perfect man. If Christ's all-present divinity robbed Him of His humanity, then His eternal mediatory office would be annulled. Thus Christ cannot be physically present in the Eucharist service as a resurrected man when He, as such, is sitting at the right hand of God in Heaven. In other words, even after the resurrection, the human attributes of Christ do not disappear. He is forever perfect Man just as He is perfect God. This led Brenz to call Bullinger a Nestorian for separating the Persons of the Godhead. Bullinger explained that he held to the full deity and full humanity of Christ but that these qualities are not merged so that Christ's divinity is lessened by His humanity or His humanity deified in any way. Though the Triune Deity is omnipresent as Spirit, Christ cannot be carnally omnipresent as He would then not be true man. Luther and Benz, however, argued that Christ, as true man, need not be present *locally* and *spatially* if he were present *definitively*, that is in His capacity of Man. Bullinger rejected this as a sophistic speculation and self-contradiction with no Scriptural backing at all and which could not justify the erroneous doctrine of consubstantiation i.e. the teaching that after the

[48] These dukedoms were friendly to the Swiss Reformation. See *Zürich Letters*, First Series, p. 98.

consecration, the real flesh and blood of Christ co-exist in and with the natural elements of bread and wine. The picture Luther had given to illustrate the Lutheran view was to take a smoothing iron and heat it. The iron was then still the same but it had received another attribute, that of heat. Thus the bread and wine receive the further attribute of Christ's flesh and blood after the consecration. Brenz died in 1570 and Bullinger in 1575 but this war of definitions and semantics still goes on between Lutherans and the Reformed.

Meanwhile, Bullinger's works against Brenz and the Lutheran doctrine of the Lord's Supper were being eagerly read in England where the bishops were following Bullinger's advice not to be influenced by the Lutherans' wish to remain in debate with Rome and work out some mutual compromise with the findings of Trent.[49] John Jewel responded with his massive volume *Apologia Ecclesiae Anglicanae* which he quickly sent to Bullinger,[50] apologising for the large amount of printer's errors in it. Bishop Parkhurst described the work to Bullinger jokingly as 'a little book' which shows, "why we have gone over from the pope to Christ, and why we refuse to acknowledge the council of Trent."[51] In the same letter, Parkhurst tells Bullinger that he had a clergyman friend, almost ninety years old, who 'strenuously and obstinately' defended Brenz doctrine of the Lord's Supper. The bishop lent the good man his copy of Bullinger's recently published work against Brenz and the old man confessed himself completely converted to the Reformed teaching through Bullinger's work.

Peter Martyr wrote from Zürich on 24 August, 1562 to tell Jewel of the warm reception of the work in the Swiss Reformed churches. He said of the *Apologia*:

"It hath not only in all points and respects satisfied me (by whom all your writings are so wonderfully well liked and approved,) but it appeared also to Bullinger, and his sons and sons-in-law, and also to

[49] Bullinger had already criticised Trent in his dedication to Henry VIII in *Concerning Sacred Scripture* and had criticised such councils in his *Decades* dedication to Edward VI.
[50] *Zürich Letters*, First Series, p. 101.
[51] Ibid, p. 121.

Gualter and Wolfius, so wise, admirable, and eloquent, that they can make no end of commending it, and that nothing in these days hath been set forth more perfectly. I exceedingly congratulate your talents upon this excellent fruit, the church upon this edifying of it, and England upon this honour; and beseech you to proceed in the same way you have entered."[52]

Less than a year later, we find Jewel writing to Bullinger on 5 March, 1563 confessing his grief at the sudden death of Peter Martyr who had died at Zürich and now left Bullinger to combat Brenz alone. Martyr had been one of Jewel's closest friends as they had served at Oxford together and lodged at Strasburg together when exiled. Most of the pioneer Reformers were now dead and Jewel wrote, "May our great and good God mercifully look upon his church, and raise up for her other defenders in the room of the departed. Ye are few, my father, ye are but few, upon the whole matter rests; and I have always reckoned yourself amongst the foremost. Oh that there may always be some, to whom you may transfer your duties with satisfaction."[53] Jewel was thinking of the coming generation, using the picture in the original Latin of a runner carrying a lighted torch which he handed over to the next runner after covering his set distance. However, Bullinger's work on Brenz had obviously made his fingers itch to be writing again himself. So we find him telling Bullinger:

"I do not wonder that your Hercules of Tübingen, the forger of monstrosities, is now triumphing at his ease: I wonder whether he is able to confine himself within the ample limits and regions of his Ubiquitarian kingdom. Should he make any attack on our departed friend, and his writings come to my knowledge, unless some of you should be before hand with me, I shall think it my duty to reply to him, as far as my engagements will permit; if for no other reason, at least to let the world know, that England and Switzerland are both united against these Ubiquitarians."[54]

---

[52] Ibid, p. 339.
[53] Ibid, p. 122.
[54] Ibid, p. 123.

Jewel's energies for the next few years, however, were mostly taken up with combating the attacks of Arch-Papist Thomas Harding and other servants of Rome who singled Jewel out as the main English spokesman for the Reformation. This resulted, nevertheless, in Jewel writing extensively on the Lord's Supper, very much as if Brenz were his target and, indeed, Jewel confessed to Bullinger that he had written a work specifically against Brenz when combating Harding, but in English.[55] Jewel's printed works ran into many thousands of pages, most of which was preserved in Legh Richmond's *The Fathers of the English Church*, Vol. VII of 1811, and the Parker Society four-volumed large format edition of 1845. As Jewel has a most lively, imaginative, vivid and clear style and his doctrines are all gold, it would be of immense profit to our present-day Church if he could be reprinted or put on the Internet.

Bullinger's son Heinrich travels to Germany for further education

In 1555, just when relations between the Lutherans and the Reformed were so strained, Bullinger's eldest son Heinrich (1534-1583) and shortly later his son Hans Rudolf (1536-1582), begged their father to keep to the family tradition and send them to Germany to further their education. Bullinger was not at all pleased with the idea as he was frightened that the Germans would use the opportunity to win his boys over to Lutheranism which would be a major victory for them. As a compromise, Bullinger sent the two boys to Strasburg in Upper Germany to study under the Italians and friends of many years Peter Martyr and Jerome Zanchi. Their church stood nearer Zürich in doctrine than Wittenberg. Martyr and Zanchi, however, advised Bullinger to send his son Heinrich to Wittenberg for his post-graduate education. Bullinger then arranged for Henry to study there under Philip Melanchthon and Paul Eber. Bullinger told his son that he did not wish to hinder his academic progress but that he might not be well received at Wittenberg because of the Saxons' antipathy to Zürich's theology. On 23 June, 1555 Bullinger thus wrote to Heinrich, "You must be careful (I say this in strict confidence, my son)

[55] Ibid, p. 139.

that you being my son might not prove a handicap and a vexation to you. It is said that the name of Bullinger from Zürich has an evil reputation in Saxony. You must be careful that you are not put under pressure to accept a faith which stands in stark opposition to our true belief."[56] Nevertheless, Bullinger tells his son to attend the preaching services but see that they respect his views concerning the Lord's Supper. Before giving his final permission, Bullinger asks Henry to find out discretely what the true position is regarding Swiss Protestants in Saxony. He also tells him that there are rumours of the pest in Germany and he did not want to send his son into any kind of danger.

Heinrich Jun. stays with Melanchthon

When news reached Zürich that the plague was not rampant in Saxony, the initial inhibitions that Bullinger had against Wittenberg disappeared. He then arranged that Henry should stay at the home of Melanchthon who was considered the more tolerant of the Lutherans. Bullinger sent an introductory letter with his son to Melanchthon, saying:

"Trusting entirely in your friendliness and good nature, I am sending to you pious and learned sir Philip, honourable, most beloved Brother, my son Heinrich and beseech you to be a father to him in your house and take him into your care. I will pay you what is good and proper and what his fellow-students pay you. Besides this, I pledge myself to do the same for you and yours and offer you every possible service in return. Should it not be convenient for you to take him into your home, please assist him with your wise advice to find a true and pious host and keep an eye on him. He will be a burden to no one, cause no bother and quarrel with nobody. He will keep himself to himself, God and the sciences. He will follow you and choose you as his mentor and attend your lectures. I would like him to live peacefully and acceptable at your home and learn pure good, sincere Christianity because I have dedicated him to God and to academic studies. If you will combine your efforts with mine to make

[56] *Merkwürdige Züge*, p. 96.

him acquainted with God, virtue and the sciences, our Lord God will reward your endeavours and my family and I will be for ever grateful to you and your family. On this subject our dearest brother Calvin will soon write to you, so I shall be brief as I know you are always so busy. I enclose for your edification, three sermons in German which I published this year and last year, the latter one is mainly against the Schwenckfelders. May the Lord Jesus keep you in good health for the blessing of our troubled Church. My brethren and fellow-warriors greet you with their full hearts,
Yours truly,

Henry Bullinger
Servant of the Church in Zürich

Bullinger's sermon against the teaching of Casper Schwenckfeld von Ossig (1490-1561) would have been of special interest to Melanchthon who called a special convention in 1540 to brand Schwenckfeld as a heretic. This caused the German aristocrat to set up an alternative 'Lutheran' church called 'The Confessors of the Glory of Christ' which practised another form of the Lord's Supper. They also developed a different Christology by teaching the deification of Christ's humanity and practised a different church discipline. The movement first became more radical after it was forced out of the Lutheran fold. The Schwenckfelders were severely persecuted by Protestants and Romanists alike. Small communities of Schwenckfelders have survived in the United States of America, in Pennsylvania but they have given up practising the Lord's Supper. Speaking of the intolerance of the churches and reflecting his own and his followers' experiences, Schwenckfeld said in his *Corpus Schwenckfeldianorum*, "The papists damn the Lutherans; the Lutherans damn the Zwinglians … ; the Zwinglians damn the Anabaptists and the Anabaptists damn all others."[57]

[57] Leipzig, 1907 ff, IV. 818.

Bullinger's rules of strategy and conduct for his son

Bullinger advised his son to attend lectures at Wittenberg and study industriously but sit for the examinations elsewhere as Wittenberg demanded that their students should sign the *Augsburg Confession* before being allowed to take higher examinations. He thus suggested obtaining reports and recommendations from his Wittenberg professors and then taking them to the less strict Marburg University where he could sit for the Master's examination without having to state of what theological party he was. Through his friend Sebastian Fabrizius, Bullinger had discovered that one could sit for higher degrees in Marburg without having to attend previous courses there and the university only charged a fee of 10-12 Thalers. This tradition still exists today, though without the fees.[58] Because of the difficulties at Wittenberg, Bullinger sent his second youngest son directly to Marburg after his studies at Strasburg had ended.

Bullinger's letters to his son Heinrich show how he was constantly worried that he might be branded as a heretic by the Saxons or accommodate himself at least externally to Lutheranism in order to gain academic honours. Thus, in the 52 rules of conduct and advice that Bullinger gave him on 1 September, 1553 concerning his studies, Bullinger says in rule 18, "Quarrel stubbornly with no one who hates our religion. Always confess that you believe your religion and do not deny this but leave disputations to those who are proficient in them."[59] In rule 21, Bullinger advises his son, "Do not comment on all things, do not listen to all things. If you must speak, say the best you can and not your worst to every thing. He who seeks peace, finds it and the quarrelsome person is a nuisance to God and mankind. Much gossip is always a sin, this is why Saint James said, 'Let every man be swift to hear, slow to speak, slow to wrath.' That is why you should not talk too much." In one of his usual long list of numbered pieces of advice to Henry, written on

[58] The author's son took his doctorate at Marburg whilst working in Munich, having only to visit his Doktorvater occasionally.

[59] The full text is reproduced in J. F. Franz's collection of Bullinger's letters to his son in *Merkwürdige Züge*.

22 August, 1555 whilst Heinrich was contemplating studying at Wittenberg, Bullinger tells him:

"Visit all of Philipp's[60] lectures but from the others choose only the theological lectures of Major[61] and Caspar Peucer's lectures on mathematics. Do not load yourself up with lessons. I will not have you running from college to college or senselessly wandering from lecture hall to lecture hall. Be industrious otherwise I will soon call you back home. Learn the Latin and Greek languages, didactics, rhetorics, literature and theology. As soon as you have the opportunity, tell me where you are boarding, how expensive it is[62] and which lectures you are visiting."[63]

Henry followed his father's advice and was then allowed to add the lectures of Prof. Jacob Milich on history and Greek and Prof. Paul Eber's lectures in mathematics and Hebrew.

Superstition under the guise of science criticised

One of the main distinctions between the Swiss-German Reformed Church and the Lutherans was the latter's insistence on interpreting the Scriptures through the supposedly scientific methods of didactics, rhetoric, logic and mathematics laid down by Aristotle. Much of the work of Melanchthon in Reforming the Church was to emphasise that the papists had misinterpreted Aristotle in a metaphysical sense, whereas the Lutherans interpreted Aristotle correctly in a scientific sense which made a true exegesis of the Scriptures possible. However, Melanchthon and the Lutherans, following Aristotle all too closely, believed that astrology was a science to be believed and followed by all. Thus the Lutherans looked to the position of the stars in gauging God's will. Melanchthon never undertook anything he thought important without first consulting such

[60] Melanchthon.
[61] George Major.
[62] Bullinger always told his boys (based on his own experience as a student) to find accommodation at one address and board at another. This prevented them from becoming too negatively familiar with their hosts and gave them a degree of variety and freedom.
[63] Ibid, pp. 107-108.

constellations. Bullinger believed this was sheer paganism. Perhaps young Henry had already been influenced by the Wittenberg mentality when he reported to his father in March, 1556, that a comet was seen moving northwards over Wittenberg which looked like a rod used for disciplining children. Henry Jun. ends his description of the event in a letter to his father with the words, "O if this could only turn the people to honouring God and bettering their lives![64] In September, 1556, Bullinger heard from Henry that he was required to inform the university not only of his date of birth but also of the name of the day and the very hour he was born. As he had no idea of these details, he wrote asking for the information from his father. Bullinger immediately grew suspicious, knowing the Lutheran's Aristotelian thinking and replied:

"I would tell you the time and hour of your birth if I had not noticed why you require it. You are requested to find out about your nativity so that your future fate may be worked out. Do you not know, my son, that God forbids such enquiries? They are superstitious and those who behave in this way sin heavily against God. Think of the birth of Esau and Jacob and other twins who met different ends. Use your time for other, more profitable things so that you will not tarnish pure religion and your faith."[65]

Bullinger knew what risks Melanchthon was running in having such close connections with him. Luther and the Gnesio-Lutherans were calling him 'Anabaptists' and 'heretic', so Bullinger wrote in the same letter, "Give Dr Melanchthon my greetings. I am not writing to him personally so that he will not be hated by the others."

Bullinger pleads with Melanchthon to work for peace amongst the Lutherans and Reformed

Early in 1556, Melanchthon wrote to Bullinger to inform him of his son's progress. Sadly, the letter is lost but Bullinger's reply is extant and

[64] Ibid, p. 129.
[65] Ibid, p. 120, letter written 1 September, 1556

preserved in its German version in J. F. Franz' collection *Merkwürdige Züge*. The letter is a bid for peace when the Lutherans were doing their utmost to stifle the progress of the Reformation both in England and Europe. In this reply, Bullinger first thanks Melanchthon for his care of Henry before going on to appeal to him to use his great influence to pacify the more militant Lutherans. Neither Bullinger nor Calvin could understand why Melanchthon had chosen to remain quiet on the most important issues of peace and tolerance. Actually, it was Melanchthon's views of tolerance which prevented him from opening his mouth. If he had too much contact with the Upper Germans and the Swiss, the more militant Lutherans criticised him and if he emphasised his repeatedly changing ideas on justification, predestination and the Lord's Supper, which were usually not in the interest of his Reformed friends, he would soon hear from Strasburg, Bern, Basle, Zürich and Geneva. Melanchthon felt that if all kept quiet on controversial subjects as he did himself, there would be no problem. The trouble was that Melanchthon's tolerance was often not in the interest of the Reformation and when he became outspoken, it was usually to defend his Augsburg Confessions and his apologetic work on it rather than Reformed doctrines. Until he became disillusioned with the Council of Trent and the Emperor, Melanchthon loved to attend disputations where he would put forward his *Augsburg Confession* as if it were Scripture itself. This pleased few of the parties present who were there to bargain. Bullinger's letter to Melanchthon in full reads:

"Honourable, Most Worthy, Pious, Highly Treasured Brother in Christ!

How greatly pleasant and welcome to me was your latest friendly and cordial letter! Receive therefore my warmest, hearty thanks. My Heinrich cannot tell me enough how lovingly you have accepted him and how fatherly you are taking care of him and guide him always with your best advice. Receive therefore my special thanks. Please continue to instruct him, to encourage him, to foster him and to care for him! God knows that you will receive no lack of thanks from him for this kindness and they will not fail on my part. I continually remind him of the value of all that he needs to thank you for. The first wish of my heart is that this my son will return to his parental home, devout and well-educated so that he may be of use to his country and serve the Lord in truth.

How it grieves me, honoured father that the sad sacrament controversy has broken out again. We have been drawn once again by the hair into the arena and against our will to answer several bitter printed pamphlets. I take the liberty, to send you, my dear friend, a copy of one of our apologetic writings. I fight with all weapons but only so as to offer peace which is a thousand times more important to us than open battle. O, if you, honourable friend, are able to do anything (and your influence is enormously strong), so speak up! Step into the fray to mediate with all your power. Tame the frantic violence of those men who are well-known to you. Tell them that if they must write, to at least leave out the abuse, reproaches, bitter accusations and in a reasonably, modest, illuminating way defend themselves on Scriptural grounds. It would be a thousand times better if we could tolerate each other and stop biting each other when we do not understand each other and find a balance. What tragic consequences this time of tension brings us, this split amongst brethren. Are not our common enemies thus gaining in strength and are the weak not being discouraged?

As far as we are concerned, though this eternal battle is loathsome to us, we cannot surrender our righteous cause. For my part, I have a natural distaste for all quarrelling but at times our religion demands that those passages given us by the Lord should be contended for with all our strength. So once again I would ask you, honourable Sir, my friend, intervene. It must be very apparent to you, that we do not fight for irreligion or absurdities.

My son will present you with my latest German publication *The Sum of True Religion.*[66] It deals with all, or at least the most important doctrines of our faith. I cannot imagine that either you or other devout and modest men will think amiss of my work. If you, however, or anyone

---

[66] Published in 1556 and 1595. A Latin version was published in 1556, 1559 and 1569.

else should find anything in it which is offensive which you would like to see altered, I would ask and beg you to tell me openly. The candid judgement of godly men over my studies and work is very important for me. Friendly tips assist me being more careful in future.

Hearty greetings to you my fellow-wayfarers in the Lord and every blessing from the Lord. Love us, faithful brother in Christ, we who carry such a cordial love for you. Again, I commend my dear son to you as if he belonged to you.

The Lord be with you,

Your
Bullinger[67]

Bullinger's anxious care for his son and the Reformed faith

Bullinger's personal opinion of the Lutherans rarely comes to the surface in his exegetical and apologetic works but his letters to Henry reveal his heart. As his son was encouraged more and more by his professors both at Strasburg and Wittenberg to strive for the very highest academic attainments, Bullinger thought that he had better keep warning his son against the dangers of compromising. He thus wrote to Heinrich on 2 November, 1556:

"I know that in Wittenberg, they combine religious opinions with the honour of receiving a doctorate and demand from each person who aspires to the title that he should not depart in any way in the matter of beliefs from those of the Wittenberg Church and schools and accept and sign the *Augsburg Confession*. You know that Luther both personally and through his schools, charges us with error and heresy. The illustrious Senate of our city could not and would not sign the *Augsburg Confession*, mainly because in the tenth article the very being and corporal presence of Christ's body in the bread is upheld and defended .... At the beginning we are informed that the tenth article is 'authorised' but by whom? The

[67] *Merkwürdige Züge*, pp. 134-136.

Emperor and his papists? What do these accept and call good? That which we by all means reject."

Bullinger warns his son of the negative consequences that could arise if he returned to his native country to minister there after signing a document which the Swiss Protestants felt betrayed the Reformation. So, too, Bullinger was frank about his own fears should the Senate hear or even suspect that his son had signed a semi-papist document. Then, in spite of his office as Superintendent, Bullinger would have difficulties defending himself from the charge of aiding and abetting his son. Too drive the point home, the worried father told his son that Luther's slander (Lästerungen) against the Reformed churches of Switzerland had spread across the world and Reformed people abroad would think that the Lutherans, whose doctrines were diametrically opposed to the Swiss Protestants, had defeated them in argument which would cause the other Reformed churches to turn from the Swiss-Germans. Bullinger is thinking here mainly of the English, Hungarian and Romanian churches. In order to be on the safe side, Bullinger wrote to Landgrave Philip of Hessen and at least two of the Marburg professors, so as to pave the way for his child to take his higher examinations there. By November, 1556, Bullinger became more intent to have his son move on to Marburg as Melanchthon had written to him confessing that his position at Wittenberg had become precarious and he was surrounded by enemies and critics at the university. Andrew Osiander and Matthew Vlacich, commonly known as Flacius, were busy at the time writing pamphlet after pamphlet against Melanchthon whom they accused of betraying the Lutheran faith. In one year, Flacius published no less than ninety times against his colleague.

Article Ten of the *Augsburg Confession*

It was the Swiss-Germans' attitude to the tenth article of the *Augsburg Confession* which caused some friction between the Swiss Protestants and those of Geneva, with the latter taking a more lax attitude than the former. The article states, "The body and blood of Christ are truly present, and are distributed to those who eat the Supper of the Lord, and they reject those who teach otherwise." During Calvin's 1538-41 exile in Strasburg, Bucer had taken him to Frankfurt to dispute with Melanchthon who was revising the tenth article there in an effort to find a compromise with the papists and Reformed churches. Melanchthon discussed his views with the budding theologian Calvin who found he agreed in all respects. Thus Calvin, when, reporting on the Frankfurt meeting to William Farel, his major mentor at this time, tells him concerning Melanchthon, "You need not doubt about him, but consider that he is entirely of the same opinion as ourselves."[68] This is one of the first signs that Calvin differed in his view of the Eucharist from the German Swiss Reformers as also from their Anglican allies. After lengthy discussions following the Disputation of Worms, Eck, Melanchthon, Cardinal Contari and Gropper reached a compromise on 2 May, 1541 concerning the Lord's Supper. Melanchthon declared that the main points of the Christian faith were ratified but Luther and the Saxon elector, according to Prof. Stupperich, saw no good in the final formula. Calvin, however, wrote to Farel on 11 May to tell him that he marvelled at the success of the disputation and that the formula agreed on contained the 'substance of true doctrine'. Especially with reference to justification, Calvin even tells Farel, "Nothing can be comprehended in it which is not found in our writings". Historian Thomas M. Lindsay's remark on such statements highlights the lengths the German Lutherans and French Reformed were prepared to go in their efforts to find unity with Rome. Lindsay declares, "The discussions showed that it was possible to state Romanist and Lutheran doctrine in ambiguous propositions which could be accepted by the theologians of both Confessions."[69] Bullinger, however, was always for clarity of thought and expression so that no ambiguities remained. The truth was not a matter of playing with words or speaking relatively. Calvin scolded Bullinger at times for taking his own words at their face value. He told his Swiss friend that he should accept his words according to the meaning he placed on them and not be so exact in his interpretations. Bullinger, a brilliant linguist and exegete, believed that one should use words as

[68] Letter written March 1539, Ages Collection.
[69] *History of the Reformation*, Vol. I., p. 380.

exactly and precisely as possible and seek to avoid loose expressions and ambiguity. When reading books, few are able to ask the author what he meant. His words must express their meaning clearly. This difference in using words reflected the different ideas of tolerance between Bullinger and Calvin. The latter's tolerance was shown in accepting formulas but giving them different interpretations, which enabled him to approve what Bullinger rejected. On the other hand, Bullinger could tolerate brethren who held to different views on certain matters and even share the Lord's Table with them, yet he would not sign their various formulas if he could not accept them point for point. Calvin was not always consistent in his view as he refused to sign the Athanasian Creed.

Chapter 7

Bullinger's Special Contribution to Reformed Doctrines

To outline all the doctrines of Bullinger would take volumes as even Bullinger did not manage to cram them all into his five books of his doctrinal work the *Decades* which was published in the English version in four volumes with a total of 1,866 pages.[1] The following brief studies refer to a selection from Bullinger's literary output and doctrines which were peculiar to himself and highly influenced the Swiss and English Reformed churches and through them the Reformed churches throughout the world.

Bullinger's vast literary witness

Bullinger always complained that going from one disputation or conference to another was a poor means of spreading the good news of the gospel which could only be obtained through the preached and written word. He would have also added that the nearest the written word came to the spoken word of the exegetical sermon, the better. Contemporary catalogues of Bullinger's works run into many hundreds of pages[2] so it is only possible to deal with a few of his major works in this brief overview. Several collections of sermons from 1532 on have already been

[1] Decades, I-II, 435 pages, III, 432 pages, IV, 408 pages and V, 591 pages.
[2] See *Heinrich Bullinger Werke*, Erste Abteilung, Bibliographie, Band I and II.

mentioned. Indeed in thirteen publications from 1532-1546, Bullinger covered all the books of the Bible. Recognising Revelation as a worthy member of the New Testament canon, contrary to the view of notable Reformers such as Zwingli and Calvin, Bullinger wrote a commentary on the book and published a collection of sermons entitled *100 Predigten zur Offenbarung* in 1557. In the same year, he published an eschatological work *Ueber das Ende des Weltzeitalters und das künftige Gericht unserns Herrn Jesus Christus.*[3] The exact date of his commentary on Revelation is a matter of debate as the Zürich Council forbade its original publication for a number of years. It was finally published in 1561.

The hundred sermons on Revelation went through 30 editions before the end of the century and were translated into Latin, German, English, French and Dutch. Bullinger taught that the book of Revelation was the mother of Christian theology and dedicated his work to "All who live in Germany and the Confederacy and those out of France, England, Italy and other kingdoms who are exiled for Christ's sake and all believers wherever they might live who are waiting for the return of Christ." For Bullinger, Revelation was the book of comfort *par excellence* for the elect believer and demonstrated that Christ would never leave His Church no matter what difficulties and calamities they would have to go through. Bullinger prefaced all his commentaries and writings with Matthew 17:5, "This is my beloved Son, in whom I am well pleased; hear ye him."

Added to all these sermons were 18 more on the Christian festivals published in 1558; 174 sermons on Jeremiah which appeared between 1557 and 1561; 66 sermons on Daniel in 1565 and 190 sermons on Isaiah in 1567, apart from a few dozen single sermons published on special occasions. Bullinger differed in his convictions concerning Christian festivities to his friends in Geneva who had little interest in them. As an historian and one who had to deal all his life with enthusiasts who wished to spiritualise away outward signs and historical events, Bullinger felt that a minister should emphasise the nature of Christ as the Word who became flesh and all the historical occasions of his incarnated life in his preaching

[3] *On the End of the World's Epoch and the Future Judgement of Our Lord Jesus Christ.*

and family worship. Thus, to him, the celebration of Christmas, Easter and Whitsuntide was a major Christian witness and especial Christmastide ought to be solemnly kept. The latter season was the time when family fellowship became especially dear to the Bullingers and the greater family always strove to be together. Thus Bullinger has preserved for us in his publications especially accounts of how the Bullinger's celebrated Christmas. Nowadays, sadly, many would-be Reformed believers who appear to have been brought up on the Stoics, campaign avidly for the abolishing of the Christian festivities as if they were valueless in Christian teaching and worship. Thus we are told that celebrating the historicity of Christ's life, especially His incarnation, is not important as this has been too misused by papists and commerce. The main thing, we are told, is to celebrate the fact that Christ is born in our hearts and resurrected in our lives. Bullinger believed as Paul who in 1 Corinthians 15 stressed the importance of remembering the historicity of salvation without which there can be no spiritual work in man.[4] So, too, through remembering the sojourn of Christ on this earth, we come nearer to understanding that He came 'in the fullness of time'.

In all, there are 618 known sermons published by Bullinger but more sermons published or unpublished are being discovered from year to year. Fritz Büsser, on examining all the extant sermon manuscripts and outlines in German and Latin left by Bullinger and the large number of transcriptions made by Rudolf Gualter, besides Bullinger's references to his preaching activities meticulously kept in his diary, states that they add up to some 7,000 sermons.

Amongst his published work for his *Prophezei*, two of his earliest were his lectures on Romans (1525) in which he emphasised the faithfulness of God in the life of the believer and the differences between law, nature and grace, and his lectures on Hebrews (1526-7) in which he stresses the uniqueness of Christ and the right usage of Biblical typology.

---

[4] See Pastor Christoffel's fine depicture of Christmas in Zürich in his chapter 'Wie Bullinger und seine Gattin ihre eigene und die Ihnen anvertrauten Kinder erziehen und versorgen' (How Bullinger and his wife educated and cared for their own children and those placed in their care) in *Heinrich Bullinger und seine Gattin*.

During this early period, Bullinger published major works on the Lord's Supper (1528), against images (1529) and on the Catabaptists (1531). In 1534, he dealt the dispensationalist views of the Catabaptists who rejected the Old Testament and emphasised the one covenant of grace in the entire Bible.

During the 1530s and 1540s, Bullinger published commentaries on separate books and his complete New Testament commentary came out in 1554. These works were all printed in Latin so they could be used throughout Europe. Though Bullinger preached most of his works in Swiss German, that language was limited to a few Swiss cantons and even they had their special local spoken and written forms of the language. Thus Swiss-German was most inappropriate for spreading the gospel throughout the world. On the other hand, Latin was spoken all over Europe including the British Isles in the seventeenth century, and there were many German, Dutch, French, Polish and English who could read and write better Latin than their mother tongue. William Cowper, writing in the following century, still confesses that his fellow pupils at Westminster could compose an essay in Latin but not write home to their parents in plain English.

Bullinger's first published work outlining his doctrine of the Scriptures, entitled *Ueber die Autorität der Heilige Schrift*, came out in 1538 and a further work on the subject, *Gründlicher Bericht über die Hoheit, Würde und Vollkommenheit der Heiligen Schrift*[5] followed in 1572. However, in 1991 Hans-Georg vom Berg, Bernd Schneider and Endre Zsindely published a number of hitherto unpublished works of Bullinger's from the 1520s such as *De scripturae negotio* showing that Bullinger was one of the very earliest Reformers to develop the understanding of the Scriptures now shared by Reformed Christians all over the world. So, too, we have Bullinger's earliest thoughts on the Lord's Supper, which Zwingli told him not to publish at the time as they were so innovating.[6] From 1549-51, Bullinger published his *Decades*,

[5] *Thorough Report of the Sovereignty, Dignity and Perfection of the Holy Scriptures.*
[6] *Heinrich Bullinger Theologische Schriften*, Dritte Abteilung, Band 2, Unveröffentlichte Werke der Kappeler Zeit, TVZ.

called such as the four volumes were divided into five collections of ten books each. This collection of sermons on the doctrines of the Christian Church was translated into German in 1558 and then quickly translated into English, French and Dutch.

As Christians were being persecuted all over Europe, Bullinger published his *Der Rechte Vollkommenheit der Christen* as a plea to the secular powers for tolerance.[7] In 1559, he published a manual for persecuted Christians, helping them deal with questions put to them by their persecutors.[8]

Bullinger's most popular and widespread work the Second Helvetic Confession (1566), or *Confessio helvetica posterior*, as it was originally called, was translated into almost all European languages and used as a standard of orthodoxy throughout East and West Europe and in regions of North America. The First Helvetic Confession of 1536 was a Swiss-Strasburg confession of which Bullinger was only one, although the leading compiler, of several esteemed authors. The confession was initially merely drawn up as a basis for cooperation with the Lutherans – a plan which, as outlined above, came to nought. The Second Helvetic Confession was solely the work of Bullinger and designed initially as Bullinger's own statement of faith. Indeed, it was completed during the Black Death of 1564 and placed with Bullinger's will as he, struck by the plague, prepared himself for his home-call. However, Bullinger recovered. Friedrich III, the Elector of the Palatine left the Lutheran Church and approached Bullinger as the leading Continental theologian to draw up a creed showing that the Reformed faith was the true, apostolic belief. Bullinger sent him his own declaration of faith. Friedrich found the confession ideal and had it translated into German, printed and distributed. It thus came to the notice of all the Swiss churches, the most prominent being Bern, Zürich and Geneva, and was adopted as a pan-Swiss confession. It was quickly translated into French by Beza and adopted by the French Swiss and Protestants of France. It probably

[7] *The True Perfection of Christians*, initially written as a plea to Henry II not to persecute the French Protestants.

[8] *Anleitung, wie die Verfolgten antworten sollen.*

reached Scotland in its French form where it was accepted as a standard creed by the Scottish Reformed churches in 1567. However, when their General Assembly wrote to Beza in September 1566 concerning the Confession which was most positively received, the Assembly pointed out that the news that there were still holders of the 'syncretism of Augsburg' in Geneva at the time was 'painful and distressing'.[9] In 1571, the Hungarian Reformed Church adopted the confession, then the Poles and Czechs.

Next to the Heidelberg Catechism which developed from it, Bullinger's confession became the most generally recognised in all the Reformed Church. Indeed, the 120 editions in 13 languages which have ensued over the years make the *Second Helvetic Confession* the most published work of the Swiss Reformation, including the Genevan. On reading through the confession, one is immediately struck by its relevance to the theological problems of today. Here, one finds the faults of Arminianism dealt with alongside the errors of Antinomianism. Those who build their faith around Old Testament case-law will find their bubbles burst in the confession but also those moderns who reject the Old Testament or tell us that Christ did not put Himself under the law for the sake of His elect. Modern half-baked New Covenant teaching, so different from the old, could be put into better shape by consulting Bullinger's confession. On dealing recently with those who say that God does not use means to convert people, not even the preaching of the Gospel, but regenerates the soul directly through inward revelation, I was struck by the clear answer Bullinger gives to such views in his very first chapter entitled *Of the Holy Scriptures Being the True Word of God.* Of these people Bullinger says:

"Inward illumination does not eliminate external preaching. For he that illuminates inwardly by giving men the Holy Spirit, the same one, by way of commandment, said unto his disciple, "Go into all the world, and

---

[9] *The Works of John Knox*, Laing edition, Vol. 6, pp. 544-550. Beza suggested to Bullinger that the testimony of the Scottish churches should be added to the Latin and German reprints and that he would add it to the French version, ibid, p. 550.

preach the Gospel to the whole creation" (Mark 16:15). And so in Philippi, Paul preached outwardly to Lydia, a seller of purple goods; but the Lord inwardly opened the woman's heart (Acts 16:14). And the same Paul, after a beautiful development of his thought, in Romans 10:17 at length comes to the conclusion, "So faith comes from hearing, and hearing from the Word of God by the preaching of Christ."

At the same time we recognise that God can illuminate whom and when he will, even without the external ministry, for that is in his power; but we speak of the usual way of instructing men, delivered unto us from God, both by commandment and example."

Preaching 'outside of the temple'

Apart from his theological writings, Bullinger penned works on caring for the sick and dying and a number of history books on the history of Switzerland and the Reformation. He also kept a journal from his youngest days to his death, outlining family news and commenting on current events. Like the English Reformers, such as John Foxe, Bullinger believed that the gospel could be preached *profanus* (outside the temple) in the form of drama, so, from his early twenties on, Bullinger, amidst his vast theological writing, composed several stage plays which reached national and international renown. *Lucretia and Brutus* is the most well-known and might shock even modern Christian minds. In order to impress on his audiences the Christian responsibility of every man great or small, rich or poor, Bullinger tells the story of Lucretia, a happily married woman who is raped by Sextus, the son of the tyrant king Tarquinius. Lucretia, in her shame, commits suicide before her gathered family. The people elect Lucretia's husband, Collatinus, and Brutus as consuls, depose the tyrant and proclaim a republic. Tarquinius strives to regain control through bribing Brutus' two sons. Throughout the play, one is reminded of Schiller's *William Tell*, which most probably received its inspiration from Bullinger's much earlier work. Tragically Brutus is forced by law to sentence his traitor sons to death. The moral is that countries can only be happy if they are ruled by the people for the people and only in such a social order can peace reign and the gospel be preached freely. However, the fame of this literary master-piece was not sought for by its author. An unknown person obtained possession of Bullinger's play and took it to Basle and had it printed, distributed and performed without Bullinger knowing anything about it. Jakob Bächtold in his *Geschichte der deutschen Literature in der Schweiz,*[10] says "Bullinger's *Lucretia and Brutus*, alongside *Manuel*, belongs to the most exquisite dramatical works of the sixteenth century that Switzerland possesses."

Bullinger's letters to his own sons who studied abroad in the middle fifteen fifties have been preserved and are full of wise, Christian and pedagogic advice both regarding humanistic and theological studies. Bullinger had, however, begun to do research into educational methods and curricula as soon as he took over the abbey school at Kappel and by 1527, at the early age of twenty-three, he had compiled his famous *Studiorum ratio* or study guide, originally written for the private use of a friend, Werner Steiner (Wernherus Lithonius), but later published in a shortened form by Pellican and in its full length years later in 1594 by a descendent of Zwingli's. Although Erasmus and Zwingli wrote on the subject of education and curricula, there does not appear to be signs of any influence by them on Bullinger. However, in 1525, Bullinger had prepared a work for the printer's entitled *De propheta libri duo* which was never published and modern scholars such as Susi Hausammann find in this work the forerunner of his *Studiorum ratio*.

The lengthy thesis is divided into thirty-three chapters in roughly two parts.[11] The first covers the entire realm of humanistic learning of the age including philosophy, poetry, rhetoric and history. Bullinger, however, adds a guide to understanding mathematics and the natural sciences. This part is accompanied by a list of textbooks and literature to be carefully studied. The second part starting with Chapter 15 deals with the critical analysis of literature, in particular that which cultivates a deeper

[10] History of German Literature in Switzerland. Bächtold deals with Bullinger's play on pp. 303-307.

[11] Büsser, in his comments on the work refers to thirty-two chapters (ibid, pp. 52-53) but the Peter Stotz TVZ edition gives thirty-three chapters with the Peroration as Chapter 33.

understanding of the Scriptures. Bullinger deals in detail with the full canon of the Bible and emphasises the importance of learning Hebrew and Greek and being open to the illuminating work of the Holy Spirit. Here, Bullinger outlines his doctrine of the covenant as the central axis of the Scriptures and God's revealed will to mankind. In this comprehensive work, Bullinger maintains that thinking comes from reading and the more one digs into the literary past, the more one is able to think in a way which will solve the problems of the future. In short, he who will not read about the past and understand literatures' *genres* cannot possibly think in any way useful to the education and advancement of mankind whether in natural or spiritual knowledge. Bullinger thus sees the minister as the teacher and foreseer of the future, who, through his exegetical work, acquaints the reader and hearer with the thoughts of God and the way to God and prepares him for his future life with God. The structure of Bullinger's work is typically humanistic and thus follows a pattern common to Bullinger's age. The originality of the work is found in its application of known literary methods of analysis to Biblical literature and its emphasis that the good, well-qualified student can only be truly such if he is at least as versed in the Scriptures as he is in secular literature. It is obvious that Bullinger holds that learning how to think and how to study at school and college and what aims one should have in life is more important than merely learning by rote. Particularly useful to students is Bullinger's practical advice on how to divide the day and portion out the time for eating, studying, recreation and sleeping and how to fit out a study-room and one's own personal library. His advice on the methodics of learning is also excellent as also his teaching on how to deal with the works of the experts. Bullinger's own expert advice on how to become a successful pastor and how to approach the Word of God in order to make its truth plain to one's sheep, are, this author believes, the great highlights of the *Studiorum ratio*.

Bullinger's international correspondence

Letter writing was considered a form of art in 16th century Europe and was a main feature of Renaissance life and the humanism that developed from it. Erasmus had written his *De conscribendis epistolis* in 1522, classifying letters into their various types and giving advice as to how a letter should reflect its topic and the character of the writer. He laid great stress on the correct form of salutation, greeting and ending and emphasised the importance of correctly dating and addressing letters. Our Reformers took over the art of letter writing and used it to spread the gospel. Bullinger, in keeping with Luther, Melanchthon, Zwingli, Bucer, Calvin and others, certainly wrote letters with a view to collecting them later and publishing them in book form to heighten and further their usage. Thus we find Bullinger making copies of letters and re-acquiring letters after the decease of correspondents. This explains why many of Bullinger's letters do not contain the usual personal problems and joys of every day life with comments on health and the weather but are often theological theses which were obviously meant for a wide readership.

Bullinger's enormous correspondence has not received the attention it deserves. For instance, when discussing Calvin as a letter writer in his Courtenay Studies in Reformation, Jean-Daniel Benoît speaks of Calvin's eleven *Corpus Reformatorum* volumes of letters as if this were an unrivalled feat. Though Bullinger corresponded regularly with Calvin and Beza and well over 600 letters between them are extant, Benoit hardly mentions Bullinger amongst Calvin's correspondents though only Farel and Viret corresponded more with the Genevan Reformer. So, too, Bullinger corresponded with many other contemporary Reformers, at least tripling Calvin's endeavours. However, when all Bullinger's letters are eventually published as planned, Fritz Büsser, their present Zürich editor, believes they will run into at least 60 similar volumes to the Calvin collection, but more probably 100.[12] Indeed, if the amount of extant letters written by our Reformers is anything to go by, Bullinger must have been the greatest letter-writer known to the Reformation. Of Erasmus' own correspondence, to and from his correspondents, only 3,100 letters have been preserved. There are around 4,200 extant letters preserved from Luther's correspondence and the same amount from Calvin's. There are,

[12] *Die Prophezei*, pp. 209-212.

however, 12,000 letters extant between Bullinger and his 700-1,000 correspondents in the Zürich archives alone and known collections in many other state and city archives hold at least three thousand more. Fritz Büsser confesses that there is still much research to be done in this field.[13] As Bullinger corresponded with people ranging from students to kings throughout Switzerland, Germany, Holland, Belgium, France, Italy, Poland, Austria, Hungary, Romania, Bulgaria, Denmark and England, one can imagine that these countries might still have many of Bullinger's literary and spiritual gems in their possession. Furthermore, Bullinger's works were available in all these languages and also even Turkish and Arabic. Zürich was of such international influence, however, that Bullinger even with his vast energies could not keep up with the demands for advice which came in from all over Europe. Thus Bullinger divided Europe into sections amongst his colleagues, allotting a part of Europe to each of them. Conrad Pellican corresponded with Italy, Johannes Wolf (1521-1571) and Josias Simler (1530-1576) with Poland, Peter Martyr and Rudolf Gualter with England, Gualter, Wolf, Simler and Johann Wilhelm Stucki (1542-1607) with Germany, Graubünden and the Swiss Eidgenossenshaft (confederacies). These hundreds of letters must be added to the 15,000 and more letters attributed to Bullinger's personal correspondence as he and his work was the main interest of these correspondents and his letter-writing team wrote on his behalf. Only then is it possible to obtain some idea of the enormous international importance of Henry Bullinger. In the nineteenth century, the English Parker Society printed a large number of letters between Bullinger and his English correspondents besides a number addressed to important Continental Reformers such as Calvin. His English correspondents included giants of the Reformation such as Archbishops Cranmer and Grindal, Foxe, Hales, Hooper, Humphrey, Lever, Jewel, Sampson, Traheron, Parkhurst, Pilkington, Ponet, Coverdale, Horne, Sandys, Cheke, Cox, Lady Jane Grey and King Edward VI besides many lesser

[13] See Büsser's introductory essay to *Heinrich Bullinger Werke*, Zweite Abteilung, Briefwechsel, Band I, Briefe der Jahre 1524-1531, Theologischer Verlag Zürich, 1973.

known men and women.[14] A large amount of Bullinger's correspondence with these English Reformers is available in English in Gilbert Burnet's *Collection of Records of Original Papers*, which is Vol. 5 of the 1830 edition of his *History of the Reformation* and the four volumes of Parker Society Letters – *Zürich Letters* 2 volumes, 1842 and *Original Letters*, 2 volumes, 1847. It is because of this massive Europe-wide pastoral witness that Bullinger received the title 'Shepherd of the Churches'.

The uniqueness of Bullinger's *Decades* in the Reformed Church.

Bullinger's most popular larger work was undoubtedly his *Decades* which was originally written as a handbook for preachers but quickly became a theological text book for students and even a manual of theology and devotion for household use. The latter usage is reflected in the German name for the *Decades* which is simply *Hausbuch* (House Book). The work, published between 1549 and 1551, began years before in separate sermons, a number of which were published. They were then collected together and issued as a collection of fifty sermons in five books of ten each, hence the name *Decades*. Bullinger was not a pioneer in bringing out such a collection when compared with Roman Catholic and Lutheran preachers. The Dominicans had been diligent in compiling works over a century before and Bullinger refers to their *Sermones Discipuli et Pelbarti* in his preface to the first two books. So, too, the Lutherans had already published several collections of sermons and homilies since the early 1530s. Indeed, Luther began to regret that this had happened and in 1543 protested that lazy pastors and preachers, instead of praying, reading the Scriptures and studying were content with merely reading other men's sermons to their flocks.[15] Bullinger emphasised the positive aspect of reading and studying sermons in his own Preface to the first two books of the *Decades* and this was echoed by the author of *A Preface to the ministry of the Church of England, and to other well disposed readers of God's Word* prefaced to the English

[14] *Zürich Letters* 2 Vols., 1842 and *Original Letters* 2 Vols., 1846.
[15] Luther's Preface to Johann Spangenberg's *Postilla.*

editions. Bullinger was, however, a pioneer amongst what came to be called the Reformed churches as opposed to the Lutheran.

Zwingli's contemporaries at Zürich were unanimous in affirming that he was a mighty preacher but he preached without notes and did not write down his sermons either before or after delivering them. Thus only a handful of his sermons have survived. Oecolampadius of Basle had published a few sermons in 1524 on 1 John but his successor Oswald Myconius preached only to his own sheep and never thought of printing and distributing his sermons. The same can be said of Berchtold Haller the Bern Reformer. Nor did William Farel of Geneva and Neuchâtel or Peter Viret of Neuchâtel and Lausanne ever produce any printed sermons, though both these men had a high reputation as preachers. Up to around 1550, Calvin at Geneva had only published two sermons. The mystery is complete when one realises that Martin Bucer who can truly be said to have rocked Farel, Viret and Calvin in their Reformed cradles, in spite of the great mass of other works he produced, published none of his sermons himself, though three or four were published by others. Indeed, it is astonishing that until the middle of the sixteenth century the only member of the Reformed Churches to produce a major work on doctrinal preaching was Henry Bullinger.

The reception of the *Decades* in England

No single work affected the English as much as Bullinger's *Decades*. Single sermons and component parts of the *collection* had appeared in English since the early forties and the complete German version was being used by students in England by 1566,[16] but the full work was probably not translated until 1577 when a 'H. I. student in Diuinite'[17] had the five books printed in three volumes by 'Ralphe Newberrie dwelling in Fleete-streate a little aboue the Conduite'. They immediately became the standard work in England on 'the chiefe and principall pointes of Christian Religion'. The English version of the *Decades* was reprinted in

[16] Letter from John Abel to Bullinger dated London, 6 June, 1566, ibid, p. 117.

[17] The Latin version gives '*impensis Radulphi Newberii et Hugonis Jaksonii*' so possibly Hugh Jackson was the translator.

full in 1584 and 1587 but the Latin version was regularly printed in England from 1551 on. Froschauer's versions were also widely distributed in England.

Richard Cox, Bishop of Ely, friend and correspondent of Bullinger's, though they never met, was an avid reader of Bullinger's works and obviously introduced these to his chaplain Thomas Cooper. When Cooper became Bishop of Lincoln in 1573, he began to promote the reading of the *Decades* in his diocese and by 1577 had made it compulsory reading for all the clergy below an MA degree. In 1583, Bishop Middleton of St David's had a copy placed in every parish church in his diocese and by 1584 Archbishop John Whitgift had made the *Decades* compulsory reading for the junior clergy of his entire archbishopric of Canterbury. In the year 1586 the Archbishop drew up instructions for all candidates to the ministry which he entitled *Orders for the better increase of learning in the inferior Ministers*. In this official statement of procedure, Whitgift ruled:

"Every Minister having Cure, & being under the Degrees of Master of Arts, and Batchelor of Law, and not Licensed to be a public Preacher, shal before the second day of *February* next provide a Bible, & *Bullinger's* Decads in *Latin* or *English*, and a Paper-Book, and shal every day read over one Chapter of the *Holy Scriptures*, and note the principal Contents thereof briefly in his Paper-Book, and shal every Week read over one Sermon in the said *Decads*, and note likewise the chief Matters therein contained in the said Paper (Book) And shall once in every Quarter, Viz. within a fortnight before or after the end of the Quarter, shew his said Notes to some preacher neer adjoyning, to be assigned for that Purpose.

Item, The Bishop, Archdeacons, or other Ordinary, being a public Preacher, shal appoint certain grave and learned Preachers: who shall privately examine the Diligence, and view the Notes of the said Ministers: Assigning six or seven Ministers, as Occasion shal require, to every such Preacher, that shal be next adjoyning to him. So as the Ministers be not driven to travail, for the exhibiting of their Notes above

6 or 7 Miles, if it may be. And the said preacher shal by Letters or otherwise, truly certify to the Archdeacon, or other Ordinary of the Place, themselves being public Preachers, & Resident within, or neer to their Jurisdiction, and for want thereof, to the Bishop himself, who do perform the said Exercises, & how they have profited therein, and who do refuse or neglect to perform the same.

The Archdeacons & others receiving the said Certificates, shal signify the same once in the Year, to the Bishop: And that about *Michaelmas*.

Item, Such as shal refuse to perform the Exercises, or shall be negligent therein; and shal not after Admonition by the Bishop, Archdeacon, or other Ordinary aforesaid, reform himself, if he be Beneficed, shal be compelled thereunto by Ecclesiastical Censures. If he be a curate, shal be inhibited to serve within the jurisdiction, etc..”[18]

It is concluded that the exercises above written, and no other, shall be henceforth publicly or privately used within any parts of this province.”[19]

At the seventh sitting of the Convocation on 10 March, Whitgift called for prayer concerning his plans to build the education of the lower clergy around Bullinger's *Decades* and again ‘exhorted all the clergy to do their duty’. From then on, during Whitgift's administration, the bishops and clergy were admonished to keep up the training system which rapidly began to mold the teaching of the Church of England. Whitgift's move was entirely in the spirit of his predecessor, Thomas Cranmer, who had invited Continental theologians such as Martin Bucer, Jan Laski and Peter Martyr to England with the express purpose of forming a church whose confessions reflected the entire European Reformation. The only other thrust in this direction was the Synod of Dort at which both the English and Scottish churches, with the strong backing of James I, piloted the synod into international theological waters.

---

[18] The following four paragraphs refer to the duties of the clergy in catechising, preaching both within and outside the parish. The ministers were recommended to preach once a month outside their own parishes.

[19] Taken from Appendix of Original Records, Number XXXII in Strype's *The Life and Acts of John Whitgift*, 1718.

The English Preface to the *Decades* laid the blame for the need to use a foreign manual of instruction at the feet of the British bishops who had been less than diligent in educating candidates for the ministry themselves, or had prescribed the works of Calvin, Gualter, Musculus, Peter Martyr and Marlorat[20] which were too complicated for the theological novice. No British authors were mentioned![21] Bullinger, the writer explains, has neither Calvin's obscurity, nor Musculus' scholastical subtlety but is able to pack much sound, perspicuous doctrine into comparatively little space and make it interesting to read and easy to remember. As Whitgift was having great difficulty with the Precisians or Ultra-Puritans at this time who denounced catechisms and instructive reading other than the Bible, the writer says that such are like physicians who forbid their patients the very diet that does them good. Besides, he adds, we have not yet the clergy to undertake a comprehensive teaching ministry for students. The very idea of Whitgift's attempt to instruct such men was to provide sound preachers and teachers for the future.

The Word of God in Reformed Theology

Bullinger held to a uniquely pure doctrine of the word of God which was not shared by either Zwingli, Wittenberg, or Geneva but found its nearest allies in the Reformers of the Church of England. Susi Hausammann shows in her Festschrift essay commemorating the 400th anniversary of Bullinger's death how his *De scripturae negotio*, written at the age of nineteen, shows marked and important difference between Bullinger's understanding of the Word of God and that of Luther.[22] For Bullinger the full canon of the Old and New Testaments was the full Word of God, Spirit breathed and given to the Church for her sole authority in matters of faith and doctrine. The entire Scriptures point to Christ and His salvation, therefore the entire Scriptures are Christ's

[20] A French Protestant and writer of commentaries, born in Lorraine and martyred in 1562 in Rouen by order of the Duke of Guise.

[21] Whitgift had already made Puritan Nowell's Catechism mandatory in spite of Thomas Cartwright's protests

[22] Anfrage zum Scriftverständnis des Jungen Bullinger im Zusammenhang einer Interpretation von 'De Scriptrae Negotio', *Gesammelte Aufsätze zum 400. Todestag*.

gospel. Luther had great difficulty in accepting all the books of the canon as like-inspired and thus distinguished between what he believed was the Word of God and Scripture. Furthermore, he could not easily reconcile the condemning with the saving aspects of the Scriptures and thus could not accept Bullinger's thorough-going Christological interpretation. This view led him to isolate what he believed was the shadowy and wrathful side of God from the sunny side presented in the gospel of Christ. Law was one thing and gospel was another. Therefore, Luther taught that there were passages of Scripture which did not promote Christ (Christus treiben). If they did not promote Christ in this way or did not touch certain individuals, then the Scriptures were not a Word of God (Verbum dei) to them. Luther could thus speak of a passage of Scripture being 'a Word of God for me' or 'a Word of God for you'. Bullinger, on the other hand, looked on all Scripture as the Word of God for everyone which enabled him to emphasise more than the other Continental Reformers that the Word of God to all was the sole reference to the Christian for all matters of faith and Christian practice. What was right for one in the eyes of God was right for one and all.

Both Zwingli and Calvin had their difficulties with the Book of Revelation and did not publish commentaries on it. Zwingli started his *Exposition of the Christian Faith* with the doctrine of God and His worship, and though he added an article on the Catabaptists on the grounds that they did not use Scripture rightly, he did not include an article on the Word of God itself. Calvin started his 1536 *Institutes* with the knowledge of God and the Law but did not add a section on the Word of God. In the 1559 edition, Calvin deals with Scripture in Book I, Chapter VI-X after dealing with natural theology. In summing up his doctrine of Scripture in Chapter X, Calvin returns to natural theology stating that 'in Scripture, the Lord represents himself in the same character in which we have already seen that he is delineated in his works'. Such expressions of what he calls 'the virus of natural theology'[23] are seen by Arthur C. Cochrane as signs of Stoicism latent in Humanism

[23] *Reformed Confessions of the 16th Century*, p. 139.

which found its way into the French Confession of 1559. Article II states, "God reveals himself to men; firstly in his works, in their creation, as well as in their preservation and control. Secondly, and more clearly, in his Word." Arthur C. Cochrane argues that natural theology otherwise played no part in the Reformed Confessions of the 16th century but gained entrance into the Belgic Confession of 1561 from the French Confession which was then taken over by the Westminster Confession of 1643. Cochrane points out that the churches had to wait until the Barmer Confession of 1934 before the joint committee of Lutheran, Reformed and Evangelical Free Churches rejected natural theology, chiefly because of the importance placed on it by the so-called German Christians whose aim was to bring the Protestant churches into line with Fascism and the National Socialist Party.

Calvin had very little to say about the divine inspiration and literal inerrancy of the Scriptures and does not mention the subject when outlining his doctrine of Scripture in his *Institutes*. Furthermore, he speaks continually of the Word of God being found in the Scriptural writings rather than being those writings themselves,[24] and emphasises the need for the Scriptures to be knit with the Spirit before becoming the Word of God.[25] So, too, Calvin always emphasises the deadness of the Scriptures in themselves before being taken up and applied by the Spirit. Calvin, in fact, views the Scriptures as he does the ordinances. The bread and wine are nothing in themselves until the Spirit takes them and uses them,[26] so it is with the Word of God. Contrary to such a position, Bullinger stressed that the Scriptures as such were the true, complete and perfect Word of God in themselves, so that nothing could be added to or subtracted from them. All Scripture is authored by the Spirit and no Scripture is superfluous to the Word of God. The one is a synonym for

---

[24]See *Institutes* IV:8, 5-9 for one of Calvin's more explicit references to the status of the Word of God.

[25]Ibid, Book I:9, 3.

[26]See Niesel's *The Theology of Calvin*, Scripture and Spirit, pp. 30-39; McGrath's *John Calvin*, Der christliche Glaube nach Calvin: das Medium, pp. 171-180 and Warfield's *Calvin and Calvinism*, The Knowledge of God, pp. 29-130 for studies in Calvin's doctrine of the Scriptures viewed from various angles.

the other. This truth which became the foundational doctrine of the Scriptures for the Reformed churches is outlined in Bullinger's *Second Helvetic Confession* and in the first three sermons of the *Decades*. Bullinger was so convinced of the inspiration and inerrancy of the Word of God that he believed it was still the inspired Word of God when applied to the consciences of sinners in preaching. He argued that when a courier read out a pronouncement from the King, no one in their right mind would say that the pronouncement was the courier's. Bullinger believed that the Scriptures were never dead, awaiting to be brought to life by either the Spirit or the sinner's acceptance as one could not separate the fact of being breathed out by the Spirit from the words which were breathed out. This strong and quite revolutionary view of the Word of God in papist times moved teenager Bullinger to start the Reformation in Kappel and Bremgarten by expounding the Word of God systematically in a teaching capacity long before he was ordained for the ministry. Thus by the time Calvin, whom Professor Fritz Büsser sees as being strongly influenced by Bullinger in his method of exposition,[27] had written his first NT commentary in 1539 on the Letter to the Romans, Bullinger had already authored two complete series of all the NT letters from the early 1520s on. His 1537 edition of the epistles included an exegesis of the Acts of the Apostles. These works were to be re-printed at regular intervals afterwards (1539, 1543, 1549, 1558 etc.). During the 1540s commentaries on the gospels and other books appeared yearly.

Jud, Bibliander, Pellican and perhaps even Zwingli had worked diligently on the Zürich Bible, which appeared in German some years before the Luther Bible of 1534.[28] Bullinger never admitted to having taken part in the translation but Professor Fritz Büsser maintains that he was just as much engaged in the work as Jud, Pellican, Bibliander, Colin

[27] See *Heinrich Bullinger: Leben, Werk und Wirkung*, Band I, p. 243m n.5.

[28] See ibid, p. 248. English-speaking Christians are brought up to believe that the Luther Bible was the first Bible to be produced in German. There is, however, a long history of Bible work in German prior to that date and Prof. Büsser points out that the Zürich ministers had produced German Bibles in 1530 and 1531, now known as the Froschauer or Zürich Bible. Luther would not recognise the Zürich Bible and denied the scholarly and spiritual competence of its translators, though they were arguably far more competent than Luther to perform such a task. The Lutherans argued that two German Bibles would cause strife in the churches.

and Gualter.[29] Bullinger wrote the Foreword to the 1539 edition, stressing how expounding the Word was the first and foremost goal of theology. He entitled his introductory words, *Concerning all the Books of the Holy and Divine Scriptures and Also Their Dignity and Excellency: A Lucid Account To the Christian Reader.*[30] In his Preface, Bullinger emphasised that the Scriptures do not merely display the divine wisdom of God but also many things that can be comprehended by the human mind such as right conduct and virtue and how to live an honest and upright life. Also, they show how one should rule one's house, how the Church should be ruled, what is useful and what is not, in short, things that the best of philosophies cannot teach. The Bible also teaches man to look to God's wisdom revealed in Christ for his guidance and salvation and not to his own, which, as human philosophy in general, has not a word to say on the subject. Then Bullinger outlines the general and central themes of the Bible by expounding Proverbs 8:6-9, 14 and then gives an overview of each of the Biblical books, comparing their wisdom with that of worldly men's philosophies and dealing with their authorship, origin and scope. Bullinger makes it clear that his aim is to show that the Scriptures are the true Word of God with which no human wisdom can compare as he outlines the method and aims of Moses, the Writings and the Prophets and goes on to deal with the culmination of salvation in the work of Christ.

Bullinger refers in detail to the great works of the greatest philosophers, men of science and men of letters, urging his learned critics to make themselves as familiar with the Scriptures as they are with the works of the likes of Aristotle, Seneca and Homer and find out for themselves how superior God's Word is to them. All true knowledge, for Bullinger is merely a handmaid to assist the mind in pointing to the Scriptures, yet the simple man who has been given grace to comprehend the Word, need not turn to the knowledge of the philosophers for added wisdom as they had none to give.

---

[29] Ibid, p. 251.
[30] Author's translation from the Swiss-German.

Because Bullinger always emphasised that the Word of God must be expounded regularly before the gathered church, he realised he was open to the criticism that his form of preaching was a new form of law. His hearers were told how to think and how to behave. In his Preface to the 1537 edition of the *New Testament Epistles*, Bullinger explains to his readers the difference between law and commentary. Showing how a commentary is couched in the words of man's wisdom and must always be accompanied by prayer, study, a love for the well-being of the reader and a determination not to speculate. Nevertheless, Bullinger believes he is called to expound the Scriptures in this way so as to show his readers the meaning of the text and to warn them against false teaching and help them come to an understanding of how a Christian ought to organise his life so that he might be a useful citizen and witness.

His five rules for his own Bible exegesis are to be gathered from his *Studiorum ratio* (1527), *De testamento seu foedere* (1534) and *Assertio utriusque in Christo natura* (1534), *Decades* (1549) and *Second Helvetic Confession* (1550s to 1556). These are:

1. Seek out the exact meaning of the text using all linguistic aids possible.
2. Use the same method for all books, that is (a) Examine the full textual account before going on to analyse individual words and expressions, paying due regard to grammar and rhetoric. (b) Study the context and topics with which the text deals. (c) Compare the text with similar passages.
3. Compare the exposition worked out with that of exegetes both contemporary and historical on the same text.
4. Use the rule of faith and love with God's honour and the salvation of sinners always in mind.
5. Christ is the beginning, centre and end of all exegetical work.

The Second Helvetic Confession

Bullinger's most commonly known definition of the Word of God is to be found in his *Second Helvetic Confession* where he affirms:

"Of the Holy Scripture Being the True Word of God

Canonical Scripture. We believe and confess the canonical Scriptures of the holy prophets and apostles of both Testaments to be the true Word of God, and to have sufficient authority of themselves, not of men. For God himself spoke to the fathers, prophets, apostles, and still speaks to us through the Holy Scriptures. And in this Holy Scripture, the universal Church of Christ has the most complete exposition of all that pertains to a saving faith, and also to the framing of a life acceptable to God; and in this respect it is expressly commanded by God that nothing be either added to or taken from the same.

Scripture Teaches Fully All Godliness. We judge, therefore, that from these Scriptures are to be derived true wisdom and godliness, the reformation and government of churches; as also instruction in all duties of piety; and, to be short, the confirmation of doctrines, and the rejection of all errors, moreover, all exhortations according to that word of the apostle, 'All Scripture is inspired by God and profitable for teaching, for reproof,' etc. (1 Timothy 3:16-17). Again, 'I am writing these instructions to you,' says the apostle to Timothy, 'so that you may know how one ought to behave in the household of God,' etc. (1 Timothy 3:14-15).

Scripture Is the Word of God. Again, the selfsame apostle to the Thessalonians: 'When,' says he, 'you received the Word of God which you heard from us, you accepted it, not as the word of men but as what it really is, the Word of God,' etc. (1 Thessalonians 2:13). For the Lord himself has said in the Gospel, 'It is not you who speak, but the Spirit of my Father speaking through you;' therefore 'he who hears you hears me, and he who rejects me rejects him who sent me' (Matthew 10:20; Luke 10:16; John 13:20).

The Preaching of the Word of God Is the Word of God. Wherefore when this Word of God is now preached in the church by preachers lawfully called, we believe that the very Word of God is proclaimed, and received by the faithful; and that neither any other Word of God is to be invented nor is to be expected from heaven: and that now the Word itself which is preached is to be regarded, not the minister that preaches; for even if he be evil and a sinner, nevertheless the Word of God remains still true and good.

Neither do we think that therefore the outward preaching is to be thought as fruitless because the instruction in true religion depends on the inward illumination of the Spirit, or because it is written 'And no longer shall each man teach his neighbour … , for they shall all know me' (Jeremiah 31:34), and 'Neither he who plants nor he who waters is anything, but only God who gives the growth' (1 Corinthians 3:7). For although 'no one can come to Christ unless he be drawn by the Father' (John 6:44), and unless the Holy Spirit inwardly illumines him, yet we know that it is surely the will of God that his Word should be preached outwardly also. God could indeed, by his Holy Spirit, or by the ministry of an angel, without the ministry of St Peter, have taught Cornelius in the Acts; but, nevertheless, he refers him to Peter, of whom the angel speaking says, 'He shall tell you what you ought to do'.

Inward Illumination Does Not Eliminate External Preaching. For he that illuminates inwardly by giving men the Holy Spirit, the same one, by way of commandment, said unto his disciples, 'Go into all the world, and preach the Gospel to the whole creation' (Mark 16:15). And so in Philippi, Paul preached the Word outwardly to Lydia, a seller of purple goods; but the Lord inwardly opened the woman's heart (Acts 16:14). And the same Paul, after a beautiful development of his thought, in Romans 10:17 at length comes to the conclusion, 'So faith comes from hearing, and hearing from the Word of God by the preaching of Christ.'

At the same time we recognize that God can illuminate whom and when he will, even without the external ministry, for that is in his power; but we speak of the usual way of instructing men, delivered unto us from God, both by commandment and examples."

The Word of God; the Cause of It; and How and by Whom, it was Revealed to the World.

In Bullinger's opening sermons of the *Decades*, he goes into far more detail. In his first sermon, the author examines the Scriptures under the title *The Word of God; the Cause of It; and How and by Whom, it was Revealed to the World.* Bullinger starts by saying that nothing can be known about the decrees of God without the Word of God. That is, either applied to God's revelation of Himself or to His plan for man. He adds that we must distinguish between different uses of 'word' in the Scriptures. The word can mean 'thing' as in "With God shall no word be impossible" (Luke 1:37).[31] It can also mean anything uttered by man whether a word, sentence or speech.

When 'word' is used with the name of the deity as in 'the Word of God', it can mean the virtue and power of God or even the Person and Office of the Lord Jesus Christ as in 'The Word was made flesh' (John 1:14). In this sermon, Bullinger explains that he is dealing with the Word of God as the speech of God and the revealing of God's will in the words of Christ, the prophets and the Apostles as recorded in that book we call The Holy and Divine Scriptures. The reason and cause of the Word is that it is God's will that He should reveal His mind character and demands to man. God speaks to man in the way of men, that is, through words so that he might best understand. As God is just, without deceit, and guile, without error or evil affection, holy, good, immortal and everlasting, so the Word of God possesses all these attributes. The Word of God is Truth (John 17:17) and is for everlasting (Isaiah 40:8; 1 Peter 1:25). Thus, going through the entire history of the world from Adam to the Word of God becoming flesh and throughout New Testament times until the last times, Bullinger shows how there was never a time in the history of man and never would be a time when God did not communicate to him in words.

Of the word of God. To whom, and to what end, it was revealed; also in what manner it is to be heard; and that it doth fully teach the whole doctrine of godliness.

In this second sermon on the Word of God, Bullinger has a special word of warning to say here to those of his day who believed like the

[31] See Greek text.

Zwickauer Prophets in spiritual teaching from God not contained in His Word or who rejected the Old Testament, stating that they were Christians and not to be taught by 'Jews' such as Abraham, Isaac, Jacob and the prophets. Bullinger saw these 'Jews' as standing under God's word as all Christians stand and, what is more, they were used by God to record His Word just as the Apostles were. The Old Testament was the Word of God to Christ, followed by Peter and the Apostles, just as the words given Peter and the Apostles are God's Word to us, telling us of God's attitude towards us, what we must do to be saved and how we can live a worshipful life in God's service. Thus the Word of God is revealed to man so that he might see the whole scope of salvation from God's covenant with Adam through to the Christian's entering into his eternal inheritance. This Word is perfect as its Speaker, God, is perfect and thus its doctrine is perfect in all points. There is nothing outside of the Scriptures which can tell us anything about God of itself. Thus Bullinger warns against those teachers who profess to patch up the Scriptures with little extras of their own invention. Here Bullinger shows the danger of arguing that because the early church followed the Word of God, we can follow their traditions as being a Word of God to us, also. This is poison, says Bullinger. The only way we know if a saint has left us a Word of God is by comparing it with the written Word of God that we have received, because:

"They which had one and the same spirit of truth, left not unto us one thing in writing, and taught another thing by word of mouth. Furthermore, we must diligently search whether those traditions do set forward the glory of God rather than of men; or the safety of the faithful, rather than the private advantage of the priests. And we must take heed of men's traditions, especially since the Lord saith, 'In vain do they worship me, teaching as doctrines the precepts of men.' So that now the surest way is, to cleave to the word of the Lord left to us in the scriptures, which teacheth abundantly all things that belong to true godliness."[32]

Though Bullinger never ceases to emphasise the Spirit breathed nature of the Word, he equally emphases the need of faith without which sinners cannot hear and respond to that Word and bring forth fruit due to its being implanted within us. Here, he quotes Paul who says, "To us also is the word of God declared, even as unto our fathers. But it availeth them nothing to hear the word, because it was not joined with faith in them that heard it: for they died in the desert." He therefore warns his hearers so that, "no man die in the same example of unbelief." Thus every man ought to pray that God would grant him faith that the seed of God's Word may be quickened in his heart. Those who receive such a quickening can now say, "The word of God doth feed, strengthen, confirm, and comfort our souls; it doth regenerate, cleanse, make joyful, and join us to God; yea, and obtaineth all things for us at God's hands, setting us in a most happy state: insomuch that no goods or treasures of the whole world are to be compared with the word of God."[33]

Of the sense and right exposition of the word of God, and by what manner of means it may be expounded.

Bullinger contends in his third sermon on the Scriptures against the popish notion that the Word of God is too dark and difficult for ordinary people who are thus better left in that darkness. There is nothing in the Scriptures, Bullinger argues, that cannot be read, understood and expounded. Even people of low intelligence can understand the scriptures as their authors did not use highfaluting, pseudo-language but the language of the people. The Scriptures are full of proverbs, anecdotes, wise sayings and parables, comparisons and narratives which suit even the most common of wits. The few difficulties which there are in the Bible can be removed by the diligence, study and faith of sound

[32] *Decades*, Books I/II, Parker Society, p. 64
[33] Ibid, pp. 66-67.

teachers. To be unlearned in Scriptural matters has nothing to do with the schooling of the reader or hearer but whether faith is within him so that he can act on what he hears. If the gospel is hid, it is hid from them to whom it has not been given to see 'the light of the gospel of the glory of Christ, who is the image of God."[34] Thus all Christians can say with David, "Thy word is a lantern unto my feet, and a light unto my paths." Therefore, if any controversies arise in the Church, they must be resolved by a careful, mutual study of the Scriptures.

However, the Scriptures are designed, Bullinger claims, to be expounded. He argues in this way because the sects of the day were maintaining that a Bible ministry was superfluous as the Spirit spoke to each Christian directly in order to lead him. Bullinger points out that in the Old Testament, Moses, the Levites and the Prophets instructed the people and this was continued in the New Testament with the Apostles as witnessed by Peter expounding Isaiah to the Eunuch. He told those who were arguing that Paul never expounded the Scriptures that they must have neither read of the deeds of Paul nor studied his written works. He also warns these 'Spiritualists' against claiming that the Scriptures need not be read and expounded in Christian worship as their function is to move the individual Christian in his daily reading without superfluous notice given to the contextual background, occasion for the word being given and who was speaking at the time. Bullinger judges such men as fighting against the use of the Scriptures appointed by God. This means that expounders of the Word must be most careful so as not to bring anything into their expositions which is contrary to the general teaching of Scripture. They are there to expound the Word, not to add to it. The minister who adds to the Word in this way tramples the true Word underfoot and destroys the pasture on which the sheep are to graze. "The true and proper sense of God's word must be taken out of the scriptures themselves, and not to be forcefully thrust upon the scriptures, as we ourselves lust."[35] We must thus beware of thinking that we have some new doctrine that quite contradicts the faith of our

---

[34] Ibid, p. 71
[35] Ibid, p. 75.

fathers, gained through viewing one passage of Scripture as contradicting another. Thus when we read that Christ says that His Father is greater than He is (John 14:28), we must note the context and reason for Christ saying this and not automatically conclude that the passages which state that the Father and the Son are equal must be wrong. So, too, when we read that 'Flesh and blood cannot inherit the Kingdom of God' (1 Corinthians 15:50), we are not to immediately believe that there will be no bodily resurrection. This is why it is important to have Scripture teach Scripture and not act on one isolated passage of Scripture as if it were God's special revelation for a special occasion without due regard to what the rest of Scripture says. All Scripture must be contextualised before acting on it. What goes before and what follows should be taken into consideration as also the circumstances given. Our interpretation of Scripture must not be repugnant to the love of God and our neighbour and it must be motivated by a zealous heart after earnest prayer.

Bullinger's preaching

That Bullinger was widely acclaimed as a great preacher has already been illustrated by the description of Bullinger's first sermons at Bremgarten and Zürich mentioned above. Bullinger's main concern in preaching was to bring the gospel to the numerous workers and ordinary citizens of his parish. This fact was something of an embarrassment for the Council who often wished to show off their Superintendent when foreign state visitors arrived. Bullinger's fame as a great scholar and student of the ancient languages was widespread but when noblemen and church dignitaries were given a place of honour in the gallery appointed for prominent people, they invariably heard Bullinger preaching in the local dialect. The story is told that one very prominent guest from Germany asked to attend one of Bullinger's sermons and was given a prominent VIP pew in the gallery. Looking down from his vantage point, he saw what appeared to be a peasant, in ordinary, everyday clothing,[36]

[36] Bullinger is often depicted wearing an ecclesiastical robe, actually he preached in his cathedral in ordinary attire. He never, however, condemned his colleagues who wore special ecclesiastical

speaking in an uncouth language. Afterwards he complained that Bullinger was a simple country-yokel and decided to tell him so. The learned Superintendent listened to the criticism and then said to the noble guest, "Did not Your Grace look down from above and see the filled and cramped pews full of rough caps and old wives' headscarves? I preach for them and not for great lords and learned scholars."

The great Reformer and Professor of Hebrew and Greek, Conrad Pellican, is our authority for affirming that Bullinger had one of the greatest minds of his age yet was the simplest of preachers. Pellican had visited most of Europe's leading universities and taught at the best of them, so he knew what he was talking about. As a preacher, Pellican tells us in his *Chronikon*, Bullinger had no equal anywhere and he was easily the best and most important preacher that he had ever heard. Pellican confessed that there was no difficult passage in Scripture which Bullinger could not master by studying the original texts and make comprehensible in the simplest of language which enabled him to preach through the entire Bible in twelve years without a single person ever complaining that he could not follow the preacher.[37] Pellican affirmed:

"Now Moses, when he speaks to our countrymen is better understood by citizens, old people and young boys and girls than when formerly doctors from Paris, Scottist and Thomist monks preached. The Prophets, Christ, the Evangelists and Apostles speak to our people in the German language so that no text in the Biblical canon is too dark not to be illuminated with great light bearing much fruit by our Bullinger and readily absorbed by our people."[38]

Indeed, we know that Bullinger during his ministry preached through a number of books two, three and even, as in the case of Hebrews, four

---

attire, counting such clothing 'things indifferent'. Thus he took the side of the Church of England in the vestment controversy as he felt the Precisians were making a sacramental issue of vestments and placing externals on a par with saving doctrines.

[37] Pellican was not quite exact as Bullinger once wrote in his notebook that someone had complained that he was too mild with his people and ought to be more severe with the Senate.

[38] Quoted by Schulthess-Rechberg, p. 42.

times. During this time, less than one person per year had ever left Bullinger's church before he was finished with his sermon. Pellican points out that none of the learned scholars who heard Bullinger could point out a single flaw in his exegesis of the Biblical text. He put this down to Bullinger's immense industry and the fact that he never gave up careful study. Indeed, he attended Professor Bibliander's lectures on the canon year after year in order not to rust. This was alongside preaching many times a week, corresponding with between 700 and 1,000 people all over the known world, entertaining a never-ending stream of guests and writing book after book. The fact that Bullinger could use his great learning to teach the common man in terms that he could understand is also attested by Calvin when explaining to Simon Grynaeus in November 1539 how his predecessors had helped him in writing his commentary on Romans. After mentioning the light that Melanchthon had shed on the epistle, he continued, "Then comes Bullinger, who also received much praise; and that rightly, because he has combined simplicity with learning, and for this he has been highly approved."[39] Calvin rejects the accusation that he is entering into 'odious rivalry' with his mentors who will be offended at his undertaking because, he argues, Melanchthon merely kept to essentials and left much out, Bullinger was too simple, though learned and Bucer was both too learned and too complex though "by his tireless labours, has just about said the last word," therefore there was room for his own as "nothing is so perfect among men that those who come after them will find no room for refining and clarifying it, and adding to its beauty.[40]

The English editor of his *Decades* ended his introductory Preface to the 1587 edition with the words:

"These sermons of master Bullinger's are such as, whether they be used privately or read publicly, whether of ministers of the word or other God's children, certainly there will be found in them such light and instruction for the ignorant, such sweet and spiritual comfort for

[39] *Calvin's Commentaries*, The Library of Christian Classics, Vol. XXIII, pp. 74-75.
[40] Ibid, p. 75.

consciences, such heavenly delights for souls, that as perfumes, the more they are chafed, the better they smell; and as gold mines, the deeper ye dig them, the more riches they shew; so these: the more diligently ye peruse them, the more delightfully they will please; and the deeper ye dig with daily study in their mines, the more golden matter they will deliver forth to the glory of God: to whom only be praise, for ever and ever, Amen."

The *Decades*, a textbook for preachers

Bullinger had set up institutions for the training of evangelical, reformed pastors since the fifteen twenties – long before reformers in other countries even attempted the same. England had to wait until the late 40s, German universities such as Heidelberg the late 50s and Calvin was first able to set up his Geneva Academy in 1559. Bullinger's *Decades* (or Housebook) was designed to help theological students obtain a basic grasp of the Reformed faith and the duties and necessities of Christian witness. Through Hooper's fellowship, Bullinger gained access to Edward VI's ear and dedicated two volumes in the series to the English king. A volume was also dedicated to the Marquis of Dorset, Henry Grey, father of Jane Grey who was murdered and martyred by Mary. Lady Jane had corresponded with Bullinger since her earlier childhood and had testified to her deep faith. Soon the *Decades* were translated into German, French, Dutch and English (perhaps also Italian) and had become the set books for Reformed theological students throughout Europe. Bullinger regularly pressed on his hearers the need for a sound, Christian education before ever attempting to enter a pulpit. So, in his last and fiftieth sermon of his *Decades*, he begins with the fact that no church can have lasting strength until it cares well for its youth and tells us that after the setting up of a true church, "Christian schools have the first place, which bring forth a plentiful increase of prophets or ministers of the church." Bullinger bases this conviction on the fact that when the commonwealth of Israel was set up as a pattern of a true godly kingdom, forty-eight

Levitical schools were set up in the towns of the realm.[41] Furthermore, we have the example of Christ in the New Testament who called twelve students to instruct them personally in the ways of righteousness. Bullinger's last words of his *Decades* are an appeal to the learned to use their learning for the establishing and spreading of the Church to whom he says:

"I trust that in these fifty sermons I have, as shortly and conveniently as might be, comprehended the whole matter of faith, godliness or true religion, and also the church. That which I do often repeat in all my sermons and my books, that do I also repeat in this place; that the learned will with my good-will and thanks gather and embrace better things out of the scriptures. Unto the Lord our God, the everlasting Fountain of all goodness, be praise and glory, through our Lord Jesus Christ. Amen.

Dedication to the Zürich ministers

Bullinger originally intended publishing 60 didactic sermons (Lehrpredigten) in his *Decades* but closed the volumes after the fifth book of ten sermons each. He planned the first two books together and originally intended them to be a compendium of instruction for the junior clergy, presenting them with material from his own sermons from which they could gain the basics of Christian doctrine and a feeling for homiletics and didactics. In the interim time between the fall of papist power and the firm establishment of the Reformed faith, colleges, seminaries and even churches had been closed down, salaries not paid and many sound men were forced to enter into secular employment to support themselves and had no opportunity either to gain or impart Christian knowledge. Whereas the elder ministers had learnt at least how to study and use the Classical languages in searching out the deep meanings of the Bible text, the young men had no education of this kind to build on. Bullinger thus dedicated the first two Decades to his 'dear brethren and fellow-workers'. His aim is not to give model sermons for

[41] Bullinger appears to be basing this conviction on Numbers 35:7 and Joshua 21:41 which he believes speak of places of Levitical instruction.

all as different churches at different times are faced with different problems and possibilities. He believes that "the part of a wise pastor is, to consider diligently what is adapted for each church, what is proper for it, useful, and necessary; and to insist upon that." In such preaching, "no sin must be palliated or explained away but the preacher should call a spade a spade and a fig a fig, and speak with plainness though withal soberly and modestly." Freedom of speech is, to the Christian minister, honesty of heart and he must make known to his flock his love for them. Thus Bullinger says, "Let it appear to impartial hearers, that we reprove with the feeling of a father, and assail sinners of mankind from a desire to save and not to destroy them; that we attack the crime and not the person of the criminal."

Bullinger opened Book I with a dedication to his own fellow pastors in the words: "To the most illustrious men, Masters Rudolf Gualter, Peter Simler, John Strumphius, John Blumen, John Seiler, Hadrian Hospinian, Nicholas Schneider, and John Hugo, Deans or Archpresbyters: and to all the ministers of Christ and of the churches of the classes of the Zürich-See, Freyamt, Stein, Winterthur, Elgg, Werikon, and Regensburg, in the territory of Zürich; his reverend and very beloved fellow-ministers and brethren; greeting."

Bullinger's opening words to his brethren in the ministry show what a difficult time the Swiss churches were going through. Luther died in 1546 and the Emperor's Schmalkaldian war against the Protestants ended in victory for the papists.[42] The Augsburg Interim restrictions made it almost impossible for the Protestants in the Emperor's vast domains to evangelise and spread into Roman Catholic territories. So, too, Bullinger, now forty-five years of age, was burdened with a work load which would have rendered any other man quite helpless to undertake such a task. Bullinger's letters to his friends Myconius in Basle and Vadian in St Gallen show that he often wrote in a state of exhaustion but the iron-

[42] The Swiss confederacies, including Zürich had remained neutral during the wars. This was to preserve their independence from imperial influence and prevent their confederacies from breaking up into Roman Catholic and Protestant camps and thus causing further wars in Switzerland. In Zürich, public prayer was held for the Protestants and refugees from the wars were given asylum.

willed man, confident that he was fulfilling a godly and important task, kept on. His letters to Vadian alone fill several folio volumes. The only departure from his original plan to write a work which would provide a series of teaching sermons and a doctrinal compendium was the reduction of the intended sixty sermons to fifty.

The *Decades*, however, were not merely intended as a textbook for the edification of ministers and their congregations but also as a reminder that Protestant Zürich had greatly sinned in the years leading up to the Kappel wars and the only remedy against such sin was a renewed turning to the full gospel of the Lord Jesus Christ and His covenant with mankind. Thus Bullinger writes:

"If any other age has furnished a fruitful subject for discourse, this time present of ours furnishes the most fruitful; for what happens and what threatens Christendom at this day, is too evident to require many words to declare it. The just Lord is angry at our sins, and punishes them also; nay, he is preparing far heavier calamities to pour out on the heads of the impenitent: Our duty is then to watch for the Lord's flock, and on the approach of the sword to give timely warning to all the sheep committed to our trust, that the blood of those who perish be not required at our hands. Methinks, therefore, I shall do a profitable work, if I talk with you, reverend fellow-ministers and most dear brethren, of the right discharge of our duty in this dangerous age, and of the sure method whereby we may piously appease the anger of God provoked by our sins. I know with whom I speak; even with men, who are perfectly skilled in the things of God. I shall therefore study to be brief.

That the most righteous Lord is angry at the sins of men, is beyond a doubt: and it follows therefore, that to wash away sins is the only way of appeasing the divine wrath. But sins are not washed away without being acknowledged first, and afterward put away by faith and repentance. Wherefore, if we desire according to our office that anger and severe punishments be taken off from the Lord's flock, we must of necessity shew and accuse the sins of men, and also teach faith and enforce repentance."

Using Ezekiel 22:15 as an illustration of the plight of Zürich, Bullinger nevertheless warns against judgmental preaching which merely displays the gall of bitterness. Pastors who think that they have not done their duty "unless they have poured forth and emptied out upon their unfortunate hearers whole cart-loads of abuse without all measure of and discrimination," are not feeding their flocks aright. Bullinger goes on to explain:

"The examples of the prophets give no support to such ravings as these; and they are wrongly applied, because circumstances are overlooked. Let the rebuke or fault-finding of the ministers of the truth be prudent rather than daring; sober and well-weighed, and not light and loose: let it glow not with passion, but with fervency of spirit; let it be chaste, modest, and holily tempered with a just severity, and come down upon the guilty individual and hold him fast rather by matter-of-fact plainness, transparency, and majesty, than pierce by profusion of ill words: I mean, wound the guilty conscience by a lively setting forth of sin, and by exposing the foulness or enormity of bad deeds, rather than exasperate it by scoffings and impure quips. And certain is it, men are deeply moved, whenever they are brought to understand clearly, that the things they go about are directed against God, and tend to the destruction of their body and the eternal ruin of their soul.

Still in vain and fruitlessly shall we have attacked sin, if we do not at the same time urge faith and repentance. When he has been provoked, God is not appeased by a few ceremonies and commonplace acts, which are trifling and brought to us by human tradition. 'In vain do they worship me,' saith the Lord, 'teaching for doctrines the commandments of men.' Nay, the Lord is highly indignant, when we persist in seeking reconciliation with him by some absurd worshipping of God. For he cries by Jeremiah: 'Amend your ways and your doings, and I will cause you to dwell in this place. But behold, ye trust in lying words that cannot profit. Will ye steal, murder, and commit adultery, and swear falsely, and walk after other gods, and come and stand before me in this house, which is called by my name, and say, We are delivered to do all these abominations? Is this house which is called by my name become a den of robbers in your eyes?' Wherefore let us lay aside false doctrine, and learn from God's word what kind of conversion pleases him, and what is true repentance and faith."

Bullinger goes on to argue that all the repentance in the world will not suffice, as it did not suffice in Judas' case, if that repentance is not carried out in the full assurance that Christ is the only One who can take away the sins of the world. Thus the faithful preacher must urge his flock to believe that their sins are forgiven them freely for Christ's sake. He then points out to his fellow-ministers how such assurance comes as a full conviction to some and to a small glimmer of hope to others so that the pastor must deal with his sheep individually and according to their various needs. He finishes by stating that he expected his brethren to use the *Decades* wisely and that:

"These sermons truly I have written, that I might bestow my labours upon you, assist your own studies, or even stimulate each one of you to think and find out more; but not that every one should use them word for word in the church confided to his care: For selection and judgment is needed, that we may not speak to our own church what is foreign to it, or little profitable and necessary for it. Let the wise pastor consider well of what kind are the morals of the people of his charge, and what things are most requisite for them, and so set them before them, having regard always to edification, true faith, piety, charity, and innocence. For we must both teach and admonish, that the church over which it hath pleased the Lord to set us may be godly and holy. Certain forms of sermons, therefore, I put forth, by which I desire also to gratify those who have for many years asked this of me. And in all these, and with regard to all points, I would have that most just rule of the apostle to prevail with all readers: "Prove all things; hold fast that which is good". Nor am I much affected by the slanders of those who cry out, that such sermons make the brethren idle; as was the case formerly when the sermons of Discipulus[43] and Pelbart[44] were read. For I have on my side the example of the greatest luminaries in the church: I mean, the most eminent bishops in the church, who themselves also wrote sermons and homilies to the great profit of the church. The idle are always idle, even though nothing at all be written."

Bullinger and the Covenant

Covenant Theology is widely thought today, especially amongst Presbyterians, to be a product of Calvin's genius but Bullinger's covenant teaching is far more developed, comprehensive and meticulously perfected than Calvin's and was presented to the public some fourteen years before Calvin took up the theme. As Prof. Büsser points out, Bullinger's covenant teaching first became widely known in the mid-twenties when Zwingli and Bullinger were combating the Anabaptists and reached various other countries long before it reached Geneva. Büsser argues in his 1994 work on the subject that 'without a doubt' it was Bullinger's teaching which Calvin took up in his 1539 and 1559 *Institutes* and that the Germans and English followed the teaching 'a long time before Calvin'.[45] He can thus conclude concerning God's covenant of grace which embraces the entire Bible:

"Although this is commonly thought to be typically Calvinistic, its origin is in Zürich. It is to be found since around 1925 as a decisive term in the controversies Zwingli and Bullinger had with the Baptists (Täufern), and it was Bullinger who, in answer to a booklet of Schwenckfeld's on the Difference between the Old and New Testaments, wrote his fundamental thesis on covenant theology in his tract *De Testamento seu foedere Dei unico et aeterno* (On the One and Eternal Testament or Covenant of God)."[46]

---

[43] John Herolt the Dominican.
[44] Pelbart Oswald the Franciscan
[45] Längst vor Calvin. *Die Prophezei*, p. 215.
[46] Bundesbegriff in *Die Prophezei*, p. 214.

It is equally 'without a doubt' that the greatest and lasting contribution Henry Bullinger made to the Reformed churches is his doctrine of the covenant. Indeed, Bullinger can be truly called the Father of Reformed Covenant teaching as he alone pointed out to such an all-embracing degree how the essential message of salvation is seen throughout the entire Bible from Genesis to Revelation, providing a focusing point for all the doctrines of grace which other Reformers tended to present in their preaching and teaching as self-contained entities. For Bullinger, baptism, the Lord's Supper, predestination, election, reprobation, law and gospel, the forgiveness of sins, justification, sanctification and the perseverance of the saints, are all to be understood in a covenant context. Furthermore, this covenant centres alone in the work and offices of the Lord Jesus Christ through whom all believers have access to all covenant blessings. Bullinger's covenant teaching also had far reaching political consequences as it was not only the basis on which the Zürich view of the state was based but became the foundation for the United States of America's democratic system.[47] Indeed, Büsser argues that it was Bullinger's optimistic apocalyptic thinking based on his covenant teaching and much of its fulfilment in the Zürich of Bullinger's day, that gave rise to what has become commonly known as 'the Puritan hope' which motivated the Protestants of England and the European Continent to seek a 'New Jerusalem' at the other side of the Atlantic. This Christian optimism is certainly one of Bullinger's major aims in writing his *Decades*.

Trying to prove exactly who was first in reviving the Scriptural teaching that God's one covenant was revealed in both Testaments is fraught with difficulties but Bullinger's major rival as a re-discoverer of covenant theology during Reformation times was not Calvin but Zwingli. Bullinger's predecessor at Zürich also developed a covenant theology in the fifteen-twenties and it is not easy to date a number of each writers'

[47] See Büsser's *Die Prophezei*, pp. 214-217. Büsser mentions John Winthrop's speech written on board the Arabella whilst voyaging to the new world in 1630. The entire speech is to be found in Peter Miller's and Thomas H. Johnson's two volumed anthology *The Puritans: A Sourcebook of their Writings*, Vol. 1, pp. 194-199 amongst other documents from Winthrop's pen.

early works bearing on the subject. We know, for instance, that several very early works of Bullinger are lost or preserved merely in fragments, and this is most likely the case with Zwingli's seminal Reformed works, too, so one cannot be too dogmatic. Furthermore, Bullinger's *Von dem Touff* (On Baptism) which refers to one covenant of grace throughout the Scriptures has recently been dated immediately after Zwingli's arguments referring to a covenant in his *Reply to Hubmeier* of 5 November, 1525 and not in late 1524 as formerly supposed. Hans-Georg vom Berg in his 1991 edition gives between 5 November and 10 December, 1525 as a possible date for *Von dem Touff.* Similarly Bullinger's *Answer to Burchard*, which also deals with the covenant to a high degree, previously dated 1525, is now believed to have been written a year later. Zwingli is thus thought, by a very slim margin of mere days, to be the first to use the word 'covenant' to describe God's one saving plan outlined in both Testaments.

Who influenced whom on the doctrine of the covenant of grace?

This modern view, however, is not above criticism. The methods used appear to be like dating what came first, the hen or the egg and, in reality, are merely based on the assumption that Zwingli, being twenty years older than Bullinger, had had a longer time to ripen in his Reformation ideas. Thus, the criterion used for placing Bullinger's works on the covenant after Zwingli's *Reply to Hubmeier* is merely one of assumed dependence. In fact, it appears difficult for some scholars to see any similarities between the two men's works without claiming that Bullinger must have relied on Zwingli for his material merely because they suppose that Bullinger was Zwingli's pupil. The evidence brought forward to back up this hypothesis is meagre. For instance, Hans-Georg vom Berg believes that he has discovered in Bullinger's *Von dem Touff*, (notes 20, 25, 38, 54, 78, 79, 92, 108 etc.), evidence that Bullinger followed Zwingli. Bullinger refers to baptism as a 'Pflichtzeichen' or sign of commitment, a term Zwingli also uses, so the deduction is made that Bullinger copied Zwingli. So, too, it is argued, Bullinger likens Anabaptist practice to the baptizing of geese and thus must have taken over the idea from Zwingli as the older man likens Anabaptist re-baptism to bathing geese. But all this proves is that the two Swiss-Germans, who both spoke the same kind of idiomatic German, used much the same terminology and imagery. This proves that Bullinger must have taken his theology from Zwingli as little as it proves that Zwingli took his language from his younger friend.

In the case of Zwingli's *Reply to Hubmeier*, we are asked to believe that as soon as that letter was sent off to Hubmeier, Bullinger was given a copy which he immediately used to compose a far more detailed, extensive, and in important parts quite different work, which he finished on the very next day or very shortly afterwards. The truth is that Bullinger was often ahead of Zwingli in his Reformed works and he was clearly often the one who influenced Zwingli, or at least beat him to writing on the subject. This had very much to do with the fact that Bullinger saw his calling at the time in writing and not preaching, whereas Zwingli saw his calling in preaching and only took to his pen when circumstances compelled him. So, too, Bullinger's works on the covenant were more detailed and developed than Zwingli's ever became. On 10 December, 1525, for instance, Bullinger sent off his *De institutione et genuine eucharistiae* to Bartholomäus Stocker emphasising the importance of the Lord's Supper in God's covenant for His people. Again, Bullinger was ahead of Zwingli here as the Zürich Superintendent had not involved the Eucharist in his references to a covenant anywhere near as clearly as Bullinger, nor presented any full-scale plan of how the covenant as a whole worked. So too, in the coming year, Bullinger was far more productive than Zwingli on the topic of the covenant and Zwingli only began to teach a more detailed doctrine in his *Elenchus* (Refutation of the Tricks of the Re-Baptisers) which appeared in July, 1527. This work, however, was still less comprehensive than Bullinger's previous works on the subject.

Oddly enough, the idea that Zwingli might have been dependent on Bullinger as the two men worked diligently together at this time appears not to have been raised by other scholars. Yet Bullinger's influence over Zwingli grew rapidly and we have Bullinger's own testimony that he was the one who wished to inform the public quickly on newly discovered Reformed principles, whereas Zwingli pleaded for caution. We do know for certain, however, that when Zwingli wrote his *Reply to Hubmeier* in November of 1525, he must have been influenced in some way by Bullinger or at least had asked him for help. Evidence for this is found in a letter from Leo Jud, dated 1 December, 1525 thanking Bullinger for drawing Zwingli's attention to quotes from Tertullian and Lactantius supporting the covenant unity of the Scriptures which Zwingli had used in his November work. Bullinger was in Zürich from June to November, 1525 and the two men consulted each other often during this period, especially concerning the Eucharist. So it is very likely that Bullinger had discussed his views on the covenant in conjunction with the Eucharist and Jud's remark referred to these discussions. Bullinger's departure from Zürich coincided with Zwingli's publication of his *Reply to Hubmeier*. So, too, there is scarcely any evidence that Bullinger ever stood in Zwingli's shadow and learnt his doctrines from him. Indeed most of the available evidence points to independence of thought in Bullinger which always caused him to pursue Reformed paths either in front of or abreast of Zwingli.

Bullinger emphasised the unity of the Testaments before Zwingli

There is far more to a doctrine, however than the word that describes it. Bullinger's teaching on the subject was worked out in conjunction with his studies of the two Testaments so that when looking back on his rise to faith through reading the Scriptures in his *De Scripturae negotio* of 30 November, 1523, Bullinger could write, "In brief, I discover that the New Testament is nothing other than the interpretation of the Old, in that the latter promises, the former teaches what has been made real; the latter more concealed, the former more open; the latter in veils and figures, the former with clear evidence and the things itself."[48] In a footnote, he adds "The New Testament is a commentary".[49] In this passage, Bullinger also shows that Christ based His calling on the Old Testament Scriptures and

[48] Unveröffentliche Werke aus der Kappeler Zeit, *De Scripturae negotio*, p. 25.
[49] *Novum testa(mentum) est commentarius.*

proclaimed that the Old Testament bore witness to Him (John 5:39-47). Likewise, Acts 15:14-21 shows that the Apostles saw their work as carrying out the message of the Old Testament. So, too, Paul, when he told Timothy that all Scripture was written on inspiration of God, he was chiefly referring to the Old Testament (2 Timothy 3:16-17).[50] If we, however, compare Zwingli's teaching with Bullinger's at this time, we find the older man, on the appearance of his *Taufbüchlein* in late May 1525, still emphasising the distinctions and contrast rather than the unity of the two Testaments. He must have thus moved from a belief in two separate Testaments with contrasting teaching to a unity of doctrine regarding God's plan of salvation in both Testaments between late May and early November of 1525. By that time, however, Bullinger had been teaching the unity of the Testaments for at least two years, though he did not use exactly the same terms as Zwingli. Indeed, it is clear from Bullinger's works that he rarely uses a fixed *terminus technicus* to describe the eternal covenant of grace but speaks sometimes of a '*punt*', sometimes of a '*gmecht*', sometimes of a '*testament*'. He also uses various Latin equivalents such as '*foedus*', '*testamentum*' and '*pactum*', the words being used as synonyms at times and at other times with divers meanings.

Peter Opitz in his *Habilitationschrift* on Heinrich Bullinger's theology agrees that in *Von dem Touff*, which Bullinger wrote for Henry Simler to help him contend with the Catabaptists, Bullinger deals with elements concerning baptism which Zwingli had also discussed earlier in the year but adds that in his doctrine of the covenant outlined in that work, he takes on a position and emphasis (Stellung und Prägung) which can be traced back to his work before meeting up with Zwingli.[51] In *Von dem Touff*, Bullinger emphasises God's covenantal requirements concerning His creatures, a point almost totally left out by Zwingli. Unlike Zwingli, Bullinger anchors baptism firmly in God's covenantal dealings with man and relates how God by His mercy alone first made a covenant of grace with Adam, then Enoch, then Noah and then with Abraham and his seed

---

[50] *De Scripturtae negotio*, p. 25.

[51] Opitz, p. 320.

for ever. Zwingli saw the idea of covenant simply in the form of how God obliged Himself in mercy to serve man, whereas Bullinger adds how obliged man is to walk uprightly before God. There is thus a bilateral aspect in Bullinger's doctrine lacking in Zwingli and most especially in Calvin. Furthermore, in outlining this bilateral responsibility, Bullinger sees one of Abraham's major covenantal tasks being to institute circumcision as a covenant sign pointing to the grace God offers. In the same way, Christian parents are obliged to have their children baptised as a covenant sign. Similar comparisons provided by J. Wayne Baker make him also conclude that:

"This does not mean, however, that Bullinger then became Zwingli's student any more than he had previously been bound to Luther and Melanchthon. Rather, he worked on his own point of view with some intellectual and spiritual freedom. Indeed, the single time Bullinger mentioned a theological matter in connection with Zwingli in his *Diarium*, he emphasised his own independence."[52]

Be this as it may, in Bullinger's 1527 work *Studiorum ratio*, Bullinger points out that all the books of the whole Bible point to the one eternal covenant which is thus the central theme of God's Word. Furthermore, Bullinger goes down in history, as far as we know at the present time, as the Reformer who first penned a complete work solely on the topic of the covenant. This was his *De testamento seu foedere dei unico et aeterno expositio* or *On the One and Eternal Testament or Covenant of God* of 1534 which quickly went into 15 editions and in which Bullinger outlines that all God's covenant promises in both the Old and New Testaments are centred in the eternal son of God and are thus 'one and eternal' in themselves. The subtitle of this work is Bullinger's most used text, "This is my beloved Son in whom I am well pleased; hear ye him," (Matthew 17:5).

[52] This was the reference on 12 September, 1524 when Zwingli asked him not to publish his findings on the Lord's Supper.

Bullinger's covenant doctrine developed through his dealings with the Catabaptists

Bullinger tells us in his diary for 1534 that he wrote his work on the covenant chiefly against the Catabaptist views of the day. Many of these varied movements rejected the entire covenant idea as being merely Jewish and part of an Old Testament which had no relevance to Christians. Bullinger pointed out that in rejecting the Old Testament, Catabaptists rejected not only the covenant and the signs pointing to the work of grace in Christ but to a right use of the ordinances and the central themes of law and gospel. Bullinger's *On the One and Eternal Covenant* is divided into three parts, the first of which is taken up with a Biblical definition of the term 'covenant' which Bullinger sees as being synonymous with 'testament'. This testament is bi-lateral because it outlines not only the eternal inheritance of God's people through an act of grace, but also the binding duties of believers in living according to the covenant. The German word for covenant is *Bund* which is similar in meaning to the English word 'Bond'. It includes not only the idea of the covenant itself as used in English but also the idea of '*keeping* the covenant'. Then, secondly, Bullinger shows that through this covenant, God first unbinds the sinner from his bondage to sin and then binds him to Himself, placing him under a mutual obligation to serve his God. Thus Bullinger emphasises not only Psalm 103:8 ff. and Romans 11:36 when stressing that the covenant is all of grace, but he equally emphasises Genesis 17:1 which states that the believer must walk before God and be perfect. The Zürich Bible translates Genesis 17:1 as "I am the almighty God, walk before me then you will be unpunishable." For Bullinger, the perfect man is the man whose condemnation has been removed from him and who has been justified and sanctified in Christ. The covenant people are those whom God has no cause to punish eternally because our Covenant Head, the Lord Jesus Christ, has sealed the covenant in His own obedience to the law and His vicarious death under its penalties. Then, thirdly, Bullinger deals with all the questions which might arise during a study of his covenantal doctrines such as the relationship between the Old and New Testaments, body and spirit, law and gospel and also the relationship of baptism to the covenant gospel. As Bullinger explained in *Von dem Touff*, he sees the covenant sign of circumcision as pointing ahead to the blood sacrifice of Christ. After that sacrifice was made once and for all eternity, the covenant sign became the unbloody sign of water baptism demonstrating the fulfilment of the covenant in the cleansing powers of Christ's work on the cross and the outpouring of the Spirit of God on His people.

Justification in the theology of Henry Bullinger

As we have seen in the previous section, Bullinger believed that there can be no right understanding of justification unless one is clear on the doctrine of the covenant. Just as the two are inseparable in a right Reformed faith, so also, for Bullinger, sanctification is a corollary of justification and one cannot have the one without the other. Bullinger outlines this comprehensive doctrine in the first book of his *Decades*, after dealing with the nature of the Word of God and faith. Sadly nowadays, the Reformed doctrine of justification has again fallen into oblivion and, as far as this doctrine goes, we are back in pre-Reformation times. The dominant theory within the so-called *Reformed Establishment* today is not that of Bullinger and the Reformation but that of Philip Melanchthon in his efforts to build a systematic theology on the analytical, and one might also say 'pagan' didactics of Aristotle. This resulted in Melanchthon, in contrast to Luther, viewing justification merely as a secular, forensic declaration which brought with it no spiritual, transforming causative effect. The emphasis on being made just which was so much part of Luther's and Bullinger's preaching, has been dropped and the whole procedure of justification has been reduced to a figurative, forensic declaration of punishment withheld from the point of view of the Great Judge, but which leaves the former condemned sinner where he had always been. It was a form of God's changing His attitude to sinners without changing sinners. Justification, modern would-be Reformed theologians tell us, is a *status* and not a *state*. Sadly, nowadays, most books on the subject of justification[53] fail to capture the true Reformed doctrine of justification by faith alone applied by grace alone with all its transforming powers. The forensic, legal doctrine of justification proclaimed by so many evangelical legalists today which sees the doctrine as a mere declarative, judicial, formal act, leaving the sinner to deserve it by the hard work of sanctification and holiness, is quite different to the all-transforming total work of justification which Bullinger and the bulk of our Reformers taught. Bullinger knows nothing of a mere legal fiction in justification but looked on the doctrine as embracing the whole scope of salvation. He teaches that justification is a *status* given us by grace through Christ's righteousness imputed to us, but this does not rule out the new *state* which this *status* brings with it. That changed state is that we were lost but have been found and we were sinners but now all our sins are covered and we have new life as children of God and are no longer children of the devil. Thus he taught in this sermon, "To justify is as much to say as to quit from judgment and from the denounced and uttered sentence of condemnation," and he goes on, "It signifieth to remit offences, to cleanse, to sanctify, and to give inheritance of life everlasting."[54] Bullinger sees justification as the proof of Christ's intercession for His elect, drawing our condemnation upon Himself and transferring His own guiltless state before God to ourselves. Thus justification for Bullinger is not only the passive forgiveness of sins but the active adoption of the forgiven-one into the number of the sons of God. The word used by Bullinger which is translated 'sanctification' is '*beatificationem*' which he links with both the state and status of one whose sins are covered, i.e. of one who was accursed but is now made blessed. Bullinger is emphatic on the point that God has not only freed us from punishment but he has made us guilt-free in justification and heirs

[53]The following works may be consulted for an overview of modern views of justification which differ radically from those of our Reformers: *Collected Writings of John Murray*, BOT, Vol. ii, IV:17; Justification by Faith Alone, John F. MacArthur et. al., Soli Deo Gloria; *Justification: What's at Stake in the Current Debates*, Mark Husbands and Daniel J. Treiber (eds), IVP; *Right With God*, D.A. Carson (ed), Paternoster Press; The Apostolic Preaching of the Cross, Leon Morris, Tyndale Press; *Justification and the Call of the Gospel*, George M. Ella, Go Publications.
[54] Sixth Sermon, Book I, *Decades*, That the Faithful are Justified by Faith Without the Law and Works.

of the glory that is in Christ. This means that the sinner is not merely declared just but he is made just so that he may remain just and act justly. Thus, for Bullinger though justification is solely by faith given by God which is the sole instrument of justification, what Bullinger calls 'post faith', i.e. faith once it is given, is never alone but accompanied by the fruits of justification in our lives because we are now, "the workmanship of God, created unto good works, which God hath before ordained that we should walk in them." Therefore justification comes to sinners without respect to just works which sinners cannot perform anyway, but justification does not leave the sinner without just works. Justification in the sinner does not leave itself without active evidence of its work. Justification then for Bullinger is to be re-created for the good works that God performs through His justified ones. In this sense, and in this sense only, is "true faith the well-spring and root of all virtues and good works," and "all that is born of God overcometh the world: and this is the victory that vanquisheth the world, even your faith." Bullinger can therefore conclude his sermon on justification by saying:

"Ye have heard, dearly beloved, that true faith is the justification of the church or faithful of God; that it is, I say, the forgiveness of all sins, a receiving into the grace of God, a taking by adoption into the number of the sons of God, and assured and blessed sanctification, and finally the well-spring of all good works. Let us therefore in true faith pray to God the Father, in the name of our Lord Jesus Christ, that he will vouchsafe to fill our hearts with this true faith; that in this present world, being joined to him in faith, we may serve him as we ought; and, after our departure out of this life, we may for ever live with him in whom we believe. To him be praise and glory for ever. Amen."[55]

Providence and Predestination in Reformed Theology

The fourth sermon of Book IV in Bullinger's *Decades* is on God's providential predestination. As interpretations of this latter doctrine was

[55]Ibid, p. 121.

the cause of much strife in the 16th century and separates the so-called Hyper-Calvinists from the so-called Moderate Calvinist today, it will be most instructive to examine Bullinger's views on the subject. Bullinger entitles his sermon *That God is the Creator of all things, and governeth all things by His Providence: Where mention is also made of the goodwill of God to usward, and of predestination.* Here, he looks at the reason for God creating the earth and furnituring[56] it as the realm of man's stewardship under God's dominion. Bullinger thus sees the Providence of God in His general good will to His creation, and especially to mankind whom He has fashioned to be earth's stewards. However, though man is earth's administrator, God is earth's Governor and He has given man strict, though benevolent, rules as to how his stewardship should proceed. Thus every man is obliged to trust in God's benevolence and just government in providence. Whoever appeals merely to God's providence in the form of benevolence for His gospel and excludes His providence in the form of justice preaches a false Gospel. Rejecting philosophical (scientific) and astrological speculations concerning the origin and purpose of the earth, Bullinger says:

"We content ourselves in the only word of God; and do therefore simply believe and teach, that God by his providence doth govern all things, and that, too, according to his own will, just judgment and comely order, by means just and equal: which means whosoever despiseth, and maketh his boast only on the bare name of God's providence, it cannot be that he should rightly understand the effect of God's providence."[57]

Two extremes in evangelism considered

Here Bullinger has a word to say to two extremes in today's evangelism. On the one hand, we have those evangelists and preachers who believe they are motivated to offer salvation on the basis of a benign providence alone and on the other hand those who equally erroneously

[56] Bullinger's phrase. The Reformer obviously compares Eden to a mansion as Christ did Heaven.

[57] Parker Society, Book IV, p. 181.

leave out God's purposes, government and justice in placing man on the earth in their doctrine of the eternal decrees regarding predestination and election. It is, according to Bullinger, erroneous to work out one's gospel of salvation without taking into account man's pre-fallen duties in a benevolent creation and how he failed them. It is equally erroneous to conceive of a gospel of salvation without respect to God's just government of creation and how man was damned because of his misuse of these duties. Bullinger believed that Calvin was always in danger of forgetting this Biblical view of God in creation in his doctrine of predestination.

To Bullinger, the very idea that God would reprobate a man to hell irrespective of his failure as God's steward and irrespective of God's governing justice in creation was unthinkable. Furthermore, he saw election as stemming from the elects' union with Christ and His vicarious work for them so that any doctrine of election based on the mere *a priori* idea that God can do as He likes is ignoring the doctrine of election outlined in Scripture. This tells us not what God may do if He likes, which is beyond our comprehension but what God has done for His elect in Christ. There is thus no dichotomy between God's providence and God's justice and any doctrine of predestination and election must be centred in God's original plan for mankind as a just steward and his restoration to a higher Eden in Christ.

Another serious error, which Bullinger rejects, is the modern, but ever so old, idea that a benign providence can lead sinful man directly to God. For Bullinger, this is a futile faith because providence, because it is a just providence, brings with it both curses and blessings. Thus, though modern evangelists lay great emphasis on stressing that God's providence in nature, which they often call 'Common Grace', shows sinners that God has provided for their salvation, they omit to tell us, like Paul in Romans 1-2, that God's providence leaves all men accursed because they have sinned against the just providence of God. Thus a gospel that is not based on a true understanding of creation and the Fall is a false gospel which goes against providential justice and is thus to be shunned.

Bullinger's and Calvin's views of pre-fallen Adam

Here there is a clear difference in apologetics between Bullinger's view of Adam's special case as a man created upright and who fell and begot fallen offspring and Calvin's teaching that Adam though created initially upright had a sinful virus in him which was timed to one day break out. Calvin tells us in his *The Secret Providence of God*, "From all that has been said, we can at once gather how vain and fluctuating is that flimsy defence of the Divine justice which desires to make it appear that the evil things that are done, are so done, not by the will of God, but by His permission only."[58] The doctrine of predestination according to Bullinger is a saving doctrine and thus applicable to men in a fallen state. To be elect is not through a direct belief in God's Person. No man can attain to such a belief. It is a belief in the Lord Jesus Christ, the only way, the truth and the life. Thus one of Bullinger's favourite evangelistic texts was Philippians 2:12-13, i.e. those who work for their salvation are those in whom God is working and drawing to Christ.

Bullinger does not teach, however, that predestination to salvation has no parallels with providence. Providence is God working out his purpose from eternity in a world whose time-flux is constantly before Him from the beginning to the end. He has fore-appointed who are to be saved and who are to be condemned but the end of that fore-appointment is Christ who becomes the Saviour of those who are fore-appointed to salvation. Therefore God's predestination or fore-appointment can only be known in Christ and it is futile to speak of a predestination apart from Christ. Indeed, for Bullinger it is futile to speak of either providence or predestination in Christ without seeing the one in relation to the other. The one condemns and the other justifies. Bullinger continues:

"The end of predestination, or fore-appointment, is Christ, the Son of God the Father. For God hath ordained and decreed to save all, how many soever have communion and fellowship with Christ, his only-begotten Son; and to destroy or condemn all, how many soever have no part in the

[58] *Calvin's Calvinism*, Sovereign Grace Union, p. 244.

communion or fellowship of Christ, his only Son. Now the faithful verily have fellowship with Christ, and the unfaithful are strangers from Christ. For Paul in his Epistle to the Ephesians saith: 'God hath chosen us in Christ, before the foundations of the world were laid, that we should be holy and without blame before him through love: who hath predestinate us into his sons through Jesus Christ into himself, according to the good pleasure of his will; that the glory of his grace may be praised, wherewith he is pleased with us in his beloved.' Lo, God hath chosen us; and he hath chosen us before the foundations of the world were laid; yea, he hath chosen us, that we should be without blame, that is, to be heirs of eternal life: howbeit, in Christ, by and through Christ hath he chosen us. And yet again more plainer: he hath 'predestinate us,' saith he, 'to adopt us into his sons,' but by Christ; and that too hath he done freely, to the intent that to his divine grace glory might be given. Therefore whosoever are in Christ are chosen and elected: for John the apostle saith: 'Whoso hath the Son hath life; whoso hath not the Son of God, hath not life.' With the doctrine of the apostles agreeth that also of the gospel. For in the gospel the Lord saith: 'This is the will of him that sent me, the Father; that every one which seeth the Son, and believeth in him, should have everlasting life: and I will raise him up in the last day.' Lo. This is the will or eternal decree of God, saith he, that in the Son by faith we should be saved. Again, on the contrary part, touching those that are predestinate to death, the Lord saith: 'He that believeth not is condemned already, because he hath not believed in the name of the only-begotten Son of God. And this is the condemnation, that light is come into the world, and men have loved darkness more than light.' Therefore, if thou ask me whether thou art elected to life, or predestinate to death; that is, whether thou art of the number of them that are to be damned, or that are to be saved; I answer simply out of the scripture, both of the evangelists and the apostles: If thou hast communion or fellowship with Christ, thou art predestinate to life, and thou art of the number of the elect and chosen: but if thou be a stranger from Christ, howsoever otherwise thou seem to flourish in virtues, thou art predestinate to death, and foreknowledged, as they say, to damnation. Higher and deeper I will not creep into the seat of God's counsel. And here I rehearse again the former testimonies of scripture: 'God hath predestinate us, to adopt us into his sons through Jesus Christ. This is the will of God, that whoso believeth in the Son should live; and whose believeth not should die.' Faith therefore is a most assured sign that thou art elected; and whiles thou art called to the communion of Christ, and art taught faith, the most loving God declareth towards thee his election and good-will.

The simpler sort, verily, are greatly tempted and exceedingly troubled with the question of election. For the devil goeth about to throw into their minds the hate of God, as though he envied us our salvation, and had appointed and ordained us to death. That he may the more easily persuade this unto us, he laboureth tooth and nail wickedly to enfeeble and overthrow our faith; as though our salvation were doubtful, which leaneth and is stayed upon the uncertain election of God. Against these fiery weapons the servants of God do arm their hearts with cogitations and comforts of this sort fetched out of the scripture."[59]

Bullinger then goes on to comfort those who have been frightened away from the gospel by metaphysical speculations concerning a God who elects some and reprobates others without regress to a Saviour who calls not the righteous but sinners to repentance. Bullinger thus says that no one has cause to despair if they seek Christ but do not find a ripe and mature faith in themselves. Those who hear Christ's voice calling them to salvation will be saved but the call of Christ can be likened to the Scriptures (Mark 4.) "Of her own accord doth the earth bring forth fruit; first the blade, then the ear, and afterwards the full corn in the ear." So faith often comes little by little as we pray, "I believe Lord; help mine unbelief," and as we follow the Scriptural advice, "Ask and it shall be given you; seek, and ye shall find; knock and it shall be opened unto you." Nobody asks God for bread only to receive stones.

---

[59] *Decades*, Book IV, pp. 188-189.

Providence and predestination cannot be separated in God's salvation plan

Thus, Bullinger preaches election and predestination Biblically in the full framework of the whole gospel. This is where it belongs and from here it should never be isolated. On the other hand, instead of merging the doctrines of predestination and providence together and centring them in Christ, Calvin separates predestination from the rest of the gospel and subordinates everything else to it, including God's saving covenant with man. He obviously does this because he cannot envisage his sovereign God bending down and entering into any dialogue or agreement with man or interaction with him. This was no problem to Bullinger who emphasised that God's providence, the covenant and Christ's priestly work were all communicatory channels of God's grace. Thus when one looks at Bullinger on providence, it is all the story of God's patience with man but Calvin's providence shows an arbitrary God and his one refrain is the mind-breaking hypothesis that though God is the first cause of all things, He is not the author of evil, He merely decrees, ordains and directs it and, "Those things which are vainly or unrighteously done by man, are rightly and righteously the works of God." Calvin here adds that if such sentiments seem paradoxical or self-contradictory, two Scripture references will prove him right. However, Calvin's use of Scripture here is most questionable. He gives Proverbs 16:33, "The lot is cast into the lap, but the whole disposing thereof is of the Lord". Taking the first and obvious meaning as being the safest, this text is saying that God overrules in all things, in spite of man's foolishness. Here, there is a great distinction between man's foolishness in casting the lot and God's wisdom in overruling. It would be blasphemy to say that God's wisdom overrules over the foolishness He instills in man, a foolishness that comes from God. Calvin's next text is Deuteronomy 19:5 which says that if a branch falls from a tree or an axe slips from someone's hand and kills a person, this is because God willed that the man be killed. This again is a far cry from saying that man as a sinful agent is a product of God's will. Sin is a rebellion against God and not God's rebellion against His own self. Calvin adds here that it is most unworthy and most disgraceful to think that he (Calvin) is arguing like a Stoic here. He goes on to argue that God can make the wicked mad if it is in His purpose. Few Christian's would deny this. But it is a far cry from this to say that God made righteous Adam mad because God wanted Adam to fall, which is what Calvin is getting at all the time. [60]

Two contrary positions regarding predestination

Sadly, the doctrine of predestination was to divide the still young Reformed Church because of two positions which quickly formed. The first was the argument from revelation and experience. This is based on the entire ways of God with man and does not separate predestination from salvation, justification, sanctification and glorification. Instead of separating the gospel's doctrines and the commands of the Great Commission, they are synthesised and placed in the comprehensive unity of thought to which they belong. This was Bullinger's standpoint. The second view was based on a logical sequence deriving from a subjective, philosophical view of God's absolute sovereignty, greatness, honour and majesty. It was a strictly analytical position but also strictly theoretical. Taken in isolation, such doctrines can never be complete. William Cowper compares the critic with his analytical philosophy to a butcher dressing and carving a bird. He plucks the feathers, cuts out the giblets, dresses the meat, removes the bones and the beautiful bird is lost. This is very much the state of our systematic theologies. Thus, whereas Bullinger could not contemplate predestination outside of creation, the fall, the mission of Christ and the salvation of the elect, Calvin, from time to time, put his doctrine of predestination into what he believed was a strictly logical, analytical and *a priori* mould. In Calvin's doctrine, given that his commentaries and sermons occasionally disagree with his *Institutes* on this issue, he can ignore man and especially his sin fully and see God merely picking out those whom He wished to save and those whom He wished to reject. Bullinger never viewed God's decrees in isolation from the way God chose to effect them, namely in the Person and Work of

---

[60] *Calvin's Calvinism*, pp. 232-237.

Christ. It is in Him and the grace given in salvation which reveals God's saving and electing decrees to man and it is through God-given faith in Christ that election is made known to him. We are never called to believe in decrees for salvation but to believe in Him who fulfils God's decrees, the Lord Jesus Christ. Furthermore, as Calvin leaves the freedom God gave to Adam completely out of his predestination story, one is led to believe that Adam was really innocent of the fall because God willed, ordained and decreed him to sin. The poor man had no choice! Thus, in this Hyper-Calvinistic system, man by nature was never upright, and this nature never fell in deciding to disobey God but God placed disobedience from the start into his very nature. Thus Calvin can claim that Adam's ordained purpose in life was to sin. Complaining of those such as Bullinger who believed that though God permitted Adam to sin, He did not make Him sin, Calvin says:

"They deny that it is ever said in distinct terms, God decreed that Adam should perish by his revolt. As if the same God, who is declared in Scripture to do what ever He pleases, could have made the noblest of his creatures without any special purpose. They say that, in accordance with free-will, he was to be the architect of his own fortune, that God had decreed nothing but to treat him according to his desert. If this frigid fiction is received, where will be the omnipotence of God, by which, according to his secret counsel on which everything depends he rules over all?

Then, turning to Adam's fallen offspring, Calvin says "It was *not* owing to nature that they all lost salvation by the fault of one parent."[61] Bullinger, on the other hand, argued that we must distinguish between what God permits in His mercy to happen and what He makes in His mercy out of it. Thus God can use man's fall to a greater rising in Christ. This does not mean that He decrees sin but it does mean that He decrees its healing.

---

[61] *Institutes*, Book III, Chapter XXIII, paragraph 7.

Calvin's mistake was that he hid his own idea of what majesty and justice entail behind the *a priori* postulate of an arbitrary God who acted purely out of analytical, logical reasons instead of finding his understanding of God in the gospel.

By the 1550s, the extreme view of Calvin regarding a God who decreed the fall had reached England. Ironically enough, it was pioneered by those whom Bullinger had introduced to Calvin to allow Calvin to broaden his horizons. Bartholomew Traheron, who had found asylum in Bullinger's house in 1537 when he fled from Oxford under the persecutions of Henry VIII, had been corresponding with Bullinger since that time and his letters had been full of concord with Bullinger's theology. However, on 10 September, 1552, Traheron wrote to Bullinger from London saying:

"I am exceedingly desirous to know what you and the other learned men, who live at Zürich, think respecting the predestination and providence of God. If you ask the reason, there are certain individuals here who lived among you some time, and who assert that you lean too much to Melanchthon's views. But the greater number among us, of whom I own myself to be one, embrace the opinion of John Calvin as being perspicuous and most agreeing to holy Scripture. And we truly thank God, that that excellent treatise of the very learned and excellent John Calvin against Pighius and one Georgius Siculus should have come forth at the very time when the question began to be agitated among us. For we confess that he has thrown much light upon the subject, or rather so handled it, as that we have never before seen any thing more learned or more plain. We are anxious to know what are your opinions, to which we justly allow much weight. We certainly hope that you differ in no respect from his excellent and most learned opinion. At least you will please to point out what you approve in that treatise, or think defective, or reject altogether, if indeed you do reject any part of it, which we shall not easily believe."[62]

---

[62] *Original Letters*, Vol. I, pp. 325-326

Traheron's letter has all the audacity of a student who thinks he has grown beyond his tutor's care and can turn the tables on him. He neither says what he does not accept in Melanchthon, nor how he understands Calvin. Actually, Traheron found out that he had interpreted Calvin in too severe a way but instead of apologising to both Calvin and Bullinger, he rebuked them for not being so steadfast in their teaching as he. Also, Melanchthon chopped and changed his views on predestination and fluctuated almost permanently between believing as Luther and believing as the Pelagians, sometimes harmoniously finding a balance and often not. So it was rather unfair of men such as Traheron who had been given asylum by Bullinger to come up with such unfounded criticism. At this time in England, however, a number of fiery spirits who came to be known as Precisians, were grouping together to form what they thought was an elite group amongst the Reformed men. Traheron thus felt free to challenge his tutors on predestination and started a most controversial dispute against John Hooper, Bullinger's most intimate friend and soon to be martyred, on the subject. John and Anne Hooper had been won over for the Reformation by reading Bullinger's works and were much influenced by Bullinger's doctrine of predestination as centred in and worked out in the Person of Christ. They also followed Bullinger in his doctrine of sanctification in connection with justification and the work of Christ as Priest.[63] The young couple had sought asylum under Bullinger's roof from 1547-49 and Bullinger became god-father to their daughter Rachel who was born in Zürich. It was thus clear that those Precisians in England who viewed predestination as a logical postulate *per se* and not in its Christological aspects as Bullinger taught would find fault with the experimental theology of such as his disciple Hooper.

John Hooper, like Bullinger, believed that election was election out of sin and not without reference to sin, seeing electing grace as that which extends mercy to certain lost ones. Thus in Article X of his private *Confession of Faith*, Hooper says:

---

[63] As distinct from Prophet and King.

"I believe that this corruption of nature, otherwise called original sin, is the fountain and root of all other sins: for the which all the miseries and adversities that we endure in this present life as well in body as soul, do come to us; yea, and in the end double death, that is to say, both of body and soul. These be the fruits and rewards of sin. But although the same be due and common to all men generally, nevertheless the Lord through his mercy hath reserved to himself a certain number (which are only known to himself), the which he hath drawn from his corrupt heap, and hath sanctified and cleansed the same in the blood of his Son Jesus Christ, and by means thereof hath made them vessels of election and honour, apt unto all good works."[64]

This was as near as makes no difference the doctrine of Bullinger and the bulk of our Reformers. On the other hand, Traheron was convinced that he was following Calvin in believing that God condemned some men to reprobation and others to salvation irrespective of creation and the fall. Calvin, of course, had a fine Christology but here the grave weakness of his analytical system in comparison to the synthesising system of Bullinger and Hooper is displayed. If one isolates predestination and election from Christology, one is bound to end up believing in a form of theological fatalism. The theologian is lost in the philosopher. Traheron was by no means the most extreme of such fiery spirits but he had begun to develop a strict form of Calvinism which spread for a while throughout England and Scotland which the reign of Mary dampened considerably and which Calvin and even Beza, besides Bullinger, Martyr and Gualter condemned. Traheron merely felt that the Swiss and Genevans were now soft-pedalling on essential issues. Oddly enough, it is such as hold to Traheron's idea of being elected outside of Christ and reprobated irrespective of sin who still claim nowadays that they are true Calvinists and claim that their Bullingerite brethren are 'Hypo-Calvinist' which they define as 'Sub-Calvinist'.

---

[64] *Later Writings of John Hooper*, Parker Society, p. 25. Hooper's authorship is questioned.

Bullinger replied to Traheron's letter on 3 March, 1553.[65] First Bullinger emphasised that he had nothing to do with Melanchthon's ever-fluctuating teaching on predestination and held to the orthodox view which had existed since Biblical days. This affirmed that all sin is of the Devil and God is not its author but the author of all that is good and merciful. Bullinger tells Traheron that he must distinguish between three forms of man. First we have unfallen man with his free will, then we have fallen man with a will in bondage to will sin and then we have the born again Christian who has a restored free will but not through the power of his nature but through the power of God's grace in his being placed in Christ. By nature fallen man is bound to sin, by grace redeemed man is lifted up by the power of God. Those who are given God's grace to become new creatures are His elect. Bullinger defines predestination as "that ordination (*ordinatio*) of God whereby He from eternity has destined everything, but especially man, the lord of all, for a certain end (*finitio*) and that according to his holy and just council, rule (*iudicio*) and decree. Furthermore, there is an election of God from eternity, through which he chooses the one to life and the other to destruction. The reason for election and predestination is solely the good and just will of God which saves the elect with no reference to their merit, but rejects the reprobate because of their own demerits … God chose from eternity those whom He wanted. He wanted, however, according to His resolution and design, believers …. We do not regard belief as if it were our work … but belief is included in the divine decree."[66]

Bullinger adds that he has high respect for Calvin but he would not dare say as Calvin that "God not only foresaw the fall of man and the misery of his offspring but ordained it by His will." For Bullinger, sin did not come to Adam by force but of his own free will. Fallen man is

[65] I have consulted this letter in Latin and German forms but various sources claim that Zürich Letters III contains a copy in English. I have sought diligently for such a work for many years in vain. Perhaps the work was planned but never printed.
[66] Translated from the German version provided by Walter Hollweg in his *Heinrich Bullinger's Hausbuch*, pp. 300-302.

accursed because of his own sinful nature. For Calvin man is accursed because God wished to curse him and therefore created him to fall.

All Bullinger's fine and pastoral theology which holds up the responsibility of man for his depravity and the sovereign grace of God for his mercy left Traheron cold and rebellious against his tutor. He replied on 3 June, 1553:

"I acknowledge, my excellent Bullinger, your especial kindness, who for the sake of satisfying my earnest request have thought it no trouble to write to me so fully and accurately respecting the providence and predestination of God. But though I admire both your exceeding learning and moderation in this writing of yours, nevertheless, to say the truth, I cannot altogether think as you do. For you so state that God permits certain things, that you seem to take away from him the power of acting. We say that God permits many things, when he does not renew men by his Spirit, but gives them up to the dominion of their own lusts. And though God does not himself create in us evil desires, which are born with us; we maintain nevertheless, that he determines the place, the time, and mode (of bringing them into action), so that nothing can happen otherwise than as he has before determined that it should happen. For, as Augustine has it, he ordains even darkness. To be brief, we ascribe all actions to God, but leave to men whatever sin there is in them; which Augustine has, I think, stated in these words: "To sin is in the power of men, but to produce this or that effect by sinning belongs not to them, but to God, who ordains darkness." Again, "God fulfils his own good purposes by the evil purposes of evil men." And to this belongs that saying, that in some wonderful and ineffable manner that does not take place without his will, which is done even against his will.

But I am acting very indiscreetly in reminding you of these things, to whom all the writings of Augustine are so well known. You do not approve of Calvin when he states that God not only foresaw the fall of the first man, and in him the ruin of his posterity, but that he also at his own pleasure arranged it. And unless we allow this, we shall certainly take away both the providence and the wisdom of God altogether I do not indeed perceive how this sentence of Solomon contains any thing less than this: "The Lord hath made all things for himself: yea, even the wicked for the day of evil" (Proverbs 16:4). And that of Paul: "Of him, and through him, and to him, are all things" (Romans 11:36). I pass over other expressions which the most learned Calvin employs, because they occur every where in the holy scriptures. But I cannot think it either foolish or dangerous to follow that mode of speaking which the Holy Ghost useth. And did it not seem superfluous, I would entreat you again and again, to beware lest any disagreement be occasioned between you by reason of these things. For it will retard the course of the gospel not a little; and unless I am altogether mistaken, you will not be long able to support a cause that is tottering of itself."

Obviously, Traheron has misunderstood Bullinger concerning God's overruling of evil that good might come of it and Calvin would certainly have agreed to differ on several points with Traheron's rather naïve interpretation of his theology. Indeed, Traheron was taking a pro-Calvin stand against Bullinger, just when Calvin was taking a pro-Bullinger stand himself regarding Bolsec. Calvin said clearly that Bolsec lied in arguing that Bullinger took his side. No matter how Traheron seeks to show that though God ordains man's sinning, He does not create his sin, in affirming that God creates everything, including evil, he cannot avoid the accusation that this is tantamount to saying the same thing, i.e. God is the author of sin. Traheron strives to dodge the issue of who ordained sin by saying that sin is born in man and thus sin is solely man's fault. The moot question is how man became sinful and Traheron's answer is because he was made such by God and not that he became such through the exercise of his will. Nevertheless, Traheron has rightly quoted from Calvin's *Institutes* concerning Calvin's belief that God 'arranged' the fall.

As is often the case when students suddenly feel that they have progressed beyond their tutors and found another and better mentor, they are prone to alter their minds again, so we find Traheron only a few years after he turned against Bullinger, now turning against Calvin whom he finds is not consistently Traheronian. Writing to Calvin with a group of

Reformers of the 'old school', he tells the man he had praised so much in his letters to Bullinger that Calvin is gullible, acts on the advice of deceivers and those who really shamefully abuse him and accuses people of great offences of which they are fully innocent. Calvin is told that his deceitful friends are a disgrace to their country for feeding him with 'barefaced and impudent falsehoods'. The whole tone of the lengthy letter is that Calvin is a foolish busy-body who does not know a good man when he sees one and allies with nigh criminals. This must have been one of the most condemnatory letters Calvin ever received.[67]

Traheron died prematurely around 1558 so he did not experience Bullinger's *Second Helvetic Confession* of 1566 in which the Swiss theologian affirmed his belief in predestination and election, saying in X.1.:

"1. God has from the beginning freely, and of His mere grace, without any respect of men, predestinated or elected the saints, whom He will save in Christ, according to the saying of the apostle, 'According as He hath chosen us in Him before the foundation of the world' (Ephesians 1:4); and again, 'Who hath saved us, and called us with an holy calling, not according to our works, but according to His own purpose and grace, which was given us in Christ Jesus, before the world began, but is now made manifest by the appearing of our Saviour Jesus Christ' (2 Timothy 1:9-10).

2. Therefore, though not for any merit of ours, yet not without a means, but in Christ, and for Christ, did God choose us; and they who are now ingrafted into Christ by faith, the same also were elected. But such as are without Christ were rejected, according to the saying of the apostle, 'Examine yourselves, whether ye be in the faith; prove your own selves. Know ye not your own selves, how that Jesus Christ is in you, except ye be reprobates?' (2 Corinthians 13:5).

3. To conclude, the saints are chosen in Christ by God unto a sure end, which end the apostle declares when he says, 'According as He hath

[67] Letter CCCLVII, *Original Letters*, pp. 755-763.

chosen us in Him before the foundation of the world, that we should be holy and without blame before Him in love: having predestinated us unto the adoption of children by Jesus Christ to Himself, according to the good pleasure of His will' (Ephesians 1:4-5).

4. And although God knows who are His, and now and then mention is made of the small number of the elect, yet we must hope well of all, and not rashly judge any man to be a reprobate: for Paul says to the Philippians, 'I thank my God upon every remembrance of you,' (now he speaks of the whole Church of the Philippians), 'always in every prayer of mine for you all making request with joy, for your fellowship in the gospel from the first day until now; being confident of this very thing, that He which hath begun a good work in you will perform it until the day of Jesus Christ: even as it is meet for me to think this of you all' (Philippians 1:3-7).

5. And when the Lord was asked whether there were few that should be saved, He does not answer and tell them that few or many should be saved or damned, but rather He exhorts every man to 'strive to enter in at the strait gate', (Luke 13:24): as if He should say, It is not for you rashly to inquire of these matters, but rather to endeavor that you may enter into heaven by the strait way.

6. Wherefore we do not allow of the wicked speeches of some who say, Few are chosen, and seeing I know not whether I am in the number of these few, I will not defraud my nature of her desires. Others there are who say, If I be predestinated and chosen of God, nothing can hinder me from salvation, which is already certainly appointed for me, whatsoever I do at any time; but if I be in the number of the reprobate, no faith or repentance will help me, seeing the decree of God can not be changed: therefore all teachings and admonitions are to no purpose. Now, against these men the saying of the apostle makes much, 'And the servant of the Lord must not strive; but be gentle unto all men, apt to teach, patient, in meekness instructing those that oppose themselves; if God peradventure will give them repentance to the acknowledging of the truth; and that they may recover themselves out of the snare of the devil, who are taken captive by him at his will' (2 Timothy 2:24-26).

7. Besides, Augustine also teaches, that both the grace of free election and predestination, and also wholesome admonitions and doctrines, are to be preached *(Lib. de Bono Perseverantiae,* chap. 14).

8. We therefore condemn those who seek otherwhere than in Christ whether they be chosen from all eternity, and what God has decreed of them before all beginning. For men must hear the gospel preached, and believe it. If thou believest, and art in Christ, thou mayest undoubtedly hold that thou art elected. For the Father has revealed unto us in Christ His eternal sentence of predestination, as we even now showed out of the apostle, in 2 Timothy 1:9-10. This is therefore above all to be taught and well weighed, what great love of the Father toward us in Christ is revealed. We must hear what the Lord does daily preach unto us in His gospel: how He calls and says, 'Come unto Me all ye that labour and are heavy laden, and I will give you rest' (Matthew 11:28); and, 'God so loved the world, that He gave His only begotten Son, that whosoever believeth in Him should not perish, but have everlasting life' (John 3:16); also, 'It is not the will of your Father in heaven, that one of these little ones should perish' (Matthew 18:14).

9. Let Christ, therefore, be our looking glass, in whom we may behold our predestination. We shall have a most evident and sure testimony that we are written in the Book of Life if we communicate with Christ, and He be ours, and we be His, by a true faith. Let this comfort us in the temptation touching predestination, than which there is none more dangerous: that the promises of God are general to the faithful; in that he says, 'Ask, and it shall be given you; ... every one that asketh receiveth' (Luke 11:9-10). And, to conclude, we pray, with the whole Church of God, 'Our Father which art in heaven' (Matthew 6:9); and in baptism, we are ingrafted into the body of Christ, and we are fed in His Church, oftentimes, with His flesh and blood, unto everlasting life. Thereby, being strengthened, we are commanded to 'work out your own salvation with fear and trembling,' according to that precept of Paul, in Philippians 2:12."

How more evangelistic and more pastoral is such a definition of predestination! Here the doctrine is embedded in the entire scope of the gospel and it is in such a position that the Scriptures place it. Sadly, the Traheron-type doctrine of predestination is little more than an attempt to define the shape and contents of a cake by speculating on the icing.

Bullinger's Cup presented by Queen Elizabeth I

Chapter 8

Bullinger's Vast Importance for the English Reformation

Bullinger's early contacts with England

When dealing with Calvinism in England during 1558-1640, Patrick Collinson, the acclaimed expert on the Elizabethan Age, has an interesting point to make. He states, "If we were to identify one author and one book which represented the centre of theological gravity of the Elizabethan Church it would not be Calvin's *Institutes* but the *Common Places* of Peter Martyr, described by his translator, Anthony Marten, as 'a verie Apostle'. And at least equally influential was Bullinger."[1] This is all the more interesting as Martyr had served in England for several years, yet Bullinger had never even set foot on English soil. In spite of this, he was still considered as sharing the top rung of the ladder of fame with Martyr. Bullinger's English contemporaries, however, tended to place Bullinger even higher than the Italian Reformer. Indeed, Bullinger's importance to the English Reformation can scarcely be exaggerated and there are many good, solid reasons for this as will be seen below.

Numerous Reformers were forced into exile during Henry VIII's reign mainly because of resistance to Henry's notorious Six Articles. A number

[1] *International Calvinism* 1541-1715, pp. 214-215.

of these found shelter in Switzerland. These were followed by many hundreds who fled from Mary's England. Bullinger and his fellow ministers in Zürich, as also many councilmen, merchants, farmers and craftsmen, opened their private houses to these refugees and arranged for accommodation for those wishing to settle in Aarau, Vevey, Basle or Geneva. Not only did Bullinger provide from his own funds in order to aid the English refugees but he persuaded the Zürich Senate and his fellow-Reformers scattered throughout Europe to do likewise. Even when Mary was striving to smother the Reformed Church in England, he knew of men and women in England who were able to provide funds for their exiled brethren and appealed to their generosity. On 24 August, 1554, for instance, Bullinger wrote to 'certain Englishmen' to remind them of their Christian duties to their brethren:

"Our Lord Jesus Christ not only requires believers to befriend his banished ones themselves, but also to procure, for them the favour of all godly persons, and by pleading their cause in all quarters to aid them in every possible way. For this reason we do not hesitate to commend to your kindness your English exiles, whom our most honourable magistrates here have taken into their protection, and to whom we wish well from our hearts. They have hitherto lived among us in the sincere fear of God, in true godliness, in constant prayer, in godly discipline, and in purity and innocence of life. They have, as far as we know, afforded no occasion of offence to any one; they have not injured or been troublesome to any one; they are beloved by all godly persons; they are so devoted to, and so greatly profit by, their literary and theological studies, that it is impossible not to expect from them the most abundant fruit. Should they go on as they have begun, there is no doubt but that they will be a benefit and advantage to the renowned kingdom of England. For though England at this present time neither regards nor requires them and their progress in learning and godliness, we nevertheless entertain the hope that other and happier times will at length arrive; especially when we see that changes in kingdoms are of very frequent occurrence, and in a word, that the grace of Christ is denied to none, so that the man who has lately been a most active persecutor of Christ and his gospel, may soon perhaps become a most zealous preacher of the gospel.

You will therefore, honoured friends and brethren, act with the greatest wisdom as well as godliness, by not withdrawing your support from the deserving and hopeful members of Christ, who stand in need of your assistance. You know what praise and honour in the sight of God and men Obadiah, the governor of the house of the ungodly king Ahab, procured to himself, because, at the utmost risk both of his life and property, (living as he did in those most perilous times, when queen Jezebel purposed to destroy all the prophets of God, either by the sword, or to make them perish with hunger,) he fed even whole schools of the prophets in caves and secret places. And indeed these your countrymen are so far from abounding in luxury, that they seem to the most careful observers to deny themselves even what is necessary for their support, and live far too sparingly. And I wish that many among ourselves had the same power of shewing kindness to them, as we should otherwise have the inclination; for they would then be richer than they are at present. But inasmuch as God has blessed you. and has not only bestowed upon you more ample means, but has also afforded you this seasonable opportunity of benefiting your countrymen; your charity will understand how acceptable a sacrifice you will offer to God, and how greatly you will improve your own circumstances, if you continue to shew liberality to these your countrymen, who are true members of Christ. For you are aware that Paul, the holy apostle of Christ, in more than one place calls the collection made by the rich, on behalf of those who were in banishment and poverty by reason of the gospel of Christ, 'an odour of a sweet, smell, a sacrifice acceptable, well-pleasing to God.' (Philippians 4:18). The same apostle too adds: 'My God shall supply all your need according to his riches in glory by Christ Jesus.' And again, in another place: 'God is able,' he says, 'to make all grace abound towards you, that ye, always having all sufficiency in all things, may abound to every good work; as it is written, He hath dispersed abroad, he hath given to the poor; his righteousness remaineth for ever.' (2 Corinthians 9:8, 9). And the Lord Jesus himself expressly declares in his gospel: 'He that receiveth you, receiveth me; and he that receiveth me, receiveth him that sent me. He that receiveth a prophet in the name of a prophet, shall receive a prophet's reward; and whosoever shall give to drink unto one of these little ones a cup of cold water only in the name of a disciple, verily, I. say unto you, he shall not lose his reward.' (Matthew 10:40-42). For the same Lord declares in another place: 'I was an hungered, and ye gave me meat; I was thirsty, and ye gave me drink; I was a stranger, and ye took me in; naked, and ye clothed me,' &c. 'Verily, I say unto you, inasmuch as ye have done it unto one of the least of these my brethren, ye have done it unto me.' (Matthew 25:35, 40). And Christ our Lord promises to such persons all manner of blessing, and a happy life. And we read also that David sung: 'Blessed is the man that considereth the poor and needy; the Lord will deliver him in the time of trouble. The Lord preserve him and keep him alive, and make him blessed upon the earth, and not deliver him into the hands of his enemies. The Lord comfort him on his bed of languishing; thou wilt make all his bed in his sickness,: etc., Psalm 41:1 etc.. All the words of God are true, steadfast, and undoubted. For heaven and earth shall pass away, but the eternal word of God shall never perish, nor shall one jot or tittle fall from it.

Believing therefore in those most certain declarations of God, earnestly endeavour, brethren and friends beloved in the Lord by a plenteous sowing and liberal contribution to prepare for yourselves against that day an abundant harvest, and one that will satisfy you for eternity, through Christ our Lord. Fare ye well, and receive this our exhortation with kindness as from your friends and brethren.

Henry Bullinger,
In the name of all the pastors, readers, and ministers of the church of Zürich."

John Hooper witnesses to Bullinger's Reforming influence in Britain

The martyr John Hooper, with his entire family, was sheltered two years in Bullinger's home. He became deeply influenced by the beautiful character and plain but profound teaching of the Reformer. Hooper had begun to correspond with Bullinger during the reign of Henry VIII and it was through reading Bullinger's commentaries which began to appear in England in the early thirties that Hooper was won for the Reformed faith. When Hooper had to flee from Henry's wrath, he sought asylum in Zürich after writing the following words in a letter (here abridged) dated January, 1546:

"These singular gifts of God exhibited by you to the world at large, I was unwilling to neglect, especially as I perceived them seriously to affect the eternal salvation and happiness of my soul: so that I thought it well worth my while, night and day, with earnest study, and an almost superstitious diligence, to devote my entire attention to your writings. Nor was my labour in this respect ever wearisome to me: for after I had arrived at manhood, and by the kindness of my father enjoyed the means of living more unrestrainedly, I had begun to blaspheme God by impious worship and all manner of idolatry, following the evil ways of my forefathers, before I rightly understood what God was. But being at length delivered by the goodness of God, for which I am solely indebted to him and to yourselves, nothing now remains for me in reference to the remainder of my life and my last hour, but to worship God with a pure heart, and know my defects while living in this body, since indeed the tenure of life is deceitful, and every man is altogether as nothing; and to serve my godly brethren in Christ, and the ungodly for Christ: for I do not think that a Christian is born for himself, or that he ought to live to himself; but that, whatever he has or is, he ought altogether to ascribe, not to himself, but to refer it to God as the author, and regard every thing that he possesses as common to all, according as the necessities and wants of his brethren may require. I am indeed ashamed beyond measure, that I have not performed these duties heretofore; but that like a brute beast, as the greater part of mankind are wont to do, I have been a slave to my own lusts: but it is better to be wise late, than not at all.

By reason of my love and respect towards you, I had often proposed to visit you, though I have always been prevented hitherto, partly by my ill-health, and partly because I am mistrustful of the favour of fortune; for my father, of whom I am the only son and heir, is so opposed to me on account of Christ's religion, that should I refuse to act according to his wishes, I shall be sure to find him for future, not a father, but a cruel tyrant. Shortly however, in about a month's time, I mean to go down to my native place[2] to bid farewell to the honours, pleasures, and friends of the world; and I will then endeavour, if possible, by the assistance of my friends, to obtain at least some portion of what I am entitled to, wherewith I may be able to subsist upon my slender means among you at Zürich: and should God order it otherwise, and see fit to visit me with poverty and want, or in any other way, I will bear it with an undisturbed mind, and choose rather, as an exile, to suffer affliction with the people of God, than to enjoy the pleasures of sin for a season; esteeming the reproach of Christ (I use the words of St Paul) greater riches than the treasures in Egypt; for I have respect unto the recompence of the reward, and hope for eternal life, obtained, not by my merits, but by the blood of Christ. I entreat you, therefore, O man of God, by our Lord Jesus Christ, that you aid me in this journey by your prayers to God for me. For I am in fear, and not without reason, of those perfidious bishops, to whom nothing is more acceptable than the spilling of the blood of the godly, and whose temper and disposition I have often experienced to the great peril of my life. I desire therefore, to defend myself against their treachery and tyranny with the remedies that God has given me; and I seek the aid of your church, that by the help of her prayers I may derive some comfort, according to the promise of God, who is ever present with all who call upon him in truth, and from whom alone assistance is to be sought for in every kind of danger. For there cannot be a more powerful safeguard than believing prayer: by this Hezekiah overcame the king of the Assyrians, Elijah called down fire from heaven, and Jehoshaphat obtained a signal victory. But I will dilate no longer upon this subject, for fear of offending your pious and learned ears by so rude and unpolished a letter. Accept, my very dear master, in few words, the news from England. As far as true religion is concerned, idolatry is no where in greater vigour. Our king has

[2] Somersetshire.

destroyed the pope, but not popery; he has expelled all the monks and nuns, and pulled down their monasteries; he has caused all their possessions to be transferred into his exchequer, and yet they are bound, even the frail female sex, by the king's command, to perpetual chastity. England has at this time at least ten thousand nuns, not one of whom is allowed to marry. The impious mass, the most shameful celibacy of the clergy, the invocation of saints, auricular confession, superstitious abstinence from meats, and purgatory, were never before held by the people in greater esteem than at the present moment …

The chief supporters of the gospel in England are dying every hour: many very illustrious personages have departed within these two years; the lord chancellor Audley, the duke of Suffolk, (Sir Edward) Baynton, the queen's first lord of the bedchamber; Poinings, the king's deputy at Boulogne; Sir Thomas Wyatt, known throughout the whole world for his noble qualities, and a most zealous defender of yours and Christ's religion; Dr Butts, a physician who had the charge of the king's person: all these were of the privy council, and real favourers of the gospel, and promoted the glory of God to the utmost of their power. They all died of the plague and fever; so that the country is now left altogether to the bishops, and those who despise God and all true religion …

The conference at Ratisbon, as far as I understand by a letter from master Bucer, is suspended: I am more inclined to believe this, because Philip Melancthon is neither yet come to them, nor does he intend it. And Bucer, as I hear, is about to come to us sooner than I expected: but as yet we have nothing certain; as soon as this shall be the case, I will inform your reverence forthwith, and you may expect a more copious letter whenever any new tidings shall require it. The count Palatine has lately provided for the preaching of the gospel throughout his dominions: but as far as relates to the eucharist he has descended, as the proverb has it, from the horse to the ass; for he has fallen from popery into the doctrine of Luther, who is in that particular more erroneous than all the papists; and those who deny the substance of bread to remain in the sacrament, and substitute the body of Christ in its place, come more closely to the truth than those who affirm that the natural body of Christ is with the bread, in the bread, and under the form of bread, and yet occupies no place. God I hope will at length give him a better mind …

Salute affectionately in my name those excellent men masters Bibliander and Pellican, with the other godly brethren. Farewell, most learned and godly sir, and suffer me, I pray you, to be numbered amongst those who truly and from the heart admire the majesty of your religion. Strasburgh, Jan. 27, (1546).

Yours entirely,
John Hooper, Anglus."[3]

Hooper wrote to Bullinger, several times in 1549, asking him for permission to copy his unpublished works for general distribution. Hooper's sudden arrest and execution under Mary, though he regarded her as the rightful Queen and had supported her, put an end to Hooper's plan to distribute the bulk of Bullinger's works throughout all England.

Further influence of Bullinger's works

Bullinger's Latin commentaries and a number of German and English translations filled a large gap in Reformation literature for the struggling English Church so that they became bestsellers and even made English booksellers rich. Many letters of thanks from Englishmen for Bullinger's expositions of the word of God have been preserved such as the one written by Nicolas Eliot as early as 1537. Eliot says amongst many more compliments:

"Not only the church of Zürich, but all other churches which are in Christ, bear witness to the skill, and purity, and simplicity of faith, with which you have expounded the whole Bible, and especially the epistles of St Paul. And how great weight all persons attribute to your commentaries, how greedily they embrace and admire them, (to pass over numerous

[3] *Original Letters*, Vol. I, pp. 33ff.

other arguments) the booksellers are most ample witnesses, whom by the sale of your writings alone, from being more destitute than Irus and Codrus, you see suddenly becoming as rich as Croesus. May God therefore give you the disposition to publish all your writings as speedily as possible, whereby you will not only fill the coffers of the booksellers, but will gain over very many souls to Christ, and adorn his church with more precious jewels."[4]

One of the most famous of the English exiles in Germany and Switzerland who became positively influenced by Bullinger's Reforming works was Miles Coverdale, commonly called by his contemporaries *Superintendent At-Large of the Reformation.* Coverdale was a brilliant linguist and pastored a German-speaking church himself during his Marian exile. We soon find him therefore translating Bullinger's German and Latin works into English. His first known translation was from *Der alt gloub* or *The Old Faith* published in 1541 which was a summary of the Old and New Testaments and the faith once committed to the saints. This proved very popular and was reprinted and modernised by Coverdale a number of times and also revised and retranslated by others in the 17th century. In 1541, Coverdale also translated and published Bullinger's work on Christian marriage of 1540 entitled *The Christen statye of Matrimonye. The orygenall of holy wedlock: whan where how and of whom it was instituted & ordeyned: what it is: how it ought to proceade: what be the occasions fruit and commodities thereof.* This work went through at least eight editions in a few years. By the early forties, Bullinger was so loved in England that even single letters which anyone received were quickly snapped up, translated, printed and distributed in tract form. Sadly, however, private letters of Bullinger were often reduplicated and distributed without the knowledge of either the author or the recipient. This caused Bullinger some anxiety as altered or abridged versions of his letters, especially during the vestment controversy, were used by both friends and foes for their own purposes.

[4] Ibid, Vol. II, p. 620.

When Bullinger heard that Henry VIII had separated from the pope, he wrote his *The Authority, the Certitude, the Stability and the Absolute Perfection of Holy Scripture* and *The Institution and the Function of Bishops* which he dedicated to the King and sent copies to him and to Cranmer and Cromwell via former students Nicolas Eliot and Nicolas Partridge. Both the King and Cranmer requested that the Latin works should be translated into English and Eliot wrote:

"Your books are wonderfully well received, not only by our king, but equally so by the Lord Cromwell, who is keeper of the king's privy seal and vicar general of the church of England ... but your writings have obtained for you a reputation and honour among the English, to say nothing of other nations, beyond what could possibly be believed."[5]

By the 1550s Bullinger was ranked as the number one theological author in England so that when Jan Laski, pastor of the Stranger's Church in London, approached Archbishop Cranmer in 1551 concerning publishing Bullinger's *Absoluta de Christi Domini et catholicæ ejus ecclesiæ Sacramentis tractatio*, Cranmer told Laski to go ahead, saying that he had no need to examine the work first as all Bullinger's works were the very best.

One of Bullinger's most popular works in England was his collection of sermons on Revelation, a book hitherto avoided by English and Swiss commentators. When the English translation appeared in 1561, English Bishop Parkhurst ordered all the clergy in his large diocese of Suffolk and Norfolk to purchase and study either the Latin or English text. Parkhurst had spent no less than four years in exile under Bullinger's roof and remained a very ardent friend and disciple of the Swiss Reformer. Bullinger wrote his *The True Christian Sacrifice* of 1551 at Parkhurst's prompting.

---

[5] Ibid, p. 618.

King Edward's interest in Bullinger

The great kindness shown by Bullinger and the Zürich Senate to former exiles caused Edward VI on coming to the throne to write to him thanking him as a personal friend and saying, "In addition to which, there is also a mutual agreement between us concerning the Christian religion and true godliness which ought to render this friendship of ours, by God's blessing, yet more intimate. We therefore return you our warmest thanks for your singular and favourable disposition towards us, which you shall always find to be reciprocal on our part, whenever an opportunity shall present itself."[6] This more intimate friendship was to make itself apparent when Edward died amidst rumours of being poisoned by the papists and his half-sister forced thousands of the Lord's people who had escaped martyrdom out of England. Many of these exiles kept close contact with Bullinger, not only because of his own person but also because he had access to Christopher Froschauer's printing press at Zürich who stood with Bullinger at the side of the English exiles, making sure that Reformed works in English were smuggled into Britain.

Whilst Bullinger was compiling Books III and IV, of his famous *Decades*, the Reformation on the Continent was going through difficult times as Emperor Charles V consolidated his enormous powers. The independent, nigh-democratic nature of the Swiss cantons gave the Protestant districts some measure of religious liberty but in England the Reformation was making leaps and bounds unparalleled in the larger nations on the Continent and it appeared that soon the entire country was well on its way to becoming thoroughly Reformed. Bullinger's works had helped to bring about this change and the Swiss Reformer was in intimate contact with most of the leading lights of the English Reformation including the clergy, the nobility, the politicians and secular scholars, tradesmen and even a number of servants who were strong in the new faith. Foremost amongst these were John and Anne Hooper, Johann ab Ulmis, Richard Cox, Sir John Cheke, Richard Hilles, John Abel, Christopher Hales, Bartholomew Traheron, Nicolas Partridge, John

[6] Original Letters, Vol. I, p. 1.

Butler and John Burcher. These English friends told Bullinger of the faith and godliness of their new young King and urged him to encourage Edward in his Reforms as much as was in his power. The letters of these Englishmen and women and ex-patriot Swiss in England concerning the compilation and reception of the *Decades* have happily been preserved in the fifth volume of Gilbert Burnet's *History of the Reformation* and the Parker Society's *Original Letters Relative to the English Reformation 1537-1558* and *The Zürich Letters 1558-1602*. It thus appeared natural and strategic for Bullinger to dedicate Books III and IV of his doctrinal sermons to Edward VI, the boy King in the words: "To the most renowned Prince Edward the Sixth, King of England and France, Lord of Ireland, Prince of Wales and Cornwall, Defender of the Christian Faith." Indeed, Bucer of Strasburg, Bullinger of Zürich, Jan Laski of Poland and Peter Martyr and Jerome Zanchi of Italy all believed that the Church of England was now leading the Reformation of the ancient Church which had gone astray from God after the pattern of the Jews.

Bullinger's action in honouring the English King moved other Continental church leaders to follow his example. Later in 1550, Martin Bucer dedicated his magnum opus *De regno Christi* to Edward. Calvin followed him in 1551 by dedicating his commentary on the catholic epistles to Edward. John Hooper wrote to Bullinger in March, 1550, shortly before conferring with the King and told his mentor concerning his beloved sovereign:

"Believe me, my much esteemed friend, you have never seen in the world for these thousand years so much erudition united with piety and sweetness of disposition. Should he live and grow up with these virtues, he will be a terror to all the sovereigns of the earth. He receives with his own hand a copy of every sermon that he hears, and most diligently requires an account of them after dinner from those who study with him. Many of the boys and youths who are his companions in study are well and faithfully instructed in the fear of God, and in good learning."[7]

---

[7] *Original Letters*, Vol. 1, p. 82.

The *Decades* preface to Edward

In his Preface to the boy-king, Bullinger instructs him in the ways of God with earthly monarchs and goes through the divine instructions to them in the Scriptures, particular regarding Saul, David and Solomon so that Edward, in taking heed to their follies and triumphs may have a prosperous and successful reign. After dealing with the Scriptures, Bullinger proceeds throughout church history up to the time of Edward's father, Henry VIII, explaining in one of Bullinger's rare positive references to himself that it was a book he had dedicated and sent to Henry some twelve years previously which had helped to bring forth 'no small fruit' to the English Reformation and now gave Bullinger the courage to address Henry's son on similar topics.[8] Bullinger continues by saying:

"In these sermons I handle not the least and lowest points or places of Christian religion, the law, sin, grace, the Gospel, and repentance. Neither do I, as I think, handle them irreligiously. For I use to confer one scripture with another; than which there is no better way and safer to follow in the handling of matters touching our religion. And for because you are the true defender of the Christian faith, it cannot be but well undoubtedly, to have Christian sermons come abroad under the defence of your majesty's name. My mind was, according to my ability and the measure of faith which is within me, to further the cause of true religion, which now beginneth to bud in England, to the great rejoicing of all good people."

As the Reformation progressed and people became used to gospel preaching, sermons grew longer and longer until ministers began to suspect that they were expected to be like the Wittenberg Reformer Bugenhagen who would preach for as long he felt a congregation could take it. Even Luther, who usually expounded his text thoroughly and at

---

[8] Dedication to King Edward the Sixth, *Decades*, Book III, p. 15. The book sent to Henry was on the Word of God, the institution and function of bishops and the folly of Rome's superstitions and tyranny.

length had to tell Bugenhagen to think of his hearers' delicate ears and not preach for seven hours as he once did in Denmark. Farel and Viret were famous (or notorious) for their lengthy sermons, as was also Bucer. Two to three hours preaching was no exception in those days. Bullinger and Calvin usually strove to leave the pulpit within an hour of opening up their subject. Bullinger's sermons in his *Decades*, however, became longer and longer and it is difficult to think that he really preached those recorded in his third to fifth books. We need not think he did. Bullinger told Edward that he had been careful to write long sermons:

"and handled the matter so, that of one many more may be gotten: wherein the pastor's discretion shall easily discern what is most available and profitable for every several church. And the pastor's duty is rightly to mow the word of truth, and aptly to give the fodder of life unto the Lord's flock.[9] They will not think much, I hope because in these sermons I do use the same matter, the same arguments, and the very same words, that other before me, both ancient, and late writers, (whom I have judged to follow the scriptures), have used before now, or which I myself have elsewhere alleged in other books of mine own heretofore published. For as this doctrine, at all times and in all points agreeable to itself, is safest to be followed, so hath it always been worthily praised of all good and godly people."

The Threat of the Council of Trent to the Reformation

On the Continent, the Lutheran Reformation was suffering major setbacks by the way Melanchthon, in an effort to maintain peace with the Roman Catholics and Emperor Charles V, favoured joining the Council of Trent and was willing to accept any joint Protestant-Roman Catholic pronouncements which might ensue from that council. This filled Bullinger and his English allies with great apprehension. Since 1548, the Emperor had set up his policy known as the *Interim* as a basis on which the Council of Trent could meet and as a display of his own freedom from

[9] 2 Timothy 2:15. Erasmus and Beza give 'secare' here. Beza "*et qui rectè sermonem veritatis secat.*

the pope's control. This allowed the Lutherans some freedom in doctrine but not in church rites, though the various dukes of the German states managed to modify the *Interim* proposals to give them an appearance of independence from the Emperor. Charles demanded that the Protestants kept to the *Interim* compromise but not the Roman Catholics. Melanchthon accepted this state of affairs for two reasons, (a) the Lutherans thus obtained a limited toleration and (b) Melanchthon was obsessed with the idea that as the powers that be are ordained of God and are God's regents on earth, then the Emperor must one day accept the Reformation. To save his own reputation, in a letter to Christopher von Carlowitz, Melanchthon blamed Luther for the break in the church, forgetting that his *Augsburg Confession* had caused not only a necessary break with Rome but a most unnecessary break with the Swiss-German and English Reformation. That the German Lutherans lagged way behind the Swiss in their Reforming zeal is illustrated by the fact that there was scarcely a word of protest against the Emperor's ruling. Brave Palatine rejected the *Interim* and proceedings were eventually made with Bullinger to use the Second Helvetic Confession and with Zacharias Ursinus and Caspar Olevanus to use the Heidelberg Catechism. This development, however, was to take another decade.

Bullinger's lack of interest in and even suspicion of councils had developed in his Bremgarten days when he saw his colleagues regularly leaving their sheep to dash off to councils which were invariably pointless as each delegate merely visited them to put forward his own view. In 1532, Bullinger authored an essay on *Wie man in ein Concilium einwilligen möge* (On Accepting a Council) in which he listed a number of points which could possibly lead to an acceptable council. Such a council should be voluntary, Christian and free from papal control. Its purpose must be to find the truth to the glory of God and the edification of the people. The criteria used must be centred in the Word of God in faith and brotherly love. Scripture must be explained by Scripture and not via the rule of the Roman Church. The venue must be a place where no party may expect betrayal or even murder and a guarantee for one's personal security is given. The Council of Trent did not fulfil any of these criteria for Bullinger so there was no point in taking part in it. This Bullinger explained in his 1546 *Antwort der Predigeren zu Zürich uff des Papst Laden in das Concilium zu Trient* (Answer of the Zürich Preachers to the papal invitation to the Council of Trent). Bullinger pointed out that from Leo X to Paul III, the papists had condemned the Evangelicals (Protestants) as 'heretics' and the Council of Trent was specifically called to exterminate 'heretics', so going there was akin to suicide. When the invitation to the Council came in 1551, Zürich had no qualms in refusing it as with the invitation came no promise of free discussion but the command that the Swiss should accept the invitation and thus demonstrate their humble submission to the pope.[10] On hearing what was happening at the Council, Bullinger, Bibliander, Vergerio and Calvin composed a number of works against Trent.

Thoughts of such a development on Rome's side grieved Edward VI and the Church of England so Edward decided to turn to Bullinger for help. One day in 1550 a stranger knocked at Bullinger's door and asked for hospitality. He refused to say who he was and where he was from at first but this did not stop Bullinger making sure that the stranger was fed and housed. It appeared that the stranger wished to sound out his hosts before revealing his identity. Actually, Bullinger had corresponded with the man for years but had never met him face to face. Once the stranger was satisfied that he would receive a brotherly hearing, he confessed that he was none other than Christopher Mount, Edward's personal ambassador to Germany and Switzerland and one of his closest advisers. Mount had brought with him a letter from the English King requesting the aid of Bullinger and the Zürich Council in determining what course England and the Church of England should take in face of the Imperial and popish pressure on England to take part in the Council of Trent. The letter from Edward suggested that the Swiss and the English should call a joint Council as alternative to Trent which should be binding for the Reformed Churches of the two countries and for others who might wish to join. So, too, Edward begged Bullinger to use all his powers in

[10] See Rudolf Pfister's anniversary article Zu Bullinger's Beurteilung des Konzils von Trent, Gesammelte Aufsätze zum 400. Todestag, Erste Band, pp. 123-140.

working out a reconcilliation between France and England, who were now facing hostilities, and also help form a peaceful alliance between Switzerland and England against the Emperor. In February, 1551, the Reichstag met at Augsburg and the Emperor rejected all Protestant arguments against the Council of Trent. Bullinger immediately wrote to Calvin to say that this could be the end of the German Reformation and the Emperor would now seek to suppress Swiss and English resistance. He urged Calvin to work with him to help the English deal with Henry II of France and warn them against joining the Council of Trent. Bullinger told Calvin that he was in principle for a political and Church union with England but did not think the idea would gain general acceptance. Bullinger was obviously only half-heartedly for a political union but his warnings against Trent did not go unheeded in England and King and Church rejected the idea of a common council with the Roman Catholics.

Book V of the *Decades* dedicated to Lord Henry Grey

In his letter of March, 1550 mentioned above, John Hooper also suggested to Bullinger that he should dedicate a volume of his *Decades* to one of England's most influential noblemen, Lord Henry Grey, the Marquis of Dorset. This nobleman's influence has been recorded in history as being due to the schemes he was party to whilst campaigning to have his daughter, Lady Jane Grey (1537-1554) either wedded to the King or become Queen in her own right rather than for his zeal for the Reformation. However, his letters show a fervent faith and an eagerness to promote the gospel. John ab Ulmis who was something of a protégé of Lord Grey's and often a guest at his mansion home, had already suggested that Bullinger should honour Grey with a preface at least as early as August of the preceding year and, indeed, Bullinger had already decided to dedicate Book V to Lord Grey before Hooper had written his March letter.[11] Ulmis sketched a pen-portrait of Lord Grey for Bullinger in the words:

---

[11] See ab Ulmis' correspondence with Bullinger in *Original Letters*, Vol. II during the period 1548-1552.

"He is descended from the royal family, with which he is very nearly connected; and is the most honourable of the king's privy council. He has exerted himself up to the present day with the greatest zeal and labours courageously to propagate the gospel of Christ. He is the thunderbolt and terror of the papists, that is, a fierce and terrible adversary. He spoke most nobly in defence of the eucharist in the last parliament. He is very much looked up to by the king. He is learned, and speaks Latin with elegance. He is the protector of all students, and the refuge of foreigners. He maintains at his own house the most learned men: he has a daughter, about fourteen years of age, who is pious and accomplished beyond what can be expressed; to whom I hope shortly to present your book on the holy marriage of Christians, which I have almost entirely translated into Latin."[12]

It was also Ulmis who informed Bullinger how to address Grey which resulted in his dedication "To the most illustrious Prince and Lord, Henry Grey, Marquis of Dorset, Baron Ferrers, of Groby, Harrington, Bonville and Astley; one of the Privy Council of his most serene Majesty, the King, and of the Famous Kingdom of England; Henry Bullinger wisheth grace and peace from God the Father through our Lord Jesus Christ."

Lord Grey was away in Scotland on a diplomatic visit when Book V of the *Decades* reached England, so Ulmis took it up to Scotland to make sure that the nobleman would definitely receive the gift in person. On his return to England, Lord Grey wrote to thank Bullinger, saying:

"That you have not received, my very dear Bullinger, any letter from me before now, by which I might testify towards you that good-will which you have on so many accounts deserved, and also thank you most heartily for your exceeding courtesy to me, which I most entirely appreciate, has been solely attributable to those affairs of state, upon which I had to bestow all my zeal, labour, and diligence, unless I would

[12] *Original Letters*, Vol. II, 406.

fail in satisfying my duty to God, my own dignity, and the expectation of the public. You will therefore, I know, easily pardon my delay, especially as I would have you assured that my regard for you can be diminished by none and much less by time. For the book which you have published under the auspices of my name, I return you not only for my own sake, but for that of the whole church of Christ, the thanks I ought; and I acknowledge the divine goodness towards his church, and, as Paul expresses it, the love of God to man, that he has chosen to adorn and illuminate his church with such lights, as that we who are less enlightened, may follow those guides in the beaten path of true religion, who may both be able, by reason of the gifts they have received from God, and willing, by reason of their affection to their brethren, diligently to point out the way in which we ought to walk. It would indeed have been all over with us, had not he provided pillars of this kind to support his church, which otherwise would beyond all doubt have been overthrown.

I acknowledge myself also to be much indebted to you on my daughter's account, for having always exhorted her in your godly letters to a true faith in Christ, the study of the scriptures, purity of manners, and innocence of life; and I earnestly request you to continue these exhortations as frequently as possible. Farewell, most accomplished Bullinger, and may Almighty God prosper your endeavours in the church, and evermore defend you! From my house in London. Dec. 21, 1551.

Henry, Duke of Suffolk.[13]

A good friend of England's in times of persecution and revival

In the days of Mary the Bloody, Bullinger kept an open home for the English and exercised his pan-European influence, enabling the English to set up churches throughout the Continent. He gave advice on who should pastor them, how to get on with the state authorities and how to defend the faith when placed under pressure to renounce Christ. The largest Continental English church during 1554-1559 was at Frankfurt

[13]*Original Letters*, Vol. I, pp. 3-4.

where Charles V had given the English the freedom of the city. It was Bullinger who sent Thomas Lever there with the recommendation that he should pastor the church; a recommendation which was wisely followed. It was through Lever's diplomacy and moderation and his keeping to sound Reformed principles in the face of several 'fiery spirits' which enabled the so-called *Liturgy of Compromise* to be drawn up which subsequently united the conflicting parties and became the basis for English worship throughout Germany and Switzerland. Lever also served as a go-between in Bullinger's correspondence with Calvin.[14] The letter that Lever and eleven of his friends sent to the Zürich magistrates in 1554, requesting asylum in Zürich has been preserved in the Parker Society's *Original Letters* and reads:

"Forasmuch as we are exiled, most honourable magistrates, from England, our beloved country, and for the sake of that light of divine truth by which she was lately distinguished, we humbly request of your worthiness, that we may be permitted to sojourn in this most famous city, relying upon and supported by your sanction, decree and protection against the violence of those, should any such be found, who would oppose and molest us. The Lord knoweth, for whose sake we have left our all, that we seek for nothing besides himself. And for this reason chiefly we have unanimously and with ready minds come to this place, where he is most sincerely preached and most purely worshipped. This being the case, we entertain the hope that, as you are most zealous defenders of the true Christian religion, so you will protect us by your authority, who by reason of the same are exiled and homeless. May the Lord Jesus long preserve you and this your industrious state in safety and prosperity! Your most humble petitioners, Robert and Margery Horne, James Pilkington, Thomas Lever, John Mullins, Thomas Bentham,

[14] See, for instance, Calvin's letter to Bullinger dated 28 April, 1554 which was a reply to a letter Bullinger had entrusted with Lever for Calvin. *Calvinism in Europe 1540-1610: A Collection of Documents*, pp. 38-41.

Richard Chambers, Thomas Spencer, Henry Cockraft, Michael Reniger, Laurence Humphrey, William Cole."[15]

These twelve saints were given the best of hospitality and it is said that they lived in Zürich 'with great glee'. The hospitality of the Zürich believers was enormous. Printer Froschauer took all twelve into his own home as most of the other Reformer's houses such as Pellican's were already full to bursting point with English refugees. The homeless saints for whom they opened their doors were to become the pillars of the Reformation under Elizabeth, filling important places in church, state and the universities. Once settled in his pastorate at Frankfurt, Lever wrote to Bullinger, thanking him with the words:

"Everlasting health in Christ Jesus! As I always found in you, when I was at Zürich, godly counsel, learning, and example, to my exceeding comfort and advantage, so now, most reverend father in Christ, I hope that I shall obtain the benefit of your pious prayers for the edification of the church of Christ of the English at Frankfurt. And as many others of my countrymen regard you as their patron, so do I acknowledge you to have been a father to myself, as I hope and desire that you will continue to be. And since I perceive that I am destitute of all power and opportunity of returning my obligations, I write this, that you may understand me to be neither unmindful nor ungrateful."[16]

Lever received a plea from the barely tolerated refugee church at Wesel, who were undergoing fierce Lutheran opposition, to help them find a more peaceful home and Lever led the majority to Frankfurt and Aarau whilst Whitehead took over the pastorate at Frankfurt again in his absence. Whitehead wrote to Bullinger on behalf of the Frankfurt church on 17 September, 1557, thanking him for his great support of the exiles:

[15] *Original Letters*, Vol. II, pp. 751-752.
[16] *Ibid*, Vol. I, letter written from Frankfurt, 12 February, 1555, p. 159.

"Health in Christ Jesus. Others inscribe the monuments of their genius to men of rank, by whose authority they may obtain protection, or by whose wealth they may become enriched; but you, most learned and most excellent sir, consecrate your most godly studies to the miserable and afflicted churches of the exiles, from whom no human support or worldly advantage can be expected. In this truly you have followed the rule of perfect charity, which seeketh not her own, but the things of others. For you have not sought for any benefit to yourself, but the comfort of the churches groaning under the cross; placing your hand as it were under the burden, and partaking and sympathising in our calamities. And this purpose of your most compassionate mind you have, as far as we can judge from ourselves, most abundantly accomplished. For having been introduced through the door opened by you into the revelation of the Lord concerning his churches, as if to behold an object immediately present before our eyes, we have derived indeed very much comfort, both from the will of Almighty God, by whose permission and allowance these things are taking place, and also from this your kindness and favour, whom we regard as a messenger of God to us. For which your deservings towards us, as you in no wise expect any return from us, so we are unable to afford any other, except that (as is the duty of men who are not ungrateful) we return you our most hearty thanks to the utmost of our power, and will in the mean time entreat God the Father of our Lord Jesus Christ in our earnest and constant prayers, that he may be pleased evermore to defend and preserve to his flock such a pastor, and to his afflicted church such a comforter.

Your piety's most devoted, the minister, elders, and deacons of the church of the English exiles at Frankfort on the Maine. (Signed) David Whitehead, John Hales, John Wilford, William Master, Thomas Sowerby, Gregory Railton, Jo. Taverner and Edmund Sutton.[17]

News of Mary's death reaches Bullinger

It was through correspondence with one of the English exiles, Edwin Sandys, that Bullinger first heard of Mary's death. Sandys had settled

[17] Ibid, Vol. II, pp. 763-764.

down on the Continent, taken out Frankfurt citizenship with his friend John Ponet and had dropped thoughts of ever returning to England as Mary was relatively young. He was sitting down at dinner with John Foxe and Peter Martyr when news of Mary's death reached the Reformed friends. Sandys, who had been imprisoned under Mary, refused to return, complaining that he had experienced enough misery in England but Grindal who also had grown to love Germany and was ever after termed 'Germanical' in his theology, persuaded him to return and help build up the Protestant church in England. Sandys thought it his duty to inform Bullinger immediately of Mary's death and wrote to him in his usual jovial manner:

"We yesterday received a letter from England, in which the death of Mary, the accession of Elizabeth, and the decease of cardinal Pole[18] is confirmed. That good cardinal, that he might not raise any disturbance, or impede the progress of the gospel, departed this life the day after his friend Mary. Such was the love and harmony between them, that not even death itself could separate them. We have nothing therefore to fear from Pole, for *dead men do not bite*."[19]

Bullinger who had raised so much money to support the deprived refugees on the Continent, now used his vast international influence to make sure that monies were provided so that the English refugees could return home. When Queen Elizabeth came to power, she wrote to Bullinger and the Zürich church, conveying her thanks and sent them a gigantic silver cup in token of her friendship.

Bullinger's works help the Church of England's defence against the Anabaptists

The Anglican Church did not have to encounter the Anabaptists until almost twenty years after the German and Dutch-speaking countries but

---

[18] Mary's relation and henchman and fellow-persecutor of the saints. Mary had made Pole Archbishop to replace Cranmer whom she had burnt at the stake.

[19] *Zürich Letters*, Vol. I, p. 3.

by the late forties Bullinger's anti-Catabaptist writings were being translated into English such as his *An holsome Antidotus against Anabaptistes*, translated by John Veron in 1548 and *A Dialogue between the seditious Anabaptist and the true Christian, about obedience to Magistrates*, printed first in English in 1549 and which went into several editions. William Ames mentioned that he had a work with a similar title from Bullinger's pen which was printed at Worcester in 1551. This he calls *Three Dialogues between the seditious libertine or rebel Anabaptist, and the true obedient Christian: wherein obedience to magistrates is handled*, which may have been a new translation by Veron with added material.

The only time Bullinger appears to have retracted any of his theology was very early in 1530 when he dabbled in prophecy and produced his *De hebdomadis quæ apud Danielem sunt, opusculum* on Daniel's visions. This was almost immediately corrected in his homilies on Daniel but not before the work had been banned in England. This, however, gives some indication of how swiftly Bullinger's works were translated into English and widely read within a year of their appearing in Latin or German.

Advising England's educators

Bullinger's reputation as an educator spread very early in England and a number of university men and tutors of the Royal family and higher nobility corresponded regularly with him on educational and spiritual matters, recognising him as their mentor who had become their close friend. Amongst these were Dean Richard Cox, Chancellor of Oxford University and tutor and almoner to Edward VI; Sir John Cheke who was also Edward's tutor and secretary; John Aylmer, private teacher to the Marquis of Dorset's children, including Lady Jane Grey and later Bishop of London; and Bartholomew Traheron, who taught the young Duke of Suffolk. All of these had been exiles during Mary's reign.

Richard Cox (1500-1581), who became Bishop of Ely under Elizabeth, remained one of Bullinger's most devoted friends from the time of Henry VIII, throughout the reigns of Edward and Mary and well into the reign of Elizabeth I. He outlived Bullinger by six years. Cox's great contribution to the Reformation in England was really made outside of England's shores. During the Marian persecutions, Reformers of various persuasions fled to the Continent and carried their controversies with them. Cox was almost unanimously looked to as a mediator in these controversies and managed to procure such a measure of peaceful agreement that when Elizabeth gained the throne, she found in the exiles a united front against the papists and no less than 17 of those whom Cox had helped to unite became bishops in the Church of England and many others became Reformed ministers. Indeed, a number of those influenced by Cox became leading members of the Government. Writing to Bullinger from Westminster Palace on 22 October, 1549, Cox confessed:

"There are many things, my very dear friend in Christ, which ought justly to inspire me with veneration for yourself; namely, your singular erudition and piety, so renowned throughout all Christendom. Many and splendid are the monuments of your talent, which have everywhere most clearly set forth the glory of God. These things however, important as they are, being of general interest, are not so likely to affect individuals: but the instance of your kindness with which you have lately favoured me, has more intimately and powerfully impressed my mind; I mean, your having done me the honour of presenting me with your most learned letter, and a jewel of a book. For there shine therein the jewels, not of earth but heaven; not those which attract the sight, but which wonderfully delight the mind. I thank you therefore most heartily, and I implore the great and good God very long to preserve both yourself and those like you, as the most solid pillars of his church."[20]

Sir John Cheke (1514-1557) was appointed first Regius Professor of Greek at Cambridge University and quickly became known and respected throughout Europe as a pioneer in reintroducing Greek studies. He was greatly loved by his pupil, England's Boy-King Edward and when Cheke

[20] Ibid, pp. 119-120.

was gravely ill in 1552, it was reported that he would surely die. On hearing of this, Edward said, "No, Cheke will not die this time; for this morning I begged his life in my prayers, and obtained it."[21] Cheke recovered. Because of his connections with Edward and Lady Jane Grey, he was stripped of all his titles by Mary, robbed of all his wealth and property and confined for a year to the Tower. Cheke fled to Germany but became such a strong supporter of the Reformation that Mary had him kidnapped on the Continent and under most severe tortures and sufferings brought to England where he was forced under further torture to recant and died soon later broken in body and spirit. John Strype (1643-1734), Cheke's fine biographer, closes Cheke's 'Life' with the words:

> Condemn not thy poor brother,
> That doth before thee lay;
> Since there is none but falls:
> I have, thou dost, all may.[22]

On 7 June, 1553, Cheke wrote to Bullinger concerning books he had sent for the King's use. After giving Bullinger his assurances of true friendship, Cheke continues:

"The books which you have written to the king's majesty, have been as acceptable to him as they deserved to be. A large portion of them I delivered to him myself, and am able therefore to inform you how kindly and courteously he received them, and how greatly he esteems them, and I can offer you my congratulations upon the subject. But since the king's majesty, debilitated by long illness, is scarcely yet restored to health, I cannot venture to make you any promise of obtaining a letter from him to yourself. But should a longer life be allowed him, (and I hope that he may very long enjoy it,) I prophesy indeed, that, with the Lord's blessing, he

---

[21] *The Life of the Learned Sir John Cheke, Kt.: First Instructor, afterwards Secretary of State, to King Edward VI,* Clarenden Press, 1821, p. 88, bound and published with Strype's *Life of Sir Thomas Smith.*
[22] Ibid, p. 181.

will prove such a king, as neither to yield to Josiah in the maintenance of true religion, nor to Solomon in the management of the state, nor to David in the encouragement of godliness. And whatever may be effected by nature or grace, or rather by God the source of both, whose providence is not even contained within the limits of the universe, it is probable that he will not only contribute very greatly to the preservation of the church, but also that he will distinguish learned men by every kind of encouragement. He has long since given evidence of these things, and has accomplished at this early period of his life more numerous and important objects, than others have been able to do when their age was more settled and matured. He has repealed the act of the six articles; he has removed images from the churches; he has overthrown idolatry; he has abolished the mass, and destroyed almost every kind of superstition. He has put forth by his authority an excellent form of common prayer; he has published good and pious homilies to lessen the ignorance of uneducated ministers. He has invited the most learned men to teach at the universities, and has done many other things of the same kind, every one of which would be considered as a great action in other men, but as nothing in him, by reason of the magnitude of what he has accomplished. Besides this, he has lately recommended to the schools by his authority the catechism of John,[23] bishop of Winchester, and has published the articles of the synod at London, which if you will compare with those of Trent, you will understand how the spirit of the one exceeds that of the other. Why should I say more? I send you the book itself as a token of my regard, and believe me yours in Christ. Fare thee well.
Greenwich, June 7, 1553. 7 Ed. VI.

Yours in the Lord, John Cheke.
Salute, I pray you, masters Rudolf Gualter, and Conrad Gessner, to whom I am shortly about to write.

[23] Bishop Ponet's Catechism. Ponet was also an exile and correspondent of Bullinger's.

A note in Bullinger's hand says that this was the last letter Cheke sent to him before the King died and Cheke was committed to the Tower. The last letter sent to Bullinger before Cheke's second imprisonment and his very last letter as a free man was sent from Strasburg on 12 March, 1556. In this letter, Cheke thanks Bullinger for his great hospitality to the English refugees and affirms his allegiance to the Reformed doctrine of the Lord's Supper and rejects that of the Lutherans. In his opening paragraphs, Cheke writes:

"Our people frequently converse respecting the kindness not of yourself alone, but also that of men of all classes, and of your whole commonwealth, towards the English who came to reside among you by reason of the change of religion in their own country: I consider this not kindness merely, but hospitality, to be especially acceptable to God, and approved of men; and that it will never perish from the memory of any of our countrymen. As to me, should I ever have it in my power to render any service to yourself, or your godly friends, or your commonwealth, I pledge myself to be so ready to perform it, as that the anxiety of a grateful mind and the desire of returning an obligation may evidently appear. I ought also upon other grounds to shew both to yourself, and to masters Bibliander and Bernardine, as much respect as is due to learned, pious, and friendly persons, who have deserved well of the church of Christ. This your hospitality, therefore, is not only praise-worthy in itself, but is yet more so by comparison with the ill-treatment of others. For I suppose you are not ignorant, that those parties who maintain the body of Christ to be every where can nowise endure the members of Christ to be any where, and have harassed them with all kinds of cruelty and atrocity, in order that with the absurdity of the opinions they have imbibed they may also join a savageness of disposition, and a brutal ferocity towards the meek children of God. But if the truth of opinions is to be judged of by their fruits, and there is as wide a difference between men's sentiments as there is in the christian life, truly they ought to have been long since convinced, and to have given up so stubborn an opinion. But of the stupidity of these parties at another time. May God enlighten their blinded mind with the light of his

Spirit, and bring them out from this thick darkness of error to a better perception of the truth, and a more harmonious consent of feelings."[24]

Cheke's reference to the inhospitality of the Lutherans was no exaggeration as they were doing their utmost to cast the Anglican refugees out of their cities such as Wesel and even out of the country.

John Aylmer (1521-1594) is little known today as a Reformer though he was one of the first to be deprived of his offices for combating the doctrine of transubstantiation in Convocation under Mary. He was compelled to flee the country and spent five years on the Continent. Whilst in exile, he assisted John Foxe in compiling and translating his *Acts and Monuments* and was spoken highly of amongst the Frankfurt and Genevan Christians, in particular those of the more 'Puritan' persuasion. Aylmer was severely criticized by the Marprelate Tracts for his adherence to the Established Church and by Ultra-Puritans for his defence of the Elizabethan Settlement against John Knox's *Monstrous Regiment of Women*. Such critics, who attack Aylmer under the mantle of Calvinism, do not realize that Knox's book was severely criticized by Calvin and Beza who had it banned from Geneva and also by the vast majority of England's Reformers. When Aylmer returned to England, Elizabeth appointed him as one of the eight disputants chosen to persuade the papist bishops to repent and choose the Reformed path. Even though Aylmer's services for the Reformation are sadly ignored by today's Reformed scholars and theologians, his services to the Marquis of Dorset and his daughter Lady Jane Grey, England's martyr Queen, have given him a sure place in the history of the United Kingdom. Through Aylmer, Bullinger and the Zürich divines became regular correspondents of his pupil Lady Jane and assisted her with sound advice, good books and study guides. Aylmer wrote on 29 May, 1551:

"Since we are accustomed, most accomplish sir, to regard any favours conferred upon our friends as extending also to ourselves, I must consider

---

[24] *Original Letters*, Vol. I, p. 145.

myself on many accounts exceedingly indebted to your kindness; and first of all, for your having so studiously and diligently exerted yourself to instruct the family of our most noble marquis by your very learned works, and by your excellent advice to retain them in the true religion. For, believe me, the letters of that holy man Bucer, whom when alive we reverenced as a father, and the remembrance of whom, now that he is no more, we most constantly retain as of a messenger of God; and also your own letters, which you sent to my most noble patron, were of great use both to confirm his stedfastness in the religion we had embraced, and also to rouse and stir up the minds of those who had begun to be either inactive through length of time, or fastidious through weariness of the subject in which we profess an interest, or careless through levity and fickleness of disposition. For they always thought it right to submit to your authority, and to follow your important admonitions. And as to myself, whenever my lord placed in my hands, either Bucer's letters, or your own, (and he always received them from both of you with the greatest satisfaction,) I used to consider myself as highly favoured in being the guardian of such valued treasures. For as often as I read them over, I seemed to myself to hold converse with the two most precious lights of the church of Christ. In the next place, the singular regard you entertain towards my pupil, compels me to declare my respect for you, if in no other way, at least by letter. For what favour more useful to herself, or gratifying to the marquis, or acceptable to me, can possibly be afforded her, not only by you, but also by any other person of equal learning and piety, than that she, whom her father loves as a daughter, and whom I look upon with affection as a pupil, may derive such maxims of conduct from your godly breast, as may assist her towards living well and happily? And you are well able to determine, in your wisdom, how useful are the counsels of the aged to guide and direct young persons at her time of life, which is just fourteen."[25]

As Jane grew in grace and a knowledge of her saviour, Mary who had been very close to Jane before she entered her teens became more alienated

[25] Ibid, pp. 275-277.

from her. Though often at court, Jane refused to adorn herself with the rich, decorative but unbecoming clothes of the court ladies. Noticing this, Mary strove to tempt her into vanity by sending her a most costly garment decorated with jewels. Jane replied, "Nay that were a shame to follow my lady Mary, who leaveth God's word, and leave my lady Elizabeth, who followeth God's word."[26] This incident and the fact that Jane refused to courtsy before the host hung up for worship in Mary's quarters, were two of Mary's reasons for martyring her relation and one time friend.

Jane's great talents did not escape Ulmis who wrote to Pellican at Zürich University on her behalf in May, 1551 as Her Ladyship had told him that she wished to learn Hebrew. In this letter, Ulmis tells the learned Reformed scholar and Bible translator:

"I am more bold in writing to you by reason of the daughter of the most noble the marquis of Dorset, a lady who is well versed both in Greek and Latin, and who is now especially desirous of studying Hebrew. I have been staying with her these two days: she is inquiring of me the best method of acquiring that language, and cannot easily discover the path which she may pursue with credit and advantage. She has written to Bullinger upon this subject; but, if I guess right, he will be very willing to transfer the office to you, both because he is always overwhelmed with affairs of greater importance, and because all the world is aware of your perfect knowledge of that language. If therefore you are willing to oblige a powerful and eminent nobleman with honour to yourself, you will by no means refuse this office and duty to his daughter. It is an important and honourable employment, and one too of great use. The young lady is the daughter of the marquis, and is to be married, as I hear, to the king. By your acceding to my request, she will be more easily kept in her distinguished course of learning; the marquis also will be made more steadfast in religion, and I shall appear to be neither unmindful of, nor ungrateful for, the favours conferred by them upon myself.

---

[26] Quoted from *Original Letters*, Vol. I, pp. 278-279.

You will perhaps say, 'I shall seem to have but very little modesty, in writing to a young lady, the daughter of a nobleman, and one too not even personally known to me.' But believe me, you need not entertain any fears of this kind. for I well know how great is the reputation of your name in this country; how influential the weight of your character, how venerated is your old age; and I wish you too to remember this, namely, that bashfulness is considered by philosophers as a defect in old men. Put away, therefore, all awkward excuses and take in hand the business itself. I promise you, indeed, and solemnly pledge myself, that I will bear all the blame, if you ever repent of this deed, or if the marquis's daughter do not most willingly acknowledge your courtesy. Write therefore a letter to her as soon as possible, in which you will briefly point out a method of learning the sacred language, and then honourably consecrate to her name your Latin translation of the Jewish Talmud. You will easily understand the extent of her attainments by the letter which she wrote to Bullinger. In truth, I do not think that among all the English nobility for many ages past there has arisen a single individual, who, to the highest excellences of talent and judgment has united so much diligence and assiduity in the cultivation of every liberal pursuit. For she is not only conversant with the more polite accomplishments, and with ordinary acquirements, but has also so exercised herself in the practice of speaking and arguing with propriety both in Greek and Latin, that it is incredible how far she has advanced already, and to what perfection she will advance in a few years; for I well know that she will complete what she has begun, unless perhaps she be diverted from her pursuits by some calamity of the times. But I have said too much upon this subject. Do you, reverend father, I pray you, only take my request in such part as my extreme respect for you or your kindness towards me requires; and I doubt not but that you will accomplish by your learning and diligence at the very first opportunity whatever shall seem most proper to be done. If you write a letter to her, take care, I pray you, that it be first delivered to me."[27]

[27] *Original Letters*, Vol. II, pp. 432-433.

Lady Jane's correspondence with Bullinger

Lady Jane had a deep trust in and knowledge of the Saviour and became so familiar with the Word of God and the original languages of the Scriptures that when she wrote to Bullinger in Latin, she quoted Scripture references from the original texts. Lady Jane had been brilliantly coached by Martin Bucer who died in February, 1551, after which she grew to depend more and more on Bullinger for her spiritual support, calling him the 'the father of learning'. Happily, several letters of Lady Jane to Bullinger have been preserved and testify not only to her great talents but also to the high respect the English Protestant nobility had for their Swiss mentor. Three of Lady Jane's original letters are preserved today in the Zürich City Library. Not yet fourteen years of age, Jane wrote the following remarkable letter to Bullinger on 12 July, 1551:

"I give you, most learned sir, unceasing thanks, and shall do so as long as I live, for I cannot engage to requite the obligation; as I seem to myself quite unable to make a suitable return for such exceeding courtesy, unless indeed you should be of opinion that I return a favour while I retain it in my remembrance. Nor are these professions made without reason. For I have received from you a most weighty and eloquent epistle, which was indeed very gratifying to me, not only because, to the neglect of more important engagements, you have condescended to write from so distant a country, and in your declining age, to me, who am unworthy of the correspondence of so distinguished a personage; but also because your writings are of such a character, as that they contain, not mere ordinary topics for amusement, but pious and divine thoughts for instruction, admonition and counsel, on such points especially, as are suited to my age and sex and the dignity of my family. In this epistle, as in every thing else that you have published to the great edification of the christian commonwealth, you have shewn. yourself not only a man of exquisite learning and singular acquirement, but also a skilful, prudent, and godly counsellor; one who can relish nothing that is not excellent, think nothing that is not divine, enjoin nothing that is not profitable, and produce nothing that is not virtuous, pious, and worthy of so reverend a father. Oh! happy me, to be possessed of such a friend and so wise a counsellor! (for, as Solomon says, 'in the multitude of counsellors there is safety;') and to be connected by the ties of friendship and intimacy with so learned a man, so pious a divine, and so intrepid a champion of true religion! On many accounts I consider myself beholden to Almighty God; but especially for having, after I was bereaved of the pious Bucer, that most learned man and holy father, who unweariedly did not cease, day and night, and to the utmost of his ability, to supply me with all necessary instructions and directions for my conduct in life; and who by his excellent advice promoted and encouraged my progress and advancement in all virtue, godliness, and learning; for having, I say, afforded me in his place a man so worthy to be reverenced as yourself, and who, I hope, will continue, as you have begun, to spur me on, when I loiter and am inclined to delay. For no better fortune can await me than to be thought worthy of the correspondence and most wholesome admonitions of men so renowned, whose virtues cannot be sufficiently eulogized; and to experience the same happiness as was enjoyed by Blesilla, Paula, and Eustochium, to whom, as it is recorded, Saint Jerome imparted instruction, and brought them by his discourses to the knowledge of divine truths; or, the happiness of that venerable matron, to whom St John addressed an exhortatory and evangelical epistle; or that, lastly, of the mother of Severus, who profited by the counsels of Origen, and was obedient to his precepts. All which personages were less indebted for their renown and celebrity to their beauty of person, nobility of birth, and large possessions, than to the glory and happiness they derived from the instructions of wise men, who, though singularly eminent for erudition and piety, did not disdain to lead them, as it were, by the hand to every thing excellent, and to suggest to them such thoughts as might especially conduce to their eternal salvation and happiness in the life to come. And I request again and again, that as you cannot be deemed inferior to any of these in understanding, or learning, or godliness, you will condescend to manifest a like kindness to myself. My unreserved requests may carry with them an appearance of boldness; but if you will consider the motive by which I am actuated, namely, that I may draw forth from the storehouse of your piety such instruction as may tend both to direct my conduct, and confirm my faith in Christ my Saviour, your goodness cannot, and your wisdom will not, allow you to censure them.

From that little volume of pure and unsophisticated religion, which you lately sent to my father and myself, I gather daily, as out of a most beautiful garden, the sweetest flowers. My father also, as far as his weighty engagements permit, is diligently occupied in the perusal of it: but whatever advantage either of us may derive from thence, we are bound to render thanks to you for it, and to God on your account; for we cannot think it right to receive with ungrateful minds such and so many truly divine benefits, conferred by Almighty God through the instrumentality of yourself and those like you, not a few of whom Germany is now in this respect so happy as to possess. If it be customary with mankind, as indeed it ought to be, to return favour for favour, and to shew ourselves mindful of benefits bestowed; how much rather should we endeavour to embrace with joyfulness the benefits conferred by divine goodness, and at least to acknowledge them with our gratitude, though we my be unable to make an adequate return!

I now come to that part of your letter which contains a commendation of myself, which as I cannot claim, so also I ought not to allow: but whatever the divine goodness may have bestowed upon me, I ascribe solely to himself, as the chief and sole author of any thing in me that bears any semblance of what is good; and to whom I entreat you, most accomplished sir, to offer your constant prayers on my behalf, that he may so direct me and all my actions, that I may not be found unworthy of his so great goodness. My most noble father would have written to you, to thank you both for the important labours in which you are engaged, and also for the singular courtesy you have manifested by inscribing with his name and publishing under his auspices your fifth Decade, had he not been summoned by most weighty business in his majesty's service to the remotest parts of Britain; but as soon as public affairs shall afford him leisure, he is determined, he says, to write you with all diligence. To conclude, as I am now beginning to learn Hebrew, if you will point out some way and method of pursuing this study to the greatest advantage you will confer on me a very great obligation.

Farewell, brightest ornament and support of the whole church of Christ; and may Almighty God long preserve you to us and to his church!

Your most devoted,
Jane Grey.[28]

In one of Lady Jane's letters, probably written in the summer of 1553, when her sufferings were increasing, we see something of herself reflected in her description of Bullinger. She tells her Swiss mentor, "For God, it seems, has looked upon you with such complacency as to have you fitted for his kingdom and for this world: for in this earthly prison you pass your days, as though you were dead; whereas you live, and this not only to Christ in the first place, without whom there can be no life, and in the next place to yourself; but also to others without number, whom you strenuously labour and assiduously endeavour to bring, by God's blessing, to that immortality which, when you shall have departed this life, you will obtain yourself."[29] At this time, Jane was more and more separating herself from the cares of the world and using the freedom of her state to learn more of the Scriptures and encourage others to follow Christ. In this letter to Bullinger, Jane reveals that she had some apprehension that her life, midst the political intrigues of her day would be short. Speaking of both Bullinger and Bibliander, she closes with the words, "And I pray God that such pillars of the church as you both are, may long enjoy good health. As long as I shall be permitted to live, I shall not cease to offer you my good wishes, to thank you for the kindness you have shewed me, and to pray for your welfare."

Soon after writing this letter, Lady Jane was committed to the Tower by her papist tormentor Mary. Various armed protests at Mary's brutal seizing of the throne took her mind off the true Queen of England for a season but on 12 February, 1554 the young girl was despatched into eternity by the woman who has gone down in history as 'Bloody Mary'.

[28] Ibid, Vol. I, pp. 4-7.
[29] Ibid, pp. 10-11.

The story goes that before being martyred, Lady Jane took off her gloves and asked that they be immediately sent to Bullinger. Büsser claims that this is a legend first aired by Johan Conrad Füessli in 1742. Nevertheless Büsser adds that Büllinger's family did indeed receive Lady Jane's gloves as if to confess that there must be some truth in the legend after all.

The Troublemakers at Frankfurt

Typical of the letters from Englishmen in exile who had profited from Bullinger's hospitality, fellowship and instruction during the Marian persecutions was that of Robert Horne and Richard Chambers dated 3 February, 1556, at Frankfurt where they had joined the English refugee church during first Lever's, then David Whitehead's pastorate. Horne was to become pastor of the church himself. The two men write:

"But if we should here attempt to enumerate all the benefits you have conferred upon us, it would probably be too disagreeable to yourself, who prefer rather to be active in doing good, than to have the reputation of it; and it would also be too troublesome a task for ourselves. For how much should we have to record of your counsel, sympathy, and protection! You it was, who conciliated to us the good will of your townsmen, and who procured the munificence of the government to be extended towards us. Nor did you content yourself merely with obtaining for us the good offices both of your family and your country; but in addition to this, by letters to those at a distance, you occasioned the liberality of other and unknown individuals to be poured out upon us from all quarters. By your writings also you sought to reach even those our friends at home, by whose kindness we have been supported; and this, that you might not be behind hand in exciting them to so godly a purpose, and in aiding us that we should not be deprived of their assistance.[30]

Frankfurt was the largest and one of the earliest English refugee churches on the Continent and drew most of the English refugees from

[30] *Original Letters*, Vol. I, pp. 129-130.

other parts of Germany such as Duisburg and Wesel where Lutheran opposition had made their sojourn impossible. A large contingent also joined them from Strasburg. The church had been set up with the strong backing of Bullinger who had arranged that Thomas Lever should pastor them. Bullinger also supported Cox who represented the majority of English refugees in bringing peace back to Frankfurt after severe troubles caused by John Knox. Wishing to set up a church on quite different lines, Knox ignored the majority vote of the church members, refused to accept the various Reformed orders used by the church[31] and protested especially against lay participation in responses and the public reading of the Word. He formed a small group of rebels who backed him for a time. To justify their action, Knox and Whittingham sent a most erroneous report to Calvin, enclosing a garbled Latin nigh-popish liturgy which they claimed was used by Lever, Cox, Foxe, Sampson, Humphrey, Grindal and the other sound men at Frankfurt. At the time the church was using a highly modified form of Edward's 1552 Prayer Book, altered to suit the needs of the French and Dutch worshippers who had joined them in Frankfurt and the specifications of the Frankfurt Senate. Knox and Whittingham withheld this information from Calvin, and, in order to stress their own innocence concerning the troubles they were causing, merely expressed their fears of how the church might evolve without their leadership as if they were based on facts. This polemical method, which William Turner called 'a literary exercise' was sadly used by both sides during the vestment controversy;[32] the idea being to paint a picture as black as possible so that people would be motivated to take an opposite stand. This method was widely used by the modern playwright Arthur Miller, who in presenting the American Puritans as representing 'Absolute Evil' in his *The Crucible*, felt that he could persuade his audiences to adopt a more liberal course. This act almost caused the English Reformed movement to split in two and the wounds are still present in today's Reformed churches, especially in circles where

---

[31] Strasburg, English, French and Genevan orders.

[32] See Turner's criticism of Bullinger's suspected 'literary exercise' in *Zürich Letters*, Second Series, pp. 124-126.

Episcopacy (the so-called Coxians) and Presbyterianism (the so-called Knoxians) are compared controversially. This, however, is a back-projecting of later troubles onto the Frankfurt situation which has no basis in historical fact. Cox was not a rigid Episcopalian by any means and Knox's views of the ministry, especially at this time, were far removed from Presbyterianism. Knox's ruse had to fail as he apparently did not know that the real confessions of the church had been printed in German in Zürich and the order of service was readily available in French for Calvin to read in his own language and thus gain clear insight into what the Frankfurt Christians really believed. The English, according to Knox, used popish ceremonies such as kneeling at communion, private baptisms, the use of crucifixes and candles and wished to maintain a hierarchy of clergy who would not allow the church members to vote themselves concerning their pastors. In a sudden dislike of all things English, Knox summed up his arguments by accusing the English of wanting to give their church 'an English face'. All these accusations were totally false.[33] Though Whittingham modified his criticism a good deal and even Knox gradually became more open to the Frankfurt Englishmen's form of Reformation which triumphed later in the Genevan English Church, a number of English Separatists continued to feed Bullinger, Gualter, Calvin and Beza with rumours of Anti-Reformed practices amongst the very best of England's Reformers so that Calvin and Beza accepted these rumours without question. After Mary's death, and as the vestment controversy continued, even Bullinger and Gualter, began to accept the malicious tales as true because they could not believe that men of good reputation would deceive them. Actually the approximately 350 English who worshipped at the Frankfurt church between 1554 and 1559 and returned to lead the Church of England were most non-conformist[34] in their worship and discipline and abhorred the

---

[33] See *A Brief Discourse of the Troubles at Frankfurt 1554-1558*, especially pp. 44-49 and my discussion of this attempt to deceive Calvin in *The Troublemakers at Frankfurt* pp. 145-170.

[34] The term 'Nonconformist' during this period did not refer to Separatists but to Anglicans who were freer with their forms of church order.

exact and absolute externalism of their critics who, they thought, mistook law for gospel. They looked upon the way the Knoxian rebels had misrepresented them as scandalous.[35] Far from imposing Roman ritualism in Latin on the Frankfort church, Cox had led the church into voting almost unanimously to adopt the Reformed French system of worship pioneered by Bucer and Poullain which was more acceptable to the other foreign churches in Frankfurt and also to the Frankfurt Senate. On returning to England, Cox risked the Queen's anger by refusing to officiate in her chapel until she removed the crucifix. On the other hand, when Knox returned to Scotland, and was required to use the Edwardian order he had declared to be 'popish' and was criticised strongly for the 'English face' he gave the Scottish church, he conformed. Indeed, one humorous critic pointed out that Knox used numerous popish ceremonies which the Protestant churches considered 'un-Reformed' and that he fought against Protestants with far greater energy than he fought against Rome.[36] Ninian Winzet listed over four score such criticisms concerning Knox's apparent neglect to follow Scriptural practices whilst professing that he based all his beliefs on Scripture.[37] It became a sad joke amongst the English Reformers that though Knox called them 'popish' and worse, there were no Roman Catholic processions in England but whilst Knox was allegedly ruling a Reformed Scottish church with an iron Reformed hand, the papists were parading through Edinburgh holding banners and effigies of St Giles high and even in Reformed churches 'creeping to the altar' was still practised.

David Whitehead and Richard Cox rectify Knox's false picture of the Frankfurt nonconformists

Thus, when Knox was asked to leave Frankfurt by the church majority and the city senate in March, 1555 for the sake of peace, both Pastor David Whitehead and Richard Cox wrote to Calvin, who had temporarily

[35] See Letter CCCLVII, Richard Cox and Others to John Calvin and Letter CCCLVIII, David Whitehead and Others to John Calvin, *Original Letters 2*.

[36] See Hugh Watt's *John Knox in Controversy*, Nelson & Sons, 1950

[37] See Winzet's *Book of Four Score and Three Question* and *The Last Blast of the Trumpet.*

backed Knox, to tell the Frenchman that his protégé had let his notorious bad temper (so John Foxe) and polemical rhetoric run away with him and that was the root of all the 'troubles at Frankfurt'. Actually, Whitehead said that Knox's behaviour had been criminal.[38] A little more diplomatic, Cox wrote:

"Though we are very loth to suspect our brethren of any thing that savours of insincerity, we are nevertheless somewhat afraid that the whole affair and case has not been set before you with sufficient explicitness. For neither are we so entirely wedded to our country, as not to be able to endure any customs differing from our own; nor is the authority of those fathers and martyrs of Christ so much regarded by us, as that we have any scruple in thinking or acting in opposition to it. And we have not only very frequently borne witness to this by our assertions, but have at length proved it by our actions. For when the magistrates lately gave us permission to adopt the rites of our native country, we freely relinquished all those ceremonies which were regarded by our brethren as offensive and inconvenient. For we gave up private baptisms. confirmation of children, saints' days, kneeling at the holy communion, the linen surplices of the ministers, crosses, and other things of the like character .... We retain however the remainder of the form of prayer and of the administration of the sacraments, which is prescribed in our book (the 1552 Book of Common Prayer, commonly called 'the Reformed Book'), and this with the consent of almost the whole church, the judgment of which in matters of this sort we did not think should be disregarded. With the consent likewise of the same church there was forthwith appointed one pastor, two preachers, four elders, two deacons; the greatest care being taken that every one should be at perfect liberty to vote as he pleased; except only that by the command of the magistrate, before the election took place, were set forth those articles lately published by the authority of king Edward, which contained a summary of our doctrine, and which we were all of us required to subscribe. For

[38] Letter to Calvin dated 20 September, 1555, *Original Letters*, Vol. II, pp. 755-763.

what kind of an election, they said, must be expected, unless the voters shall previously have agreed as to doctrine? Certain parties, who had before manifested some objection, subscribed to these articles of their own accord. Some few declined doing so, of whose peaceableness nevertheless we entertain good hope.

We have thought fit to write thus fully to your kindness, that you might ascertain the whole course of our proceedings from ourselves. Our liturgy is translated into French, and the articles above mentioned have very lately been printed at Zürich. Did we not suppose that they would easily be met with among you, we should take care that copies should be forwarded you. But we pray your kindness not to imagine that we have aimed at any thing else throughout this whole business, and this we testify before the Lord, than the purification of our church, and the avoiding of most grievous stumbling-blocks which otherwise seemed to be hanging over us."[39]

The full letter was signed not only by Richard Cox but also such Reformation stalwarts as David Whitehead, Thomas Becon, Edwin Sandys, Edmund Grindal, John Bale, Robert Horne, Thomas Lever and Thomas Sampson.

Bullinger was always frightened that the Genevans and their supporters would end up like the Anabaptists in their too close identification of external discipline with the witness of the true church. This had been Knox's grave error at Frankfurt. The Zürich pastor saw, in particular, the danger of a church wielding the sword of excommunication too freely. When Calvin, Farel and Viret strove to enforce a severe form of excommunication in their churches and reintroduced forms of auricular confession towards the end of 1543, Bullinger believed they were, in fact, putting externals before the true nature of the church and thus destroying the communion of the saints. He thus wrote to a fellow-pastor on 22 November, 1543:

---

[39] Ibid, Vol. II, pp. 753-755.

"I do not doubt, that our dear French brethren are not motivated by evil. I have read what Calvin says in his *Institutes* concerning excommunication and he will in my opinion not deny that one must be very careful in estimating the situation so that the peace of the Church will not be disturbed in which, above all, one must protect the wheat so that it will not be thrown out with the chaff. Amongst enemies of the Word, some would very much desire that we re-introduce excommunication because they hope, not without reason, that our Church will soon fall apart in numerous sects. I would prefer to retain any Church than have none .... Concerning the examining (of worshippers) before attending the Lord's Table, I can only conclude that it is a preparation for auricular confession, that corrupt evil in the Church. One introduces confession again and builds a fence around the Lord's Supper so that only a few Table guests may partake of it and the meal of thanksgiving becomes a torturing of the conscience."[40]

Bullinger could write in this way because he believed that if the Genevan and Vaud Reformers were left to themselves and pulled out of the Swiss Reformation as they from time to time threatened, they would become sacramentalists and lead their Reformed churches back to Rome. That this fear was not groundless is shown by Calvin's and Farel's own correspondence in which they discussed introducing either private confessions before attending the Lord's Supper or the full auricular confession as a church rite. Calvin wrote to Farel from Strasburg in May, 1540 to say, "I have often declared to you that it did not appear to me to be expedient that confessions should be abolished in the churches, unless that which I have lately taught be substituted in the place of it."[41] When referring to Calvin's desire to reinstate auricular confessions, Horton Davies comments: "There is little doubt that the Puritans would have regarded the re-introduction of auricular Confessions as a re-

---

[40] Kolfhaus, *Der Verkehr Calvins mit Bullinger*, p. 37.
[41]John Calvin Collection: Ages Library CD. Calvin's 'substitution' was private confessions before taking communion.

establishment of the prerogatives of the priesthood."[42] When this news reached Zürich, Bullinger told Farel:

"You stand so high in our esteem of your learnedness and integrity that we cannot suspect, let alone believe, that you are capable of such a thing. If we enforced folly so far that we allowed nobody to partake of the Lord's Supper without enquiring beforehand about their faith, what would that be, my Farel, but a preparation for a return to the auricular confessions of the papists? We must beware, honourable Farel of walking on papist paths after taking up the holy rules of the Apostles."[43]

Not realising that Zürich was keeping to Reformed paths in the spirit whereas Geneva was tending to enforce the letter, in England a small group of men led by such as Bartholomew Traheron and Thomas Cartwright began to take on a more stringent legalist and philosophical approach to theology whereas the bulk of the English Reformers followed the example of Hooper and kept close to the German-Swiss Reformation.

The dangers of dividing outward and inward conformity in church life

Once back in England, Horne and Edmund Grindal, both old friends of Bullinger's and now bishops, wrote to him often, especially during the 1560s, requesting help in restoring the Reformed Church of England. They were particularly interested in the relationship of the Christian to civil laws and the wider problems of state-Church relationships. Above all, however, they were eager to have Bullinger's advice concerning the vestment controversy which was threatening to split the Reformers. Several of the exiles were striving to introduce new forms of clerical wear which they claimed were marks of a truly Reformed Church, whereas Anglican vestments, they argued, were either Jewish or popish. Bullinger responded with his *Epistola ad Episcopos et fratres in Anglia* in which he declared that the Church of England was correct in her understanding of

[42] *The Worship of the English Puritans*, p. 44.
[43] Kolfhaus, *Der Verkehr Calvins mit Bullinger*, p. 37.

the vestments as 'things indifferent' which were a mere matter of usage. Many of these troublemakers, mistakenly believing that Calvin, who wore Continental-style vestments, supported their legalistic and separatist enthusiasm, claimed that they were 'Calvinists' and therefore true supporters of the Swiss Reformation. Bullinger, Gualter, Beza and Calvin all wrote to the rebels, appropriately named *Precisians*, telling them that they had not only misinterpreted the Swiss Reformation, but they had also misinformed their Swiss advisers as to the state of the English Church and were misusing Switzerland's good name by insisting on forcing imagined Continental externals onto the English Church. Grindal gives a minute account of this more-Calvinist-than-Calvin movement in his letter to Bullinger of 11 June, 1568.[44] It appears by this time that the Precisians in London had set up rival churches of some 200 members in all, ordained their own ministers, elders and deacons, celebrated the Lord's Supper together and emphasised church discipline and order. They had already begun to split up into various Separatist movements by exercising excommunication against one another. Grindal points out that those 'Puritans' who were thought to be the most radical of Reformers such as Dean Laurence Humphrey, Dean Thomas Sampson and Pastor Thomas Lever would have nothing to do with this rebel church. These three men were regular correspondents of Bullinger and close friends. The Separatists thus called these 'Bullingerites' 'semi-papists' and forbade them and their followers to attend their preaching. This trouble is indeed the origin of the myth that Bullinger strove to introduce another Reformation than that of Calvin, though the externals they set up as signs of a true church were not to be found in Geneva. The mention of Lever, Humphrey and Sampson is of note as they worked with Cox in bringing peace between the Anglican Reformers at Frankfurt and those at Geneva after troubles caused by John Knox during the Marian persecutions.

Some English editions of the *Decades* appended several letters of Bullinger to Laurence Humphrey, Thomas Sampson, Robert Horne, John Parkhurst and Edmund Grindal under the title *Epistles concerning the*

[44] *Zürich Letters I*, pp. 201-202. See also pp. 175-181.

Apparell of Ministers and other indifferent things. The Precisians or Ultra-Puritans in England had written to Bullinger and Gualter, complaining that ministers of the Reformed Church of England were officiating at the Lord's Table in full popish regalia. Thus Bullinger wrote condemning such a practice and the Precisians published the letter as a condemnation of the Church of England. On making enquiries, the Swiss Reformers found out that they had been misinformed as those ministers mentioned had worn the usual clerical hat as used in Switzerland, including Geneva, and a white surplice only. Bullinger discussed the subject with Sampson and Humphrey who were against vestments but would not join the militant Ultra-Puritans and had suffered much from their tongues and pens. He also wrote to the three bishops Horne, Grindal and Parkhurst as they were his close friends, moderate men and such who carried great influence in the Church of England. Bullinger's strong criticism of both those who made vestments their religion but also those who made the destruction of order equally their religion became the dominating position of the Church of England. Bullinger became irritated with the rebels' petty complaints and had little patience with their individual and changing moods and their holier-than-thou approach to Christian debate. Sampson, in particular, who joined the extremists for a time, annoyed Bullinger by his negative attitude and he told Beza on 15 March, 1567:

"I have always looked with suspicion upon the statements made by master Sampson. He is not amiss in other respects, but of an exceeding restless disposition. While he resided amongst us at Zürich, and after he returned to England, he never ceased to be troublesome to master Peter Martyr of blessed memory. He often used to complain to me, that Sampson never wrote a letter without filling it with grievances: the man is never satisfied; he has always some doubt or other to busy himself with. As often as he began, when he was here, to lay his plans before me, I used to get rid of him in a friendly way, as well knowing him to be a man of a captious and unquiet disposition. England has many characters of this sort, who cannot be at rest, who can never be satisfied, and who have always something or other to complain about. I have certainly a natural dislike to men of this stamp."[45]

Bullinger cannot be said to have been biased in any way concerning the English problem as he, unlike his Genevan counterparts, wore neither a gown, not a tippet, nor a clergyman's hat. Bullinger, however, neither quarrelled with the Genevan view of clerical dress nor the vestments used in Bern or Basle nor with the Reformed Church of England's custom, nor even with his fellow Zürich ministers over the gala gowns they sometimes wore but argued that such secondary matters were merely restricted to utility and local traditions in clothing.[46] In 1565, whilst the vestiarian controversy was raging, and to testify to his own deep fellowship with the Church of England, Bullinger dedicated his collection of sermons on Daniel (*Conciones in Danielem*) to five of his closest friends who were bishops in that Church. These were Robert Horne, John Jewel, Edwin Sandys, John Parkhurst and James Pilkington.

It is, however, not to a minister of the Church but to an English merchant friend of Bullinger's, John Abel that we are indebted for a general description of the English vestment controversy. Abel wrote to Bullinger on 6 June, 1566 in German, bringing him up to date on the topic, writing:

"Praise to God! My friendly greeting and willing service to you, my kind and dear sir. Your last letter of March 20th has come duly to hand; from which I understand that you have received my former letters. I have also received two copies of your Swiss Confession of Faith; one of which, written in Latin, I have, according to your request, given to master Richard Hilles, who expresses his best thanks. This book pleases me and many believing hearts exceedingly. But I am still more

[45] *Zürich Letters*, Second Series, p. 152.

[46] The long black gown of the Swiss-German churches and the white ruff was the usual gala dress of the upper class. As this went out of fashion, it was retained by the clergy. Bullinger did not condemn this but did not follow the usage, either.

delighted with your house-book, containing fifty of your sermons, and bearing the Latin title *Decades Bullingeri*. In this book all the articles of our christian faith are fully declared and set forth, and it is comforting, and agreeable, and instructive to me to read it.

Your letters to master Horne, bishop of Winchester, and masters Jewel and Parkhurst, I have duly forwarded; and master Horne has written me word that he has received your said letters, in which you have declared your judgment respecting the cap and surplice. And he has promised me a copy of that letter, which has been of great service to many godly preachers and others, who faithfully and diligently perform their ecclesiastical functions. Some persons, however, are not satisfied with it, those namely, who have thought fit rather to give up the office of a preacher and minister than wear a surplice in the administration of the holy sacraments, or put on a clerical cap. So rigid are they in their opinion, that they have altogether given up their ecclesiastical vocation, and are therefore deposed from their ministry: which is greatly to be regretted, especially as they need not put on a surplice when preaching, as indeed nobody is commanded to do, except in the administration of infant baptism and of the Lord's supper. Master Thomas Sampson has written you a letter upon this subject, and desires to receive your answer; because he is foremost in opposition to this practice, and his given up his preferment: and several other preachers have joined him, who are resolved rather to resign their functions than wear the cap and surplice. Five preachers have lately been deprived, and sent as prisoners, two of them to master Horne, bishop of Winchester, two to doctor Cox, bishop of Ely, and one to master Parkhurst, bishop of Norwich. These five preachers had been interdicted from preaching, but notwithstanding the prohibition, they again preached in their respective churches, in consequence of which our queen and privy council are much displeased. They were summoned before the queen's council, and when they made their appearance, much was said to them for having preached contrary to the queen's orders, and for having afforded a bad example to the common people, so as to render them disobedient. Whereupon the five preachers fell upon their knees, and asked for mercy: in reply to which the lords in council answered, that if the queen were not merciful and gracious, they would all have had to undergo severe punishment; but, seeing that they were preachers of God's holy word, they should have eight days allowed them wherein to visit their friends and connections, after which they were to proceed, two to the bishop of Winchester, and two to the bishop of Ely, and one to the bishop of Norwich, as prisoners, as above mentioned, so long as the queen and her council shall think fit. One of these preachers has also caused to be printed a book against the queen's command respecting the cap and surplice: but as soon as the authorities heard of it, the book was prohibited, the printers cast into prison, and the copies destroyed: Another book was afterwards published by order of the commissioners, wherein is declared the judgment of master doctor Peter Martyr and master Bucer, viz. that every preacher and minister ecclesiastical may wear a surplice, cap, and the other habits, without committing any sin, as you and master Gualter have also written. The opposite party are much dissatisfied with this, and, as far as they dare, write secretly against it; so that, unless our gracious God afford us his aid and support, it is to be feared that it will occasion much hindrance to the spread of the gospel. But our Lord God, I trust, is gracious and full of compassion, and will help us to establish unity and peace, so that the cruel fiend may not occasion a schism.

All things are going on pretty well in Scotland, and all the exiled nobles and lords have returned to their country, and are in possession of their lands and property. The gospel (praised be God!) is still preached, and I hope all will be quiet; for the exiled lords are magistrates in that country. The queen of Scotland, I hear, is in the family way,[47] and expects to be confined within a week. I have nothing else to write to you at present. Salute, I pray you, all my good masters and friends. The grace of God be with us all! Amen.

Yours ever,

JOHN ABEL, England.

---

[47] Mary Stuart gave birth to her son James on 19 June, 1566. After ruling over Scotland for a time as King James VI , he became James I of England, joint King of both realms.

We see from this letter that there were no rigid laws concerning vestments at the time and there was a freedom in the English Church otherwise not known in other Reformed churches outside of Zürich. However, the Precisians would not admit of this leniency and demanded strict laws in Parliament regulating the matter more thoroughly to their satisfaction and gained backing from the secular, radical nobility. This caused Archbishops Parker, Grindal and Whitgift in particular and Convocation in general to emphasise the right of clergy to wear a square cap rather than a round one and a white robe rather than a black one so much that laws were made making them statutory whereas formerly they had been voluntary except for certain occasions. Much has been made in Separatist apologetics concerning the imprisonment of the five men mentioned, describing it as severe persecution. These men, however, were disciplined by their evangelical colleagues who only differed from them in that they were less severe concerning externals. Instead of the severe penalties the law could have enforced on them, we have Archbishop Parker's testimony and that of Church Historian Strype that the discipline was most light and of a very short duration and soon all five were preaching again. Rather than Sampson having to suffer the Royal displeasure for long, he was soon granted the Queen's favour at Parker's request, became a Prebend of St Paul's and was given the mastership of William de Wigston Hospital (College) at Leicester and also was made Lecturer in Theology at Whittington College. Had these dissidents been in Geneva, they would have suffered a much sterner treatment.

Bullinger answers the critics

Sampson and Humphrey, who reflected the views of many nonconformists, bombarded Bullinger with questions concerning vestments and clerical habits from 1565 to 1573. Bullinger replied at length, sometimes writing himself, sometimes writing with Gualter and, especially in his last lengthy illness, sometimes asking Gualter to answer on behalf of the Zürich ministers.[48] On 1 May, 1566, Bullinger listed all the questions that Sampson and Humphrey had put to him and answered them in full.

"1. To the question, *whether laws respecting habits ought to be prescribed to ecclesiastics, that they may be distinguished by them from the laity,* I reply, that there is an ambiguity in the word ought. For if it is taken as implying what is necessary and appertaining to salvation, I do not think that even the authors of the laws themselves intend such an interpretation. But if it is asserted, that for the sake of decency, and comeliness of appearance, or dignity and order, some such regulation may be made, or some such thing be understood, as that which the apostle requires, namely, that a bishop or minister of the church should be *kosmios*, (I mean *decent* or orderly,) I do not see how he is to blame, who either adopts a habit of this sort himself, or who commands it to be worn by others.

2. *Whether the ceremonial worship of the Levitical priesthood is to be reintroduced into the church?* I reply, if a cap and habit not unbecoming a minister, and free from superstition, are commanded to be used by the clergy, no one can reasonably assert that Judaism is revived. Moreover, I will here repeat the answer that I see doctor Martyr made to this question, who, after having shewed that the sacraments of the old law had been abolished, and ought not to be reintroduced into the church of Christ, which has [those of] baptism and the Lord's supper, subjoined, "there were notwithstanding in the Levitical law some ordinances of such a character, as that they cannot properly be called sacraments; for they served unto decency and order, and a certain becomingness, which, as agreeable to the light of nature, and furthering some utility of ours, I judge, may not only be restored but retained. Who seeth not that the apostles for quietness sake, and for the better living together of believers commanded the gentiles to abstain from things strangled and from blood? These things were beyond dispute legal and Levitical. Also, no man is

[48] These letters are printed in an Appendix to the *Zürich Letters*, First Series, Parker Society, pp. 345-356.

ignorant that at this day tithes are instituted in many places for the support of ministers. It is most evident too, that psalms and hymns are sung in the holy assemblies, which nevertheless the Levites also practised. And, not to omit this, we have feast days in remembrance of our Lord's resurrection, and other things. Are all these things to be abolished because they are traces of the old law? You see then, that all the Levitical rites are not to be so abrogated, as that none of them may be lawfully retained." Thus far Peter Martyr.

3. *Whether is it allowable to have a habit in common, with papists?* I answer, it is not yet proved that the pope introduced a distinction of habits into the church; so far from it, that it is clear that such distinction is long anterior to popery. Nor do I see why it should be unlawful to use, in common with papists, a vestment not superstitious, but pertaining to civil regulation and good order. If it were not allowable to have any thing in common with them, it would be necessary to desert all the churches, to decline the receipt of stipend, to abstain from baptism, and the reciting of the apostles' and the Nicene creed, and even to reject the Lord's prayer. But after all, you do not borrow any ceremonies from them; for the use of the habits was never set aside from the beginning of the reformation; and it is still retained, not by any popish enactment, but by virtue of the royal edict, as a matter of indifference and of civil order.

4. The use therefore of a distinctive cap or habit in civil matters *savours neither of Judaism nor monachism*; for they affect to appear separated from civil life, and make a merit of their peculiar dress. Thus Eustathius, bishop of Sebastia, was condemned, not merely on account of his peculiar dress, but because he made religion to consist in that dress. The canons of the councils of Gangra, Laodicea, and the sixth synod are known. And if some of the people are led to believe that this savours of popery, Judaism, and monachism, let them be admonished and rightly instructed in these matters. And should any be disquieted by the importunate clamours of some individuals, lavishly poured forth upon this subject among the people, let those who act thus have a care, lest they should impose heavier burdens upon themselves, irritate the queen's

majesty, and end by bringing many faithful ministers into dangers from which they will hardly escape.

5. To the question, *whether those persons who have till now enjoyed their liberty, can with a safe conscience, by the authority of a royal edict, involve in this bondage both themselves and the church,* I reply, that in my opinion great caution is to be observed lest this dispute, and clamour, and contention respecting the habits should be conducted with too much bitterness, and by this importunity a handle should be afforded to the queen's majesty to leave that no longer a matter of choice to those who have abused their liberty; but being irritated by these needless clamours, she may issue her orders, that either these habits must be adopted, or the ministry relinquished. It appears indeed most extraordinary to me, (if I may be allowed, most accomplished and very dear brethren, to speak my sentiments without offence,) that you can persuade yourselves that you cannot, with a safe conscience, subject yourselves and churches to vestiarian bondage; and that you do not rather consider, to what kind of bondage you will subject yourselves and churches, if you refuse to comply with a civil ordinance, which is a matter of indifference, and are perpetually contending in this troublesome way; because, by the relinquishment of your office, you will expose the churches to wolves, or at least to teachers who are far from competent, and who are not equally fitted with yourselves for the instruction of the people. And can you be said to have asserted the liberty of the churches, who minister occasion of oppressing the church with burdens even yet more grievous? Are you not aware of what is the object of many, in what manner they are affected towards the preaching of the gospel, of what character will be those who are to succeed you, and what is to be expected from them?

6. *Whether the dress of the clergy is a matter of indifference?* It certainly seems such, when it is a matter of civil ordinance, and has respect only to decency and order, in which things religious worship does not consist. Thus, my most learned and dearly beloved brother, Laurence, have I thought fit briefly to reply to your letter. I now come also to the

questions of our friend master Sampson, in the discussion of which I shall probably be yet more brief.

1. Whether a peculiar habit, distinct from that of the laity, were ever assigned to the ministers of the church; and whether it ought now to be assigned to them in the reformed church? I reply: that there was in the primitive church a habit peculiar to the priests, is manifest from the ecclesiastical history of Theodoret, Book ii chap. 27, and of Socrates, Book vi. chap. 22. And no one who has but cursorily considered the monuments of antiquity, can be ignorant that the ministers always wore the *pallium* upon sacred occasions; so that, as I have before intimated, the distinction of habits does not derive its origin from the pope. Eusebius truly bears witness from the most ancient writers, that the apostle John at Ephesus wore on his forehead a *petalum*, or pontifical plate [of gold]; and Pontius, the deacon, relates of the martyr Cyprian, that when he was about to present his neck to the executioner, he first gave him his *birrus*, and his *dalmatic* to the deacon, and thus stood forth wearing only his linen garment. Besides, Chrysostom makes mention of the white garment of the clergy; and it is certain, that when Christians were converted from heathenism to the gospel and the church, they exchanged the toga for the *pallium*, on which account when they were ridiculed by unbelievers, Tertullian composed his most learned treatise *de pallio*. I could produce many other instances of the same kind, did not these suffice. I should prefer indeed, that no difficulties had been thrown in the way of the clergy, and that they might have been at liberty to follow the practice of the apostles. But since the queen's majesty only enjoins the wearing a cap and surplice, which, as I have often repeated, she does not in any way make a matter of religion; and since the same things were in use among the ancients, when the affairs of the church were yet more prosperous than at present, and this too without superstition or any thing to find fault with; I could wish that pious ministers would not make the whole advancement of religion to depend upon this matter, as if it were all in all; but that they would yield somewhat to the present time, and not dispute offensively about a matter of indifference, but modestly conclude that these things may be endured at present, but that an improvement will take place in time. For those persons come the nearest to apostolic simplicity, who are unconscious of these distinctions, or who do not urge them, while yet they do not act without a proper regard to discipline in the mean time.

2, 3. Whether the prescribing habits be consistent with christian liberty? I answer, that matters of indifference admit sometimes of *prescription,* and therefore of being imposed by force, as far as their use, so to speak, though not their moral effect is concerned; so that, for instance, something which is in its nature indifferent, may be obtruded upon the conscience as necessary, and thus made a matter of religion. In fact, the times and places of religious assemblies are assuredly regarded among things indifferent; and yet, if there is no *prescription* in such cases, consider, I pray, what confusion and disorder would ensue?

4. Whether any new ceremonies may be superadded to what is expressly prescribed in the word of God? I answer, that I by no means approve the addition of new ceremonies; but yet I am not prepared to deny that some may lawfully be instituted, provided the worship of God is not made to consist in them, and that they are appointed only for the sake of order and discipline. Christ himself observed the feast or ceremony of the dedication, though we do not read that this feast was prescribed in the law. On the whole, the greater part of the propositions or questions touching the vestiarian controversy turn upon this, whether laws concerning habits may or ought to be framed in the church? And it recalls the *general* question, namely, what regulations is it lawful to make concerning ceremonies! To these propositions I reply in few words, that though I would rather no ceremonies, excepting such as are necessary, should be obtruded upon the church, yet I must confess in the mean time that regulations respecting them, though possibly not altogether necessary, and sometimes, it may be, useless, ought not forthwith to be condemned as impious, and to excite disorder and schism in the church; seeing that they are not of a superstitious character, and also that in their very nature they are matters of indifference.

5, 6. Whether it be lawful to revive the antiquated ceremonies of the Jews, and to transfer such as were especially dedicated to the religion of idolaters, to the use of the reformed churches? I have before replied to this question, when I remarked touching the Levitical rites. But I should be loth that any idolatrous rites should be transferred to the reformed churches, without being purified from what is amiss in them. But it might also be demanded on the other hand, whether established ceremonies, void of superstition, may not be retained in the church without any impropriety, for the sake of discipline and order.

7. Whether conformity must of necessity be required in ceremonies? I reply, that conformity in ceremonies is perhaps not necessary in every church. Meantime however, if a thing is commanded, which, though not necessary, is on the other hand not sinful; the church, it seems to me, ought not on this account to be relinquished. There was not conformity in rites in all the more ancient churches; those, however, which adopted rites in conformity with each other, did not censure those who wanted such conformity. And I can easily believe that wise and politic men are urgent for a conformity of rites, because they think it will tend to concord, and that there may be one and the same church throughout all England; wherein, provided nothing sinful is intermixed, I do not see why you should oppose yourselves with hostility to harmless regulations of that kind.

8. Whether those ceremonies may be retained which occasion evident offence? I answer, that we ought to avoid offence; but we must take care in the mean time, lest we cloke our own feelings under the pretext of offence. You are not ignorant that one thing is given, and another thing received; and that offence is readily taken. I am not now inquiring whether you can, without grievous offence, desert, for a thing in itself indifferent, those churches for which Christ died.

9. Whether any constitutions may be tolerated in the church, which in their nature indeed are not impious, but do not, nevertheless, tend to edification? I answer, that if those constitutions which the queen's majesty wishes to impose upon you, are free from any impiety, they are rather to be tolerated than that the churches should be deserted. For if the edifying of the church is the chief thing to be regarded in this matter, we shall do the church a greater injury by deserting it than by wearing the habits. And where there is no impiety, and the conscience is not wounded, it is proper to submit, even if some degree of bondage be imposed. In the mean time, however, it might be demanded on the other hand, whether the imposition of the habits, as far as it tends to decency and order, may justly come under the denomination of bondage?

10. Whether any thing of a ceremonial nature may be prescribed to the church by the sovereign, without the consent and free concurrence of the clergy? I answer, if the consent of the clergy is always to be waited for by the sovereign, it is probable that those most wise and pious kings, Asa, Hezekiah, Jehoshaphat, and Josiah, and other godly princes, would never have brought into proper order the Levites and ministers of the churches. Though I would not altogether have the bishops excluded from the consultations of churchmen. But on the other hand, I would not have them assume to themselves that power, which they heretofore usurped over kings and magistrates in the time of popery. Nor again, would I have the bishops sanction by their silence the unjust ordinances of princes.

11, 12. The last two questions come more closely to the point. *Whether it is more expedient thus to obey the church, or on account of disobedience to be cast out of the ministry?* And, *whether good pastors may lawfully be removed from the ministry on account* of *their non-compliance with such ceremonies?* I answer, if in these ceremonies there is no superstition, no impiety, but yet they are imposed upon godly pastors, who would rather that they should not be imposed upon them; I will certainly allow, and that most fully, that a burden and bondage is imposed upon them; but I will not allow, and this for most just reasons, that their station or ministry is on that account to be deserted, and place given to wolves, as was before observed, or to ministers less qualified than themselves: especially, since there remains the liberty of preaching, and care may be taken that no greater bondage shall be imposed; with many other things of this kind, &c.

I have now stated what it seemed to me might be said upon the proposed questions, being well aware that others, in proportion to their erudition, might have discussed the subject with far greater elegance and effect; but since it was your wish that I myself should answer them, I have done what I could, leaving both a free pen and an unfettered opinion upon these matters to others. As to what remains, I wish not to force and entangle the conscience of any one by what I have written, but merely propose it for consideration; and I would have you beware, lest any one in this present controversy should conceal a contentious spirit under the name of conscience. And I also exhort you all, by Jesus Christ our Lord, the Saviour, head, and king of his church, that every one of you should duly consider with himself, whether he will not more edify the church of Christ by regarding the use of habits for the sake of order and decency, as a matter of indifference, and which hitherto has tended somewhat to the harmony and advantage of the church; than by leaving the church, on account of the vestiarian controversy, to be occupied hereafter, if not by evident wolves, at least by ill-qualified and evil ministers. May the Lord Jesus give you to see, to understand, and to follow what makes for his glory, and the peace and safety of the church!

Farewell in the Lord, together with all faithful ministers. We will earnestly pray the Lord for you, that you may both perceive and do what is holy and beneficial. Master Gualter salutes you most affectionately, and prays for you every happiness. We too, the other ministers, do the same,

Zürich, May 1, 1566.
Henry Bullinger, minister of the church of Zürich, in his own name and that of Gualter."

Gualter confirms the Zürich criticism that arguments over externals foster legalism

Sadly, the controversy continued throughout the Elizabethan period and English so-called 'Calvinism' continued to depart from the Reformed practice of Zürich and Geneva, setting itself up as an antagonistic alternative to the Reformed Church of England. Cox, Grindal, Jewel and many others corresponded with Bullinger and Gualter on this topic almost always accepting their advice. Grindal often entered into dialogue with these English Ultra-Calvinists, confessing that he identified himself strongly with Calvin but did not find the Frenchman's theology and church order reflected in theirs. Jewel wrote to Bullinger on 24 February, 1567:

"As to religion, the affair of the habits has at this time occasioned much disturbance. For it is quite certain that the queen will not be turned from her opinion; and some of our brethren are contending about this matter, as if the whole of our religion were contained in this single point; so that they choose rather to lay down their functions, and leave their churches empty, than to depart one tittle from their own views of the subject. They will neither be persuaded by the very learned writings of yourself and Gualter, or by the counsels of other pious men. However, we thank God that he does not suffer us at this time to be disquieted among ourselves by questions of more importance."[49]

By 1572, Bullinger was feeling his age and asked the close friend whom he had taken into care as a fatherless youth, Gualter and also his son-in-law John Simler to take over much of his vast correspondence. Gualter took the side of the Reformed Anglicans such as Richard Cox against the harsh criticisms of those who in their extremes boasted that they were following Swiss theology and that of a Calvinistic kind. Gualter condemned them for making their rigid adherence to hardly defensible externals the mark of a true Christian thus rejecting the spirituality of the Reformation for organisational and legalistic forms. On 16 March, 1574, Gualter told Cox that these More-Calvinist-than-Calvin rebels wished to 'revive' a Presbyterian system as the answer to the churches needs, but he adds, "I wish they would think about reviving that simplicity of faith and purity of morals, which formerly flourished." And adds, "I greatly fear there is lying concealed under the presbytery an affectation of oligarchy, which may at length degenerate into monarchy, or even open tyranny. Nor do I fear this without reason. For I know (to give one instance out of many) a city of some importance, in which, after this form of discipline had been introduced, within the space of three

[49] *Zürich Letters*, First Series, p. 185.

years were exhibited such instances of tyranny, as would put the Romanists to shame."[50] Here Gualter is thinking of Heidelberg which had 'progressed' from a Reformed doctrine of church discipline to the new Genevan doctrine which caused a veritable reign of terror to proceed through the churches.

Gualter wrote to Cox on 9 June, 1572, confessing that Beza, and through Beza he himself, had been hoodwinked by these Ultra-Calvinists who had sent two representatives to Geneva from England to complain about the alleged harsh treatment of supposedly Reformed men at the hands of the Anglicans. Strype, in his *Life of Parker*, identifies one of these informers as George Withers, a man who strove to erect a church disciplinary system of most severe proportions under the mantle of Calvinism. Collinson in his *The Elizabethan Puritan Movement*, after listing Withers' views says, "Here were all the ingredients of the extreme, Presbyterian puritanism of the immediate future."[51] Suggestions for the second person have been John Bartlett who caused a great controversy with Withers in the Palatine and Percival Wiburn who had enjoyed Bullinger's hospitality and teaching in the summer of 1566. Grindal and Horne had heard that malcontents in England had informed Bullinger that Latin prayers and popish rites were still practised in the Church of England but the two bishops assured Bullinger that the long list of alleged popish practices he had been given such as "prayers in a foreign tongue (Latin), oil, spittle, clay, lighted tapers etc." had been banned both by the Church and the law from England.[52] Wiburn, who was suspected of spreading such evil rumours, demanded of Horne that he should be shown this long list of supposed abuses in the English Church and then wrote to Bullinger on 25 February, 1567,[53] confessing his innocence concerning such criticisms. Although he admitted that there were still some blemishes in the Church of England, he told Bullinger that "by the grace

---

[50] *Zürich Letters*, Second Series, p. 251.
[51] See Strype's Parker, III, p. 193 and Collinson, p. 81.
[52] Ibid, p. 178 Grindal and Horne give a full list of the alleged popish practices still practised in the Church of England. They deny that this is the case.
[53] *Zürich Letters*, Vol. I, pp. 187-191.

of God she is free from these evils", i.e. those listed by Horne.[54] In his letter, Wiburn lays the blame indirectly on Beza who, like Bullinger and Gualter, confessed that they had been misled by the extreme Puritan party in England. Wiburn also warns Bullinger that 'many parties' are distorting Bullinger's works to suit radical opinions.

What ever the sources of the Ultra-Calvinist protests, Gualter said to Cox in his 1572 letter, "Who would suspect that any persons could be so barefaced, as to dare to lie with such assurance on matters of such notoriety, and the truth of which could not long be concealed?" He appears to have Withers and Bartlett in mind here as he says of them, "they were the chief authors of those changes in the Palatinate, which have inflicted such a blow upon the churches in that quarter."[55] Gualter looks upon their usage of excommunication to further their own church ends as being very questionable indeed.

Bringing new life to the English underground Church

As soon as Thomas Lever returned to England after Mary's death, he informed Bullinger that he had contacted the underground church which had become weaker and weaker under the former Queen's reign of terror but was now seeing times of revival. He continued:

"Some of us preachers, who had returned to England from Germany, being much affected with these things, and considering that the silence imposed for a long and uncertain period was not agreeable to the command and earnest injunction of Paul, to preach the word of God in season and out of season, having been requested to do so, forthwith preached the gospel in certain parish churches, to which a numerous congregation eagerly flocked together. And when we solemnly treated of conversion to Christ by true repentance, many tears from many persons bore witness that the preaching of the gospel is more effectual to true repentance and wholesome reformation, than any thing that the whole

---

[54] Ibid, pp. 187-191.

[55] This change was from an experimental approach to faith to viewing discipline in a Hyper-Calvinistic sense as a mark of the Church.

world can either imagine or approve .... Now popery is at length abolished by authority of Parliament and the true religion of Christ restored."[56]

On coming to power, Elizabeth formed a committee of eight men to debate with the papists and re-establish the Reformation in England. These were, according to Gilbert Burnet,[57] John Scory, David Whitehead, John Jewel, John Aylmer, Richard Cox, Edmund Grindal, Robert Horne and Edmund Guest. Patrick Collinson in his biography of Archbishop Grindal adds Edwin Sandys to the list.[58] With the exception of Guest who was the Queen's almoner and something of a Lutheran and free-willer, all these men had been exiles and were thoroughly Reformed. Scory was at Emden when he was called to pastor the Frankfurt Church but declined. All the rest stood close to Bullinger. Whitehead was the first to pastor the exile church at Frankfurt. He, Jewel, Cox, Grindal, Horne and Sandys represented the majority who had withstood Knox's ambitious and bad-tempered attempts to bully them at Frankfurt.

Bullinger's influence on the Elizabethan Settlement

At the Elizabethan Settlement, the Continental Reformers, especially the Church of Geneva, looked to Bullinger to lead them in their renewed association with England. Beza, after taking over from Calvin in 1564 was advised by the Genevan Council to follow as his mentors Bullinger, Bucer and Calvin, given in that order. Beza was rather worried how Elizabeth would view him as she believed that Calvin had supported Knox and Goodman in their criticism of the English Royal line in general and rule by women in particular. Beza had also very personal grounds for appealing to Bullinger. He was upset to find that Queen Elizabeth had not acknowledged a work of his and concluded with exaggerated sensitivity that this meant he was 'hateful' in her eyes, obviously because of Knox and Goodman. Beza wrote to Bullinger on 3 September, 1566, asking for

---

[56] Ibid, p. 28.

[57] *The History of the Reformation of the Church of England*, Vol. IV, pp. 374-377.

[58] *Archbishop Grindal 1519-1583*, p. 89.

his cooperation in sending a peace delegation from Zürich on behalf of Geneva to patch up old quarrels with the Anglicans and Elizabeth. Beza addressing Bullinger as 'my father', assured him that he alone in Switzerland had the authority and ability to mediate between the Swiss and Genevan churches on the one side and Elizabeth and the English Church on the other, knowing, as Adolf Keller puts it, that, "Bullinger was the oracle of the Elizabethan bishops."[59] Actually, the difficulties had only been on the Geneva side and Bullinger had maintained a spotless witness to and support for the English Reformation. The positive result was that Geneva's wish to have stronger ties with Zürich and the English Church drew the Swiss churches, well-known for their bickering past, gradually together. Beza told Bullinger:

"The reason for her (Elizabeth's) dislike is two-fold: one, because we are accounted too severe and precise, which is very displeasing to those who fear reproof; the other is, because formerly, though without our knowledge, during the lifetime of Queen Mary two books were published here in the English language, one by master Knox against the government of women, the other by master Goodman on the rights of the magistrate. As soon as we learned the contents of each, we were much displeased, and their sale was forbidden in consequence: but she notwithstanding cherishes the opinion she has taken into her head. If therefore you think the present cause worthy of being undertaken by us, it would seem the most suitable plan, and most useful to the brethren, that someone should be chosen from your congregation, if not by the express authority, at least with the permission or connivance of your magistrates, to proceed to England on this especial business, and openly solicit from the queen and bishops a remedy for these evils. This would be indeed an heroic action, worthy of your city, and, as I think, very acceptable to God, even though it should not altogether succeed according to our wish."[60]

---

[59] *Dynamis. Formen und Kräfte des amerikanischen Protestantismus*, 1922, p. 30.
[60] *Zürich Letters*, Second Series, p. 131.

Beza's description of the Knox book, which was one of the many issues why Knox was asked to leave Frankfurt by the Senate, is quite different from the evasive reply given Sir William Cecil by Calvin when he was challenged on the issue. It was also radically different from Knox's version which stressed Calvin's help and support on the project. Indeed, Calvin was plainly dissembling as he had written to Bullinger, the Republican, in April, 1554, repeating in full his discussions with Knox and Goodman on the subject and his basic agreement with them.[61] Though Cecil questioned Calvin regarding writings published in Geneva by Goodman and Knox, in his reply, Calvin briefly mentioned these, but then dropped referring to Goodman's highly revolutionary *How superior powers ought to be obeyed of their subjects, and wherein they lawfully be disobeyed and resisted* and concentrated on Knox's *The first blast against the monstrous regiment and empire of women*, About this book, Calvin told Cecil:

"I had no suspicion of the book, and for a whole year was ignorant of its publication. When I was informed of it by certain parties, I sufficiently shewed my displeasure that such paradoxes should be published; but as the remedy was too late, I thought that the evil which could not be corrected, should rather be buried in oblivion than made a matter of agitation."

Calvin goes on to say that he still had no idea of the contents of Knox's book but if he had taken action against him, this would have endangered the security of all the exiles.[62] This is quite different to Beza's version. It does appear, here, that Calvin is merely trying to wriggle out of a difficult situation. Christopher Goodman was also deeply involved in the Knox controversy and is thought to have worked with Knox at Geneva on his notorious *Blast of a Trumpet* and, at the same time, produced his own work there. Martyr had questioned Goodman on the previous August about his Genevan work and Goodman had answered:

[61] *Calvinism in Europe 1540-1610: A Collection of Documents*, p. 40.
[62] Letter from Calvin to Sir William Cecil, 29 January, 1559, *Zürich Letters*, 2nd Series, p. 35.

"I requested the judgement of master Calvin, to which you very properly attach much weight, before the book was published, and I shewed him the same propositions which I sent to you. And though he deemed them somewhat harsh, especially to those who are in the place of power, and that for this reason they should be handled with caution, yet he nevertheless admitted them to be true."[63]

What Beza did not say was that he had also made himself unpopular in Britain to both the Reformed Church of England and the would-be 'Calvinist' Separatists by first aiding and abetting the English Ultra-Puritans and Separatists and then withdrawing from them when he realised that he had been ill-informed about them. Bullinger put in a good word for Geneva and such an amiable fellowship ensued between the Church of England and the Geneva Church that when Beza became bankrupt, Archbishop Whitgift supported him from his own pocket and when Geneva's funds sank accordingly and it appeared that the Savoy would re-possess her, the Church of England took up a generous collection in 1582 on behalf of Geneva, albeit against the wishes of the Queen, for which Whitgift was reprimanded. On hearing that the Duke of Savoy was again attempting to besiege Geneva and absorb the city into his Roman Catholic state, Whitgift conferred with James I as soon as he became King and sent the following letter in 1603 to his bishops:

"SALUTEM in Christo." I have received letters from his most excellent majesty, the tenor whereof followeth: Most reverend father in God, and right trusty and right well beloved counsellor, we greet you well. The city of Geneva of famous memory, for the zeal the inhabitants have ever had to religion, and for harbouring of many persecuted for the same, as well of other nations, as of this of England in time past, hath of late been put to great charges, by extraordinary occasions happened to them more than they are able to defray, and cannot preserve themselves

[63] *Original Letters*, Vol. II, p. 771.

from some imminent danger, except they be relieved by those their friends, who for community of religion ought to hold the dangers threatening of people so well affected to be their own cause; of which sort hoping that there be in this our realm a great number, who being informed of their cause, and of our good will, that they should be relieved, will readily contribute towards the same such benevolence, as God shall put in their hearts to do; we have thought good to signify unto you, that we understand by their agent sent unto us, of their extremity, and how willing we are by way of benevolence they may be relieved; and to require you to direct your letters, in our name, to the several bishops of your province, signifying the same to them; and that our pleasure is, they shall give order to the parsons, vicars, curates, and other incumbents of the several parishes in their dioceses, to make known so much to their parishioners at their assemblies on Sundays and holy-days, and how much it shall be to the commendation of their zeal and our good liking, that in this case they shew themselves liberal and forward, and to accompany the same with such good exhortations, as they shall think meet to excite the people's devotion, to extend itself toward a city deserving so well of the common cause of religion. And for the receipt of such monies, as shall be contributed, the said bishop shall appoint the churchwardens and sidemen of each parish, with the privity of the incumbents, to take care thereof, and at every month's end to deliver the same to the archdeacon, or some other person of note or trust, by the diocesan to be appointed, who shall see the same safely conveyed unto him, and from the said diocesan the same to be conveyed unto your grace, within some reasonable time, to be by you appointed, after he shall have received it. And when the money, or any part thereof shall be sent to your hands, you shall acquaint us or our council with it, and by the advice deliver it to the agent of Geneva, or such others as they shall appoint to receive it here, and make it over to them. The said collection we think meet to begin with one month after the date of these our letters, and to continue for the space of one year. Given under our signet at our city of Winchester the eighth day of October, in the first year of our reign of England, France, and Ireland, and of Scotland the seven and thirtieth. The contents of which his majesty's said letters I doubt not but that you will perform accordingly; the intent and purpose being so charitable and Christian, and for relief of a city which maintains the gospel, and for professing thereof endureth these troubles. This collection your lordship must give order to your archdeacons and other your officers, who are by his majesty's letters to receive the same monthly of the churchwardens, that they do send it unto you within such convenient time, as that I may receive it at your lordship's hands at the end of every third month from the date hereof: provided always, that there be no deduction of charges made by any of your officers or apparitors, out of any of these collections. And so with my very hearty commendations I commit you to the protection of the Almighty.

From Croydon this 26th of October, MDCIII.
Your lordship's loving brother in Christ, JO. CANTUAR.

The Elizabethan Settlement viewed as a work of Bullinger's

When the Protestant Reformed faith was re-established under Elizabeth in 1559 with the Act of Uniformity under Elizabeth, Bullinger was hailed as the hero of the day. Thomas M. Lindsay wrote in his *History of the Reformation*:

"When the Act of Uniformity was passed by Parliament, the advanced Reformers, who had chafed at what appeared to them to be a long delay, were contented. They, one and all, believed that the Church of England had been restored to what it had been during the last year of the reign of Edward VI; and this was the end for which they (the Reformers) had been striving, the goal placed before them by their friend and adviser, Henry Bullinger of Zürich. Their letters are full of jubilation."[64]

Leading English Reformer John Jewel who called Bullinger 'the only light of our age',[65] wrote to him on 22 May, 1559 saying, "Religion is

[64] *History of the Reformation*, Vol. II, pp. 111; 402.
[65] *Zürich Letters*, First Series, p. 138.

again placed on the same footing on which it stood in king Edward's time; to which event, I doubt not, but that your own letters and exhortations, and those of your republic, have powerfully contributed."[66] Bishops Richard Cox, John Parkhurst, James Pilkington, Robert Horne, Edwin Sandys and Edmund Grindal all echo these sentiments. It is interesting to note that not only the mid-stream Reformers but quite extreme Puritans such as Percival Wiburn wrote to their 'father', Bullinger, telling him of his enormous influence in England. William Turner, a Doctor of Medicine, theologian and pioneer botanist had accused Bullinger of practising 'literary exercise' (using exaggeration to put a not-too-strong point across) in his polemics. Nevertheless, Turner told Bullinger that he was "the most learned man and best expositor of Christian doctrine in all Europe." And wrote to him as if Bullinger had only to say a word and the English would follow it.[67]

It is thus quite appropriate that Helmut Kressner, when comparing the Reformations in Switzerland and England, entitles his book, *Schweizer Ursprünge des anglikanischen Staatskirchentums* (Swiss Origins of the Anglican State Church).[68] In his 1975 essay *Theology as a basis for policy in the Elizabethan church*, David J. Keep, records Bullinger's enormous influence on the Biblical beliefs and structure of not only the Church of England but the Kingdom which it served. He sums up by saying:

"In this paper I have attempted to offer a line of defence for the elizabethan settlement, not simply as the best available between Rome and Geneva, but as a positive system based on a clear exposition of the bible. This does not emerge from the compromises of the commons, or the swingeing satires of puritan pamphleteers. It is clear only in the theological writings of the time. Nor is it sufficient to read the elizabethan apologists. I suggest that their doctrines were clearly formulated in Zürich, emerging in effect with the independence of the city, which had

---

[66] Ibid, p. 33.
[67] Ibid, Second Series, p. 125.
[68] Gütersloh, 1953.

long disregarded the German bishop of Constance. Bullinger, like Zwingli, taught that the total responsibility of the government cannot be divided. I offer this as a model of an important approach to the study of ecclesiastical history. We properly concern ourselves with the minutiae of dates and connections, of wills and statutes, but are sometimes in danger of forgetting that there is a body of faith behind these. In this instance we are able to see the elizabethan bishops as honourable christians seeking to establish the peace of Jerusalem, rather than as time-servers who were willing to cut their consciences, as well as their coats, to the whim of their mistress."[69]

In 1570 pope Pius V formally 'excommunicated' Elizabeth, claiming her Queenship was null and void. Furthermore, he piously proclaimed that the English had his papal permission to break all their oaths of allegiance to their sovereign and look to him both for their spiritual and secular leadership. Edmund Grindal, now Archbishop of York and Bishops Richard Cox and John Jewel, amongst many others, wrote to Bullinger, pleading with him to defend the Queen and the English Church against Rome. In Cox's first letter, requesting Bullinger to write against Pius V, Cox does not hesitate to call the pope 'Antichrist', who "arrogates to himself the authority of recalling, and withdrawing, and absolving subjects from their fidelity and obedience to their princes and magistrates, and commands foreign powers to invade, desolate, and destroy godly magistrates, and deprive them of every right of government."[70] Jewel wrote on 7 August, 1570 in the same vein, protesting at the 'Holy Father' alias 'the Beast', alias 'Antichrist'. But Jewel was so sure of the force of Reformed truth against popish tyranny and the strength of such pens as Bullinger's that he believed the age of Rome was now over and Pius' bull was a final effort on the pope's part to retreat with a last display of arrogance.

Bullinger responded with his *Refutatio Bullae papisticae contra Angliae Reginam Elizabetham* in which he presented his defence on

[69] *The Materials, Sources and Methods of Ecclesiastical History*, p. 269.
[70] *Zürich Letters*, First Series, p. 221.

behalf of the "true Christian Queene, and of the whole Realme of England." In this work, Bullinger traced the perfidy of the papal worldly politics through the ages, showing that the pope was the very last man who could interfere in English state affairs and religion. On completing the work, Bullinger sent the manuscript to Grindal, Cox and Jewel in his usual humble way, saying:

"By submitting to my perusal not long since the bull of Pius V, bishop of Rome, which I had not previously seen, nor indeed heard anything about it, you have afforded me an opportunity of doing, or at least attempting something for the glory of Christ our only Redeemer, and for the preservation of the church, which is with you in England, against the Roman antichrist; behold I dedicate to your reverences this my refutation in opposition to that bull, and submit it to your most exact judgments, that it may altogether stand or fall according as your reverences may please to determine. But I pray you to receive with kindness this my endeavour, and exceeding devotedness to the good cause and to your reverences. I am free to confess that my own abilities are very small, and that your learning is most profound: wherefore, had it so pleased you, you would have been able to manage this cause far more successfully than myself. But when I understood that I shall gratify your reverences by my labours, such as they are, upon this subject, I was unwilling in any measure to disappoint you. May the Lord Christ grant that my discourse may be to the great profit of many!"[71]

Bullinger ends the letter with special greetings to his former guests, colleagues and friends, Robert Horne, Edwin Sandys, John Parkhurst, James Pilkington (all now bishops), John Aylmer, Thomas Sampson, Laurence Humphrey, Thomas Lever and John Foxe. Immediately on receiving the manuscript, Richard Cox had it bound and presented to the Queen via Archbishop Parker. Strype, in his *The Life and Acts of Matthew Parker* thus looks on Parker as the initiator, writing:

---

[71] Ibid, Second Series, p. 179.

"The Archbishop did join with the rest of his Brethren the Bishops, in giving all Deference to *Henry Bullinger*, Chief Pastor of the Church of *Zurick*, who had shewn great Tenderness and Regard to many learned Exiles there, under Queen *Mary's* reign: And who rejoiced at the Reformation in *England.* This Reverend Man had lately in his Zeal for the Queen, and the Religion by her established, compiled a learned Answer to the Pope's Bull against her: And had sent it over here to some of his correspondents, the Bishops. Which was taken exceeding well by them. And Cox, Bishop of Ely, assured him that the Queen should soon be acquainted with his Good Will, and that she should have his Book to read, and that it should be put into the Press for common Good. And in the month of *September*, the Archbishop caused it to be fairly bound, and sent to her, and further procured the Printing of it in Latin, not without the Advice of the Lord Treasurer: And had it translated, and printed in English, too."[72]

John Day (1522-1584) was asked to perform the task of publishing and printing the book and Richard Cox corrected the proofs. Day was the English equivalent of Zürich's Christopher Froschauer and had supported the Reformation under Edward VI and joined the underground Anglican Church at the beginning of Mary's reign. He was discovered by Mary's spies and imprisoned at Newgate, then exiled. As soon as Elizabeth gained the throne, Day was encouraged to set up his printing works again and published the first church music book in English (1560), the earliest known collection of psalm tunes (1563), and such gems of the Reformation as Foxe's *Acts and Monuments*, better known as *Foxe's Book of Martyrs* (1563). Day had more or less a monopoly on childrens' primers and catechisms and was the first to cast Anglo-Saxon type and developed new Roman, Italic and Greek types. His sons, John and Richard, became well-known printers, translators, authors and clergymen. Most of the major English works of the Reformation and many a

[72] *The Life and Acts of Matthew Parker*, John Strype, Book IV, Chap. 6, p. 331.

Continental translation found their way to both English and Continental readers via Day, encouraged by Archbishops Parker and Grindal. On 8 August, 1571, Day wrote to Bullinger, enclosing a parcel of complimentary copies of his anti-papal work and closed his letter with the words:

"Moreover, the reverend fathers themselves will return you in their next letters their most deserved thanks for the pains you have bestowed in the composition of that book, and which is the greatest evidence of your good will to England, which is divided from you by so great a distance. Meanwhile may the Lord of glory so comfort you and his universal church by his most holy Spirit, that his truth may be advanced, and the kingdom of antichrist confounded and overthrown altogether. And may Christ the Lord grant that more persons from every part of the world may exert themselves for this object with their whole heart, and bestow their utmost pains upon it. Take, I pray you, in good part my labour, such as it is, in this work. Farewell most vigilant pastor."[73]

[73] Simler dates this letter from August, 1571. Ibid, Second Series, p. 184.

Chapter 9

The Call to Higher Service

Calvin's departure

The last ten years of Bullinger's life were sad times as he was weighed down with personal infirmities and lost not only one family member after another through the plague but also the bulk of his Christian friends and fellow ministers. One of the first major blows to Bullinger was the death of his colleague, good friend and protégé John Calvin whose life had been a hard one. The Genevan leader had come to realise that his long hope for a union of France and Geneva had no future and that union with the Swiss German states was inevitable. A confederacy of Geneva and Zürich would have been of great value to the Reformation and especially to the near future of vulnerable Geneva but Calvin had hardly considered its potentialities. Such a mutual union did occur twenty years after Calvin's death but the advantages to the Reformation had then dwindled and Geneva's Reformed position was challenged from within and without. However, the city-state, because of the great influx of French refugees was now little different from a French city itself and Calvin gained a recognition amongst his own people that he had never found amongst the patriotic Genevan citizens of the thirties and forties, nor amongst the Swiss-Germans outside of Zürich. Though Geneva had not joined France, she had become a *Petite France* in her own right. So, too, Calvin had received Genevan citizenship in 1559 and could die a

Burger of the city which he had served in almost permanent strife for twenty-five years.

Suddenly, as the fifties came to a close and Calvin's strength and health rapidly waned, he found he had become one of the most respected, internationally well-known citizens of Geneva. One of the crowning successes of Calvin's career was undoubtedly the building of the Genevan Academy which was to serve Geneva for centuries to come. He had been campaigning since 1552 to build such a centre of Christian learning, symbolising the best of Reformed education, life and piety. Shortly afterwards, the Genevan Council bought a site for the college but the following years brought little financial backing from either state or church for such a project and the plot of land remained unused. Towards the end of the fifties, at Calvin's initiative, a national subscription was organised and the citizens urged to give freely in order to provide a sound education both for their own youth and those of other nations. 10,000 florins were quickly raised and the work began. At only fifty years of age, Calvin was now physically an old man and suffering from acutely painful stomach ulcers, yet he could often be seen encouraging the workers and inspecting the swift building progress. The college was opened on 5th June, 1559. Geneva had now in the matter of further education caught up with Zürich after a delay of over thirty years.

Now Calvin made his last will and testimony. The fact that all his worldly possessions did not exceed the value of 300 crowns showed that he was a man who had lived in voluntary poverty throughout his years at Geneva and all the evil rumours that he had made himself rich at the Church's expense were proven to be base lies. After thanking God for delivering him from the darkness of Rome, Calvin revealed the two sides of his nature which had constantly made him an enigma for his contemporaries. First he stresses that he has conducted himself against his enemies without craftiness or corrupt sophistical arts but with candour and sincerity. After this self-praise, the humility of a sincere Christian comes to the surface and he continues "But alas! My study and my zeal, if they deserve the name, have been so remiss and languid that I confess innumerable things have been wanting in me to discharge the duties of my office in an excellent manner; and unless the infinite bounty of God had been present, all my study would have been vain and transient."[1]

On 28 April, 1564, Calvin called together his co-pastors in his chamber and addressed them with the words:

"Stand fast, my brethren, after my decease, in the work which you have begun, and be not discouraged, for the Lord will preserve this church and republic against the threats of its enemies. Let all divisions be removed far from you, and embrace one another with mutual charity. Consider on all occasions what you owe to the church in which the Lord hath stationed you, and let nothing draw you from it. It will indeed be easy for such as are wearied of their flocks to find means for escaping from their duty by intrigue, but they will learn by experience that the Lord cannot be deceived. On my first arrival in this city the gospel was indeed preached, but every thing was in the greatest confusion, as if Christianity consisted in nothing else than the overturning of images. Not a few wicked men arose in the church, from whom I suffered many great indignities; but the Lord our God himself so strengthened me, and banished all fear even from my mind, who am by no means distinguished for natural courage (I state the real fact,) that I was enabled to resist all their attempts. I returned hither from Strasborg, in obedience to a call, against my inclination; because I thought it would not be productive of any advantage. I knew not what the Lord had determined, and my situation was full of very many, and very great difficulties. But proceeding in this work, I perceived at length that the Lord had in reality blessed my labours. Do you, therefore, brethren, persist in your vocation; preserve the established order; use at the same time every exertion to retain the people in obedience to the doctrine delivered, for there are yet among you some wicked and stubborn characters. Affairs, as you see, are not now in an unsettled state, on which account you will be more criminal before God, if they are subverted by your inactivity. I declare my

[1] See Beza's *Life of Calvin*, Calvin's Will, pp. 53-54. Ages Ultimate Christian Library.

brethren, that I have lived united with you in the strictest bonds of true and sincere affection, and I now take my leave of you with the same feelings. If you have at any time found me too peevish under my disease, I entreat your forgiveness, and I return you my warmest thanks, because during my confinement you have discharged the burden of the duties assigned me."[2]

His biographer, an eye witness of the scene records: "After this address he reached out his right hand to each of us, and we then took leave of him with hearts overwhelmed with sorrow and grief, and eyes flowing with tears." He continues, "On the 2d of May, having been informed by Farel, in a letter, that he was determined, though now eighty years old, and in a state of health rendered infirm by age, to come and see him from Neuchâtel, for Viret's residence was at a yet greater distance, he thus answered him in Latin:

"Farewell, my best and most faithful brother! and since God is pleased you should survive me in this world, live mindful of our friendship, which has been of service to the church of God, and whose fruits we shall enjoy in heaven. Do not expose yourself to fatigue on my account. I respire with difficulty, and continually expect to draw my last breath. It is sufficient happiness for me that I live and die in Christ, who is gain to his people in life and death. Again farewell, with the brethren.

Geneva, 2d May, 1564."

Farel, physically weak and weary himself, took no heed of Calvin's concern for his health and made the strenuous journey to Geneva where he spent several hours with his old friend and assistant and then returned to Neuchâtel the very next day. After Farel's visit, Calvin spent most of his remaining days in prayer, though his voice failed at times and he had great difficulty in breathing. His biographer tells us, "He often in his prayers repeated the words of David, 'Lord, I opened not my mouth,

[2] See *Last Discourses of Calvin* and Calvin's *Biography* in Ages Ultimate Library for this and the following information.

because thou didst it;' and at times those of Hezekiah, 'I did mourn like a dove.' Once also I heard him say, 'Thou, Lord, bruisest me, but I am abundantly satisfied, since it is thy hand.'"

Many visitors came to see him, mostly to receive some words of blessing from his lips, but the number was so great that he requested his friends not to come to his house but to remain at home and pray for him. The ministers who visited him were met with a mild reproof should they have neglected their other commitments to visit their dying brother. On 19 May, the ministers were due to meet to discuss church discipline and have a meal together followed by the Lord's Supper. Calvin asked that this time, the meal should be taken in his house. When the day came, Calvin was carried from his bed to the dining-room and greeted his guests with the words, "I come to see you, my brethren, for the last time, never more to sit down with you at table." Then Calvin led in prayer and spoke for some time with his colleagues, taking a little food. He then asked to be carried back to his bed in the adjoining room saying, "This intervening wall will not prevent me from being present with you in spirit, though absent in body."

From then on, Calvin's state worsened so much that he was unable to sit up in bed and grew weaker and thinner. On Saturday, 27 May, 1564, Calvin appeared to revive somewhat and could speak almost freely. Then, at 8 o'clock in the evening, the Genevan Reformer suddenly fell asleep in the sleep of death. His biographer finishes the story of Calvin's life with the words:

"Thus this splendid light of the reformation was taken from us with the setting sun. During that night, and the following day, great lamentation prevailed throughout the city, for the republic regretted the want of one of its wisest citizens, the church deplored the death of its faithful pastor, the college sorrowed for such an incomparable professor, and all grieved for the loss of a common parent and comforter bestowed upon them by God himself. Many of the citizens were desirous to see him after he was dead, and could with difficulty be torn from his remains. Some strangers, also, who had come from a distance with a view to see and hear him, among whom was the very distinguished English ambassador to the French court, were very desirous to see only the body of the deceased. At first, indeed, they were admitted; but afterwards, because the curiosity was excessive, and it was necessary to silence the calumnies of enemies, his friends considered the best plan would be to close the coffin next morning, being the Lord's Day; his corpse, as usual, having been wrapped in a linen cloth. At two o'clock in the afternoon on Sunday, his body was carried to the common burying-place, called Plein Palais, without extraordinary pomp. His funeral, however, was attended by the members of the senate, the pastors, all the professors of the college, and a great proportion of the citizens. The abundance of tears shed on this occasion afforded the strongest evidence of the sense which they entertained of their loss. According to his own directions, no hillock, no monument was erected to his memory, on which account I wrote the following epitaph:

Why in this humble and unnoticed tomb is Calvin laid – the dread of falling Rome, Mour'n'd by the good, and by the wicked fear'd, By all who knew his excellence revered; From whom e'en virtue's self might virtue learn, And young and old its value may discern? 'Twas modesty, his constant friend on earth, That laid this stone, unsculptured with a name; Oh! happy turf, enrich'd with Calvin's worth, More lasting far than marble is thy fame!"

Anna Bullinger departs from this world

On 25 September, 1564, Anna Bullinger née Adlischwyler was called home after an illness of nine days. Her daughter Margaretha died a few weeks later on 30 October. Anna had lovingly cared for three generations of relatives smitten by the plague, including her husband, and died of the terrible illness herself. On 22 November, Bullinger wrote to his friend Fabricius in Chur who had lost his young wife and son to the plague:

"I am writing my first letter to you, I cannot say since my illness but during my illness as I still have many complaints and much sorrow to combat which this illness has brought me. If the Lord would not strengthen me in an extraordinary manner, I do not know how I would be able to recover as I am receiving blow after blow. Sorrow upon sorrow follow one another. It is five weeks since the Lord took my most beloved wife from me. You know how she was and thus can easily understand what a trial it is for me. Now, only five weeks later, the daughter of my heart Margaretha, Lavater's[3] wife was buried, torn away by the plague. She was expecting a child and gave birth to it in her illness. The little boy was born alive and received holy baptism but died the following day and in the following night his mother followed him leaving seven children behind and a husband bowed down with deep sorrow. I know that all is done according to God's council. I commit to Him, therefore, myself and all mine and beg His mercy. I would ask you, in particular, that you will commit me and my house and all the church to the Lord in your prayers."[4]

Bullinger wrote to Ambrose Blaurer in Winterthur, telling him:

"You know that the Lord has taken away the staff of my old age, my precious, elect and very godly wife. But the Lord is just and His judgments are righteous. In the last few days, He has also taken away my beloved daughter, Lavater's wife, in whom I had placed so much hope. She has left seven small children behind her. But the Lord is good and His will is good, without which this could not happen. He may continue to do what is good in His eyes if He only will keep His mercy upon me and mine."[5]

Bullinger reminded Blaurer that now he and Bullinger were the oldest serving ministers in the Swiss Church and they would meet each other soon in glory. Blaurer caught the plague on 29 November and died four

---

[3] Ludwig Lavater (1527-1586) married Margaretha Bullinger (1531-1564). He was the son of Lord Mayor Johan Rudolf Lavater and became Superintendent at the Great Minster in 1585.
[4] Taken and translated from Blanke and Leuschner, p. 283. The letter is also to be found in *Heinrich Bullinger und Seine Gattin*, p. 132-133.
[5] See *Heinrich Bullinger und Seine Gattin*, p. 133.

days later. On 6 December, 1564, Bullinger wrote to Fabricius to tell him that Ambrose Blaurer had now also become a victim of the plague. Bullinger, though only sixty years of age, was now German-speaking Switzerland's oldest serving minister. Blaurer had been in close touch with his Swiss friend since Bullinger's first years as a teacher in Kappel and a young minister in Bremgarten. He was born in Constance, the son of a town councillor, and educated at Tübingen alongside Melanchthon, becoming a Benedict monk and soon Abbot of Alpirsbach. He was converted to the Reformed faith in 1522. At first, Blaurer was strongly influenced by Luther but soon later adopted the Zürich position, though he held Bucer, too, in great respect. He served as a minister in Constance, Württemberg and Augsburg but was compelled to flee Germany in 1548 for Switzerland when the emperor's troops entered Constance. Blaurer then joined his Swiss brethren in Zürich and settled down first in Biel and then in Winterthur. There he was often visited by Bullinger and his family. He and Bullinger were in the midst of ardent correspondence when the plague struck both. Bullinger told Fabricius:

"Our brother Ambrose Blaurer left us on the sixth of this month in Winterthur. Now among my colleagues only Farel is still alive who has been longer than me in the service of the church. What is left for me other than that I too must soon tie up my bundle."[6]

Bullinger's major publisher Christopher Froschauer dies

1564 was also the year that Christopher Froschauer died. Of the twelve printers employed in Zürich from 1519-1575, the period covering Bullinger's numerous literary productions, the most well-known and most active of them was Froschauer. He was born in Öttingen, Bavaria and moved to Zürich in 1515 to be apprenticed to Hans Rüegger, a small, one-page printer. Rüegger died in 1517 and Froschauer took over the business and immediately began to work on more demanding and enterprising publications. He also married Rüegger's widow which proved to be a

[6] Quoted from Heinrich Bullinger's Efforts to Document the Zürich Reformation: History as Legacy in *Architect of Reformation*, p. 213.

great asset. His business acumen and uprightness in character and religion moved the Zürich Council to grant him citizenship in 1519. Froschauer began to expand his business quickly, adding a bookbinding department, a type-foundry, a joiner's workshop, a stationer's and a paper mill, placing the latter under the care of his brother Eustachius. He then opened up several retail stores in the city. His work took him regularly to the book fair at Frankfurt where he also met members of the Continental underground churches and Reformed refugees from England, Holland, France, Poland and Italy, passing on and receiving messages, gifts and news concerning the various churches. These international connections drew a number of Englishmen to Zürich and several, including Richard Wyer, learnt the trade from Froschauer and published English works in Zürich. William Tyndale, Miles Coverdale, John Hooper, William Thomas and Edmund Allen were further Englishmen who published via the Zürich printers in various languages. Most of Froschauer's fellow-printers in Zürich had been trained under him and there existed a great cordiality between them.[7] That Bullinger's enormous literary output and influence was the chief source of business for Froschauer and his fellow-printers is clearly seen by the fact that of the 1,570 titles published during the entire sixteenth century, 1189 were printed during Bullinger's ministry alone. Indeed, after Bullinger's death, though the Froschauer business was expanded regarding premises and staff, book production in Zürich fell by a third. It is estimated that the number of *books* published by Froschauer's printing works, as opposed to *titles*, ran into 800,000 copies.[8]

Although Froschauer printed in German, Latin, Greek and Jewish-German (Sefer ha-Jira and Sefer Josef ben Gorion) in Hebrew type, it is noteworthy that most of his titles appeared in German, though Latin was still the traditional medium for learned literature. In this, Froschauer was also a pioneer. The relative large amount of Italian literature printed in Zürich was, however, taken on by Froschauer's fellow-printers. The Froschauer family concentrated mostly on theological literature but also

[7] See Leu's Die Zürcher Buch- und Lesekultur in *Heinrich Bullinger und seine Zeit*, pp. 61-90.
[8] See Fritz Büsser, *Die Prophezei*, p. 58.

printed books on law, medicine, science, literature, linguistics, history, music and education besides school literature and lexica. This has caused Froschauer to be internationally remembered as a printer of scientific works and especially his illustrations in his books on animals and birds were widely used throughout the world for several centuries. Nevertheless, Froschauer is reckoned amongst the leading men of the Reformation, chiefly for his publication of some 87 Zwingli works, mostly initiated by Bullinger, 131 works by Bullinger himself, no less than 69 Bible editions and portions and 50 exegetical works. Froschauer reaped the enmity of the Lutherans by producing a new Bible translation from the Greek and Hebrew by Reformers Jud, Bibliander and Pellican and others. Prof. Fritz Büsser argues that though Bullinger did not append his name to the translation, (no one else did either), "His contribution especially in this area must not be underestimated. As a good spirit (guter Geist) and also as coordinator, he was hardly less engaged in bringing out the edition than Jud, Pellican, Bibliander, Colin and Gualter." Bullinger's foreword to the translation so exactly depicted the work of true scholarship in presenting the Word of God to the more general reader that it was prefixed to many other versions in either Latin or German, including the Bibles of Sebastian Münster and Leo Jud and Erasmus' *postrema editio* of the New Testament.

This early German Bible is commonly called the Froschauer or Zürich Bible. Luther declared that as the men who translated it (Zürich's greatest Reformers) were all lost, he wanted nothing to do with their work. This was most unworthy of Luther as Froschauer had been almost the sole printer of Luther's books between 1520-1529 and thus helped to spread and internationalise Luther's theology as no other. As Froschauer's two-volumed Bible had appeared in several formats and editions before Luther's own Bible translation appeared, this may have been a question of professional jealousy.

Research into the origins of German Bible translations have centred on Luther's 1534 work and even seen this work as the first presentation of modern High German extant. Many linguists and church historians have thus maintained that Luther is the father of modern over-regional New

High German. That Zwingli had used a High German version in his Bible translations and this was continued in the Zürich versions of 1529-31 by his Swiss co-translators shows that much re-thinking needs to be done in this area.[9] Furthermore, Froschauer's Bible was merely presented as a modern translation from the Greek and Hebrew without the names of any of the many translators used in the title, several of them being arguably greater linguists than Luther. Yet Luther's Bible was originally named just that, the Luther Bible i.e. the one Reformer's name was used as part of the title. Of note, too, is that from its first publication, and for the following two hundred years, the Zürich Bible became the favourite translation of German-speaking Anabaptists and Baptists. One wonders if Luther's harsh condemnation of the version and the translators as 'Anabaptists' had anything to do with this? The Humanists have also much to be thankful for in Froschauer as he, assisted by his nephew, published some twenty-three of Erasmus' works including his New Testament.

Froschauer died childless but Eustachius' son Christopher, who entered the business in 1552, was able to carry on the work from 1564-85. Other close relations set up printing businesses in cities which were of strategic importance to the Reformation such as Augsburg in Germany and Nikolsburg in Moravia. Froschauer left 700 pounds of his 22,423 pound fortune to Bullinger.

Conrad Gessner goes home

One of Bullinger's closest friends was the internationally renowned zoologist, botanist, doctor, linguist, philosopher and theologian Conrad Gessner whose talents and work has been mentioned above. From 1531 on, Gessner and Bullinger became personal friends and Bullinger called him "a prodigious adornment, not only for our Zürich but for the whole of Switzerland". Though Gessner had no call to the ministry, his enormous

[9] The present day versions of both the Luther Bible and the Zürich Bible are in a modern High German which differs greatly from the Zürich Bible of 1531 and the Luther Bible of 1534. However, in the teaching experience of this author, modern Swiss of an average education are able to understand the original Zürich Bible text better than modern Germans are able to understand Luther's German.

talents so impressed the Zürich clergy and Council that they sent him to several leading foreign universities so that he could further his education. Gessner started his occupational life as a teacher, becoming Professor of Greek at Lausanne. He then continued his studies in medicine at Basle and Montpellier and eventually was given chairs in medicine and philosophy at Zürich, becoming also the city's *Stadtarzt*, responsible for Zürich's health planning. Gessner's knowledge of all branches of learning was encyclopedical and in his *Bibliotheca universalis*, printed in 1545, he lists all known Greek, Latin and Hebrew works, some tens of thousands in all, written by some 3,000 authors. In the second part, the *Pandectae*, published in 1548, he lists all the known areas of science which then consisted of 21 main divisions with cross-references to the appropriate literature applicable to them. These volumes were followed by studies in the mammals, amphibians, reptiles, fish and birds of the world, flora, geology (especially studies on the Swiss and German spas and hot springs), pharmacology, milk and milk products. Gessner pioneered studies in experimental pharmacology, drug addiction, including smoking and chewing tobacco, and poisons. Of his theological publications, his study of the life of Pontius Pilatus gave Gessner a degree of fame. Above all, Gessner strove to rid science of the crippling effects, confusion and superstition of Roman Catholic medieval thinking and return to the clear analytical thinking of classical times and the morals of Scripture.

Gessner died in 1564 after a few days' illness. Immediately on receiving the news of his death, Bullinger wrote to a friend saying:

"Last Sunday he visited the church as he was a very diligent hearer of my sermons. The plague struck him quickly after but he did not take to his bed but worked until his last breath came. He asked me to say farewell to his friends at the Emperor's court, in Germany, France, England and Italy and to encourage them to hold fast to the Christian faith. And so the

Lord calls the most learned and upright men, one after the other, from this world."[10]

He told Fabricius, soon to be carried off by the plague himself at the early age of 39:

"What shall I write or say, my dear friend? Tribulation is heaped up on tribulation and bursts all boundaries. You know how great the pain is caused by the death of my family members. Now news of the death of that famous, learned and godly man, Dr Gessner has nigh killed me. Wretched man that I am having to follow the coffins of so many dear ones half dead myself. But with God's help I manage to keep on. I submit willingly to his disciplining."[11]

The fact that Gessner attended Bullinger's preaching service up to the week of his death, shows, too, that Bullinger, in spite of his severe illness, still kept on preaching and carrying out his pastoral duties until death closed his eyes. He was supported in this arduous and dangerous work by his son-in-law Ludwig Lavater whose family was also struck by the plague. For such Christian displays of love and care, both Gessner, Bullinger and his family were criticised by evil tongues who said that by carrying on their pastoral and medicinal duties, they were risking the lives of others by transmitting the disease. Some Reformers, such as Zanchi, thus fled as soon as they heard that the plague was spreading in their area. Of course, this criticism was not always objective but reflected the common human instinct of saving ones own skin. Gessner and Bullinger were shocked to hear that they should abandon their family, patients and flock to save themselves and called it a barbarous idea and that Christians who fled their duties to save their skins could not thus flee from the hand of God. Bullinger was particularly saddened to hear that some believed that his wife was responsible for passing on the plague to him and so endangering the life of their pastor. Actually, Anna had caught the plague

[10] Quoted from Blanke and Leuschner, p. 284.
[11] *Heinrich Bullinger und Seine Gattin*, p. 134.

whilst looking after her stricken husband. Through her sacrifice, her husband's life was saved to serve his church for another decade.

Theador Bibliander, a man before his time

Bibliander, Head of the Zürich academy, was born around 1504[12] in Bischofzell in Thurgau and died of the plague in Zürich on 26 November 1564. He studied at Zürich and Basle under such well-known and esteemed tutors as Conrad Pellican, Oecolampadius and Wolfgang Capito. After teaching in Leugnitz for several years, he was called back to Zürich to succeed Zwingli as senior professor of Old Testament studies and Oriental Philology at the Zürich academy. One of his most-well-known works is his 59 paged foreword to his 1536 edition of Zwingli's and Oecolampadius' letters in which he laid down the great principles of the Reformed faith and defended the Swiss Reformers against the charges of heresy which were raised against them both by the Lutherans and the Roman Catholics.[13] This was the first major analysis of Reformed doctrine which came from the Swiss press.

Bibliander was such an accomplished linguist that he is said to have mastered 30 languages which helped him become a leading exegete and teacher of Hebrew. His Hebrew grammar of 1535 was widely used by those training for the ministry. Bibliander had a strong missionary calling to the Mohammedans who were then close at hand because of their conquests in Austria and Hungary. He thus translated the Koran out of the Arabic into Latin for the benefit of those who wished to bring the gospel to the followers of Mohammed. This caused quite a stir in the Reformed world and the Basle Council tried to have the book banned. Luther and other missionary-minded people, including Bullinger, supported Bibliander's stance. With Gessner, Bibliander did pioneer work into the origin and spread of the Slavic languages. Bibliander had a most positive view of world missions and wrote, something in the style of Jonathan Edwards and William Cowper two hundred years later, of a united future world in which righteousness and the love of God would prevail. For him,

[12] Dates given for Bibliander's birth vary from 1504 to 1507.
[13] *Joannis Oecolampadii et Huldrichi Zuinglii epistolarum libri quatuor.*

the gospel emphasised the internationalism and universalism of the Christian's field of labour. Like Edwards and Cowper, but long before, Bibliander believed not only in the revealed language and religion of Eden as the instruments of communion with God but that after the fall and Babel, the gospel would be instrumental in bringing both language and religion back to an Edenic norm on a world-wide basis. This was part of the restitution of all things. Working closely with Gessner, Bibliander laid the foundations for the modern study of comparative linguistics which has proved so helpful to modern Bible translators on the mission field. Bibliander and Gessner not only pioneered modern linguistics but they also introduced the study of comparative religion at university level. This was rather too much for many of their contemporaries but in modern times such organisations as the Wycliffe Bible Translators and modern applied linguistics have profited greatly from Bibliander's and Gessner's work.

Somehow, Calvin never understood this fundamental optimism of Bibliander's and looked on his eschatological thinking as contradicting the doctrine of predestination. Our understanding of doctrine, however, must be subservient to the Word of God which clearly stresses both in the Old Testament (Isaiah 11:9) and in the New (Matthew 28:19-20) that the world is our parish and that Christian's must expect a great harvest of the elect before the Lord returns. Calvin was also permanently in fear that such a gifted man as Bibliander would turn against him and thus campaigned for the suppression of his works and even removal from Zürich. This was obviously an unfounded phobia on Calvin's part which proved to be a great embarrassment to the churches and almost caused a break in the relationships between the Zürich Reformation and that of Geneva. When Peter Martyr became Bibliander's colleague in 1556, taking over from the deceased Pellican, he strove to mediate between Zürich and Geneva, which led him also to adopt the position that Bibliander was unorthodox on predestination.[14] Humble Bibliander

[14] Wayne Baker in his *Heinrich Bullinger and the Covenant*, from where the quotes from Bibliander are taken, claims that Martyr took sides with Calvin against Bibliander, arguing for a double-predestination. This is, I believe, an over-simplification in the same way that it is an over-

resigned his post in 1560 to keep the peace. Alfred Schindler in his essay 'Bullinger und die lateinischer Kirchenväter', after discussing Bibliander on predestination, claims "He was not really declared a heretic which would have ruined his livelihood. But he was put on ice."[15] One might add, 'to pacify Geneva'. Against the usual practice, Bibliander was given a pension by the Zürich Council which is evidence enough that the entire affair had little to do with theology and more to do with diplomacy. Bibliander was more a humanist and linguist than a theologian and was often vague in his doctrinal utterances, never wishing to challenge either the goodness of God nor the full responsibility of man for his own plight. Calvin had early accused him of influencing Bolsec but it is clear that Bibliander viewed the free-willism of which Calvin accused him as a Pelagianism to be rejected. On the other hand, Calvin's doctrine of an election to reprobation was viewed by Bibliander as Manachianism, which he equally rejected. On viewing Pelagianism and Calvin's occasional trip into Hyper-Calvinism, Bibliander argued that "the one faction destroyed the grace of God by which alone we are saved by faith. The other settled upon God as the author of perdition and of all evil." Bibliander, however, always testified that "Faith is a gift of God so that none might boast." He also maintained soundly, "I put anticipatory (prevenient) grace prior to faith, which is the basis of the comforting election by which we have been chosen in Christ, before the foundation of the world."[16] However, Bibliander at times did come very near, but not to the same extreme, to those modern so-called 'free-offer' theologians associated today with the Banner of Truth School who

---

simplification to say that Calvin held rigidly to a double-predestination. This author is becoming more convinced on studying Martyr on predestination that he was closer to Bullinger's more balanced presentation of it than to Calvin's more philosophical definitions. However, Martyr was also a systematic theologian and strove to particularise and systematise whereas Bibliander viewed God's work in evangelism more as a total conception in God's plan for the evangelisation of the world.

[15] Heinrich Bullinger und seine Zeit (ed. Campi), p. 170.

[16] This author believes strongly in the prevenient grace of God, leading His elect by the Spirit to faith in the Son. He also believes, equally strongly in the imputation of Christ's righteousness to His elect and the imputation of their sin to Christ. Sadly, many modern and influential claimants to the name 'Reformed' are calling these doctrines, for reasons best known to themselves, 'Roman Catholic'.

emphasise God's saving wish for all mankind whether elect or non-elect. However, unlike Bibliander these modern would-be Calvinists speak paradoxically of God's desire to save all but His self-contradictory will to condemn some as if God's desire and His will were two different and contrasting characteristics. Ironically enough, these neo-reformed protagonists bare-facedly claim that they are the true 'Calvinists' in their understanding and write books striving to prove that they represent the 'Old Evangelism' and this is what Calvin believed all along, despite Calvin's testimony to the contrary and his controversy with Bibliander, Bolsec, Caroli and Castellio as outlined above.[17] Bullinger was clear in his own mind where he placed Bibliander. In his *Vita* for 1560, Bullinger, looking back over the great friendships he had enjoyed, mentions, in this order, Wolfgang Joner, Peter Simler, Ulrich Zwingli, Leo Jud, Conrad Pellican, Theodor Bibliander, Erasmus Fabritius, Kaspar Megander, Joachim Vadian, Berchtold Haller, Oecolampadius, Simon Grynäus, Ambrosius Blaurer, Jan Laski (John á Lasco), Martin Bucer, John Calvin, Conrad Fabritius and "many learned men in England, Germany and France." In view of the fact that the predestination controversy regarding Bibliander was at its height in 1560, one cannot help wondering why Bullinger mentioned Bibliander early in his list but left out Martyr entirely and placed Calvin towards the end.[18]

More deaths in Bullinger's family and amongst his friends

Within the next few months Regula Gualter died as also shortly afterwards Bullinger's daughters Anna (1530-1565), married to Ulrich Zwingli (1525-1571) and Elizabeth (1532-1565), married to Josias Simler (1530-1576). Now many members of the families of Bullinger's brothers and sisters died and also Brigitta Schmied who had been the Bullingers' faithful maid and nanny since Bremgarten times. Brigitta had done a gigantic work in the family, refusing a salary and being content with a

[17] See Iain Murray's *The Old Evangelism: Old Truths for a New Awakening*, BOT, 2005, and an excellent, well-balanced review of the book in The Gospel Standard Magazine, July, 2005, pp. 225-226.

[18] See Peter Opitz' Eine Theologie der Gemeinschaft im Zeitalter der Glaubenspaltung in *Bullinger und seine Zeit*, pp. 213-214.

little pocket-money, food and occasional clothing. The plague also hit the schools and carried off many pupils and teachers. The last of the first generation of Reformers amongst Bullinger's friends, William Farel, died in September, 1565 and in the same year Fabricius passed away. The minister from Chur had solicited in his dying hours that Bullinger would look after his motherless and fatherless children. However, Bullinger believed that he would not be spared when whole families of his loved ones were dying around him and the cream of the ministry were all gone.

The fact that Bullinger outlived the 1564-65 plague though he was struck down for months by the epidemic, appears to be a miracle of grace considering the high mortality rate in Zürich at the time. Humanly speaking, however, Bullinger had the best nurses possible in his loving wife and daughters and the best doctors possible. Gessner cared for Bullinger and his family until his own death and this care was continued by John Muralto, the famous military doctor who had fled from Locarno when the Protestant church was exiled there. Nevertheless, Bullinger realised that the chances of his being cured of the plague were small so, on 17 September, 1564, he called all the ministers of the church together to give them his last blessing and advice and commit them to the Lord.

Bullinger did not die but on recovering from the Black Death of 1564-65, he was left an old man with acute kidney trouble and difficulty in passing water and had to face many a month-long spell of acute sickness. His daughter Dorothea (born 1545) nursed him lovingly and did not think of marriage until her father had died. Then she married Lord Mayor Grossmann. Bullinger never regained the weight he lost during this illness and took on an almost spectral appearance of mere skin and bones. In view of his approaching death, he used to tell his friends who were continually advising him to put on weight, though he could not, "The worms will not find much that is delicious and juicy on me to eat." Friends advised Bullinger to marry again quickly and even scolded him when he said that there could not be a second Anna.

William Farel: Harbinger of the Reformation in the Vaud, Geneva and Neuchâtel

Farel was one of the first, if not *the* first Reformer to open up present day French-speaking Switzerland to the gospel. He embraced Reformed doctrines in 1523-4 under Oecolampadius', Zwingli's and Bucer's witness. He served for a time in Bern and was sent as a missionary to Geneva when Bern forced out the Roman Catholic government. Farel is best known nowadays for his forceful persuasion which led to Calvin assisting him in Geneva in 1536. This has led modern scholarship to view Farel as standing under Calvin's shadow but Farel's life has still not been adequately researched and, according to this writer, his work has been sadly undervalued. It was Farel (with Antoine Saunier) who was instrumental in ministering to and aiding the Protestant Waldensians of France, Bohemia, Savoy, Piedmont and Italy which led to the Contract of Chanforan in 1532, so linking the Waldensians with the French Reformed churches. This was no easy task as a powerful faction amongst the Waldensians did not wish to break with Rome. Farel also was of great influence in the Waldensian valleys in building schools and distributing and printing French Bibles. Those who were against Farel and Saunier gradually lost their identity. Calvin was to follow Farel in his solidarity with the Protestant Waldensians. Bullinger, on the German-speaking side had expressed his fellowship with the Waldensians in the early twenties and confessed that they had influenced his doctrine of the Lord's Supper.

In the drawing up of the *Consensus Tigurinus* it was Farel who steadfastly prompted Calvin to come to an agreement with Bullinger. In a letter dated 1 August, 1549,[19] Calvin tells Bullinger and the ministers at Zürich that in the matter of a union with Zürich on the Lord's Supper issue, Farel was "that indefatigable soldier of Christ, and my guide and counsellor." In a letter to Myconius recorded by Büsser, [20] Calvin states that it was at Farel's prompting that he undertook the 1549 journey to

[19] Letter 249, Ages Collection.
[20] Not in my collections. Büsser's Bullinger biography, Vol. 2., pp. 141-142. Büsser gives *Calvini opera* XIII, Nr. 1309, 456 f..

Zürich, though he was, at first, reluctant to go. Rather ambiguously, he adds that the success of the venture was purely Farel's fault.

Bullinger was less pleased with Farel's support of Calvin in wishing to form a mercenary alliance in 1547-48 between Catholic France and Protestant Zürich and Bern. The Frenchmen saw this as an opportunity to strengthen the Reformation in France, whereas Bullinger thought it would endanger the Reformation and complained that the French King's wish to employ Swiss mercenaries in his wars would again mean that Protestants would be employed to kill Protestants as in the Italian and Smalcaldian wars. Farel, Calvin and Viret had the same view of the powers that be as did Melanchthon before he was disillusioned, viewing royalty as servants, appointed by God, who must come, as a result of this, to a knowledge of the truth. Nor did Farel find any sympathy with Bullinger when he and Beza toured Germany in 1557, seeking union with the Lutherans on the Lord's Supper and putting the *Consensus Tigurinus* at risk.

Farel, though he was seventy-five years of age, visited Calvin to be with him at his death and then made the long journey to Metz to preach to the persecuted brethren there. Whilst preaching the Gospel, he collapsed, exhausted and was carried back to Neuchâtel a dying man. He remained for some months in his bed, too weak to move but his friends and brethren thronged around his bed, hoping to gain a few words from his lips. Those present went away glorifying God for what they had seen and heard. Farel died on 13, September, 1565 after labouring over fifty years in God's vineyard. He was buried in Neuchâtel churchyard but there is no stone to mark his grave. Commenting on Farel's life, ministry and home call, Frances Bevan, that golden-tongued biographer, said of Farel's transference to Glory in the poem *The Evangelist*:

> Thou shalt bring the ransomed with thee,
> They with songs shall come,
> As the golden sheaves of harvest
> Gathered home.[21]

[21] See Bevan's *The Life of William Farel.*

Called back by God from death

In 1569, Bullinger was struck down again with a most severe illness and wrote to his fervent correspondent Duke Ludwig von Sayn-Wittgenstein in a rather optimistic spirit:

"I was severely ill in May and June but recovered through the prayers of the church and called back by God from death. I am continuing to serve the church in my posts but my full strength is not yet restored but I hope to recover fully before very long and pray heartily that God will enable me according to His will to continue in the service of the church, bless me and strengthen me as He has promised."[22]

In March 1570, Bullinger wrote to Duke Sayn to tell him that he had asked his cousin, colleague and close friend Johannes Wolf to send the duke a copy of his work on Nehemiah explaining that the daily work of his ministry was so hard that he felt broken and now he wanted to encourage younger and stronger men to commit their talents to writing and to the distribution of their books. He added:

"However, I am fully satisfied with my lot and thank God that he honoured me when I, by His grace, was in full strength which He used to add glory to His Name and in the edification of the Church. I ask Him now, in my feeble old age to bless me whose boat is not far from the heavenly harbour to snatch me from the waves and take me to be with Him. I must now be satisfied with less and have just published six sermons on the subject of conversion."[23]

Indeed, Bullinger had been printing work after work since the plague hit him in 1564 and though his output was less, it was still enormous. During these years, he produced, for instance, a collection of 66 sermons on Daniel (1565), his Second Helvetic Confession (1666), his defence of

---

[22] *Heinrich Bullinger und Seine Gattin*, p. 135-136.
[23] Taken from Pestalozzi, p. 492.

Queen Elizabeth and the English Reformation against the papal bull of Pius V (1571), his *Gründlicher Bericht Über die Hoheit, Würde und Vollkomenheit der Heiligen Schrift* (1571), his *Ermahnung an alle Diener des Wortes Gottes* (1572), his *Von der schweren Verfolgung der christlichen Kirchen* (1573), his *Eidgenössische Geschichte von den frühesten Zeiten bis zum Anfang der Reformation* (1573 and 1574), his *Reformationsgeschichte* von 1519-1532 (1567 and 1574), his collection of 170 sermons on Jeremiah (1575).

Bullinger had placed so much hope in the younger generation but so many of them had died one by one whilst the old man lived on. His son-in-law, Ulrich Zwingli, son of the pioneer Zürich Reformer died in 1571 and Ulrich's son Rudolf Zwingli, Bullinger's and Zwingli's grandson died in London as a young student in 1573. In November, 1572, when Bullinger was really feeling that his work was done because of age and infirmities made worse by the constant dying of those around him, Johannes Wolf died aged only fifty-one. Bullinger wrote in his diary:

"Oh, that God would show mercy from Heaven. That I should outlive all my precious brethren, Leo, Pellican, Bibliander, Gessner, Martyr, Otto, Megander, Fries. Not a single one is left alive of all those who lived and served the church fifty years ago when the Lord called me. Oh, deliver me, oh Lord my God from this vale of tears and in thy goodness make an end of it."

He then wrote to Duke Sayn in February, 1573 to tell him, "With a most intensive feeling of pain, I must inform you, noble sir that my dear co-worker, Johannes Wolf, that unforgettable man, my faithful relative, my fervently loved brother, this truly godly, learned and humble man, who loved peace and harmony to a high degree, departed from this world last November."[24]

[24] Letter quoted in *Heinrich Bullinger und Seine Gattin*, p. 136-137.

By the following November, 1574, Bullinger was reduced and shrunk to a skeleton and was unrecognisable to those who had not seen him for a few years. After a severe bout of illness, the Bernese Statesman Niklaus Linden, who was also old and frail, wrote to Bullinger on the third of the month, expressing how shocked he was to see his friend so close to death and the churches in mourning over their beloved shepherd. He told Bullinger:

"A shiver went through my whole body, honoured father when I saw what a horrible sickness had befallen you and chiefly because I realise what a great protector the Church will lose when they are left without your sustaining help because of your sickness or death. I do not doubt that you are bearing the hand of the Lord with patience, but when I think of all our scattered friends at home and abroad and all the churches and what an impression the sickness or death of such an influential man will mean to them, I cannot keep back the tears. I find my refuge in prayer that you will be kept for us as this is the sole asylum of the distressed."[25]

Bullinger struggled on and was preaching again only days later and was able to author several apologetical works during the next few months and writing to friends such as Beza who continued to solicit his help. He was determined to work for the Lord as long as he had breath in his lungs. Bullinger continued his ministry up to the Whitsuntide service when he preached several times in rapid succession. Then, on 4 May, he felt his old kidney and bladder trouble returning and from then on was wracked day and night by severe pains. He lost his appetite entirely but would have drunk as much as he could had not passing water become so painful that Bullinger had to restrict drinking to a mere moistening of the lips. In spite of his great discomfort and having to spend night after night without sleep, his daughter Dorothea who looked after him told her brother-in-law Lavater after Bullinger's death, "I was with him every day but never heard an impatient word come from his lips. God set him up as an

[25] Pestalozzi, p. 494.

example of patience for His Church. His strength was in his continuous prayers, also when his need was greatest."[26] On 16 August, 1575 after months of acute suffering, Bullinger received sure signs that his pilgrimage was over and called all the ministers, professors and teachers in Zürich to his study for his last admonition, teaching and farewell. In a long, well-prepared speech, he exhorted his friends and brethren to keep the unity of the Spirit and remain faithful to their testimony, calling and ministry. He then sent a fitting admonition to the magistrates ending with the words: "The grace of the Father and the blessing of Jesus Christ with the power of the Holy Spirit be with you and gracefully preserve your city and state, your honour, persons and possessions under His divine care and keeping and shield you from all evil."

When friends told Bullinger that they were praying for his full restoration to health, the worn-out spiritual warrior said:

> "If the Lord will make any further use of me and of my ministry in his church, I shall willingly obey him; but if he shall please (as I much desire) to take me out of this miserable life, I shall exceedingly rejoice; as I shall be delivered from a wretched age, to go to my Saviour Christ. Socrates was glad when his death approached; because, as he thought, he should go to Homer, Hesiod, and other learned men, whom he supposed he should meet with in the other world. How much more do I rejoice, who am sure that I shall see my Saviour Christ, the saints, patriarchs, prophets, apostles, and all the holy men, who have lived from the beginning of the world. Since, I say, I am sure to see them, and partake of their joys, why should I not willingly die, to be a sharer in their eternal society and glory?"[27]

As Bullinger finished, his eyes filled with tears but he told those gathered around him that this was not because of fear of death as he was longing to be released but it was out of his deep love for all his dear friends. He emphasised that he was dying in full trust in Christ's salvation

---

[26] Ibid, pp. 137-138.
[27] Quoted in Middleton's *Biographia Evangelica*, Vol. II, pp. 169-170.

and recited the Apostles' Creed, expounding it for his hearers as he went along. After another brief exhortation to remain steadfast in the faith, he said a prayer of thanksgiving, pronounced God's blessing on his assembled brethren and gave each one his hand. After the brethren had departed, Bullinger wrote a lengthy letter to the Council, committing them to the Lord, advising them to rely on the Scriptures for their guidance in all matters. He encouraged them to continue to care for the poor, refugees, widows and orphans and keep up the care of schools and hospitals. He emphasised especially that the Council should use caution in entering into confederacies with foreign princes and dukes and warned the politicians against selling the blood of stalwart citizens to foreign potentates as mercenaries. Peace both within and without Zürich should be the Council's aim. Bullinger then wrote out his last will and testimony on 2 August, 1575.

During Bullinger's final days, he was unable to speak much and, added to his other chronic inner pains; he suffered from an acute catarrh. On 17 September, Bullinger prepared himself for the night and died peacefully in his sleep. He was buried the next day, a Sunday, in the Great Minster alongside his beloved Anna. He was seventy-one years of age and had been in full-time Christian service for over fifty-five years, forty-three of them as a minister of the gospel. On the following day, Bullinger's letter to the Council was solemnly read out before all the councilmen and hardly an eye remained dry. Bullinger's adopted son, Rudolf Gualter, was almost immediately appointed to succeed him. The choice had been Bullinger's own, and, as usual, his choice could not have been better. Seldom has there been such a great man who made so few mistakes. Pamela Biel in her *Sixteenth Century Journal* essay, 'Heinrich Bullinger's Death and Testament',[28] calls Bullinger's home-call "A well planned departure."

Bullinger's death shook the Reformed world and the peoples of many nations wrote to the remaining Zürich ministers and Bullinger's remaining children and grand-children to give them their heartfelt

---

[28] 22, 1991, pp. 3-14.

condolences at the loss of the Father of the Reformation, the Shepherd of the Churches, the Pillar of the Church and the Common Father of the Afflicted, four of the titles with which they loved to adorn Bullinger.[29] Each Reformed church from Scandinavia to the underground churches in Southern Europe sent letters of condolence and respect often accompanied by poems of remembrance which were read out in the Zürich churches. One of the most moving letters of condolence was from Bishop Richard Cox, the great consolidator of the English Reformation. Cox was four years older than Bullinger and had served the English Reformation from the days of Henry VIII. He had been Edward VI's tutor and chaplain and the Chancellor of Cambridge University and had brought peace to the exiled churches during the Marian persecutions though persecuted himself by counter-Reformation forces both on the papist and Protestant sides. Writing to Gualter, Cox says:

"My sorrow was excessive for the death of Henry Bullinger, whom, by his letters, and learned and pious writings, I had been acquainted with, and I may say, known intimately for many years, although he was never personally known to me. Who would not be made sorrowful by the loss of such and so great a man, and excellent a friend? not to mention that the whole Christian church is disquieted with exceeding regret, that so bright a star is forbidden any longer to shine upon earth.

John writes, that inauspicious stars fell down from heaven; but we are persuaded that our star has ascended up into heaven, and is fixed in heaven, and as it shone on earth, so it now shines more brightly in heaven. As to what he was on earth, his pious reputation is not silent, his pious life proclaims, his most learned writings abundantly testify: and what he now is in heaven, God knows, the angels rejoice, and the souls of the godly exult. And this is no small consolation to those who regret the loss of such a man."[30]

---

[29] The title of 'father' is still given Bullinger in Switzerland. Fritz Büsser in his *Heinrich Bullinger, Leben, Werk und Wirkung*, calls him Father of Reformed Protestantism, p. XIII.
[30]

Bibliography

Catalogues

Herkenrath, E., Heinrich Bullinger Werke, Beschreibendes Verzeichnis der Literatur über Heinrich Bullinger, TVZ, 1977.

Staedke, J., Heinrich Bullinger Werke, Beschreibendes Verzeichnis der gedruckten Werke von Heinrich Bullinger, TVZ, 1972.

Primary sixteenth century sources used

Bächtold, H. U. and Henrich, Rainer (eds), Heinrich Bullinger Werke, Briefe des Jahres 1539, TVZ, 2002.

Bächtold, Hans Ulrich and Henrich, Rainer (eds), Heinrich Bullinger Werke, Briefe des Jahres 1540, TVZ, 2003.

Bächtold, Hans Ulrich, Heinrich Bullinger vor dem Rat, Zur Gestalltung und Verwaltung des Züricher Staatswesens in den Jahren 1531-1775, Bern-Frankfurt a. M., 1982.

Blanke, Fritz, Zwingli Hauptschriften, only vols 1,2,3,4,7,9,11 issued, Zwingli-Verlag, Zürich, 1940-48.

Bray, Gerald, (ed.), Documents of the English Reformation, James Clarke & Co Ltd, 1994.

Bromiley, G. W. (ed), Zwingli and Bullinger, The Library of Christian Classics, Vol. XXIV, SCM Press, 1953.

Bucer, Martin, Common Places of Martin Bucer (ed. and trans. by D. F. Wright), The Sutton Courtenay Press, 1972.

Bullinger, Heinrich, Der Widertöufferen ursprung fürgang Secten wäsen etc., 1561 facsimile, Zentralantiquariat der Deutschen Demokratischen Republik, Leipzig, 1975.

Calvin, Jean, Calvin-Studienausgabe I.1., Band I, Reformatorische Anfänge (1533-1541), hrsg. Eberhard Busch et al., Neukirchener Verlag, 1994.
Calvin, Johannes, Unterricht in der christlichen Religion: Institutio Christianae Religionis (trans. Otto Weber), Neukirchener Verlag, 1986.
Calvin, John, Calvin's Commentaries, The Library of Christian Classics, Vol. XXIII, SCM, 1958.
Calvin, John, Institutes of the Christian Religion, (2. vols.), Eerdmans, 1979.
Calvin, John, Theological Treatises, The Library of Christian Classics, Vol. XXII, SCM, 1954.
Calvin, John, Works, Ages Digital Library, John Calvin Collection, CD, Rio, WI, USA, 2000.
Campi, Emidio et al (eds) Heinrich Bullinger Schriften, TVZ, 7 vols, 2004.

Band 1.
Das Amt des Propheten 1532.
Das Testament oder der Bund 1534.
Unterweisung der Kranken 1535
Der alte Glaube 1537.
Der Ursprung des Irrglaubens 1539
Der Christliche Eherstand 1540.
Gegenüberstellung und kurze Zusammenfassung der evangelischen und der päpistlichen Lehre 1551.

Band 2: Die Autorität und Glaubwürdigkeit der Heiligen Schrift 1538.
Band 3-5: Die Dekaden 1549-1551.
Band 6: Schriften zum Tage
Band 7: Register zu den Bänden 1-6.

Cardwell, Edward, Documentary Annals of the Reformed Church of England, (2 vols.), 1844.
Christoffel, R., Huldrich Zwingli: Leben und Ausgewählte Schriften, Elberfeld, 1857.
Clemen, O., (ed.), Luthers Briefe an seine Käthe, Berlin, 1929.
Cochrane, Arthur (ed.), Reformed Confessions of the Sixteenth Century, SCM, 1966.
Donnelly, John Patrick (ed.), The Peter Martyr Reader, Truman State University Press, 1999.
Duke, Alastair (trans. And ed.), Calvinism in Europe 1540-1610: A Collection of Documents, Manchester University Press, 1997.
Franz, Johann Friedrich, Merkwürdige Züge aus denm Leben des Zürcherischen Antistes Heinrich Bullinger, nebst dessen Reiseinstruktion und Briefen an seinen ältesten Sohn Heinrich, auf den Lehranstalten zu Strassburg und Wittenberg, Bern, 1828.
Gäbler, Ulrich and Zsindely, Endre (eds), Heinrich Bullinger Werke, Briefe der Jahre 1524-1531, TVZ, 1974.

Gee, Henry and Hardy, William John, Documents Illustrative of English Church History, Macmillan, 1910.
Harder, Leland (ed.), The Sources of Swiss Anabaptism: The Grebel Letters and Related Documents Herald Press, 1985.
Held, Friedrich (ed.), Dr Martin Luthers Vorreden zur Heiligen Schrift, Heilbronn, undated.
Hillerbrand, H. J., The Reformation in its Own Words, SCM, 1964.
Kidd, B.J. (ed.), Documents Illustrative of the Continental Reformation, Clarendon Press, 1911.
Laing, David, The Works of John Knox, 6 vols, Edinburgh, 1895.
Martyr, Peter, The Peter Martyr Library, vols. 1; 3-5; 7-8, translated and edited by John Patrick Donnelly, 1994-2003.
Melanchthon, Philipp, Loci Communes 1521, Lateinisch-Deutsch, übers. Horst Georg Pöhlman, Gütersloher Verlagshaus, 1993.
Metzger, Wolfgang (ed.), Martin Luther: Ausgewählte Werke (6 vols.), Calver Verlag, 1930.
Parker Society, Decades, 4 vols., 1849. Biography based on Bullinger's diaries in Vol. 4.
Parker Society, Original Letters Relative to the English Reformation, 1537-1558, 2 Vols., 1847.
Parker Society, Zürich Letters, First Series, 1558-1579, 1842.
Parker Society, Zürich Letters, Second Series, 1558-1602, 1845.
Parker, T.H.L. (ed.) English Reformers, The Library of Christian Classics, Vol. XXVI, SCM, 1966.
Pestalozzi, Carl, Heinrich Bullinger. Leben und ausgewählte Schriften, Eberfeld, 1858. Definitive biography, appended by the following works or part works:

Handbuch oder Summa christlicher Religion, 1556 (I. Von dem Glauben und der Predigt des heiligen Evangeliums; II. Vom Gebete der Gläubigen; III. Von den heiligen Sakramenten; Vom Tode.)
Anleitung für die, so wegen unseres Herrn Jesu Christi und seines heiligen Evangeliums ihres Glaubens halben erforscht und mit allerlei Fragen versucht werden, 1559 (I. Von der heiligen christlichen und römischen Kirche; II. Von dem freien Willen des Mernschen; III. Von Glauben, Hoffnung, Liebe und guten Werken; IV. Von dem Messopfer.)
Von dem Nachtmal des Herrn, von der Vorbereituing zu demselben, Von Schwäche und Wachstum des Glaubens. Zuschrift an Frau Anna Roist.
Von rechte Hülfe und Errettung in Nöthen. Eine Predigt aus dem heiligen Evangelio Matthai dem 14. Kap., gehalten in Zürich am 12. Juli 1552.
Denkmale von Bullingers Lebenswege (I. Bullingers Brautwerbungschreiben an Anna Adlischweiler, vom Jahre 1527; II. Bullingers väterliche Vorschriften oder Anweisung für seinen Sohn Heinrich bei dessen Abgang in die Fremde. 1553; III.

Briefe Bullingers an seinen Sohn Heinrich; IV. Bullinger Terstament oder lezter Wille an seine Herren und Obern von Zürich. 1575.)

Reformation Heritage Books, The Decades of Henry Bullinger: With new introductions by George M. Ella and Joel R. Beeke, Grand Rapids, 2004.

Schirrmacher, Friedrich Wilhelm (ed.), Briefe und Akten zum Marburger Religionsgespräch (1529) und zum Augsburger Reichstag (1530), VKW, Bonn, 2003.

Spitz, Lewis W., et al., The Protestant Reformation: Major Documents, CPH, St Louis, 1997.

Stotz, P. (trans. and ed.) Heinrich Bullinger Werke, Studiorum ratio: Studienanleitung, Teil Band 2, Einleitung, Kommentar, Register, TVZ, 1987.

Stähelin, Ernst, Johannes Calvin: Leben und ausgewählten Schriften, 2 vols, Elberfeld, 1863.

Stotz, P. (trans. and ed.), Heinrich Bullinger Werke, Studiorum ratio: Studienanleitung, Teil Band 1, Text und Uebersetzung, TVZ, 1987.

Vom Berg, H. G. And Hausammann S. (eds), Heinrich Bullinger Werke, Exegetische Schriften aus den Jahren 1525-1526, TVZ, 1983.

Vom Berg, H. G. et al (eds), Heinrich Bullinger Werke, Unveröffentlichte Werke der Kappeler Zeit. Theologica, TVZ, 1991.

Wartenberg, Günther (ed.), Martin Luther Briefe, Leipzig, 1983.

Whitaker, E. C. (ed.), Martin Bucer and the Book of Common Prayer: *Censura*; *De Ordinatione Legitima*, Mayhew-McCrimmon Ltd, 1974.

Biographies and Critical Historical Evaluations

Aland, Kurt, Die Reformatoren, GTBSiebenstern, 1976.

Anrich, Gustav, Martin Bucer, Strassburg, 1914.

Atkinson, James, Martin Luther and the Birth of Protestantism, Penguin Books, 1968.

Bächtold, Hans Ulrich, Heinrich Bullinger, Historisches Lexicon der Schweiz, Institute für schweizerische Reformationsgeschichte, 2003.

Bächtold, Hans Ulrich, Heinrich Bullinger vor dem Rat, Zur Gestalltung und Verwaltung des Züricher Staatswesens in den Jahren 1531-1775, Bern-Frankfurt a. M., 1982.

Bevan, Frances, The Life of William Farel, Alfred Holness, Glasgow, undated.

Biel, Pamela, Doorkeeper at the House of Righteousness. Heinrich Bullinger and the Zürich Clergy 1535-1575, Bern, 1991.

Blanke, Fritz and Leuschner, Immanuel, Heinrich Bullinger: Vater der reformierten Kirche, Theologischer Verlag Zütich, 1990.

Blanke, Fritz, Der Junge Bullinger, Zürich, 1942.

Booty, John E., John Jewel, As Apologist of the Church of England, SPCK, 1963.

Bouvier, André, Henri Bullinger, Réformateur et conseiller oecuménique, Zürich-Neuchâtel, 1940.

Bromiley, G.W., Thomas Cranmer, Church Book Room Press, 1956.

Bucher, Adolf, Die Reformation in den Freien Ämtern und der Stadt Bremgarten (bis 1531). Sarnen, 1950.
Büsser, Fritz, Calvins Urteil über sich selbst, Zwingli Verlag, 1950.
Büsser, Fritz, Die Prophezei: Humanismus und Reformation in Zürich, Züricher Beiträge zur Reformationsgeschichte, Verlag Peter Lang, 1994.
Büsser, Fritz, Heinrich Bullinger (1504-1575): Leben, Werk und Wirkung, Band I, TVZ, 2004.
Choisy, Eugene, L'État Chrétien Calviniste A Genève, Genève and Paris, undated, ca 1900.
Christoffel, R., Heinrich Bullinger und seine Gatin (Zur dritten Secularerinnerung an Bullingers Todestag den 17. September 1575, Zürich, 1875.
Collette, Charles Hastings, The Life, Times, and Writings of Thomas Cranmer, D.D., London, 1887.
Courvoisier, Jaques, Zwingli: A Reformed Theologian, The Epworth Press, 1964.
Dickens, A. G., Martin Luther and the Reformation, English Universities Press, 1970.
Ella, G. M., The Troublemakers at Frankfurt: A Vindication of the English Reformation, Go Publications, 2003.
Ella, G. M., Mountain Movers, Go Publications, 1999.
Ella, G. M., More Mountain Movers, Go Publications, 2005.
Evangelisches Kirchenlexikon, Vol. I, A-G, Göttingen, 1956. See entry under Bullinger, Johann Heinrich.
Fast, Heinold, Heinrich Bullinger und die Täufer, Mennonitischen Geschichtsverein e. V., Weierhof (Pfalz), 1959.
Friedrich, Reinhold, Martin Bucer - Fanatiker der Einheit?, VKW, Bonn, 2002.
Gäbler, Ulrich, Huldrych Zwingli: His Life and Work, Fortress Press, 1986.
Ganoczy, Alexandre, The Young Calvin, T. & T. Clark Ltd., 1988.
Gloede, Günter, Calvin: Weg und Werk, Leipzig, 1953.
Hollweg, Walter, Heinrich Bullingers Hausbuch, Neukirchen, 1956.
Kendall, R.T., Calvin and English Calvinism to 1649, Paternoster Press, 1997.
Koenigsberger, H. G. and Mosse, George L., Europe in the Sixteenth Century, Longman, 1972.
Köhler, Walter, Huldrych Zwingli, Leipzig, 1943.
Krahn, Cornelius, Dutch Anabaptism, Herald Press, 1981.
Kraijewski, Ekkehard, Leben und Sterben des Züricher Täuferführers Felix Manz, Oncken Verlag, 1962.
Lang, August, Zwingli und Calvin, Bielefeld and Leipzig, 1913.
Lee, Frederick George, The Church under Queen Elizabeth, 2 vols, London, 1880.
Lindsay, Thomas M., Luther and the German Reformation, Edinburgh, 1900.
Locher, Gottfried W., Die evangelische Stellung der Reformatoren zum öffentlichen Leben, Zwingli Verlag, 1950.
Locher, Gottfried W., Huldrych Zwingli und Karl V. Das Vorwort zur Fidei Ratio, 1530, Theologische Zeitschrift der Universität Basle, Jahrgang 46, 1990, pp. 205-218.

Locher, Gottfried W., Huldrych Zwingli in Neuer Sicht: Zehn Beiträge zur Theologie der Züricher Reformation, Zwingli Verlag, 1969.
MacCulloch, Diarmaid, Thomas Cranmer, Yale University Press, 1996.
McGrath, Alister E, Johann Calvin, Benziger, 1991.
McGrath, Alister E., Reformation Thought: An Introduction, Basil Blackwell, 1988.
McGrath, Patrick, Papists and Puritans under Elizabeth I, London, 1967.
Mans, Peter and Loose, Helmuth Nils, Martin Luther: Leben, Glauben, Wirkung, Herder Verlag, 1983.
Middleton, Erasmus, Biographia Evangelica (4 vols), Bullinger's biography in Vol. II, Subscription, 1784.
Müller, Patrik, Heinrich Bullinger: Reformator, Kirchenpolitiker, Historiker, TVZ, 2004.
Oberman, Heiko A., Luther: Mensch Zwischen Gott und Teufel, dtv, 1986.
Pesch, Otto Hermann, Hinführung zu Luther, Matthias Grünewald, 1982.
Plath, Uwe, Calvin und Basle in den Jahren 1552-1556, Basle and Stuttgart, 1974.
Prestwich, Menna (ed), International Calvinism 1541-1715, Clarendon Press, 1986.
Raget, Christopher, Heinrich Bullinger und seine Gattin nach ihrem segensreichen Wirken in ihrer Familie, Gemeinde und gegen verfolgte Glaubengenossen, Zürich, 1875.
Richard, James William, Philip Melanchthon: The Protestant Preceptor of Germany, G.P. Putnam's Sons, 1898.
Schirrmacher, Thomas (Hg.), Anwalt der Liebe – Martin Bucer als Theologe und Seelsorger, VKW, 2001.
Schraepler, Horst W., Die rechtliche Behandlung der Täufer in der deutschen Schweiz, Südwestdeutschland und Hessen 1525-1618, Tübingen, 1957.
Staedtke, Joachim, Johannes Calvin: Erkentnis und Gestaltung, Göttingen, 1969.
Stephens, W.P. (ed.), The Bible, the Reformation and the Church: Essays in Honour of James Atkinson, Sheffield Academic Press,1995.
Stupperich, Robert, Melanchthon: The Enigma of the Reformation, Lutterworth Press, 1966.
Suts, Johannes, Heinrich Bullinger: Der Retter der Züricher Reformation, Zürich, 1915.
Tulloch, John, Luther and Other Leaders of the Reformation, William Blackwood and Sons, 1883.
Van Campen, M., Martin Bucer en vergeten reformator, Boekcentrum, 1991.
Van der Zwaag, K., Afwachten of verwachten? De toe-eigening des heils in historisch en theologisch perspectif, Uitgeverij Groen/Heerenveen, 2003.
Von, Schulthess-Rechberg, Heinrich Bullinger der Nachfolger Zwinglis, Halle, 1904.
Warfield, Benjamin B., On the Literary History of the Institutes, Works, Vol. V, Baker Book House, 1981.
Wernle, D.P. Calvin und Basle bis zum Tode des Myconius 1535-1552, Basle, 1909.

Essay Collections

Campi, Emidio (ed.), Heinrich Bullinger und seiner Zeit: Eine Vorlesungsreihe, TVZ, 2004:

E. Campi, Heinrich Bullinger und seiner Zeit, pp. 7-35.
P. Stotz, Bullingers Bild des Mittelalters, pp. 37-60.
U. Leu, Die Zürcher Buch- und Lesekultur 1520-1575, pp. 61-90.
Th. Kruger, Heinrich Bullinger als Ausleger des Alten Testaments am Beispiel seiner Predigten über Daniel 1 und 2, pp. 91-104.
I. Backus, Bullinger als Neutestamentler. Sein Kommentar zu den Paulusbriefen und den Evangelien, pp. 105-131.
S.-P. Bergjan, Bullinger und die griechischen Kirchenvater in der konfessionellen Auseinandersetzung, pp. 133-160.
A. Schindler, Bullinger und die lateinischen Kirchenvater, pp. 161-177.
F. Bryner, Die Ausstrahlungen Bullingers auf die Reformation in Ungarn und Polen, pp. 179-197.
Peter Opitz, Eine Theologie der Gemeinschaft im Zeitalter der Glaubensspaltung, pp. 199-214.
P. Buhler, Bullinger als Systematiker - am Beispiel der *Confessio Helvetica Posterior*, pp. 215-235.
A. Muhling, Heinrich Bullinger als Kirchenpolitiker, pp. 237-249.
H. U. Bächtold, Heinrich Bullinger als Historiker der Schweizer Geschichte, pp. 251-273.
D. Roth, Heinrich Bullingers Eheschriften, pp. 275-309.
Gäbler, Ulrich und Herkenrath, Erland (eds), Heinrich Bullinger 1504-1575: Gesammelte Aufsätze zum 400. Todestag, Band I., TVZ, 1975:

Hans-Georg vom Berg: Die "Bruder vom gemeinsamen Leben" und die Stiftschule von St. Martin zu Emmerich. Zur Frage des Einflusses der devotio moderna auf den jungen Bullinger, pp. 1- 12.
Ulrich Gäbler, Bullingers Vorlesung uber das Johannesevangelium aus dem Jahre 1523, pp. 13- 27.
Susi Hausammann: Anfragen zum Schriftverstandnis des jungen Bullinger im Zusammenhang einer Interpretation von "De scripturae negotio", pp. 29-48.
Willy Rordorf: Kritik an Hieronymus. Die Schrift "Contra Vigilantium" im Urteil Zwinglis und Bullingers, pp. 49- 63.
Joachim Staedtke: Die Geschichtsauffassung des jungen Bullinger, pp. 65- 74.
Jack Warren Cottrell: Is Bullinger the source for Zwingli's doctrine of the covenant?, pp. 75- 83. Willem F. Dankbaar: Das Zurcher Bekenntnis (1545) und seine niederlandische Uebersetzung (1645), pp. 85-108.
Salvatore Corda : Bullinger e la confessione eucaristica di Goppingen (1557), pp. 109-122.
Rudolf Pf i s t e r : Zu Bullingers Beurteilung des Konzils von Trient, pp. 123-140.

J. Wayne Baker: In Defense of Magisterial Discipline: Bullinger's "Tractatus de Excommunicatione" of 1568, pp. 141-159.
István Tökés : Bullingers hermeneutische Lehre, pp. 161-189.
Hughes Oliphant Old: Bullinger and the Scholastic Works on Baptism; A Study in the History of Christian Worship, pp. 191-207.
Markus Jenny: Bullinger als Liturg, pp. 209-230.
Peter Walser : Bullingers Erklarung des Unservaters, 231-250.
Helmut Meyer: Stadt und Landschaft Zürich nach dem Zweiten Kappelerkrieg, 251-267.
Hans Ulrich Bächtold: Bullinger und die Krise der Zürcher Reformation im Jahre 1532, pp. 251-267.
Heinzpeter Stucki: Bullinger, der Ziircher Rat und die Auseinandersetzung um das Alumnat 1538-1542, 291-303.
Kurt Rüetschi: Bullinger als Schulchronist, pp. 305-322.
Erland Herkenrath: Bullinger zu Teuerung und Bettel im Jahre 1571, pp. 323-338.

Gäbler, Ulrich und Herkenrath, Erland (eds), Heinrich Bullinger 1504-1575: Gesammelte Aufsätze zum 400. Todestag, Band II., TVZ, 1975:

Gottfried W. Locher, Bullinger und Calvin - Probleme des Vergleichs ihrer Theologien pp. 1- 33.
Wilhelm H. Neuser, Die Versuche Bullingers, Calvins und der Strassburger, Melanchthon zum Fortgang von Wittenberg zu bewegen, pp. 35-55.
Beat Rudolf Jenny, Bullingers Briefwechsel mit dem Elsasser Reformator Matthias Erb (1539-1571) pp. 57- 86.
Gustav Adolf Benrath: Die Korrespondenz zwischen Bullinger und Thomas Erastus pp. 87-141.
Yasukazu Morita: Bullinger und Schwenckfeld, pp. 143-156.
Jacques V. Pollet: La correspondance inédite de Valentin Paceus avec Konrad Pellikan et Heinrich Bullinger, pp. 157-176.Oskar Sakrausky: Theologische Einfliisse Bullingers bei Primus Truber, pp. 177-195.
Mihály Bucsay: Leitgedanken der Theologie Bullingers bei Petrus Melius. Ein Beitrag zur Ausstrahlung des Zürcher Reformators nach Ungarn, pp. 197-214.
Conradin Bonorand: Die Reaktion Bullingers, Joachim Vadians und anderer evangelischer Schweizer auf die antireformatorische Tätigkeit des Johannes Cochläus, pp. 215-230.
David J. Keep: Bullinger's Defence of Queen Elizabeth, pp. 231-241.
Robert C. Walton: Bullinger's Answer to John Jewel's Call for Help: Bullinger's Exposition of Matth. 16: 18-19, pp. 243-256.

Gordon, Bruce and Campi, Emidio (eds), Architect of Reformation: An Introduction to Heinrich Bullinger, 1504-1575:

Elsie Mckee, Edward A. Dowey Jr. (1918-2003), pp. 15-16.
Bruce Gordon, Introduction: Architect of Reformation, pp. 17-32.
Edward Dowey, Heinrich Bullinger as Theologian: Thematic, Comprehensive, and Schematic, pp. 35-65.
Mark Taplin, Bullinger on the Trinity: *"Religionis Nostrae Caput et Fundamentum"*, pp. 67-99.
Peter Opitz, Bullinger's *Decades:* Instruction in Faith and Conduct, pp. 101-116.
Bruce Gordon, Bullinger's Vernacular Writings: Spirituality and the Christian Life, pp. 117-134.
Roland Diethelm, Bullinger and Worship: "Thereby Does One Plant and Sow the True Faith", pp. 135-157.
Daniel Bollinger, Bullinger on Church Authority: The Transformation of the Prophetic Role in Christian Ministry, pp. 157-177.
Emidio Campi, Bullinger's Early Political and Theological Thought: *Brutus Tigurinus*, pp. 181-199.
Christain Moser, Heinrich Bullinger's Efforts to Document the Zürich Reformation: History as Legacy, pp. 201-214.
Kurt Jakob Rüetschi, Bullinger and the Schools, pp. 215-229.
Rainer Henrich, Bullinger's Correspondence: An International News Network, pp. 231-241.
Andreas Mühling, Heinrich Bullinger as Church Politician, pp. 243-253.
Carrie E. Euler, Bullinger's *Der Christlich Eestand:* Marriage and the Covenant, pp. 255-275.

Specific Theological Studies

Adam, Gottfried, Der Streit um die Prädestination im ausgehenden 16. Jahrhundert, Neukirchener Verlag, 1970.
Baker, Joseph Wayne, Heinrich Bullinger and the Covenant. The Other Reformed Tradition. Athens (Ohio), 1980.
Battles, Ford Lewis (ed. and trans.) John Calvin's Institutes of the Christian Religion, 1536 Edition, Eerdmans, 1995.
Battles, Ford Lewis, Analysis of the Institutes of the Christian Religion, Baker Book House, 1989.
Beckwith, R. T., The Calvinist Doctrine of the Trinity, The Harrison Trust, 2001.
Bucher, Adolf , Die Reformation in den Freien Ämtern und in der Stadt Bremgarten (bis 1531), Selbstverlag, Kollegium Sarnen, 1950.
Beeke, Joel R., Puritan Reformed Spirituality, Reformation Heritage Books, 2004.
Céard, Jean (ed.), Cité des hommes, cité de Dieu : travaux sur la littérature de la renaissance en l' honneur de Daniel Ménager, Geneva, 2003.
Cochrane, Arthur C. (ed.), Reformed Confessions of the 16th Century, SCM, 1966.
Cunningham, William, *Historical Theology*, 2 vols, Edinburgh, 1870.
Cunningham, William, *The Reformers and the Theology of the Reformation*, BOTT, 1979.

Davis, Horton, Worship and Theology in England, (3 vols.), Eerdmans, 1996.
Evans, G. R., Problems of Authority in the Reformation Debates, Cambridge University Press, 1992.
Green, E. Tyrrell, The Thirty-Nine Articles and the Age of the Reformation: An Historical and Doctrinal Exposition in the Light of Contemporary Documents, London, 1896.
Kittel, Helmuth, Der Calvinismus in Westeuropa, Leipzig und Berlin, undated.
Koch, Ernst, Die Theologie der Confessio Helvetica Posterior, Neukirchener Verlag, 1968.
Krabbendam, Henry, Sovereignty and Responsibility: The Pelagian-Augustinian Controversy in Philosophical and Global Perspective, VKW, Bonn, 2002.
Lambert, Malcolm, Ketzerei im Mittelalter, Bechtermünz, 2002.
Locher, Gottfried, W., Grundzüge der Theologie Huldrych Zwinglis im Vergleich mit derjenigen Martin Luthers und Johannes Calvins, Zwingliana, Zürich, Sonderdruck aus den *Zwingliana*, Heft 7 und 8, 1967.
Lohse, Bernard, A Short History of Christian Doctrine, Fortress Press, 1978.
Mühling, Andreas, Heinrich Bullingers europäische Kirchenpolitik, Verlag Peter Lang, 2001.
Nigg, Walter, Das Buch der Ketzer, Büchergilde Gutenberg Frankfurt/Main, 1962.
Neuser, Wilhelm H. (ed.), Calvinus Sacrae Scripturae Professor, Eerdmans, 1990.
Opitz, Peter, Heinrich Bullinger als Theologe: Eine Studie zu den ‚Dekaden', TVZ , 2004.
Schaff, Philip, The Creeds of Christendom, 3 vols., Baker, 1996.
Shedd, W.G.T, Calvinism: Pure and Mixed. A Defence of the Westminster Standards, BOT, 1986.
Smithen, Frederick J., Continental Protestantism and the English Reformation, James Clarke & Co. Ltd, 1927.
Staedtke, Joachim, Die Theologie des jungen Bullinger, Zwingli Verlag, Zürich, 1962.
Sturm, Klaus, Die Theologie Peter Martyr Vermiglis während seines ersten Aufenthalts in Strassburg 1542-1547, Neukirchener Verlag, 1971.
Venema, Cornelis P., Heinrich Bullinger and the Doctrine of Predestination, Baker Academic, 2002.
Walser, Peter, Die Prädestination bei Heinrich Bullinger im Zusammenhang mit siner Gotteslehre, Zürich, 1957.
Wandel, Lee Palmer, Always Among Us: Images of the Poor in Zwingli's Zürich, CUP. 1990

Works on National and International Reformation

Baird, Robert, Sketches of Protestantism in Italy, William Collins, 1847.
Blunt, John Henry, The Reformation of the Church of England, 2 vols, Rivington's, 1882.
Bornkamm, Das Jahrhundert der Reformation, Göttingen, 1966.

Brieger, Theodor, Die Reformation: Ein Stück aus Deutschlands Weltgeschichte, Verlag Ulstein, 1913.
D'Aubigné, J. H. Merle, History of the Reformation of the Sixteenth Century, Edinburgh, 1854.
D'Aubigné, J. H. Merle, Reformationen in Europa på Calvins Tid, 2 vols., Stockholm, 1874.
D'Aubigné, J. H. Merle, The Reformation in England, Vol. II, BOTT, 1963.
De Félice, G., History of the Protestants of France, 2 vols., London, 1853.
Dickens, A. G., Reformation and Society in Sixteenth-Century Europe, Thames and Hudson, 1966.
Dickens, A. G., The English Reformation, B.T. Badsford Ltd, 1965.
Froude, James Anthony, History of England (12 vols.), New York, 1969.
Gairdner, James, History of the English Church in the Sixteenth Century, Macmillan & Co., 1904.
Green, V. H. H., Renaissance and Reformation: A Survey of European History between 1450 and 1660, Edward Arnold, 1969.
Janse, W., Grenzeloos gereformeerd, Vreije Universiteit Amsterdam, 2004.
Kidd, B.J., The Continental Reformation, Rivingtons, 1925.
Lee, Frederick George, The Church under Queen Elizabeth, 2 vols., W.H. Allen and Co., 1880.
Lindburg, Carter, The European Reformations, Blackwell, 1996.
Lindsey, T. M., History of the Reformation, Vol. 2, In Lands Beyond Germany, Edinburgh, 1951.
MacCulloch, Diarmaid, Reformation: Europe's House Divided 1490-1700, Penguin, 2004.
Ménager, Daniel, Cité des hommes, cité de Dieu : travaux sur la littérature de la renaissance en l'honneur de Daniel Ménager, Geneva, 2003.
Milner, Joseph and Isaac; Haweis, Thomas, The History of the Church of Christ, Thomas Nelson, undated.
Miles, Charles Popham, The Voice of the Glorious Reformation, London, 1844.
Moeller, Wilhelm, History of the Christian Church, Vol. III, Reformation and Counter-Reformation 1517-1648, London, 1893.
Murdock, James (ed.), Mosheim's Institutes of Ecclesiastical History, Ward, Lock & Co., 1848.
Oberman, Heiko A., Die Reformation, Vandenhoeck und Ruprecht, 1986.
Oberman, Heiko A., The Dawn of the Reformation, T. & T. Clark, 1986.
Oberman, Heiko A., Werden und Wertung der Reformation, J.C.B Mohr, 1995.
Overton, John Henry, The Church in England, 2 vols, London, 1897.
Pflugk-Harttung, Julius von, et al, Im Morgenrot der Reformation, Hersfeld, 1912.
Pill, David H., The English Reformation 1529-58, University of London Press, 1973.
Schmidt, Kurt Dietrich, Kirchengeschichte, Göttingen, 1967.
Scribner, Bob, et al, The Reformation in National Context, CUP, 1994.
Scott, John, The History of the Church of Christ, 3 vols, L. B. Seeley and Sons, 1826.

Seebass, Gottfried, Die Reformation und ihre Ausenseiter, Göttingen, 1997.
Smedley, Edward, History of the Reformed Religion in France, Vol. i, London, 1832.
Stupperich, Robert, Geschichte der Reformation, dtv, 1967.
Thulin, Oskar et al, Reformation in Europa, Berlin, 1967.
Von Ranke, Leopold, Deutsche Geschichte im Zeitalter der Reformation, Bertelsmann, undated.
Von Ranke, Leopold, History of the Reformation in Germany, London, 1905.
Wengler, J.., Die dritte Reformation, Oncken Verlag, 1963.

Journal, Magazine, Webpage and Newspaper Articles

Beeke, Joel R., Election and Reprobation: Calvin on Equal Ultimacy, BOT Magazine, Issue 489, June 2004, pp. 8-19.
Bucher, Delf, Auf Bullingers Spuren durch Bremgarten, Neue Züricher Zeitung, 2 Sept., 2004, also NZZ Online.
Bühler, Peter, Der Abendmahlsstreit der Reformatoren und seine aktuellen Implikationen, Theologische Zeitschrift, Basle, 35. Jahrgang, 1979, pp. 228-241.
Büsser, Fritz, Die Stadt auf dem Berg, Bullinger's reformatorishes Vermächtnis an der Wende zum 21 Jahrhundert. Zwingliana XXV, 1998, pp. 21-43.
Campi, Emidio, Heinrich Bullinger, 'Ein ganz normaler Mensch': Werkausgabe. Der Züricher Reformator mit auch heute noch aktuellen Ideen, Mittelland Zeitung, 23 Juni, 2006
Chadwick, Owen, Zwingli and Bullinger. Selected Translations with Introductions and Notes by G.W. Bromiley, Ph.D., D. Litt., London, 1953, Review, The Journal of Theological Studies, New Series, Vol. v., Clarendon, 1954, pp. 102-104.
Dufour, Alain, Le Mythe de Genève au Temps de Calvin, Schweizerische Zeitschrift für Geschichte, 1959, pp. 489-518.
Ella, G. M., Henry Bullinger, New Focus, Part I, Vol. 7, No. 01, Part II, Vol. 7, No. 02, 2002 and Zürich University website, www.unizh.ch.
Ella, G. M., Henry Bullinger (1504-1575), Shepherd of the Churches, The Banner of Sovereign Grace Truth, Grand Rapids, Vol. 12, No. 5, May-June 2004.
Ella, G. M., Martin Bucer: Moderator of the Reformation, New Focus, Vol. 6, No. 4, Dec.-Jan. 2002. Also MBS Texte 8, Martin Bucer Seminary, 1 Jahrgang, 2004.
Ella, G. M., Jan Laski, der paneuropäische Reformator, MBS Texte 19, Martin Bucer Seminary, 1 Jahrgang, 2004.
Ella, G. M., Philip Melanchthon (1497-1560): The Creator of Lutheranism, New Focus, Vol. 10, Nos 02-04, 2005.
Engammare, Max, Calvin: A Prophet without a Prophecy, Church History: Studies in Christianity and Culture, The American Society of Church History, Year 1998, pp. 643-661.
Faber, Eva-Maria, Zur Frage der Prädestination in der Theologie Johannes Calvins, Theologische Zeitschrift der Universität Basle, Jahrgang 56, 2000, pp. 50-68.
Kohls, Ernst-Wilhelm, Martin Bucer als Anhänger Luthers, Theologishe Zeitschrift, Basle, 33. Jahrgang, 1977, pp. 210-218.

Meyer, Bruno, Die Entstehung der Eidgenossenschaft: Der Stand der Heutigen Anschauungen, Schweizerische Zeitschrift für Geschichte, 1952, pp. 153-205.
Müller, Bernd, Bildersturm: ein Ausstellungskatalog und ein Sammelband, Archiv für Reformationsgeschichte, Jahrgang 93, pp. 391-396.
Naphy, William G., Calvin's Letters. Reflections on their usefulness in Studying Genevan History, Archiv für Reformationsgeschichte, Jahrgang 86, pp. 67-89.
Pine, Leonard, Heinrich Bullinger: The Common Shepherd of All Christian Churches, Zürich University website, www. unizh.ch..
Rabe, Horst, Zur Entstehung des Augsburger Interims 1547-48, Archiv für Reformationsgeschichte, Jahrgang 94, pp. 6-104.
Sladeczek, Franz-Josef, Die goetze in miner herren chilchen sind gerumpt!, Ein Beitrag zur Berner Reformationsgeschichte, Theologishe Zeitschrift, Basle, 44. Jahrgang, 1988, pp. 289-311.
Wilcox, Peter, The Lectures of John Calvin and the Nature of his Audience, Archiv für Reformationsgeschichte, Jahrgang 87, pp.136-48.

Indices

Index of People, Places and Names

Index of Subjects

Index of Bible Verses